The Name of the Game

The Will Eisner Library

from W. W. Norton & Company

Hardcover Compilations

The Contract With God *Trilogy: Life on Dropsie Avenue*
Will Eisner's New York: Life in the Big City
Life, in Pictures: Autobiographical Stories

Paperbacks

A Contract With God
A Life Force
Dropsie Avenue
New York: The Big City
City People Notebook
Will Eisner Reader
The Dreamer
Invisible People
To the Heart of the Storm
Life on Another Planet
Family Matter
Minor Miracles
The Name of the Game
The Building
The Plot: The Secret History of the Protocols of the Elders of Zion

Instructional Textbooks

Comics and Sequential Art
Graphic Storytelling and Visual Narrative
Expressive Anatomy for Comics and Narrative

Other Books by Will Eisner

Fagin the Jew
Last Day in Vietnam
Eisner/Miller
The Spirit Archives
Will Eisner Sketchbook
Will Eisner's Shop Talk
Hawks of the Seas
The Princess and the Frog
The Last Knight
Moby Dick
Sundiata

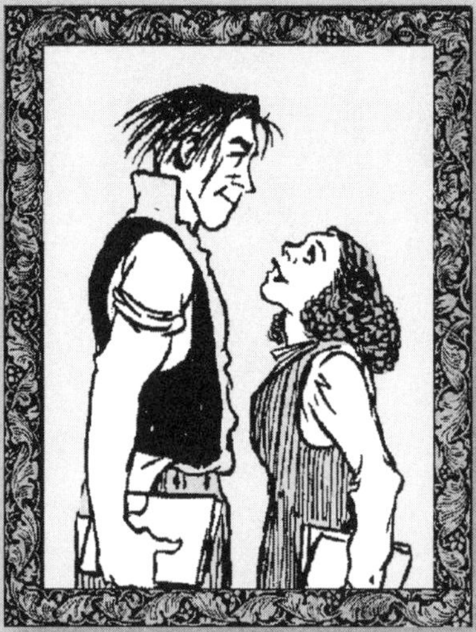

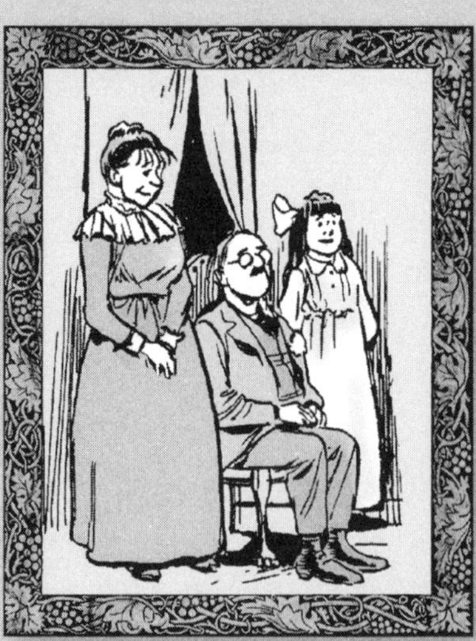

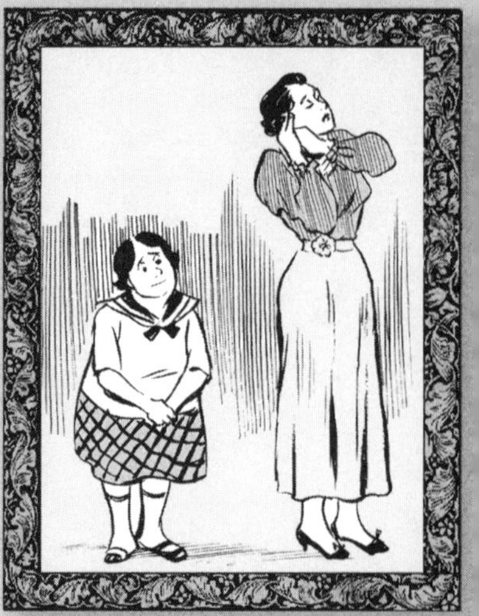

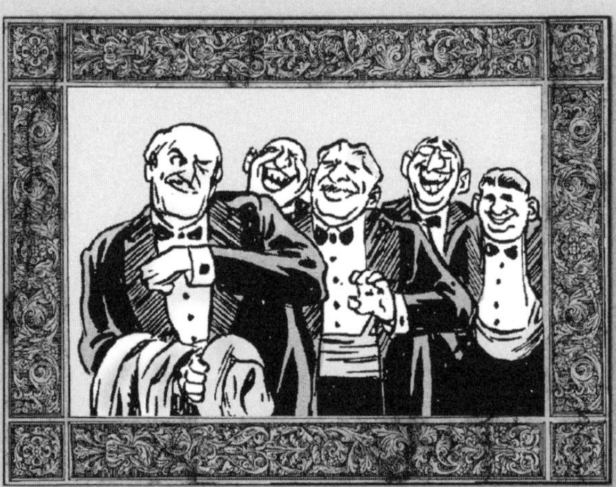

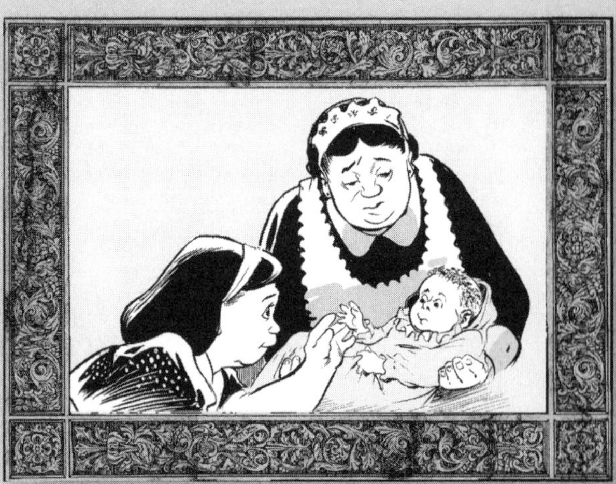

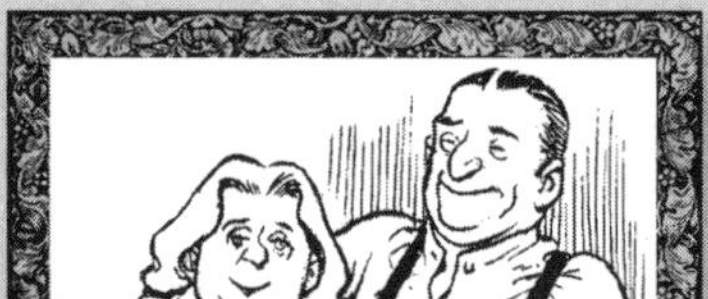

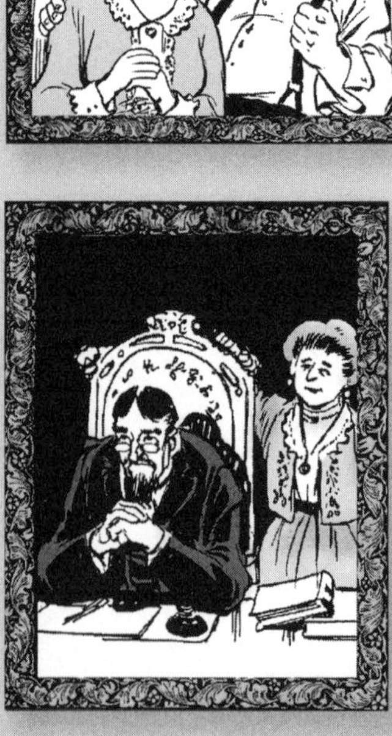

Acknowledgments

My gratitude for the years of steadfast editorial guidance and judgment of Dave Schreiner who edited this and so many of my books.

To Ann, my dear wife (and best friend), for her enduring patience and real advice drawn from her experience in the environment I've portrayed. Her help has provided me with much of the insight that is necessary to the ambiance and nuances in a work of this kind.

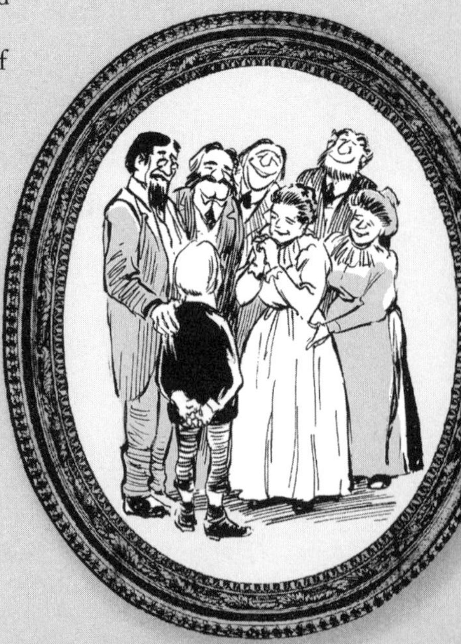

the **Name** *of the* **Game**

Will Eisner

W. W. NORTON & COMPANY
New York • London

For information about permission to reproduce selections from this book,
write to Permissions, W. W. Norton & Company, Inc.,
500 Fifth Avenue, New York, NY 10110

For information about special discounts for bulk purchases, please contact
W. W. Norton Special Sales at specialsales@wwnorton.com or 800-233-4830

Manufacturing by RR Donnelley, Willard
Production manager: Devon Zahn

Library of Congress Cataloging-in-Publication Data

Eisner, Will.
The name of the game / Will Eisner.
p. cm.
Originally published: New York : DC Comics, 2001.
ISBN 978-0-393-32815-8 (pbk.)
1. Graphic novels. I. Title.
PN6727.E4N36 2008
741.5'973—dc22

2008029328

W. W. Norton & Company, Inc.
500 Fifth Avenue, New York, N.Y. 10110
www.wwnorton.com

W. W. Norton & Company Ltd.
Castle House, 75/76 Wells Street, London W1T 3QT

1 2 3 4 5 6 7 8 9 0

Foreword

Dear Reader:

My name is Abraham Kayn. I am the father of Aron Kayn, my only son. We are very proud of him—and grateful too—because he has married into a very high-class family, the Arnheims, you know. He has lifted us up socially.

First of all, my real name is Kayinsky. I came from a little village in Poland and my wife came from a little place in Holland. We were "Nobodies," poor of course, as were my parents, grandparents and great-great-grandparents. As far back as anybody could remember the Kayinskys were never able to raise themselves up. What can I say? First of all we were never smart or lucky in trade. No, we were never better than our neighbors, so we accepted that the only other way up was by marriage.

And why not? All the stories we grew up with told us this. Whether it was history, Bible stories or fairy tales, it was always the same. A great king or nobleman would offer the hand of his beautiful daughter in marriage to the young man (from the lower classes) who performed a great deed. Generation after generation accepted this as true. Certainly for ordinary people this was a dream because any other way was not so easy.

Of course, in modern times, kings and nobles were replaced by tradesmen who accumulated great wealth and established families of power and social position.

Naturally we knew nothing about what went on in that society. Yes, we heard or believed that they all lived a life of comfort, pleasure and enjoyed the power and influence that comes with plenty of money. People from the upper class were better and happier.

How could one not be? Doesn't financial security, belonging to the best people and giving to charities guarantee a good life?? Absolutely. Marrying into such a class guaranteed living happily ever after.

What can I tell you? Marriage for us was, therefore, a game. There were bad marriages and there were good marriages. Marrying beneath oneself was bad. Marrying outside of your religon or race was worse. However, marrying a rich girl (if you were a boy) or marrying a successful man (if you were a girl) was good.

Above all, the family into which one married was most important. To marry into a socially better family would lift your family up. It would provide "connections" and you would be the envy of one's neighbors, especially when one could refer to one's in-laws on a first name basis.

So we came penniless to America, Americanized our name to Kayn, raised and educated a son who married well and changed everything for us.

Today, we are very well connected.

Yes, marriage is the Name of the Game.

Abraham Kayn

The ARNHEIM *family*

The Arnheim family was descended from Moses Arnheim, one of the many German Jews who had emigrated to America about two decades before the Civil War.

Wealthy and assimilated, they enjoyed a comfortable inclusion in American Society. By 1890, the Arnheims were a leading family in the dominant East Coast German Jewish social establishment.

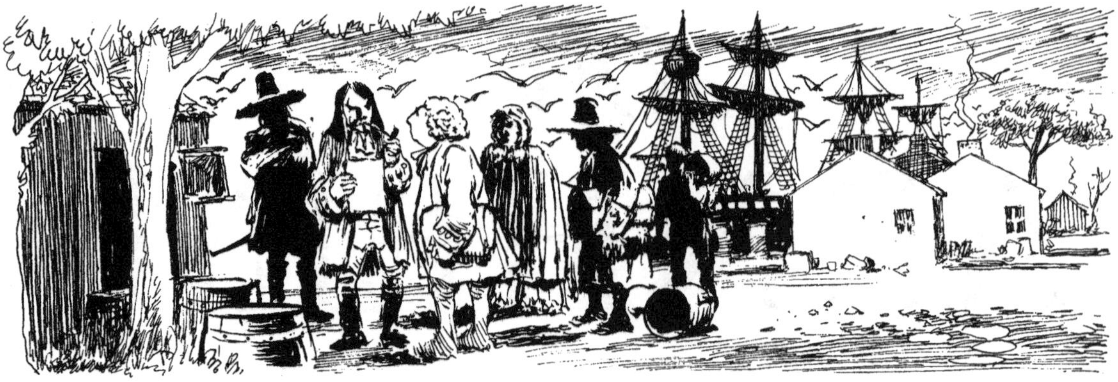

The first Jews who sought a haven in the American colonies came from Spain and Portugal via Brazil. They soon became Americanized and were well established by the time the United States became a nation. They were a cultured people who adopted community manners and quickly assimilated. As a group, they remained middle class. The more enterprising, who did not intermarry with gentiles, built important families and within the Jewish community they became the aristocracy . . . an upper class. The Sephardics.

Between 1820 and 1840, an economic depression ravaged Germany and the Austro-Hungarian Empire. This economic trouble increased the already virulent anti-Semitism there and accelerated the flight of the Jews into America.

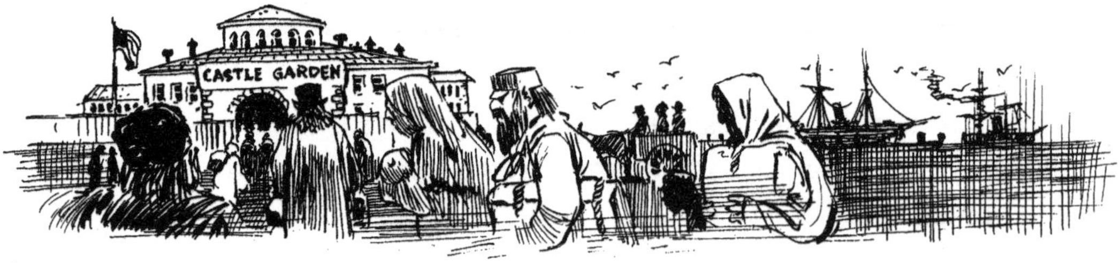
CASTLE GARDEN

These new immigrants were a crude and noisy people. But they were intelligent, resourceful and innovative, an ideal trait for life in this big and open country that was often crude and noisy itself but where opportunity was so abundant. The hard-working newcomers thrived. They were Ashkenazis, just one rung below the Sephardics on the Jewish social ladder.

It was among this wave of immigrants that the first Arnheim, Moses, arrived in America.

He was well prepared for the New World for he was well educated and had experience in trade. He came from parents who had built a small but successful clothing shop in northern Germany. While he had to abandon this shop during the pogrom, he nonetheless brought with him the experience that could be used to his advantage in the new environment.

Moses Arnheim was quick to follow immigrant countrymen who rose from peddlers to entrepreneurs, who established factories, stores and banks.

Upon his arrival in New York City, Moses immediately set up a little corset factory downtown. Moses supervised the manufacturing, and during the season traveled from city to city selling to retail shops. In 1850, corsets for women were an essential fashion element and the company grew quickly. Before long, Moses Arnheim was so wealthy he was able to gain acceptance by the established German Jewish merchant princes and bankers like the Straus, Lehman, Goldman, Loeb, Bloomingdale, Morgenthau and Guggenheim families. Moses was socially ambitious and determined to found a family that, as he always put it, "would mean something." He married well and sired three sons who joined the family business. Moses regarded his youngest, Isidore, as the most accomplished of the three. He left him with 52 percent of the stock and control of the company.

When Moses Arnheim died, Isidore inherited a well-established business with a good family name. His brothers produced four children. Three sons joined the company and the daughter "lived off" the family. Isidore joined the best clubs and married Alva Straus from one of the best Jewish families.

Isidore ran Arnheim Corset Company well. But he was less capable at bringing up his own two sons, Alex and Conrad.

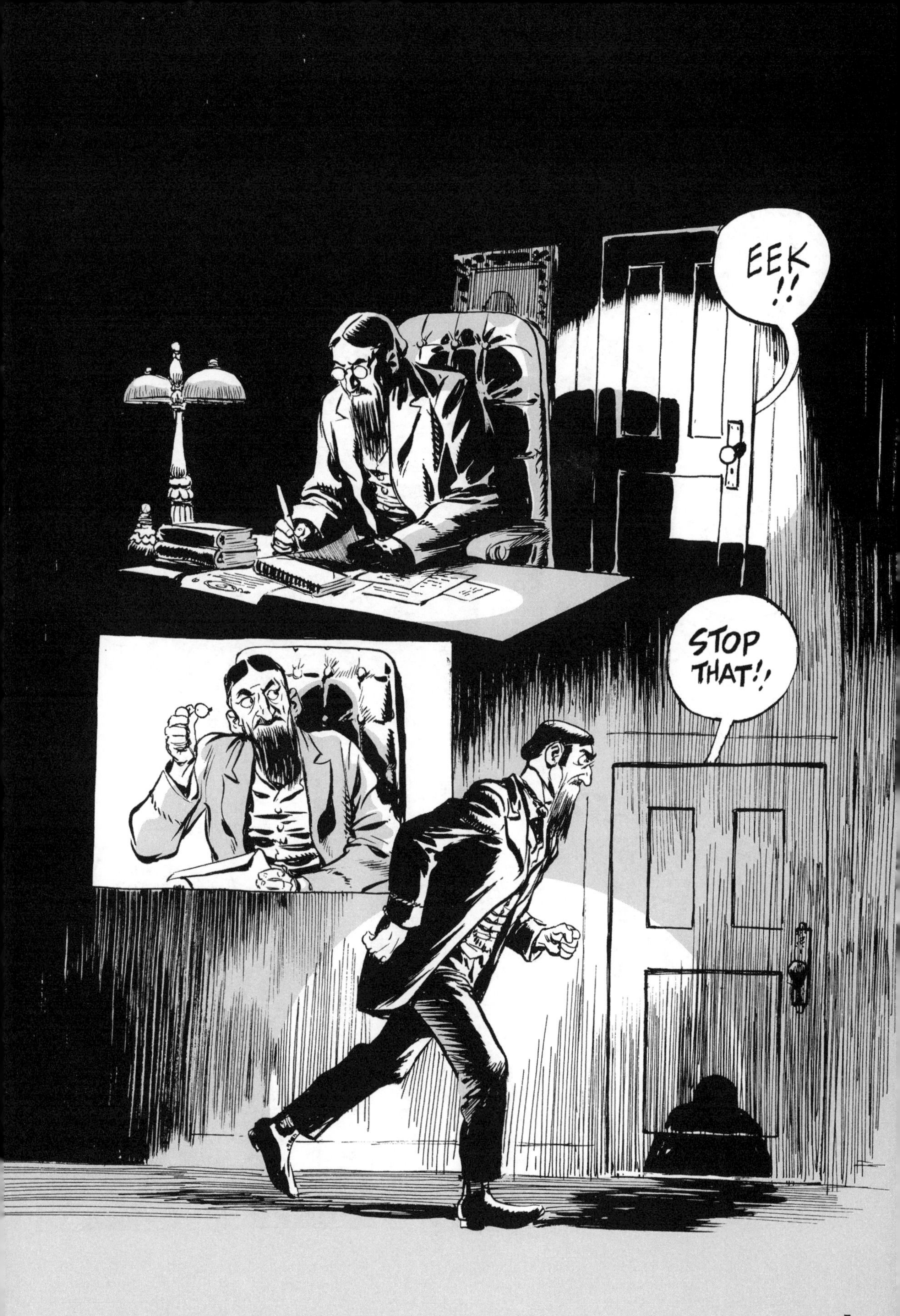
EEK!!
STOP THAT!!

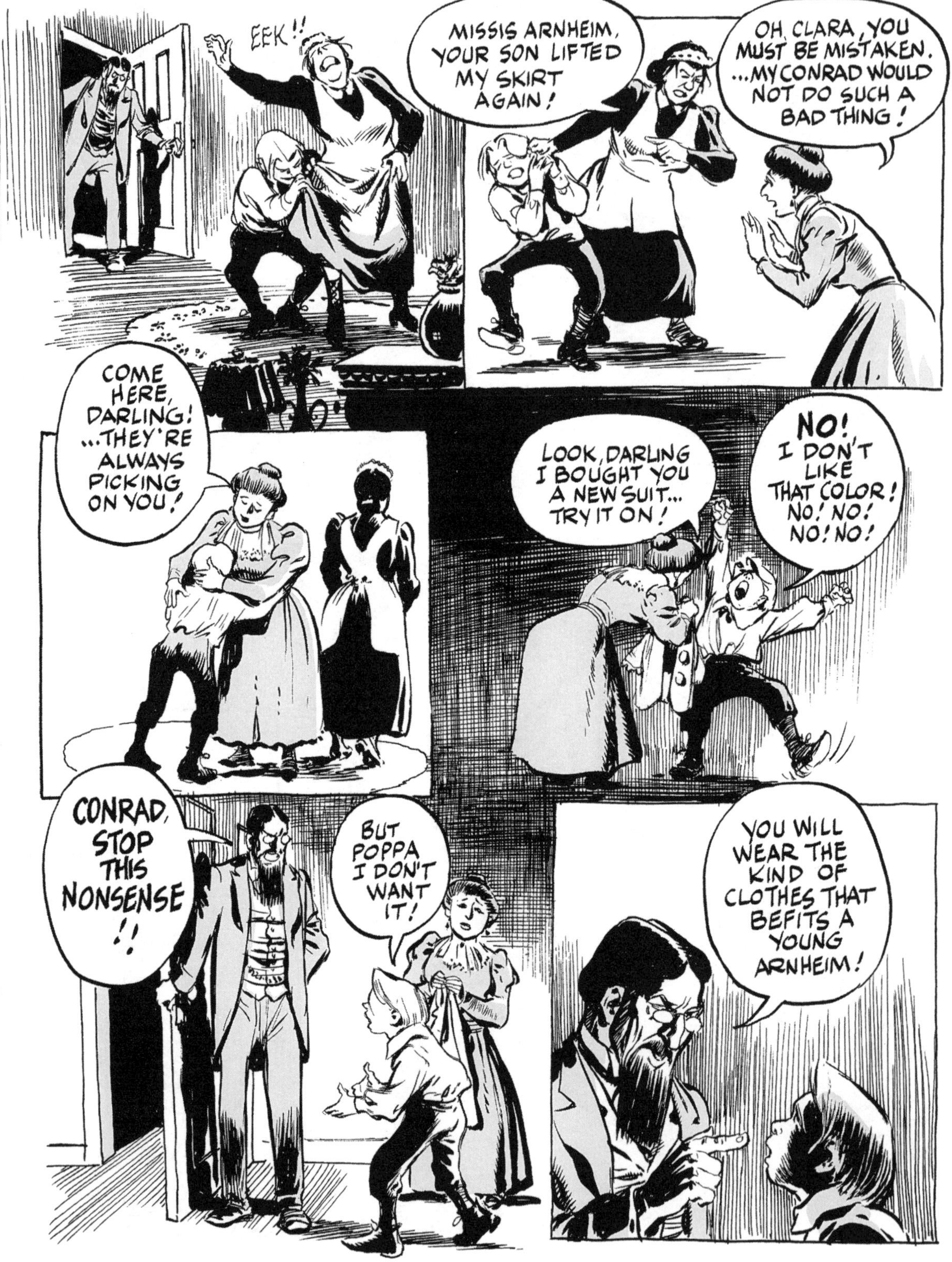
EEK!!
MISSIS ARNHEIM, YOUR SON LIFTED MY SKIRT AGAIN!
OH, CLARA, YOU MUST BE MISTAKEN. ...MY CONRAD WOULD NOT DO SUCH A BAD THING!
COME HERE, DARLING! ...THEY'RE ALWAYS PICKING ON YOU!
LOOK, DARLING I BOUGHT YOU A NEW SUIT... TRY IT ON!
NO! I DON'T LIKE THAT COLOR! NO! NO! NO! NO!
CONRAD, STOP THIS NONSENSE!!
BUT POPPA I DON'T WANT IT!
YOU WILL WEAR THE KIND OF CLOTHES THAT BEFITS A YOUNG ARNHEIM!

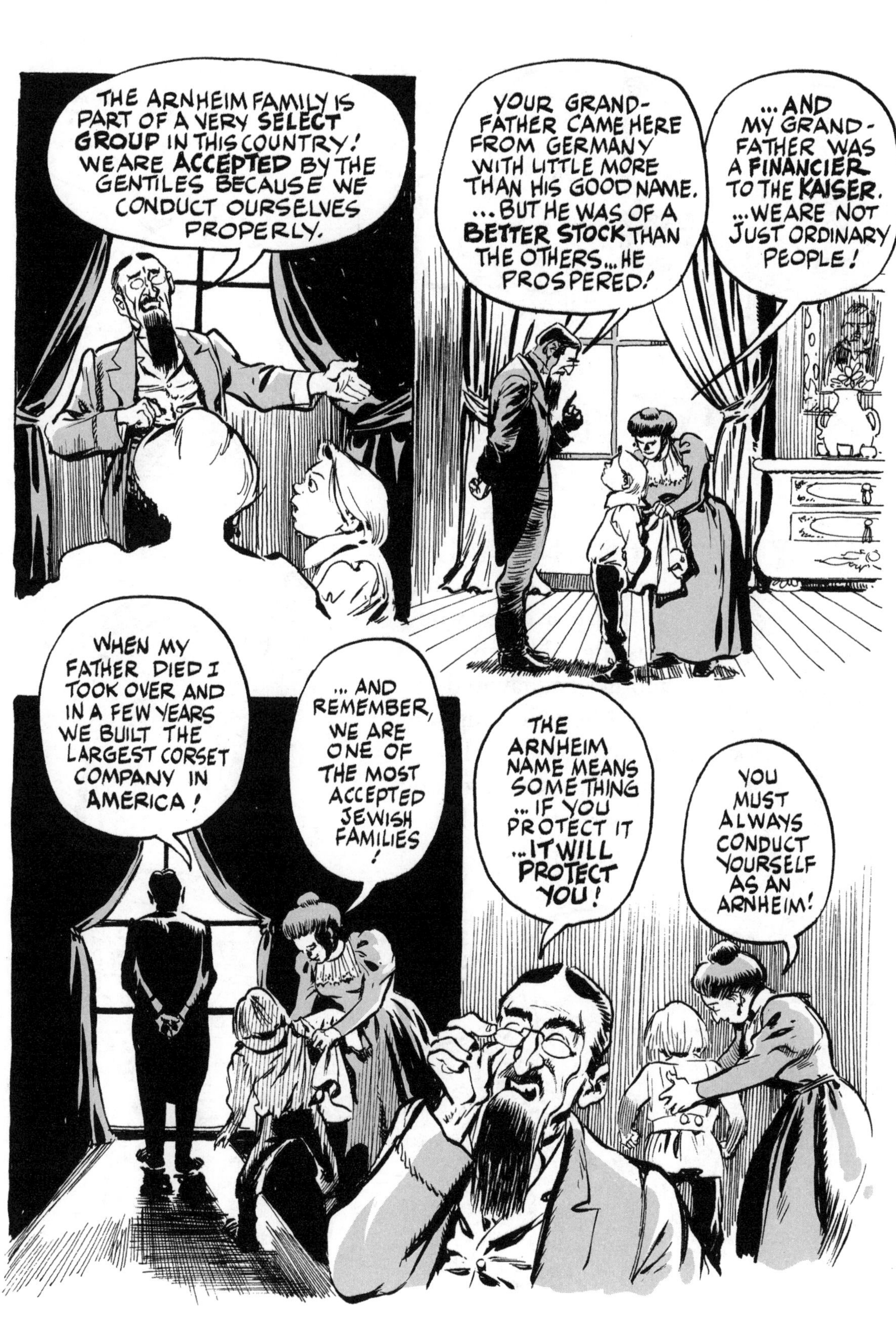
THE ARNHEIM FAMILY IS PART OF A VERY SELECT GROUP IN THIS COUNTRY! WE ARE ACCEPTED BY THE GENTILES BECAUSE WE CONDUCT OURSELVES PROPERLY.
YOUR GRAND-FATHER CAME HERE FROM GERMANY WITH LITTLE MORE THAN HIS GOOD NAME. ...BUT HE WAS OF A BETTER STOCK THAN THE OTHERS... HE PROSPERED!
...AND MY GRAND-FATHER WAS A FINANCIER TO THE KAISER. ...WE ARE NOT JUST ORDINARY PEOPLE!
WHEN MY FATHER DIED I TOOK OVER AND IN A FEW YEARS WE BUILT THE LARGEST CORSET COMPANY IN AMERICA!
...AND REMEMBER, WE ARE ONE OF THE MOST ACCEPTED JEWISH FAMILIES!
THE ARNHEIM NAME MEANS SOMETHING ...IF YOU PROTECT IT ...IT WILL PROTECT YOU!
YOU MUST ALWAYS CONDUCT YOURSELF AS AN ARNHEIM!

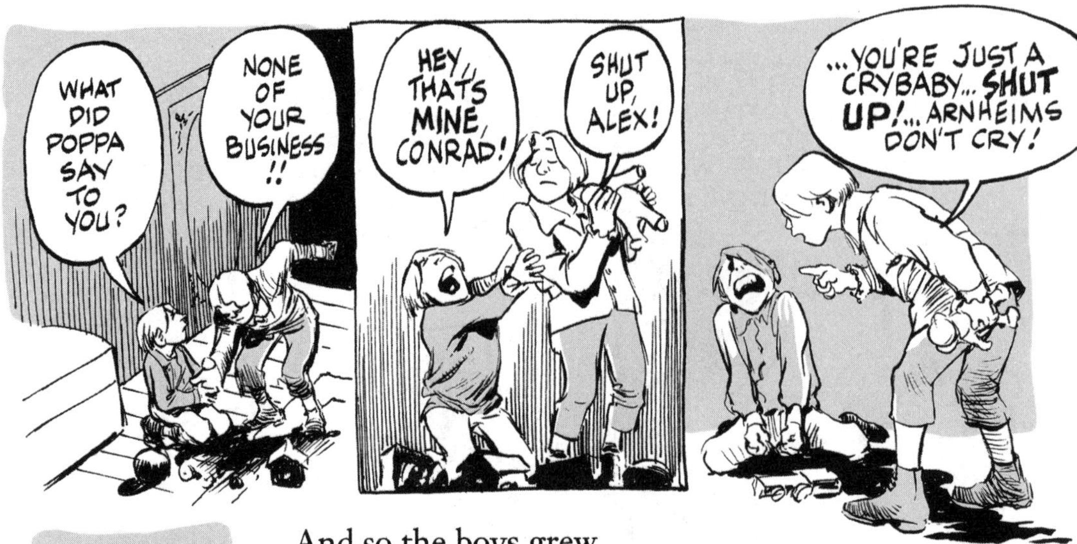
WHAT DID POPPA SAY TO YOU?
NONE OF YOUR BUSINESS !!
HEY, THAT'S MINE, CONRAD!
SHUT UP, ALEX!
...YOU'RE JUST A CRYBABY... SHUT UP!... ARNHEIMS DON'T CRY!

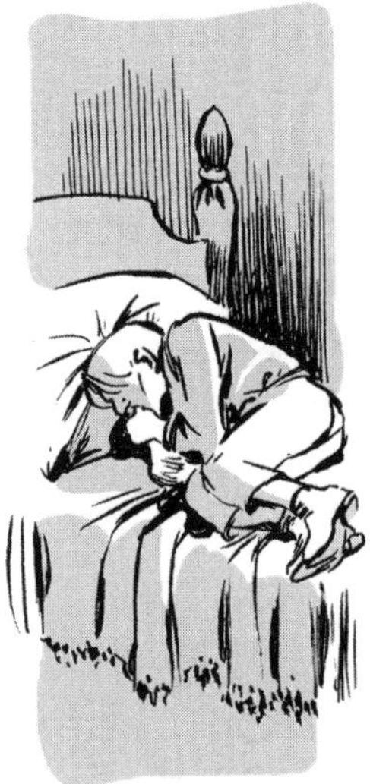

And so the boys grew up. Alex, a shy and nervous child, lived in the shadow of Conrad, an aggressive boy who was adored by his mother and favored by his father. Nothing was denied Conrad. His path through childhood was smoothed by his doting parents.

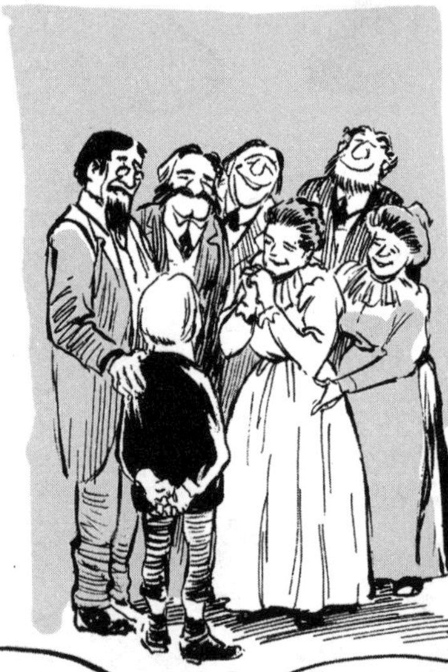

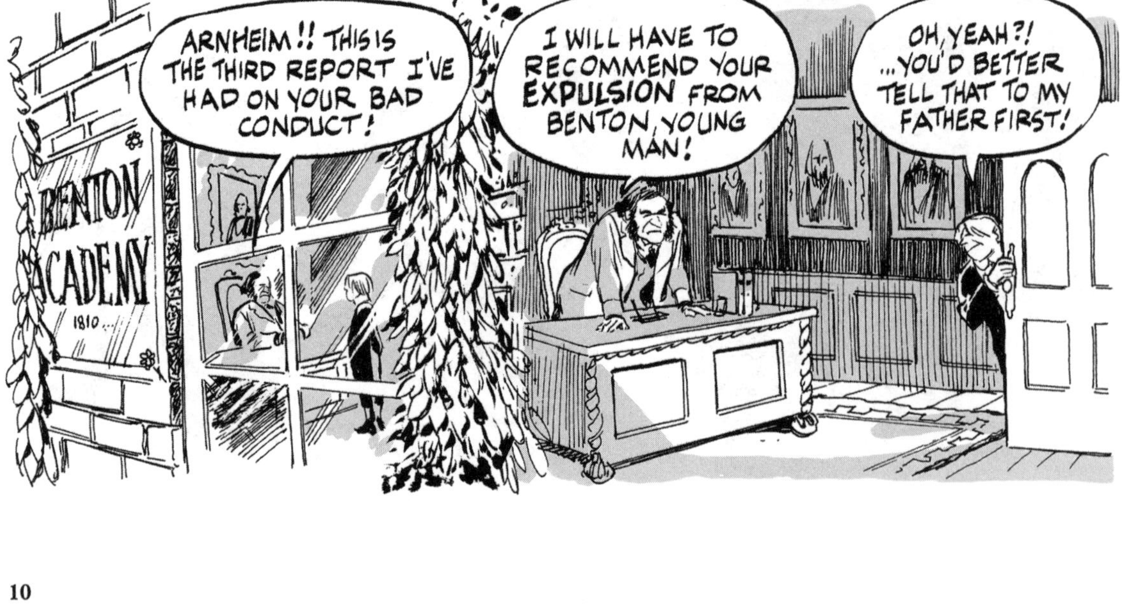
BENTON ACADEMY
1810...
ARNHEIM!! THIS IS THE THIRD REPORT I'VE HAD ON YOUR BAD CONDUCT!
I WILL HAVE TO RECOMMEND YOUR EXPULSION FROM BENTON, YOUNG MAN!
OH, YEAH?! ...YOU'D BETTER TELL THAT TO MY FATHER FIRST!

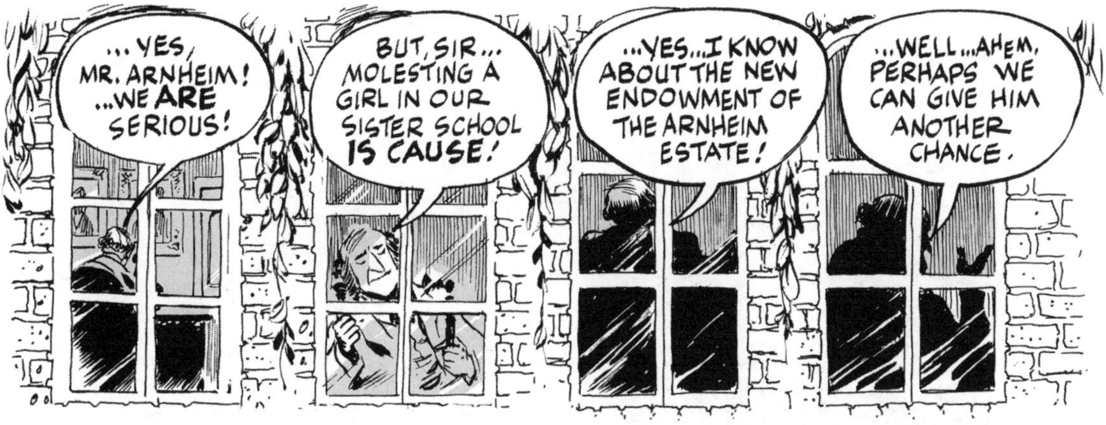
...YES, MR. ARNHEIM! ...WE ARE SERIOUS!
BUT, SIR... MOLESTING A GIRL IN OUR SISTER SCHOOL IS CAUSE!
...YES...I KNOW ABOUT THE NEW ENDOWMENT OF THE ARNHEIM ESTATE!
...WELL...AHEM, PERHAPS WE CAN GIVE HIM ANOTHER CHANCE.

The years at Benton slipped by. Conrad had a number of second chances. Finally, his graduation was negotiated and the Arnheim family could boast an academy graduate. Anything else would have been unthinkable in their social circle. Conrad's pre-manhood was typical of the other boys in his set. A year in Europe, vacations in the mountains, tennis, golf, horseback riding and parties, parties, parties.

Suddenly, one day . . .

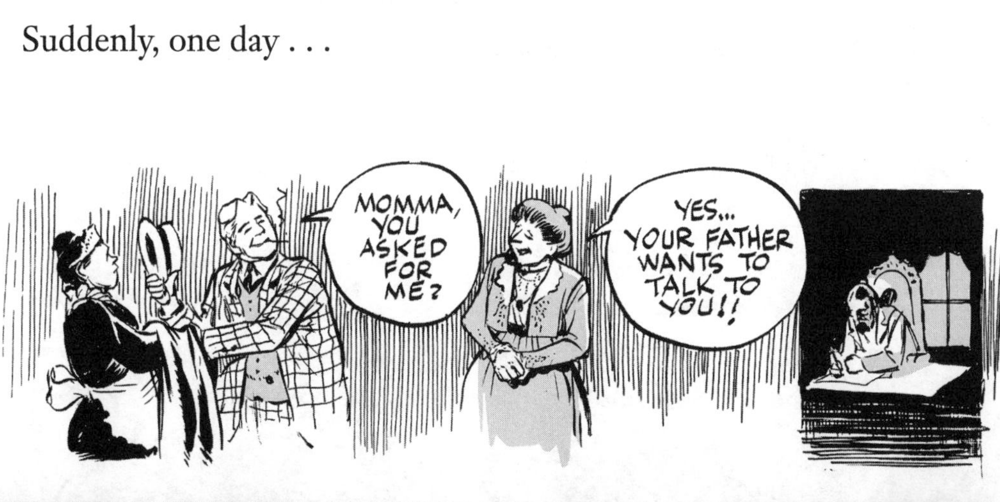
MOMMA, YOU ASKED FOR ME?
YES... YOUR FATHER WANTS TO TALK TO YOU!!

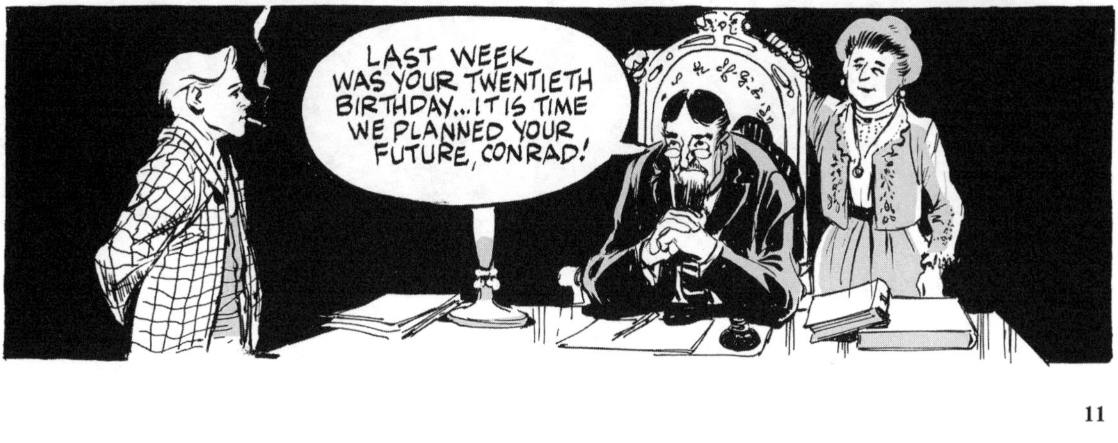
LAST WEEK WAS YOUR TWENTIETH BIRTHDAY...IT IS TIME WE PLANNED YOUR FUTURE, CONRAD!

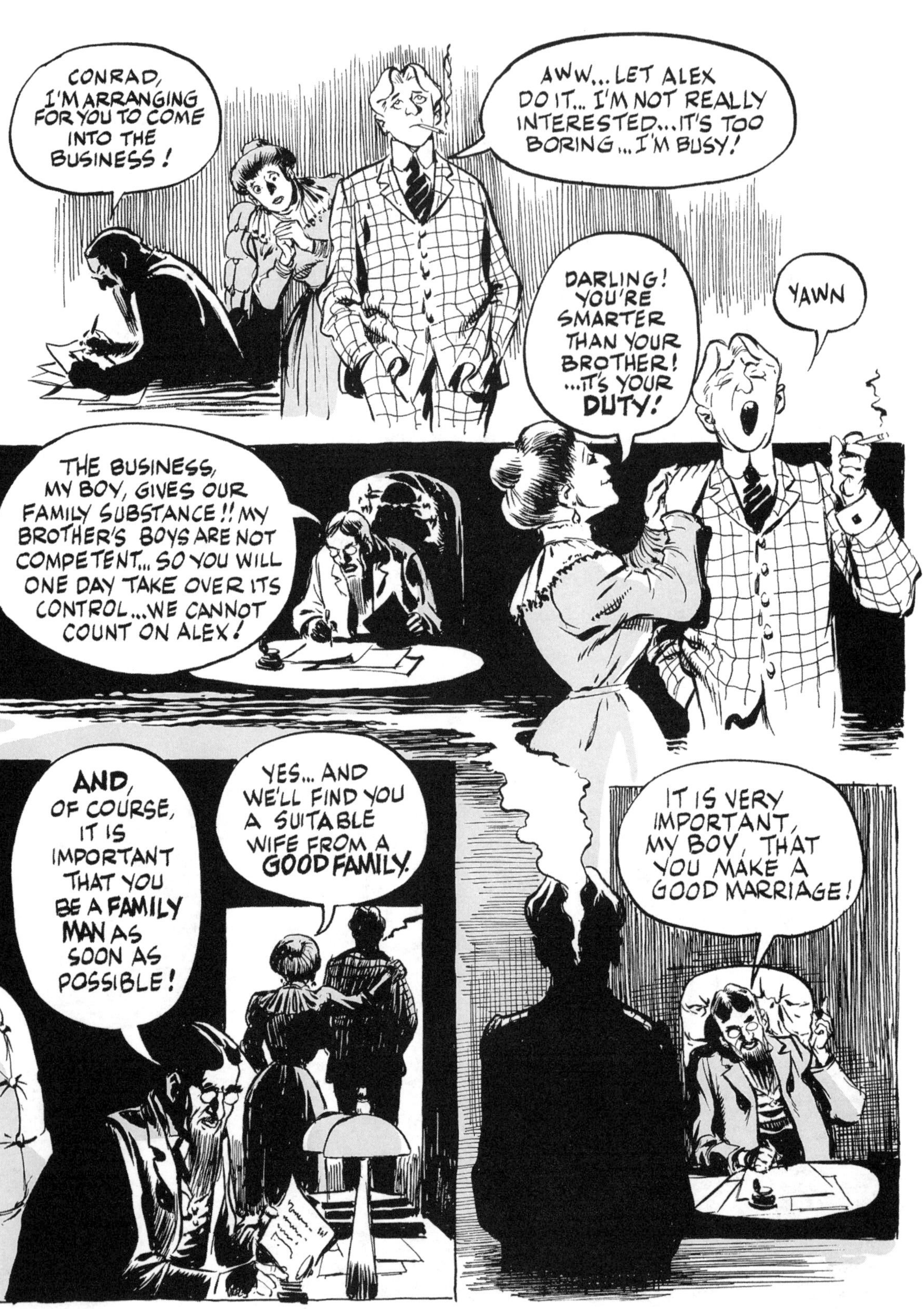
CONRAD, I'M ARRANGING FOR YOU TO COME INTO THE BUSINESS!
AWW... LET ALEX DO IT... I'M NOT REALLY INTERESTED... IT'S TOO BORING... I'M BUSY!
DARLING! YOU'RE SMARTER THAN YOUR BROTHER! ...IT'S YOUR DUTY!
YAWN
THE BUSINESS, MY BOY, GIVES OUR FAMILY SUBSTANCE!! MY BROTHER'S BOYS ARE NOT COMPETENT... SO YOU WILL ONE DAY TAKE OVER ITS CONTROL... WE CANNOT COUNT ON ALEX!
AND, OF COURSE, IT IS IMPORTANT THAT YOU BE A FAMILY MAN AS SOON AS POSSIBLE!
YES... AND WE'LL FIND YOU A SUITABLE WIFE FROM A GOOD FAMILY.
IT IS VERY IMPORTANT, MY BOY, THAT YOU MAKE A GOOD MARRIAGE!

The
OBER
Family

Not all of the immigrant German Jews remained in the big seaport cities. The more adventurous headed West and settled in the open country where small towns were in need of the enterprise and trading skills Jews had learned in Europe. Two years after the Civil War, Chaim Ober arrived in the riverhead town of Lavolier. Originally a trading post in the Ohio territory, it gradually became a farming community.

Chaim Ober opened a small dry goods store after a few years of peddling throughout the countryside. He could barely speak English, so his son Abner soon took over the management of the store.

Abner was very successful and popular. Eventually the Obers became quite wealthy and a part of Lavolier society. They were a good family.

The Ober home was one of the finest in the lower river valley. The Obers entertained often and their daughter, Lilli, was sought after by all the young swains in town. To marry into the Ober family was a dream shared by many a Jewish mother in Lavolier. They were, after all, the best family.

But the Obers themselves had dreams; privately, they had greater social ambitions.

So they willingly "sat" for local society newspaper feature stories.

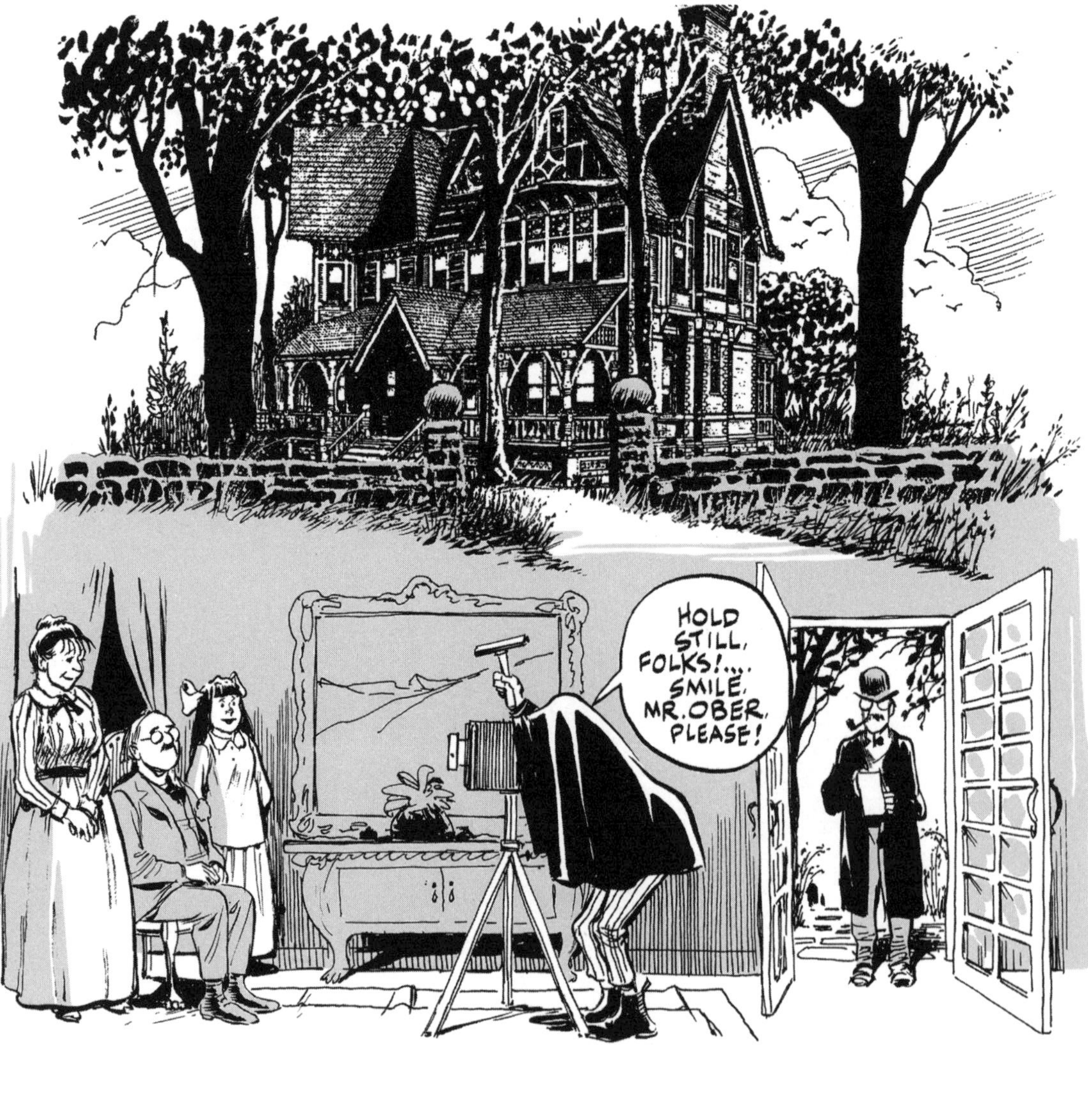
HOLD STILL, FOLKS!.... SMILE, MR. OBER, PLEASE!

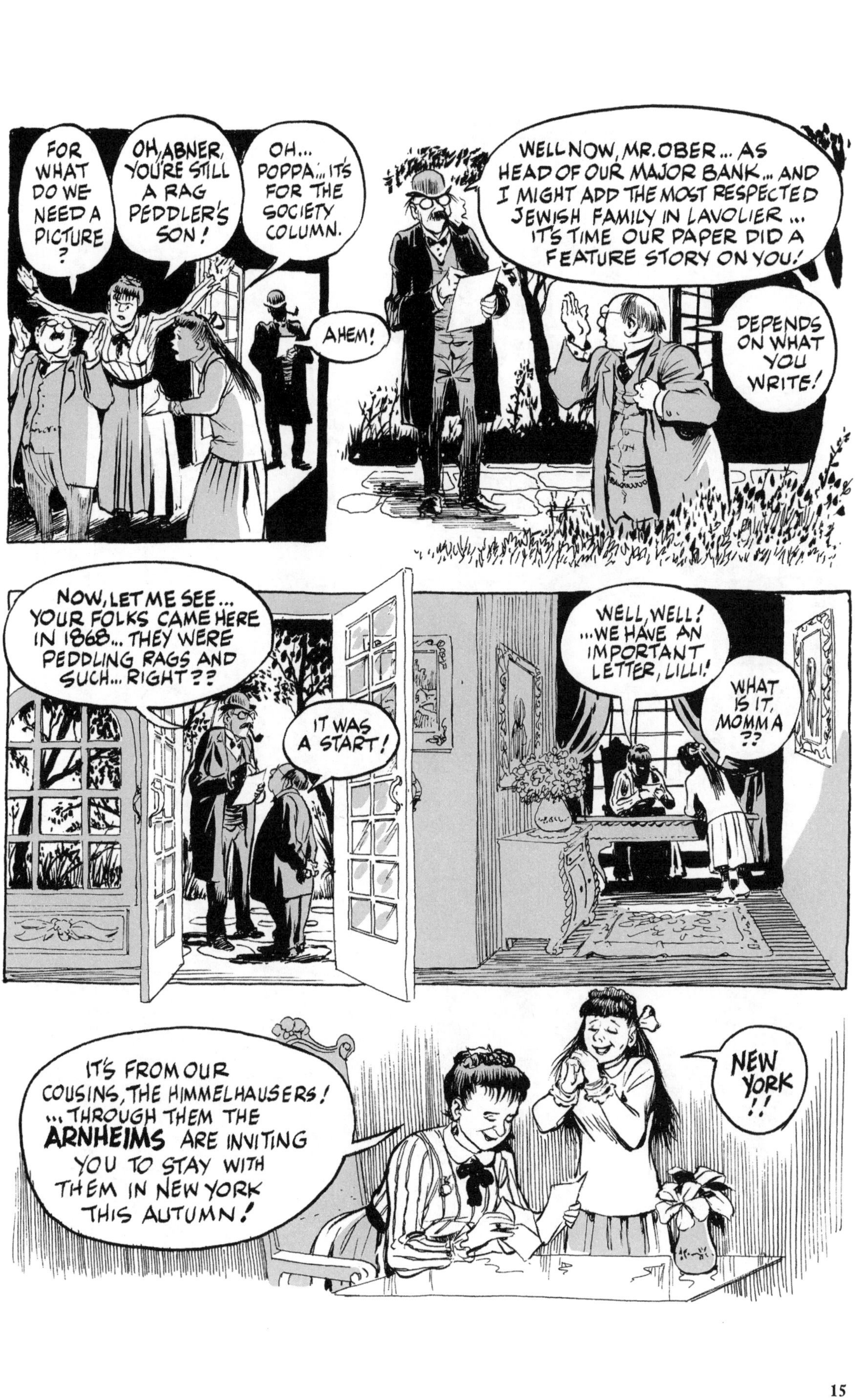
FOR WHAT DO WE NEED A PICTURE ?
OH, ABNER, YOU'RE STILL A RAG PEDDLER'S SON!
OH... POPPA... IT'S FOR THE SOCIETY COLUMN.
AHEM!
WELL NOW, MR. OBER... AS HEAD OF OUR MAJOR BANK... AND I MIGHT ADD THE MOST RESPECTED JEWISH FAMILY IN LAVOLIER... IT'S TIME OUR PAPER DID A FEATURE STORY ON YOU!
DEPENDS ON WHAT YOU WRITE!
NOW, LET ME SEE... YOUR FOLKS CAME HERE IN 1868... THEY WERE PEDDLING RAGS AND SUCH... RIGHT??
IT WAS A START!
WELL, WELL! ...WE HAVE AN IMPORTANT LETTER, LILLI!
WHAT IS IT, MOMMA ??
IT'S FROM OUR COUSINS, THE HIMMELHAUSERS! ...THROUGH THEM THE ARNHEIMS ARE INVITING YOU TO STAY WITH THEM IN NEW YORK THIS AUTUMN!
NEW YORK !!

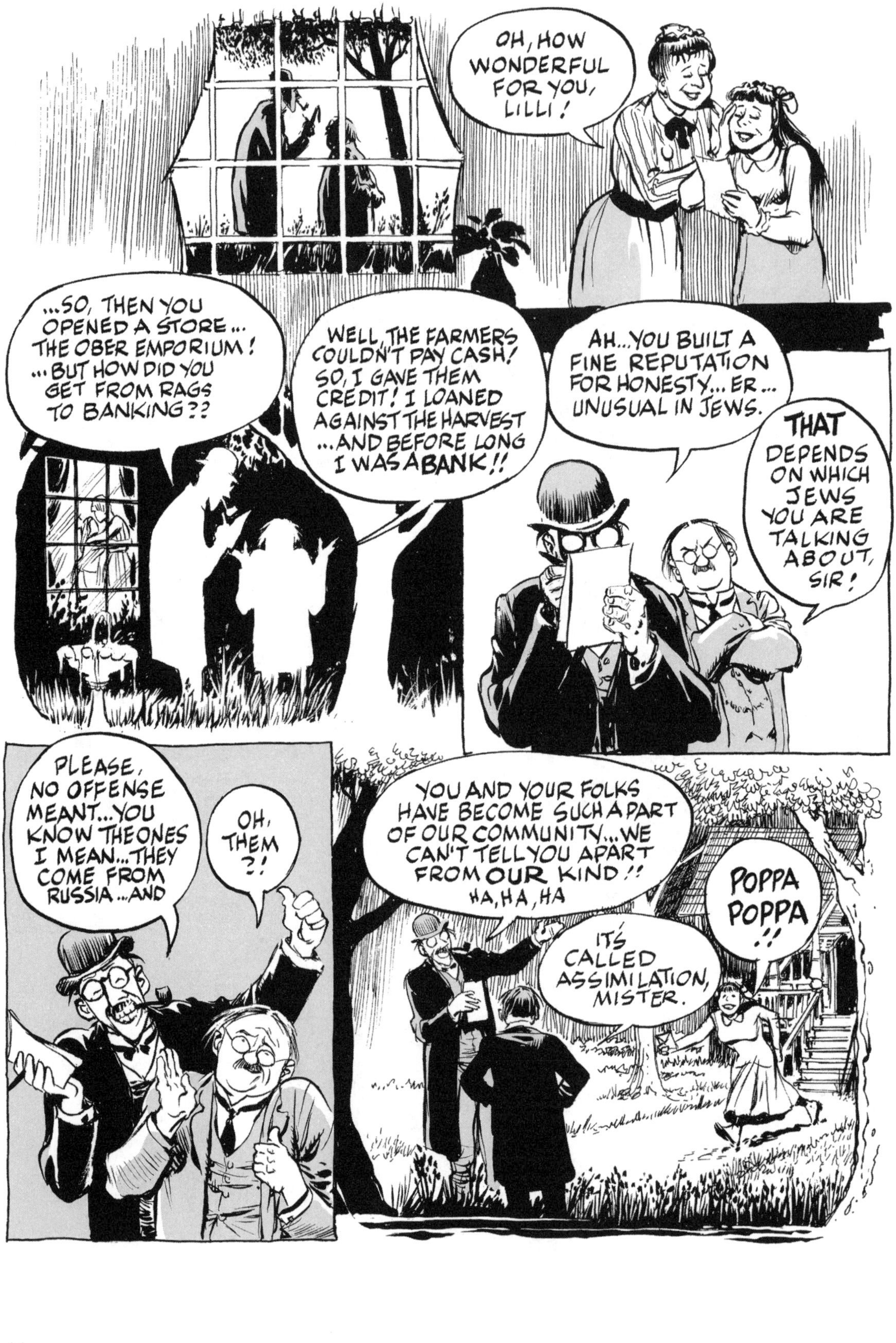
OH, HOW WONDERFUL FOR YOU, LILLI!
...SO, THEN YOU OPENED A STORE... THE OBER EMPORIUM! ...BUT HOW DID YOU GET FROM RAGS TO BANKING??
WELL, THE FARMERS COULDN'T PAY CASH! SO, I GAVE THEM CREDIT! I LOANED AGAINST THE HARVEST ...AND BEFORE LONG I WAS A BANK!!
AH...YOU BUILT A FINE REPUTATION FOR HONESTY... ER... UNUSUAL IN JEWS.
THAT DEPENDS ON WHICH JEWS YOU ARE TALKING ABOUT, SIR!
PLEASE, NO OFFENSE MEANT...YOU KNOW THE ONES I MEAN...THEY COME FROM RUSSIA ...AND
OH, THEM ?!
YOU AND YOUR FOLKS HAVE BECOME SUCH A PART OF OUR COMMUNITY...WE CAN'T TELL YOU APART FROM OUR KIND!! HA, HA, HA
IT'S CALLED ASSIMILATION, MISTER.
POPPA POPPA !!

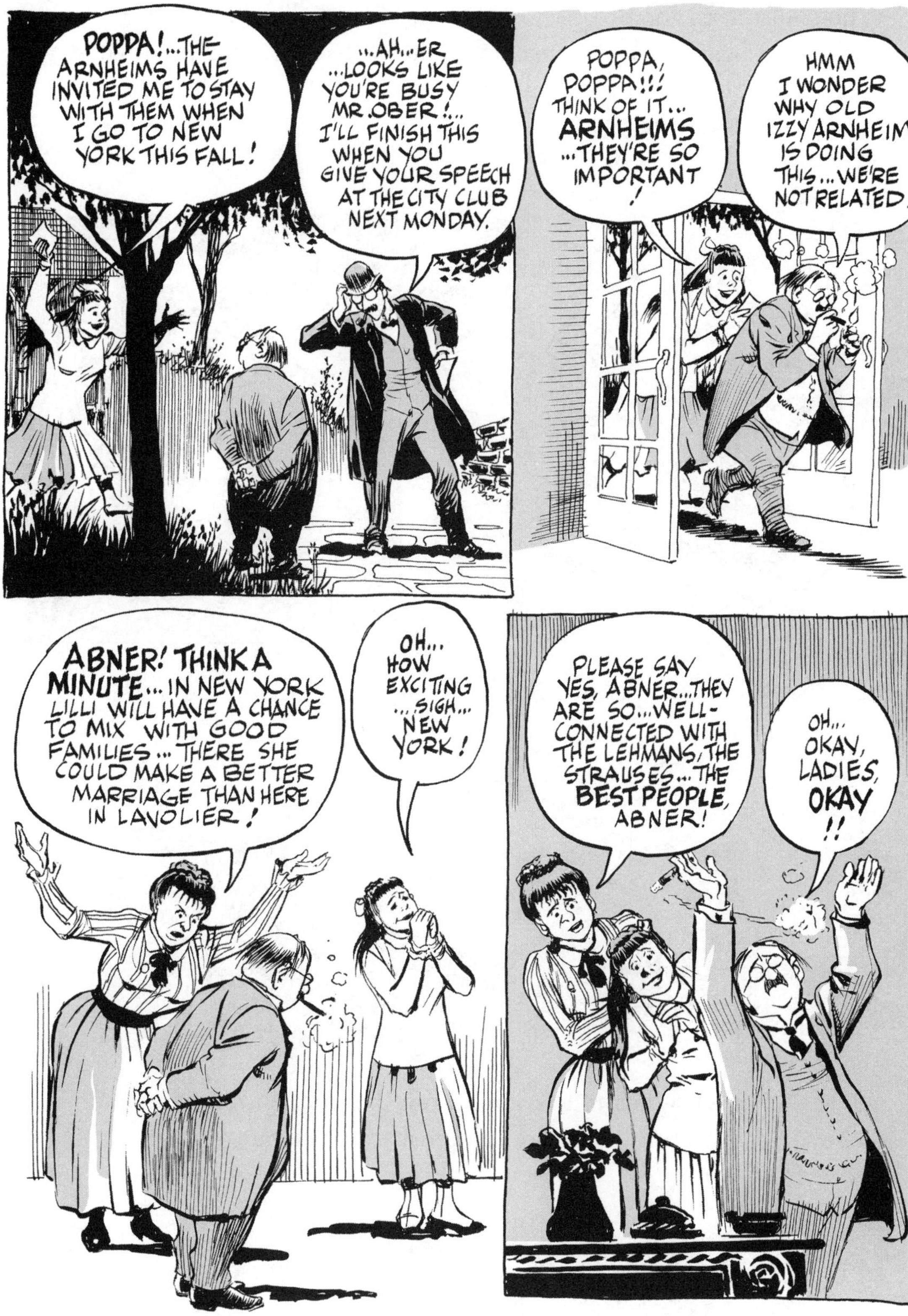
POPPA!...THE ARNHEIMS HAVE INVITED ME TO STAY WITH THEM WHEN I GO TO NEW YORK THIS FALL!
...AH...ER ...LOOKS LIKE YOU'RE BUSY MR. OBER!... I'LL FINISH THIS WHEN YOU GIVE YOUR SPEECH AT THE CITY CLUB NEXT MONDAY.
POPPA, POPPA!!! THINK OF IT... ARNHEIMS ...THEY'RE SO IMPORTANT!
HMM I WONDER WHY OLD IZZY ARNHEIM IS DOING THIS...WE'RE NOT RELATED!
ABNER! THINK A MINUTE...IN NEW YORK LILLI WILL HAVE A CHANCE TO MIX WITH GOOD FAMILIES...THERE SHE COULD MAKE A BETTER MARRIAGE THAN HERE IN LAVOLIER!
OH... HOW EXCITING ...SIGH... NEW YORK!
PLEASE SAY YES, ABNER...THEY ARE SO...WELL-CONNECTED WITH THE LEHMANS, THE STRAUSES...THE BEST PEOPLE, ABNER!
OH... OKAY, LADIES, OKAY!!

Who could resist the prospect of moving up socially? Not even a small-town banker. Most unusual was the ease with which the invitations came. Social inclusion into the upper class German Jewish society was never this easy . . .

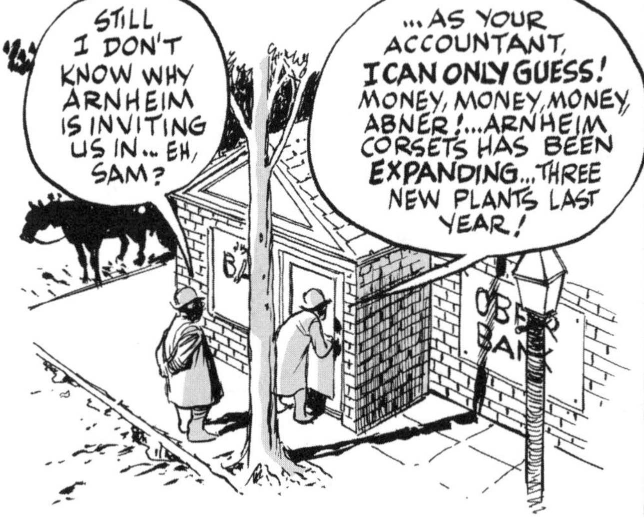

STILL I DON'T KNOW WHY ARNHEIM IS INVITING US IN... EH, SAM?
...AS YOUR ACCOUNTANT, I CAN ONLY GUESS! MONEY, MONEY, MONEY, ABNER!...ARNHEIM CORSETS HAS BEEN EXPANDING... THREE NEW PLANTS LAST YEAR!

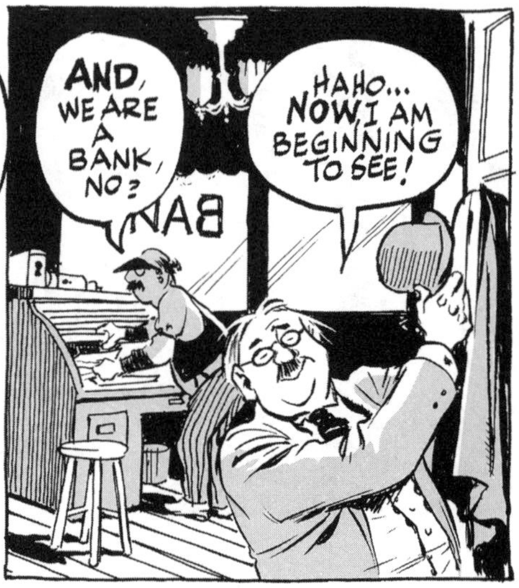

AND, WE ARE A BANK, NO?
HAHO... NOW, I AM BEGINNING TO SEE!

Late that summer Lilli left Lavolier for her new life in New York.

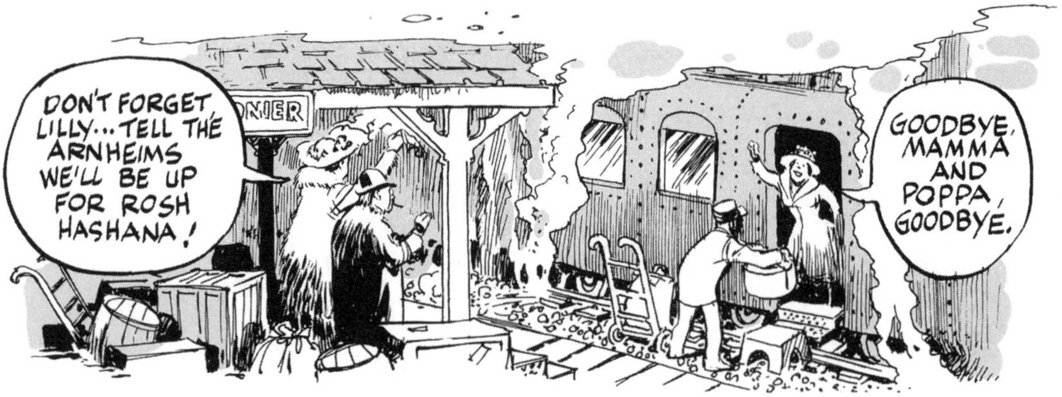

DON'T FORGET LILLY... TELL THE ARNHEIMS WE'LL BE UP FOR ROSH HASHANA!
GOODBYE, MAMMA AND POPPA, GOODBYE.

So, in the autumn during the High Holy Days, the Obers came to New York . . . not for any religious observance but to meet Isidore Arnheim.

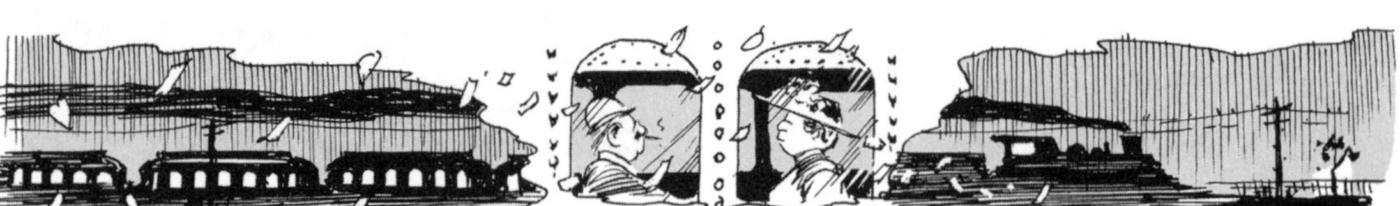

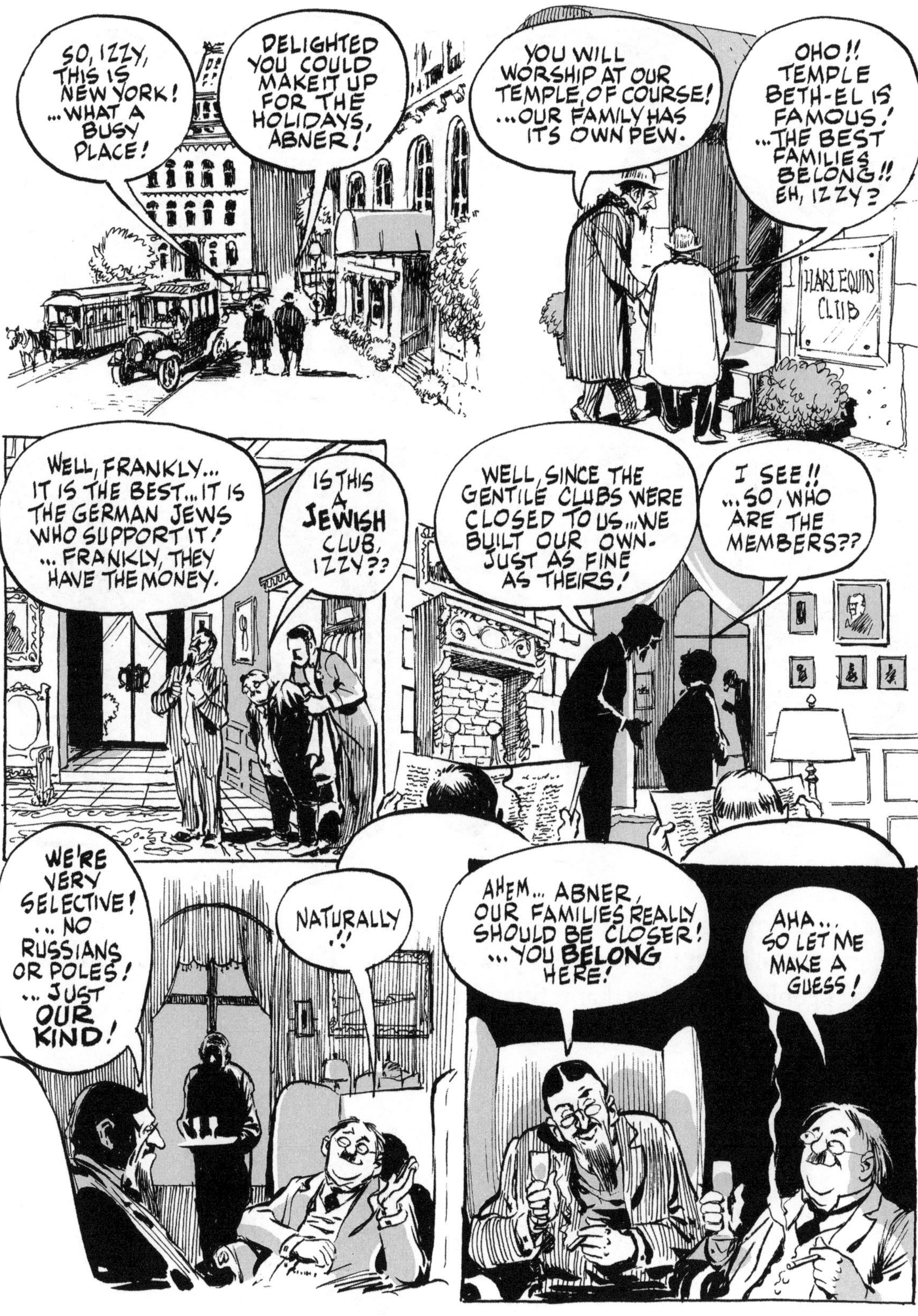
SO, IZZY, THIS IS NEW YORK! ...WHAT A BUSY PLACE!
DELIGHTED YOU COULD MAKE IT UP FOR THE HOLIDAYS, ABNER!
YOU WILL WORSHIP AT OUR TEMPLE, OF COURSE! ...OUR FAMILY HAS ITS OWN PEW.
OHO!! TEMPLE BETH-EL IS FAMOUS! ...THE BEST FAMILIES BELONG!! EH, IZZY?
HARLEQUIN CLUB
IS THIS A JEWISH CLUB, IZZY??
WELL, FRANKLY... IT IS THE BEST... IT IS THE GERMAN JEWS WHO SUPPORT IT! ... FRANKLY, THEY HAVE THE MONEY.
I SEE!! ...SO, WHO ARE THE MEMBERS??
WELL, SINCE THE GENTILE CLUBS WERE CLOSED TO US... WE BUILT OUR OWN. JUST AS FINE AS THEIRS!
WE'RE VERY SELECTIVE! .. NO RUSSIANS OR POLES! .. JUST OUR KIND!
NATURALLY!!
AHEM... ABNER, OUR FAMILIES REALLY SHOULD BE CLOSER! ... YOU BELONG HERE!
AHA... SO LET ME MAKE A GUESS!

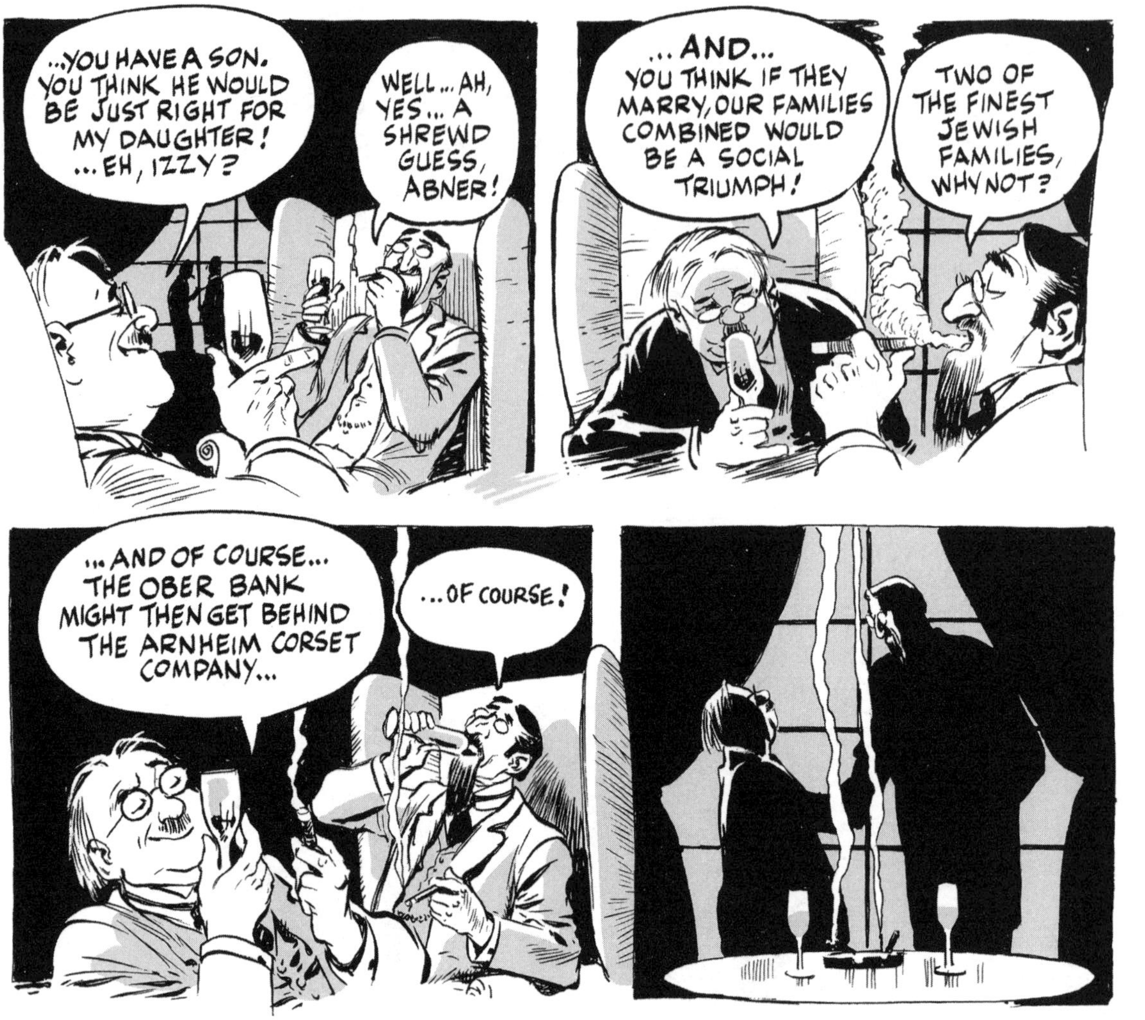
...YOU HAVE A SON. YOU THINK HE WOULD BE JUST RIGHT FOR MY DAUGHTER! ...EH, IZZY?
WELL... AH, YES... A SHREWD GUESS, ABNER!
...AND... YOU THINK IF THEY MARRY, OUR FAMILIES COMBINED WOULD BE A SOCIAL TRIUMPH!
TWO OF THE FINEST JEWISH FAMILIES, WHY NOT?
...AND OF COURSE... THE OBER BANK MIGHT THEN GET BEHIND THE ARNHEIM CORSET COMPANY...
...OF COURSE!

The following two weeks were dazzling for the Obers. They were given a place in the Arnheim pew at temple. They were introduced to people whose social and financial status was awesome.

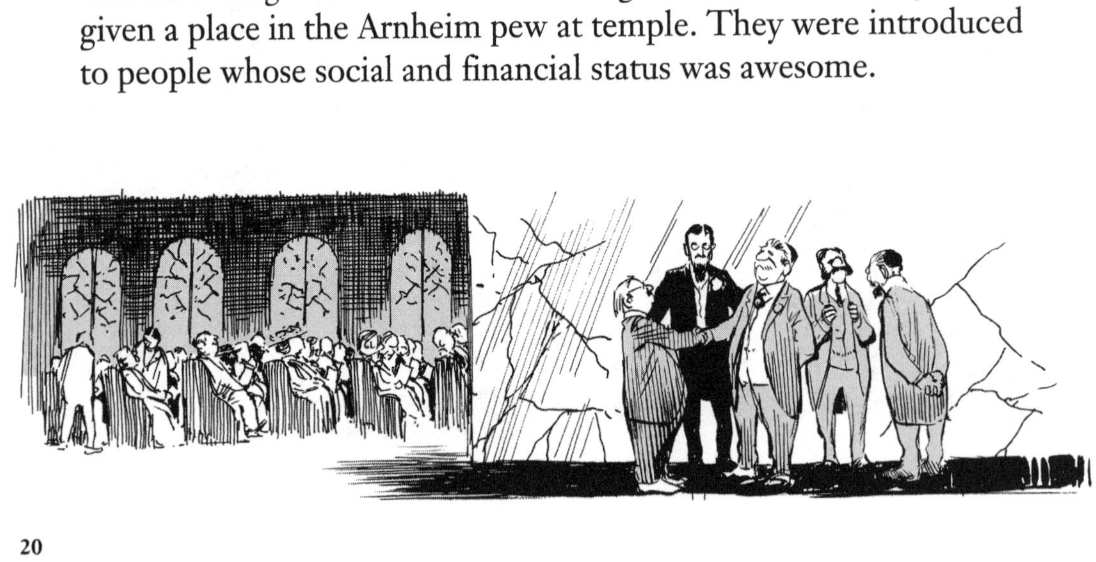

In New York, Lilli Ober seemed to grow up overnight. Under the Teutonic Arnheim tutelage, the small town girl blossomed into a "suitable" young woman who fit neatly into their society. All the next year, the Arnheims included Lilli in their social program. Not surprisingly, almost every social event included Conrad.

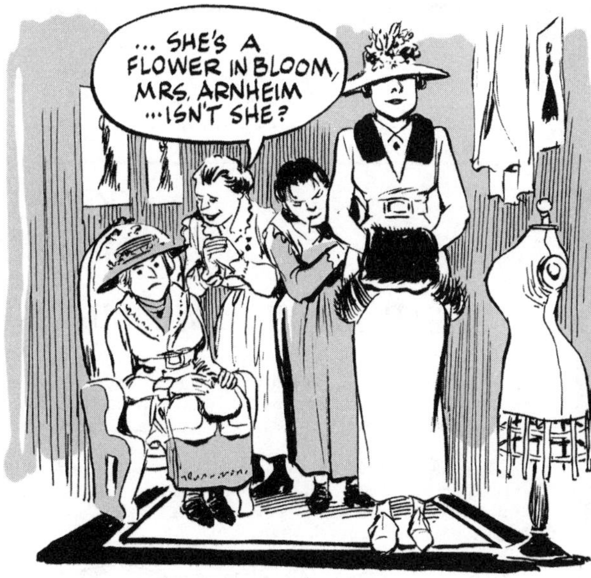
... SHE'S A FLOWER IN BLOOM, MRS. ARNHEIM ...ISN'T SHE?

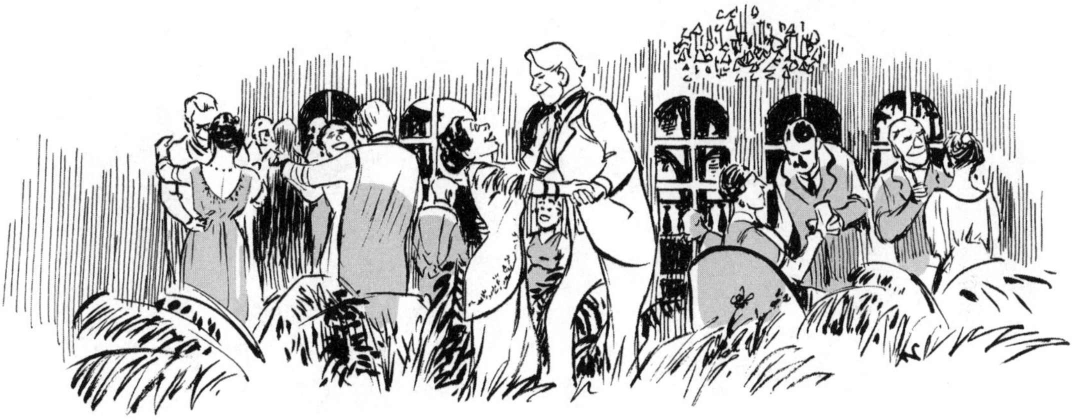

That spring, a letter arrived for the Obers in Lavolier.

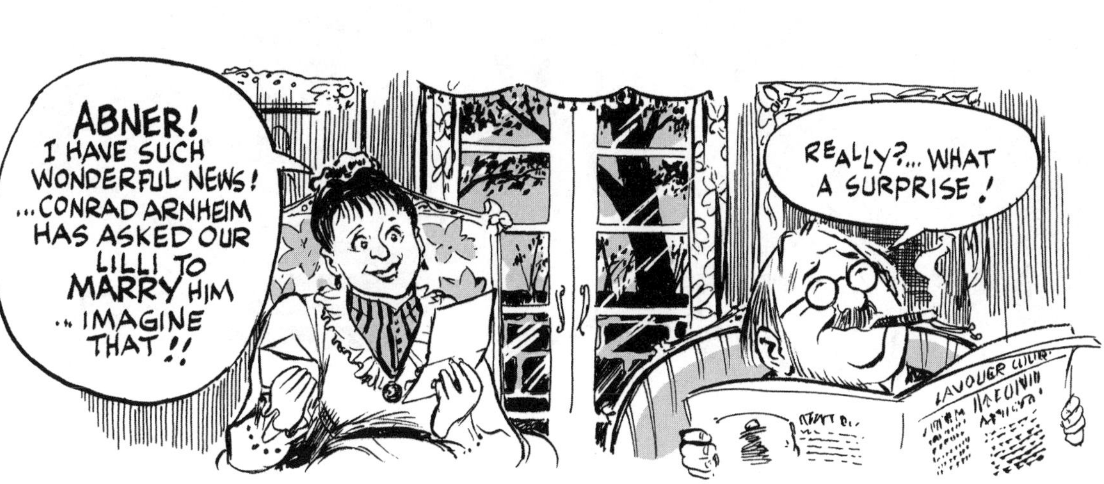
ABNER! I HAVE SUCH WONDERFUL NEWS! ...CONRAD ARNHEIM HAS ASKED OUR LILLI TO MARRY HIM .. IMAGINE THAT!!
REALLY?... WHAT A SURPRISE!

THE LAVOLIER COURIER

VOL.5 ISSUE 52 | *JUNE 19, 1910* | *TWO CENTS*

SOCIETY

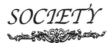

OBER-ARNHEIM WEDDING SOCIAL EVENT OF SEASON

The joining of two very prominent families brought to Lavolier two hundred guests from as far away as New York.

The Ober family, leaders of the Jewish community in our city for over two decades, celebrated the wedding of their daughter Lillian to Conrad Arnheim of New York.

Local luminaries who filled the pews of the Beth Shalom Synagogue on Elm Street came from the cream of society.

Mayor Jim Bryan, Senator Owen Hill, Rabbi and Mrs. Alex Ochs, Mr. and Mrs. Stetson, Mr. and Mrs. Cohen.

WEDDING MENU

The reception feast was the season's most sumptuous array of continental cuisine.

Beginning with a light buffet in which French truffles and baby clams were featured, the guests were then served a main course.

WHAT A LOVELY COUPLE, ABNER!
...HE'S SO HANDSOME.
THE START OF A DYNASTY, EH, ABNER?

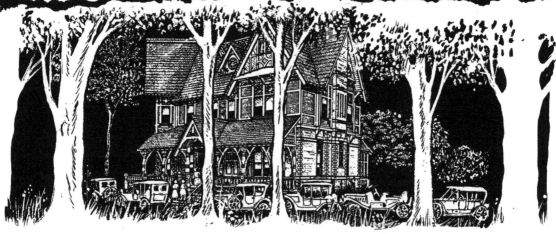

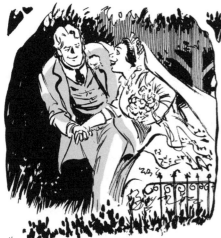

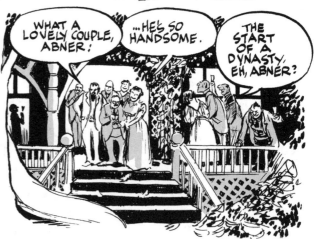

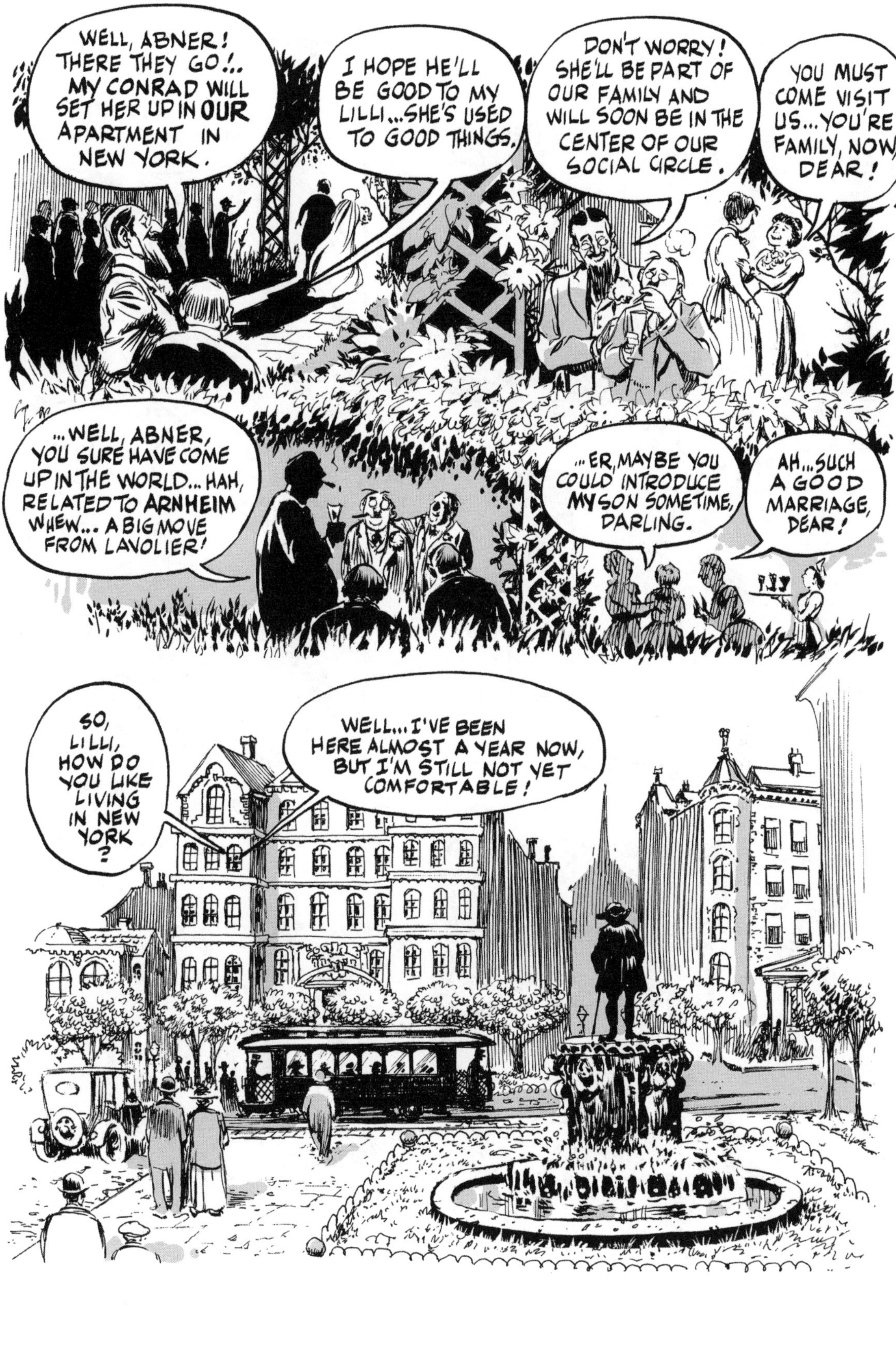
WELL, ABNER! THERE THEY GO!.. MY CONRAD WILL SET HER UP IN OUR APARTMENT IN NEW YORK.
I HOPE HE'LL BE GOOD TO MY LILLI...SHE'S USED TO GOOD THINGS.
DON'T WORRY! SHE'LL BE PART OF OUR FAMILY AND WILL SOON BE IN THE CENTER OF OUR SOCIAL CIRCLE.
YOU MUST COME VISIT US...YOU'RE FAMILY, NOW, DEAR!
...WELL, ABNER, YOU SURE HAVE COME UP IN THE WORLD... HAH, RELATED TO ARNHEIM WHEW... A BIG MOVE FROM LAVOLIER!
...ER, MAYBE YOU COULD INTRODUCE MY SON SOMETIME, DARLING.
AH...SUCH A GOOD MARRIAGE, DEAR!
SO, LILLI, HOW DO YOU LIKE LIVING IN NEW YORK?
WELL... I'VE BEEN HERE ALMOST A YEAR NOW, BUT I'M STILL NOT YET COMFORTABLE!

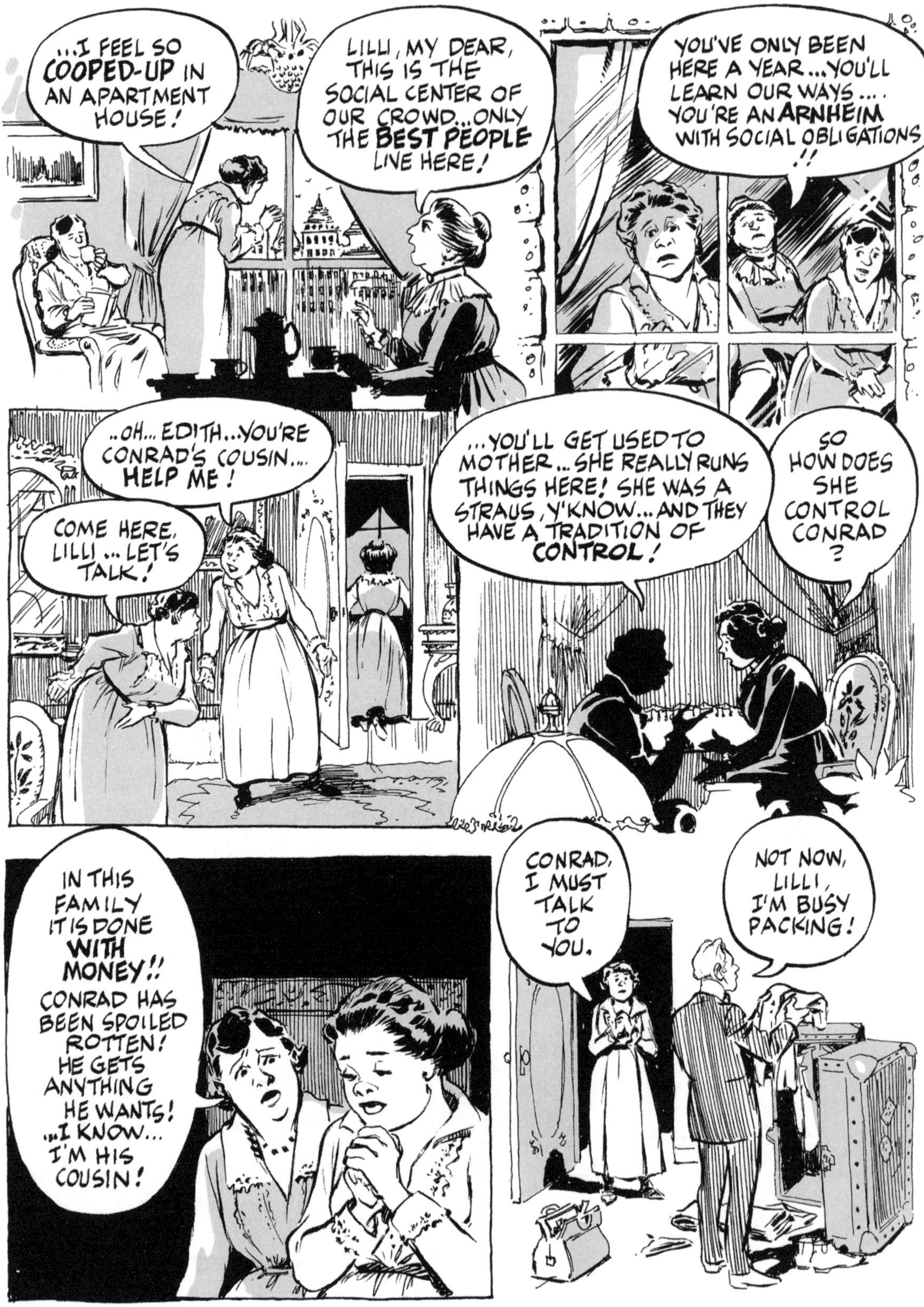
...I FEEL SO COOPED-UP IN AN APARTMENT HOUSE!
LILLI, MY DEAR, THIS IS THE SOCIAL CENTER OF OUR CROWD...ONLY THE BEST PEOPLE LIVE HERE!
YOU'VE ONLY BEEN HERE A YEAR...YOU'LL LEARN OUR WAYS.... YOU'RE AN ARNHEIM WITH SOCIAL OBLIGATIONS!!
..OH... EDITH...YOU'RE CONRAD'S COUSIN.... HELP ME!
COME HERE, LILLI...LET'S TALK!
...YOU'LL GET USED TO MOTHER...SHE REALLY RUNS THINGS HERE! SHE WAS A STRAUS, Y'KNOW...AND THEY HAVE A TRADITION OF CONTROL!
SO HOW DOES SHE CONTROL CONRAD?
IN THIS FAMILY IT IS DONE WITH MONEY!! CONRAD HAS BEEN SPOILED ROTTEN! HE GETS ANYTHING HE WANTS! ..I KNOW... I'M HIS COUSIN!
CONRAD, I MUST TALK TO YOU.
NOT NOW, LILLI, I'M BUSY PACKING!

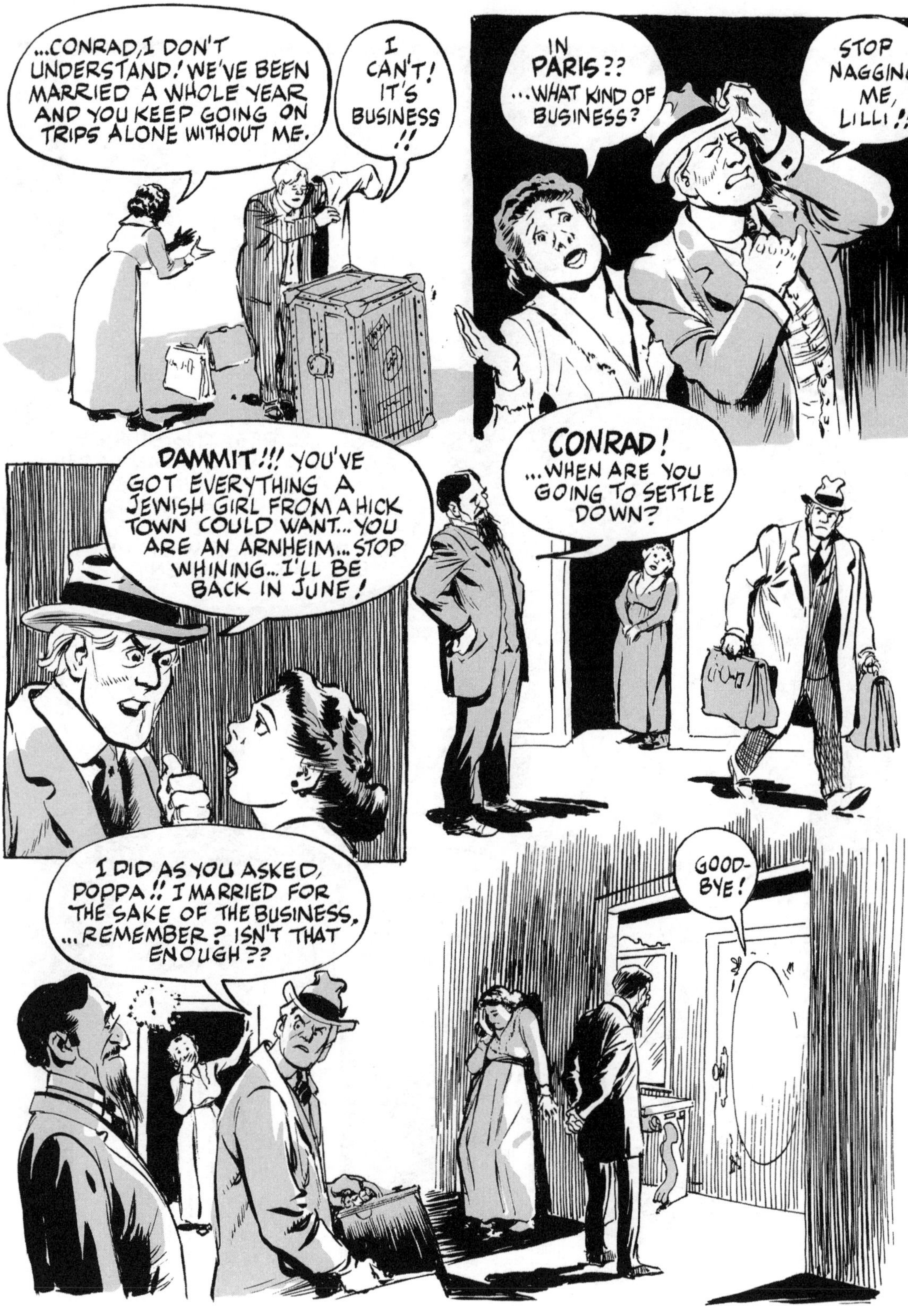
...CONRAD, I DON'T UNDERSTAND! WE'VE BEEN MARRIED A WHOLE YEAR AND YOU KEEP GOING ON TRIPS ALONE WITHOUT ME.
I CAN'T! IT'S BUSINESS !!
IN PARIS?? ...WHAT KIND OF BUSINESS?
STOP NAGGING ME, LILLI !!
DAMMIT!!! YOU'VE GOT EVERYTHING A JEWISH GIRL FROM A HICK TOWN COULD WANT... YOU ARE AN ARNHEIM... STOP WHINING... I'LL BE BACK IN JUNE!
CONRAD! ...WHEN ARE YOU GOING TO SETTLE DOWN?
I DID AS YOU ASKED, POPPA!! I MARRIED FOR THE SAKE OF THE BUSINESS. ...REMEMBER? ISN'T THAT ENOUGH??
!
GOOD-BYE!

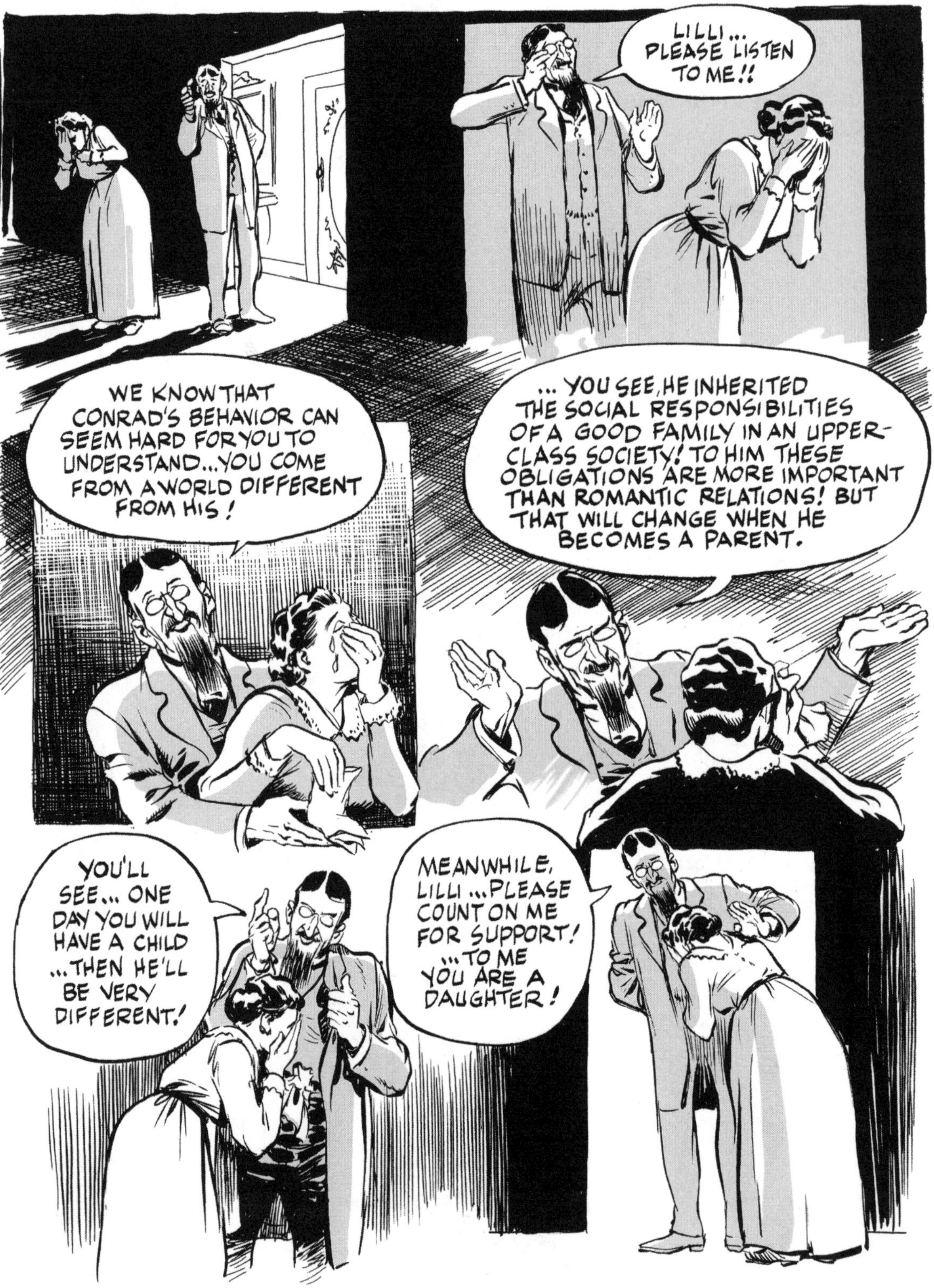
LILLI... PLEASE LISTEN TO ME!!
WE KNOW THAT CONRAD'S BEHAVIOR CAN SEEM HARD FOR YOU TO UNDERSTAND... YOU COME FROM A WORLD DIFFERENT FROM HIS!
... YOU SEE, HE INHERITED THE SOCIAL RESPONSIBILITIES OF A GOOD FAMILY IN AN UPPER-CLASS SOCIETY! TO HIM THESE OBLIGATIONS ARE MORE IMPORTANT THAN ROMANTIC RELATIONS! BUT THAT WILL CHANGE WHEN HE BECOMES A PARENT.
YOU'LL SEE... ONE DAY YOU WILL HAVE A CHILD ...THEN HE'LL BE VERY DIFFERENT!
MEANWHILE, LILLI ...PLEASE COUNT ON ME FOR SUPPORT! ...TO ME YOU ARE A DAUGHTER!

Another year passed. While Lilli immersed herself in the Arnheim social world, she enjoyed little, if any, attention from Conrad. Her only comfort was the growing closeness with her father-in-law. She now depended on old Isidore's protection.

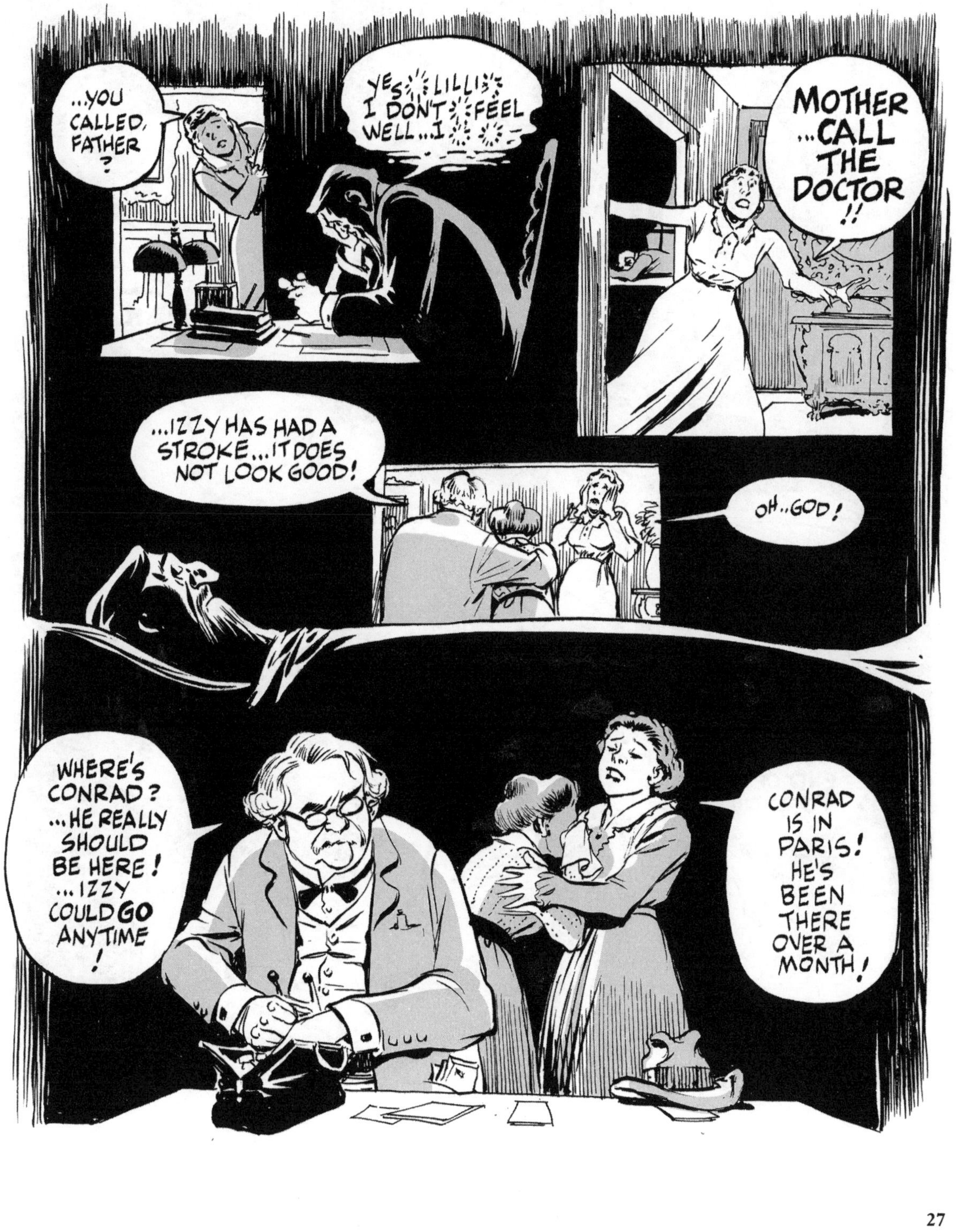

...YOU CALLED, FATHER?
YES... LILLI... I DON'T... FEEL WELL... I...
MOTHER ...CALL THE DOCTOR!!
...IZZY HAS HAD A STROKE... IT DOES NOT LOOK GOOD!
OH..GOD!
WHERE'S CONRAD? ...HE REALLY SHOULD BE HERE! ...IZZY COULD GO ANYTIME!
CONRAD IS IN PARIS! HE'S BEEN THERE OVER A MONTH!

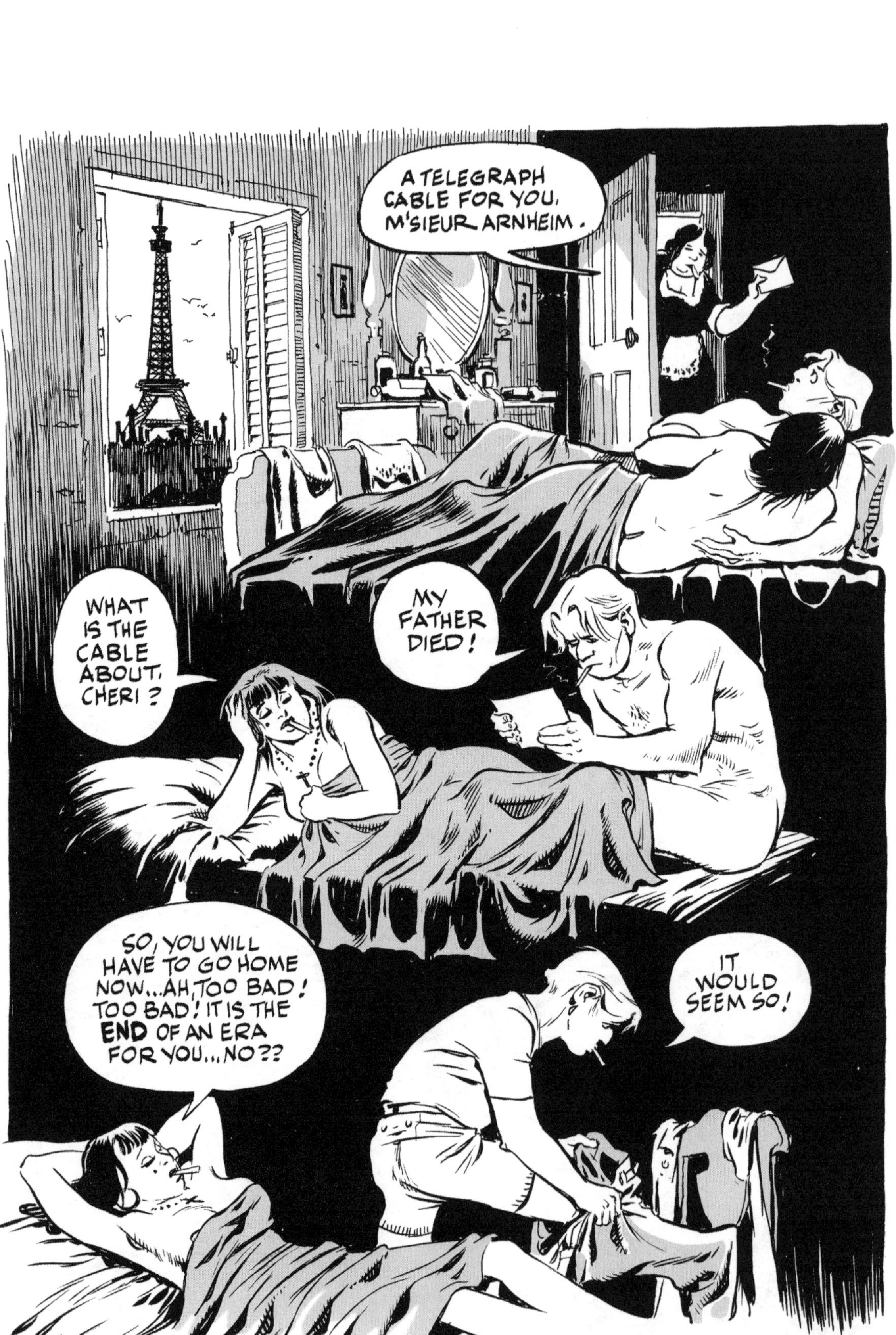
A TELEGRAPH CABLE FOR YOU, M'SIEUR ARNHEIM.
WHAT IS THE CABLE ABOUT, CHERI ?
MY FATHER DIED!
SO, YOU WILL HAVE TO GO HOME NOW...AH, TOO BAD! TOO BAD! IT IS THE **END** OF AN ERA FOR YOU...NO??
IT WOULD SEEM SO!

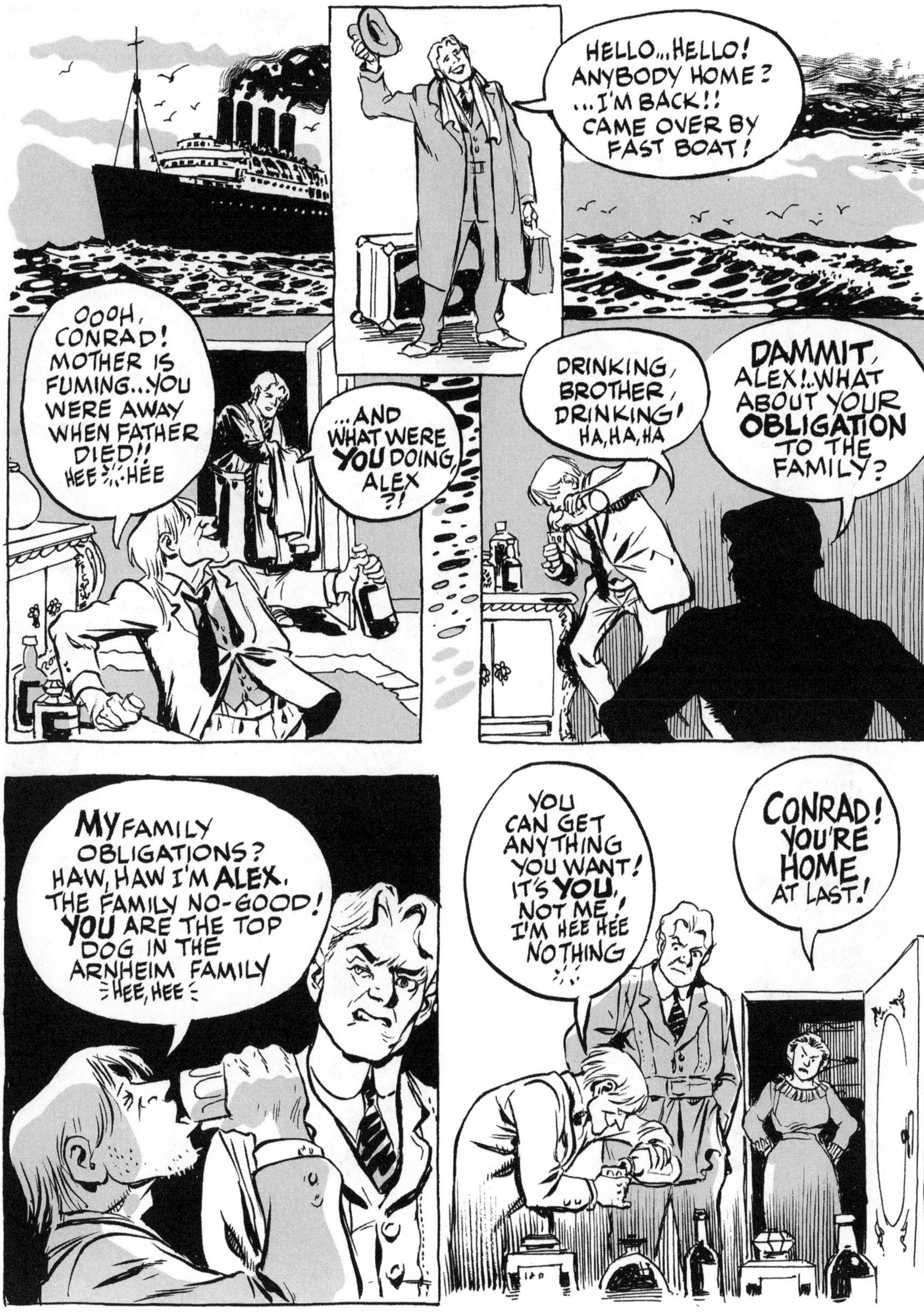
HELLO...HELLO! ANYBODY HOME? ...I'M BACK!! CAME OVER BY FAST BOAT!
OOOH, CONRAD! MOTHER IS FUMING...YOU WERE AWAY WHEN FATHER DIED!! HEE HEE
...AND WHAT WERE YOU DOING, ALEX ?!
DRINKING, BROTHER, DRINKING! HA, HA, HA
DAMMIT, ALEX!..WHAT ABOUT YOUR OBLIGATION TO THE FAMILY?
MY FAMILY OBLIGATIONS? HAW, HAW I'M ALEX, THE FAMILY NO-GOOD! YOU ARE THE TOP DOG IN THE ARNHEIM FAMILY HEE, HEE
YOU CAN GET ANYTHING YOU WANT! IT'S YOU, NOT ME, I'M HEE HEE NOTHING
CONRAD! YOU'RE HOME AT LAST!

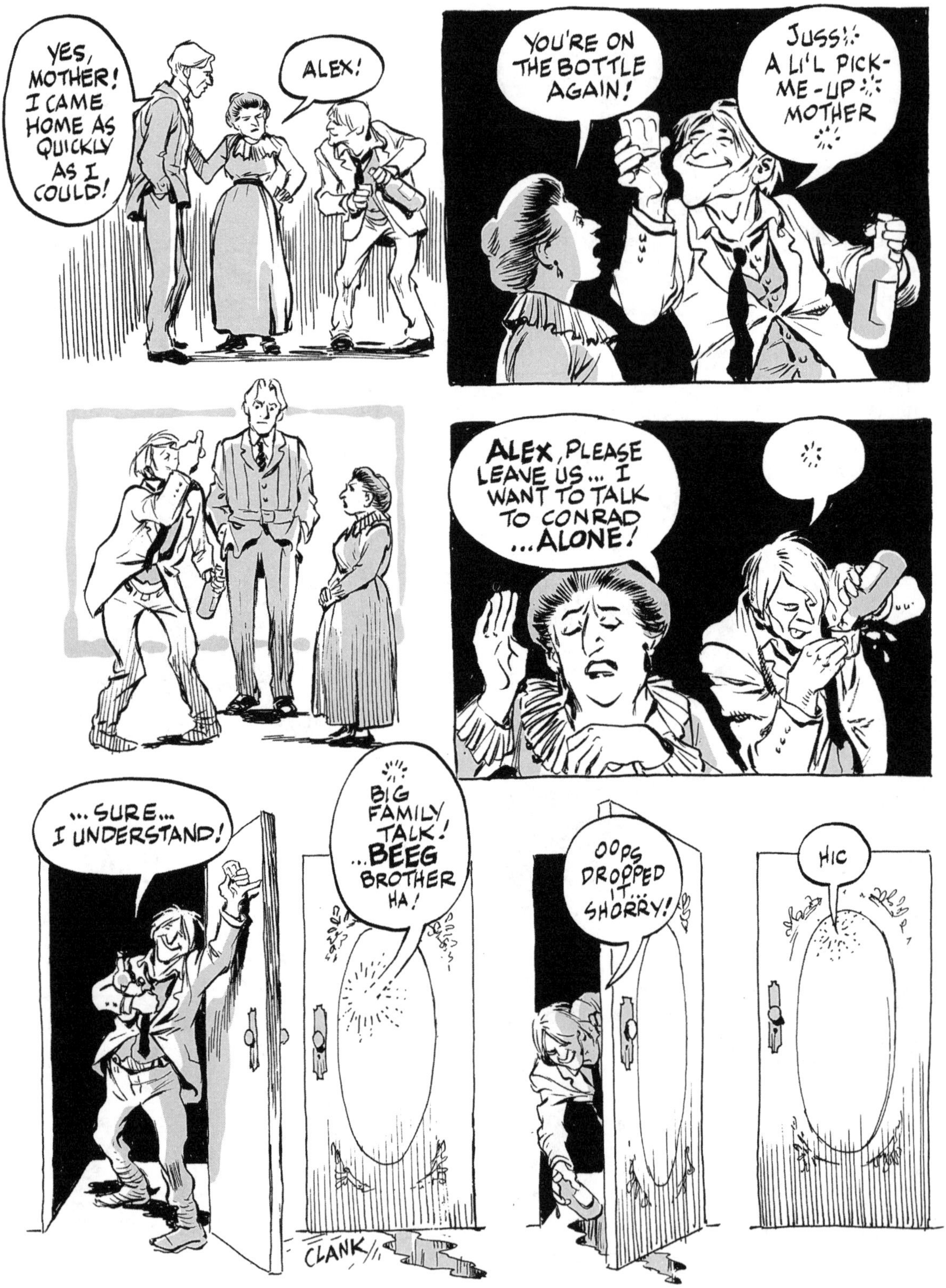
YES, MOTHER! I CAME HOME AS QUICKLY AS I COULD!
ALEX!
YOU'RE ON THE BOTTLE AGAIN!
JUSS A LI'L PICK-ME-UP MOTHER
ALEX, PLEASE LEAVE US... I WANT TO TALK TO CONRAD ...ALONE!
... SURE... I UNDERSTAND!
BIG FAMILY TALK! ...BEEG BROTHER HA!
CLANK
OOPS DROPPED IT... SHORRY!
HIC

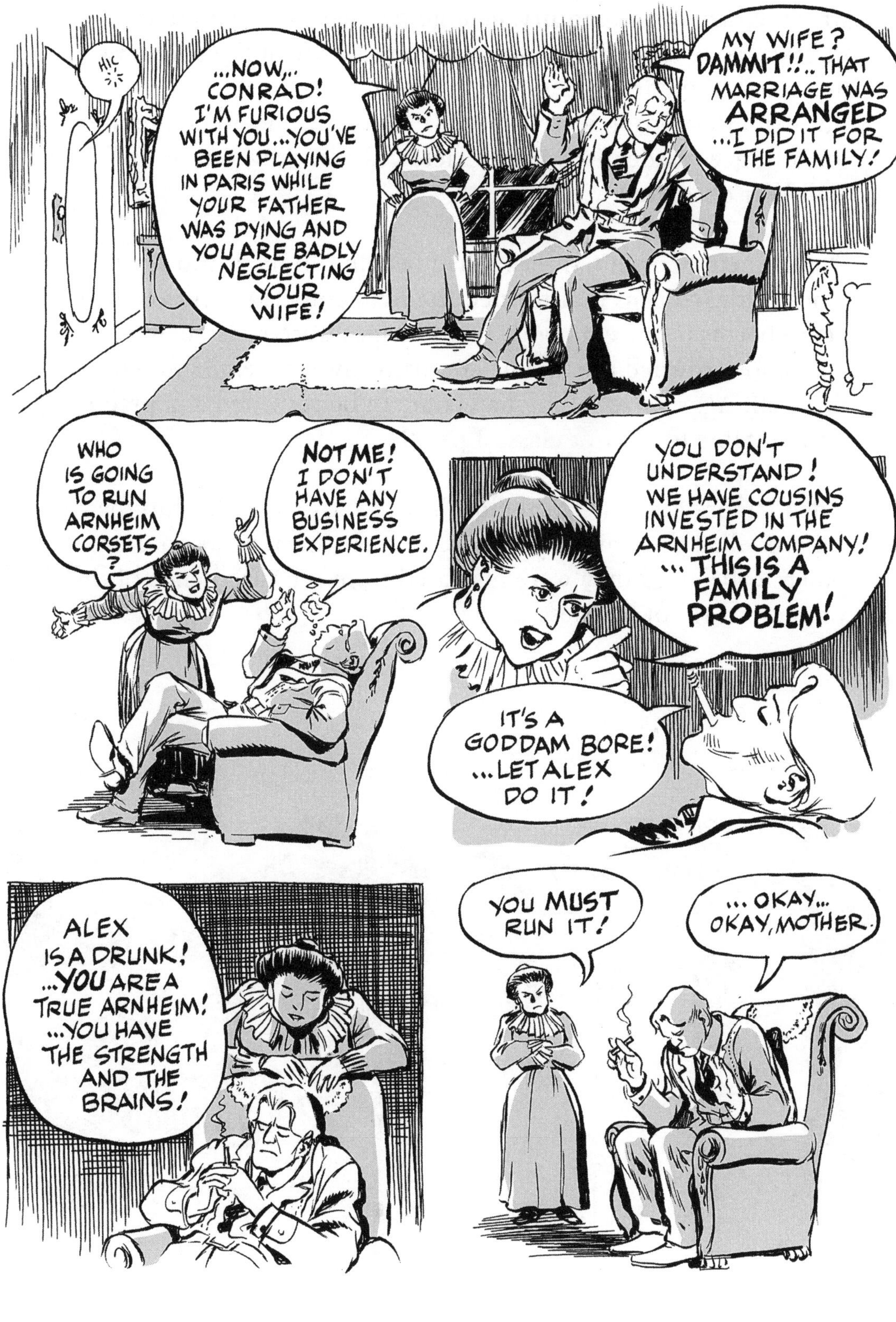
HIC
...NOW,.. CONRAD! I'M FURIOUS WITH YOU...YOU'VE BEEN PLAYING IN PARIS WHILE YOUR FATHER WAS DYING AND YOU ARE BADLY NEGLECTING YOUR WIFE!
MY WIFE? DAMMIT!!.. THAT MARRIAGE WAS ARRANGED ...I DID IT FOR THE FAMILY!
WHO IS GOING TO RUN ARNHEIM CORSETS ?
NOT ME! I DON'T HAVE ANY BUSINESS EXPERIENCE.
YOU DON'T UNDERSTAND! WE HAVE COUSINS INVESTED IN THE ARNHEIM COMPANY! ... THIS IS A FAMILY PROBLEM!
IT'S A GODDAM BORE! ...LET ALEX DO IT!
ALEX IS A DRUNK! ...YOU ARE A TRUE ARNHEIM! ...YOU HAVE THE STRENGTH AND THE BRAINS!
YOU MUST RUN IT!
... OKAY... OKAY, MOTHER.

After the turn of the century, change seemed to accelerate in America. New technology affected every sector of the country's life. Many of the manufacturing companies established in the Industrial Revolution were aging. Transportation and communication advances made many of the factories that grew out of the Civil War obsolete.

The Arnheim Corset Company had become an institution in the minds of the cousins that formed the Arnheim clan. They all had secure berths in the company. Any changes were resisted and innovation frowned upon. The company always seemed to have run itself. Aggressive selling had come to be regarded as a practice more suitable to a lower class of people.

When Isidore died, the Arnheims lost the strong leadership that had propelled the company. Secure in their social position, they somehow believed they were insulated from the turbulence of the common world of business.

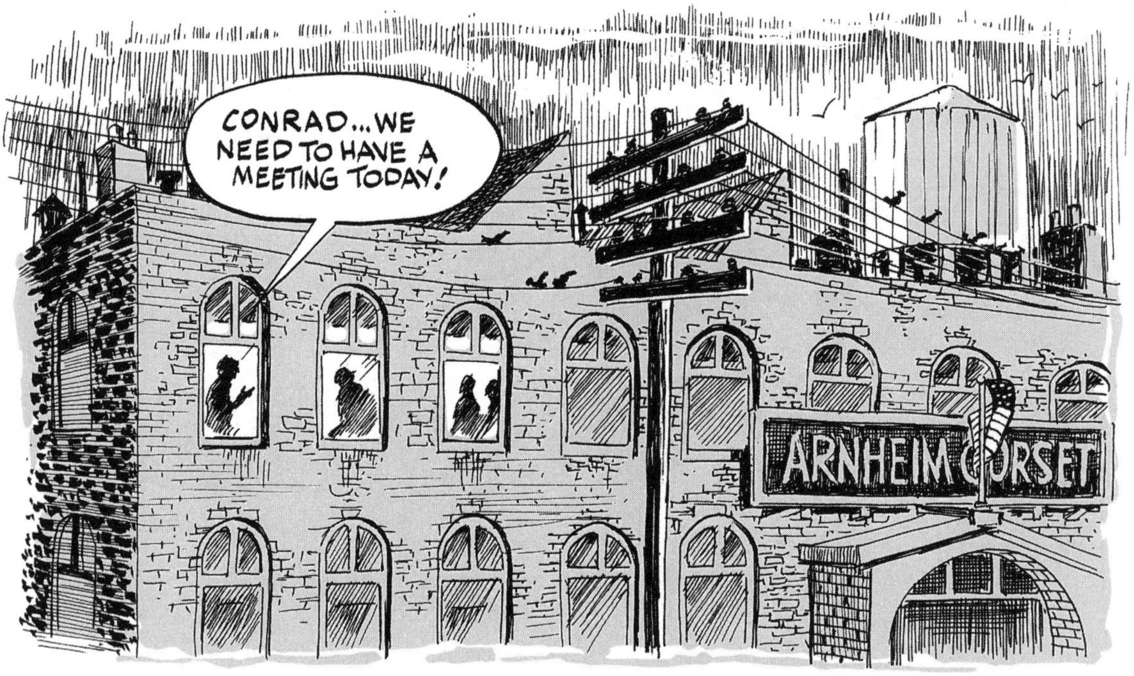
CONRAD...WE NEED TO HAVE A MEETING TODAY!
ARNHEIM CORSET

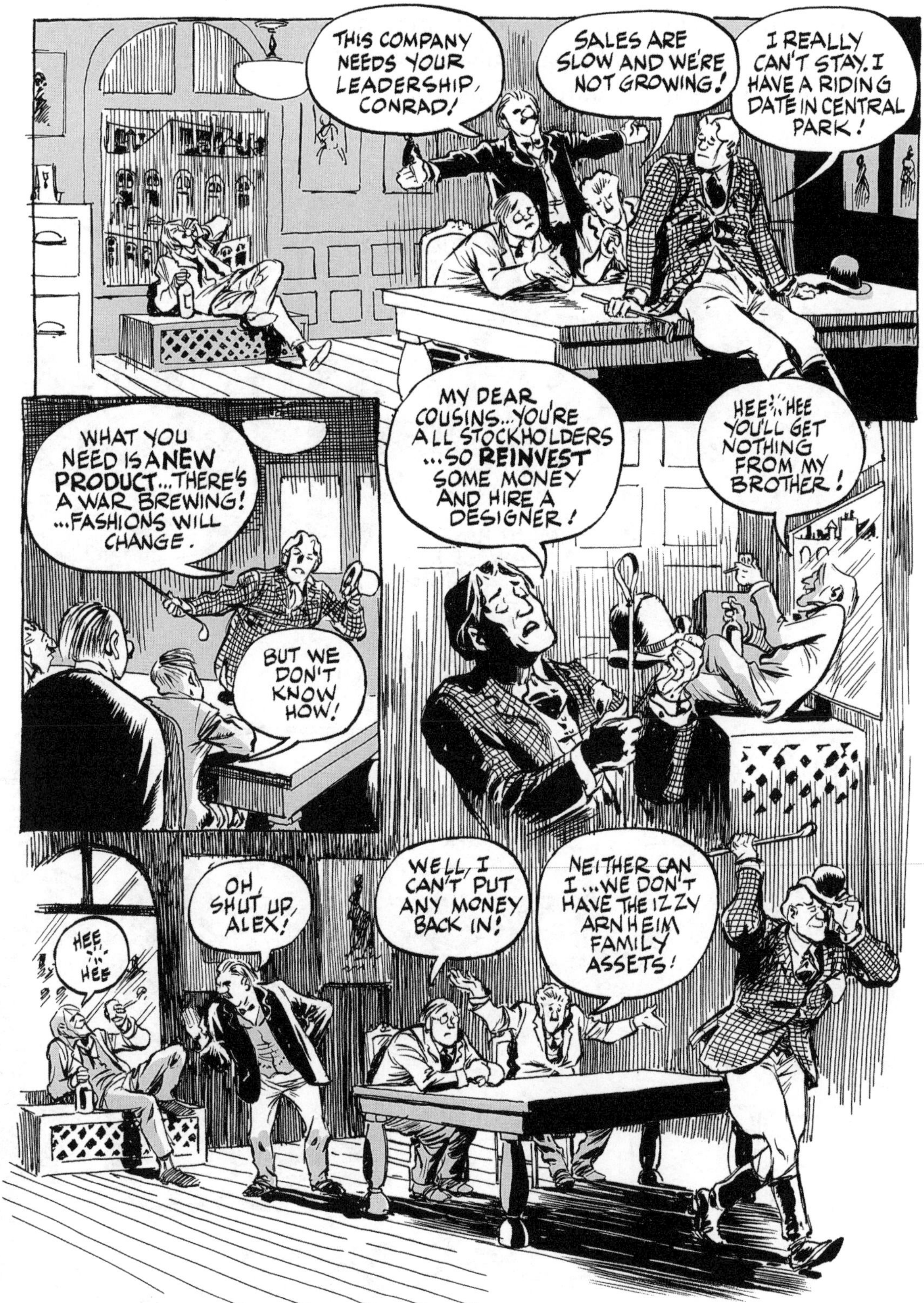
THIS COMPANY NEEDS YOUR LEADERSHIP, CONRAD!
SALES ARE SLOW AND WE'RE NOT GROWING!
I REALLY CAN'T STAY. I HAVE A RIDING DATE IN CENTRAL PARK!
WHAT YOU NEED IS A NEW PRODUCT... THERE'S A WAR BREWING! ...FASHIONS WILL CHANGE.
BUT WE DON'T KNOW HOW!
MY DEAR COUSINS... YOU'RE ALL STOCKHOLDERS ...SO REINVEST SOME MONEY AND HIRE A DESIGNER!
HEE HEE YOU'LL GET NOTHING FROM MY BROTHER!
HEE HEE
OH, SHUT UP, ALEX!
WELL, I CAN'T PUT ANY MONEY BACK IN!
NEITHER CAN I... WE DON'T HAVE THE IZZY ARNHEIM FAMILY ASSETS!

Word traveled quickly in the Arnheim social set. Rumors and gossip about business were of a particular interest, for they were, after all, the underpinnings of status in this world.

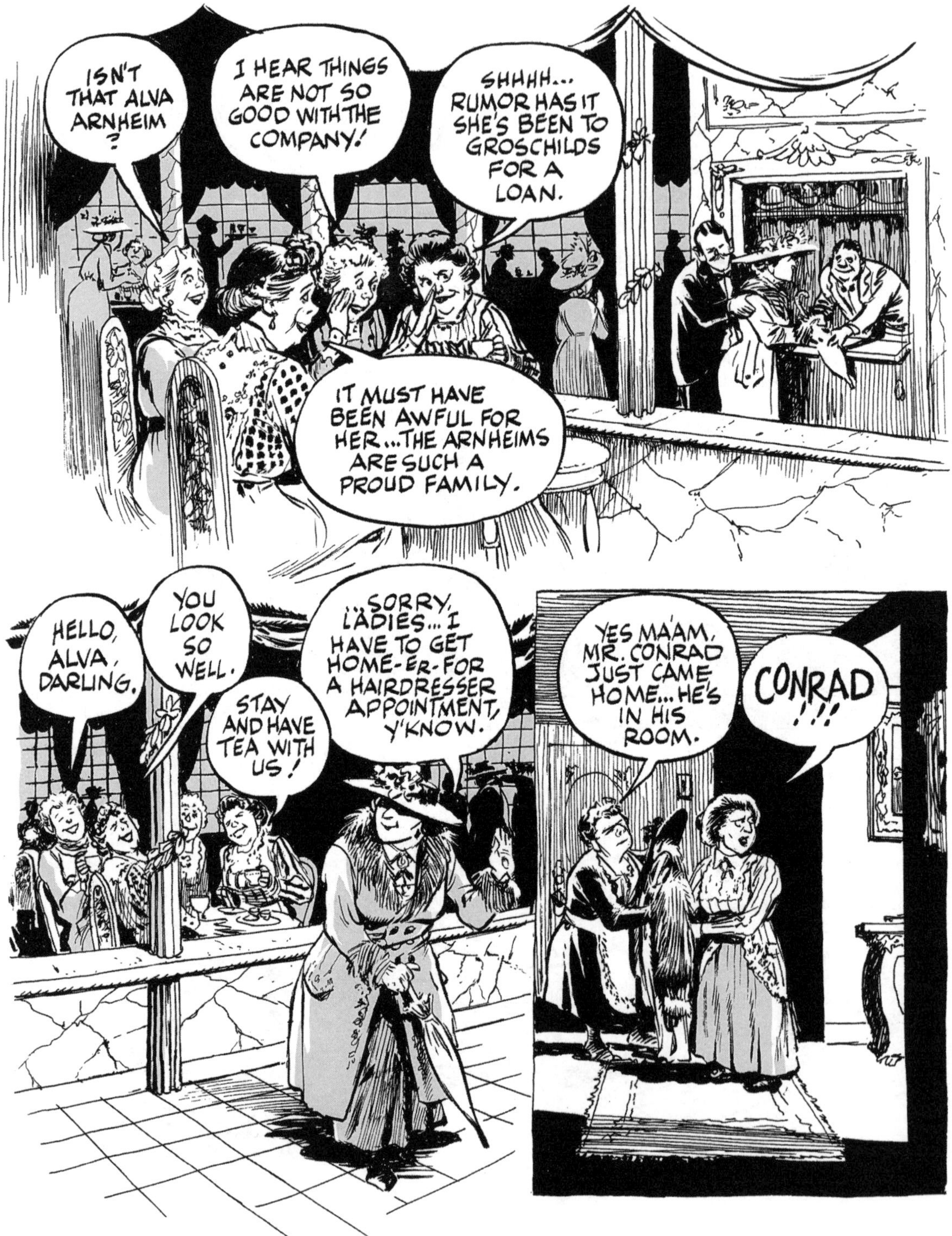

ISN'T THAT ALVA ARNHEIM ?
I HEAR THINGS ARE NOT SO GOOD WITH THE COMPANY!
SHHHH... RUMOR HAS IT SHE'S BEEN TO GROSCHILDS FOR A LOAN.
IT MUST HAVE BEEN AWFUL FOR HER...THE ARNHEIMS ARE SUCH A PROUD FAMILY.
HELLO, ALVA, DARLING.
YOU LOOK SO WELL.
STAY AND HAVE TEA WITH US!
...SORRY, LADIES... I HAVE TO GET HOME-ER-FOR A HAIRDRESSER APPOINTMENT, Y'KNOW.
YES MA'AM, MR. CONRAD JUST CAME HOME... HE'S IN HIS ROOM.
CONRAD !!!

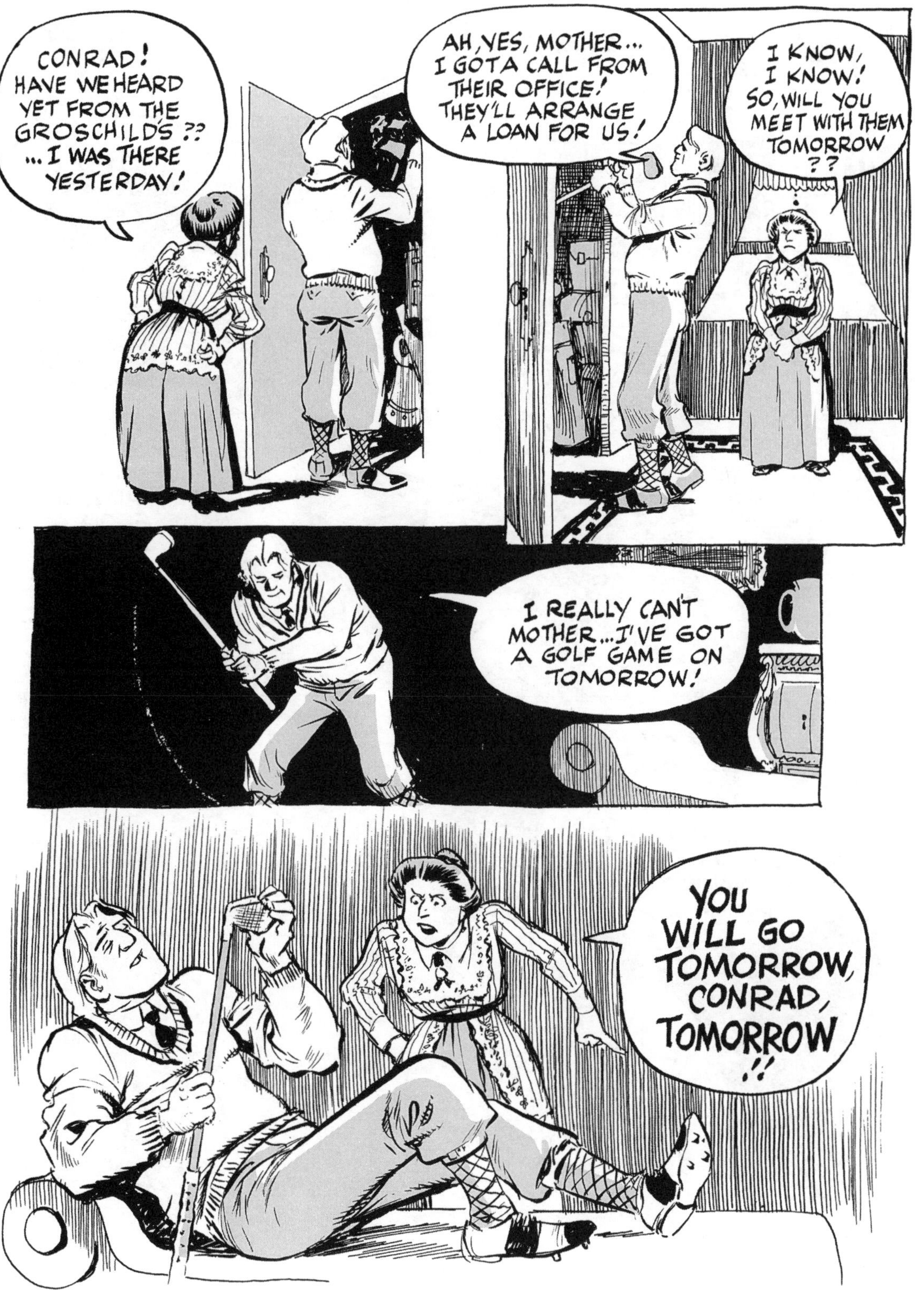
CONRAD! HAVE WE HEARD YET FROM THE GROSCHILDS ?? ... I WAS THERE YESTERDAY!
AH, YES, MOTHER... I GOT A CALL FROM THEIR OFFICE! THEY'LL ARRANGE A LOAN FOR US!
I KNOW, I KNOW! SO, WILL YOU MEET WITH THEM TOMORROW ??
I REALLY CAN'T MOTHER... I'VE GOT A GOLF GAME ON TOMORROW!
YOU WILL GO TOMORROW, CONRAD, TOMORROW !!

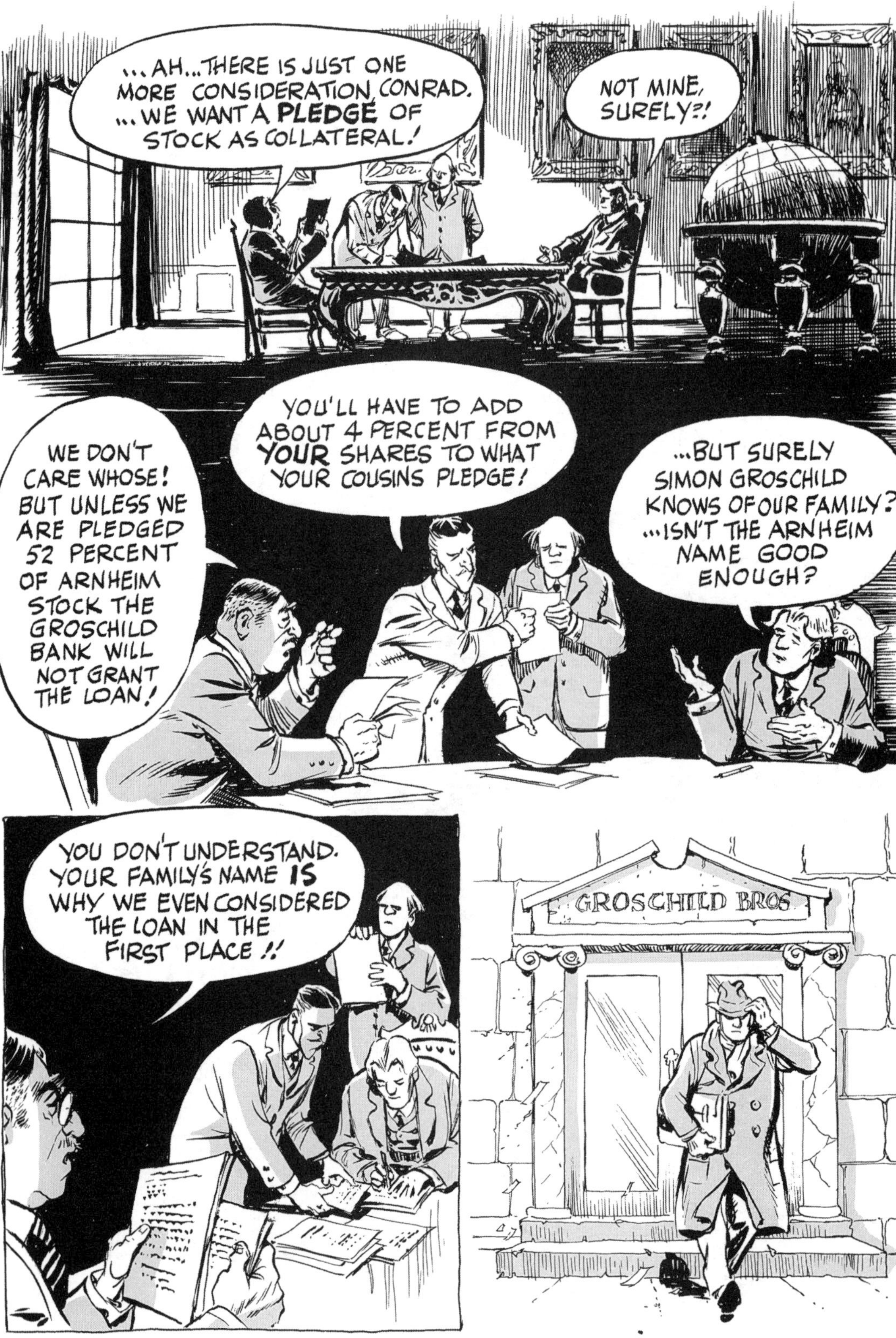
...AH...THERE IS JUST ONE MORE CONSIDERATION, CONRAD. ...WE WANT A **PLEDGE** OF STOCK AS COLLATERAL!
NOT MINE, SURELY?!
WE DON'T CARE WHOSE! BUT UNLESS WE ARE PLEDGED 52 PERCENT OF ARNHEIM STOCK THE GROSCHILD BANK WILL NOT GRANT THE LOAN!
YOU'LL HAVE TO ADD ABOUT 4 PERCENT FROM **YOUR** SHARES TO WHAT YOUR COUSINS PLEDGE!
...BUT SURELY SIMON GROSCHILD KNOWS OF OUR FAMILY? ...ISN'T THE ARNHEIM NAME GOOD ENOUGH?
YOU DON'T UNDERSTAND. YOUR FAMILY'S NAME **IS** WHY WE EVEN CONSIDERED THE LOAN IN THE FIRST PLACE!!
GROSCHILD BROS

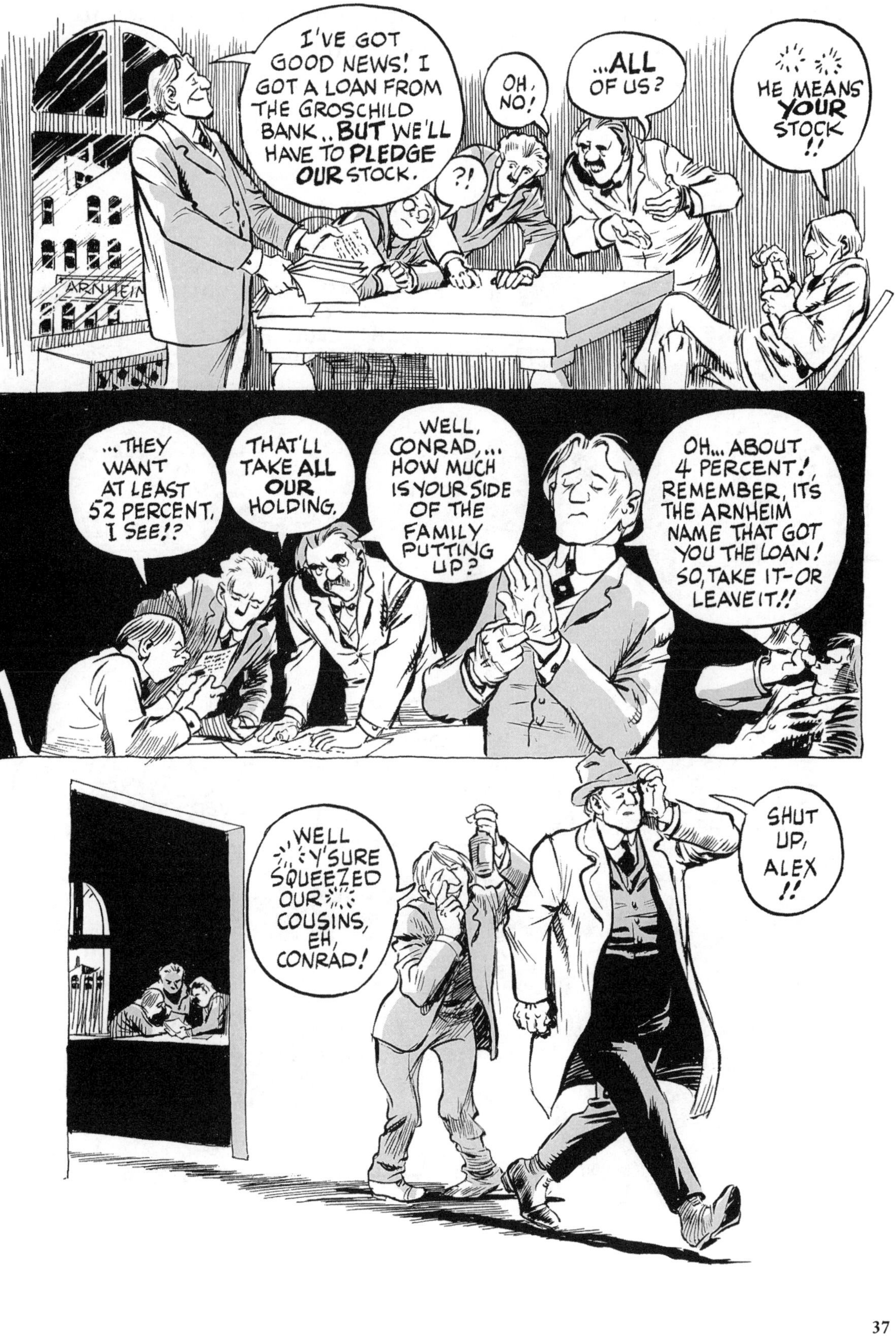
I'VE GOT GOOD NEWS! I GOT A LOAN FROM THE GROSCHILD BANK.. BUT WE'LL HAVE TO PLEDGE OUR STOCK.
?!
OH, NO!
...ALL OF US?
HE MEANS YOUR STOCK !!
ARNHEIM
...THEY WANT AT LEAST 52 PERCENT, I SEE!?
THAT'LL TAKE ALL OUR HOLDING.
WELL, CONRAD,... HOW MUCH IS YOUR SIDE OF THE FAMILY PUTTING UP?
OH... ABOUT 4 PERCENT! REMEMBER, IT'S THE ARNHEIM NAME THAT GOT YOU THE LOAN! SO, TAKE IT-OR LEAVE IT!!
WELL Y'SURE SQUEEZED OUR COUSINS, EH, CONRAD!
SHUT UP, ALEX !!

One of the requirements for maintaining a position in society was to have what others had. It was fundamental to the art of assimilation, the skill of looking like the "haves" and doing what "they" did regardless of one's real interests.

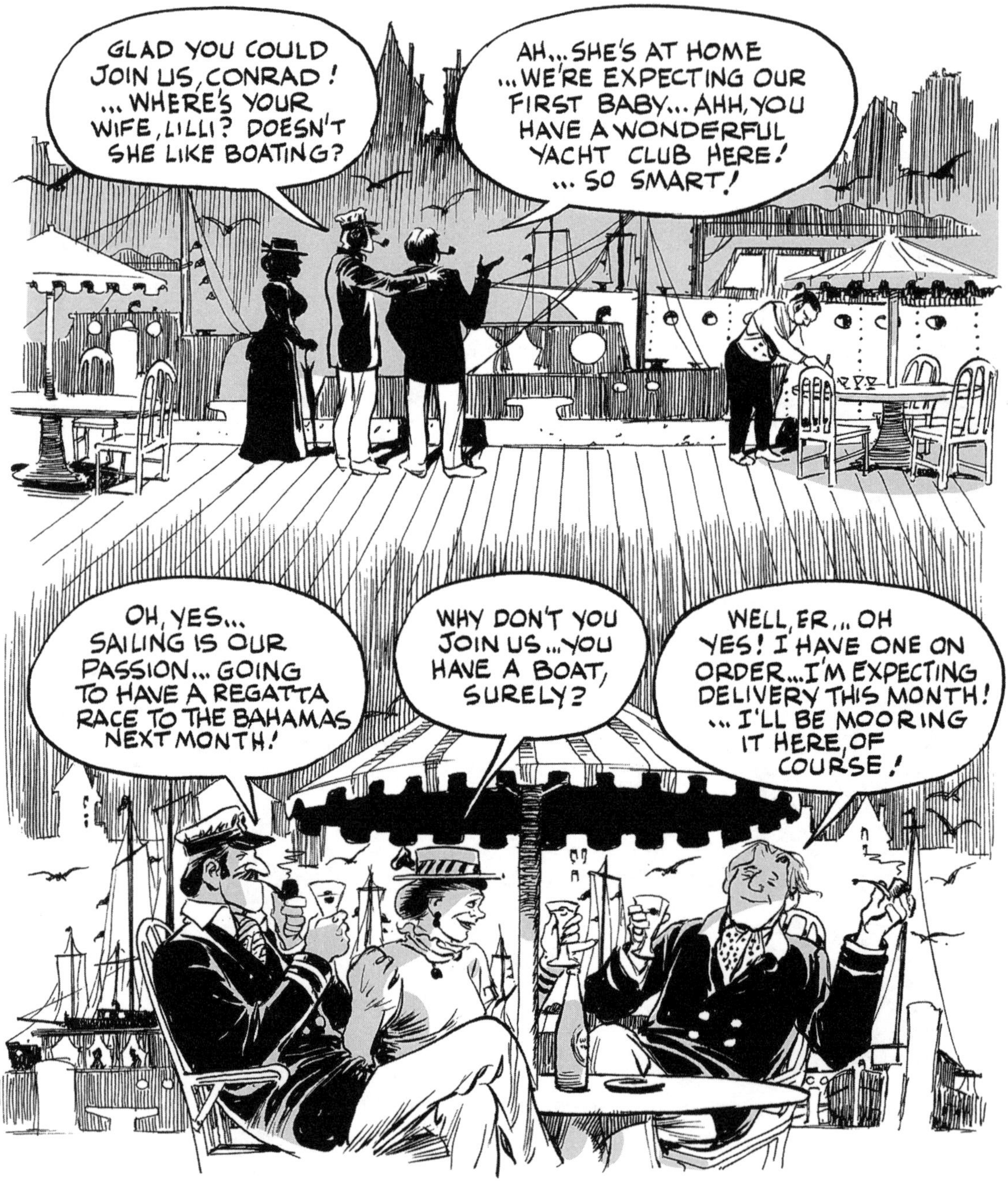

GLAD YOU COULD JOIN US, CONRAD! ... WHERE'S YOUR WIFE, LILLI? DOESN'T SHE LIKE BOATING?
AH... SHE'S AT HOME ... WE'RE EXPECTING OUR FIRST BABY... AHH, YOU HAVE A WONDERFUL YACHT CLUB HERE! ... SO SMART!
OH, YES... SAILING IS OUR PASSION... GOING TO HAVE A REGATTA RACE TO THE BAHAMAS NEXT MONTH!
WHY DON'T YOU JOIN US... YOU HAVE A BOAT, SURELY?
WELL, ER... OH YES! I HAVE ONE ON ORDER... I'M EXPECTING DELIVERY THIS MONTH! ... I'LL BE MOORING IT HERE, OF COURSE!

While people like the Arnheims understood the game, it was distasteful to them . . . after all, it was "climbing." But they played it nevertheless.

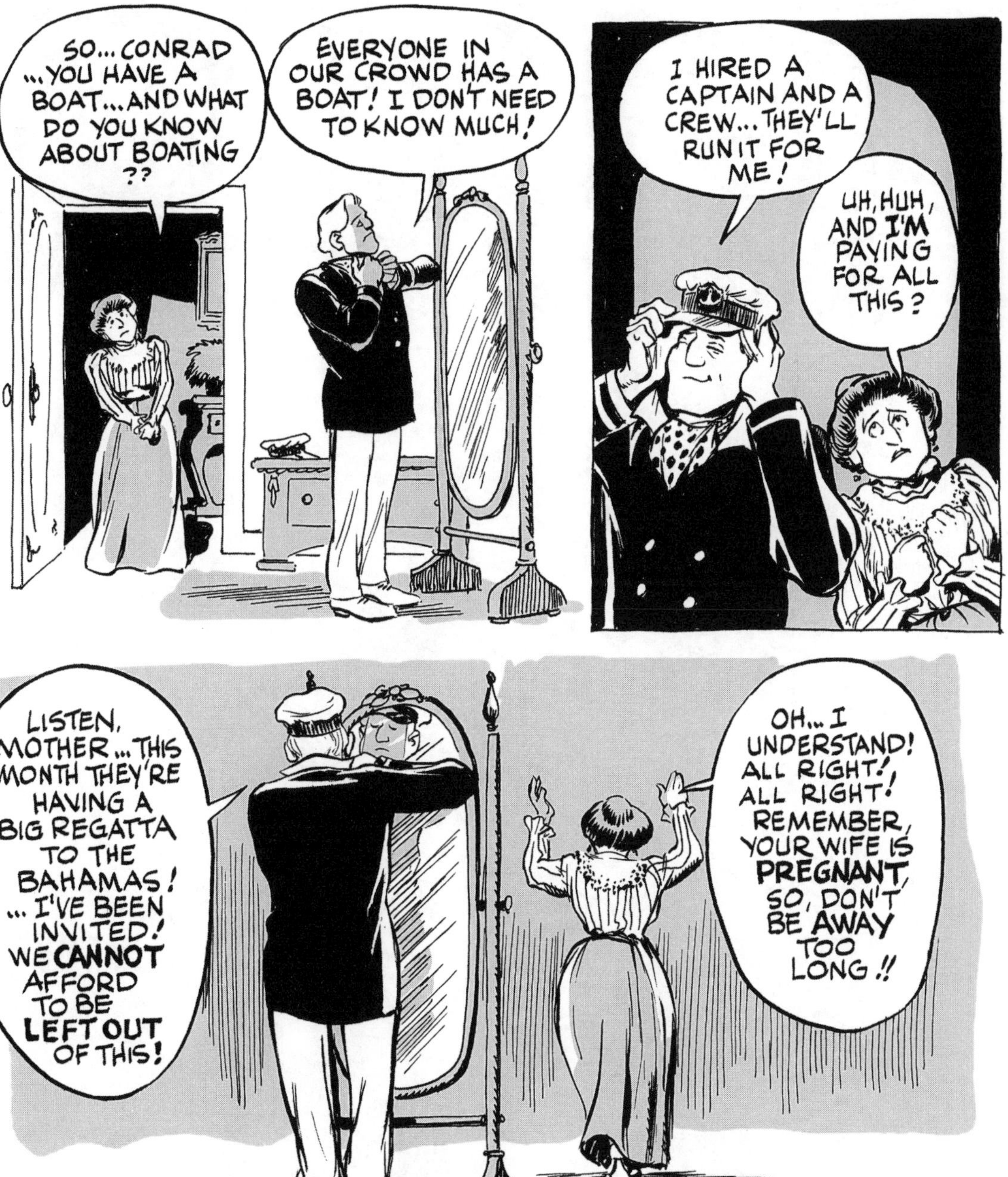
SO... CONRAD ...YOU HAVE A BOAT...AND WHAT DO YOU KNOW ABOUT BOATING ??
EVERYONE IN OUR CROWD HAS A BOAT! I DON'T NEED TO KNOW MUCH!
I HIRED A CAPTAIN AND A CREW... THEY'LL RUN IT FOR ME!
UH, HUH, AND I'M PAYING FOR ALL THIS?
LISTEN, MOTHER... THIS MONTH THEY'RE HAVING A BIG REGATTA TO THE BAHAMAS! ... I'VE BEEN INVITED! WE CANNOT AFFORD TO BE LEFT OUT OF THIS!
OH... I UNDERSTAND! ALL RIGHT! ALL RIGHT! REMEMBER, YOUR WIFE IS PREGNANT SO, DON'T BE AWAY TOO LONG!!

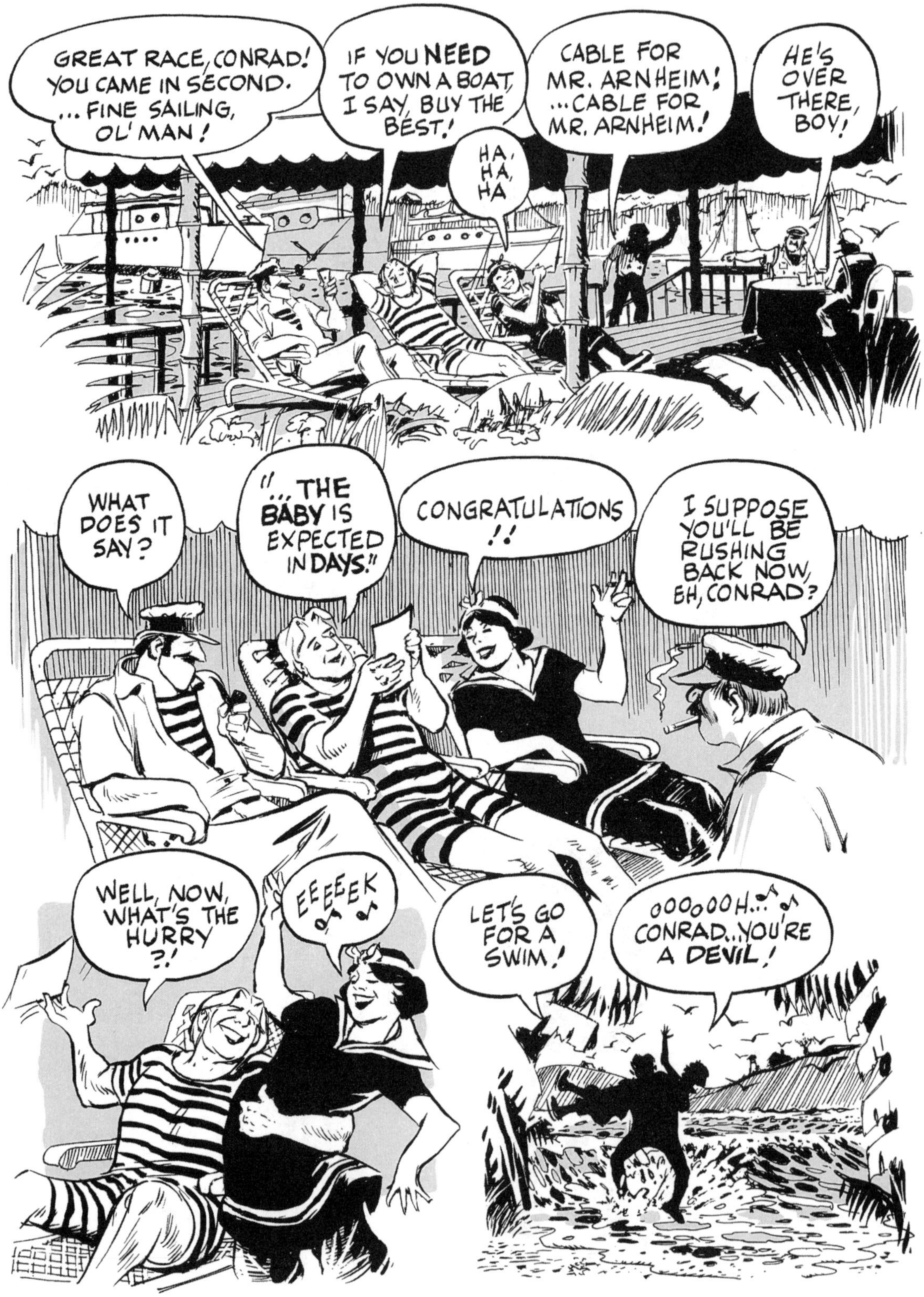
GREAT RACE, CONRAD! YOU CAME IN SECOND. ...FINE SAILING, OL' MAN!
IF YOU NEED TO OWN A BOAT, I SAY, BUY THE BEST!
HA, HA, HA
CABLE FOR MR. ARNHEIM! ...CABLE FOR MR. ARNHEIM!
HE'S OVER THERE, BOY!
WHAT DOES IT SAY?
"...THE BABY IS EXPECTED IN DAYS."
CONGRATULATIONS !!
I SUPPOSE YOU'LL BE RUSHING BACK NOW, EH, CONRAD?
WELL, NOW, WHAT'S THE HURRY ?!
EEEEEK
LET'S GO FOR A SWIM!
OOOOOOH... CONRAD...YOU'RE A DEVIL!

In Lavolier, news of Lilli's pregnancy brought the Obers up to New York to visit their daughter.

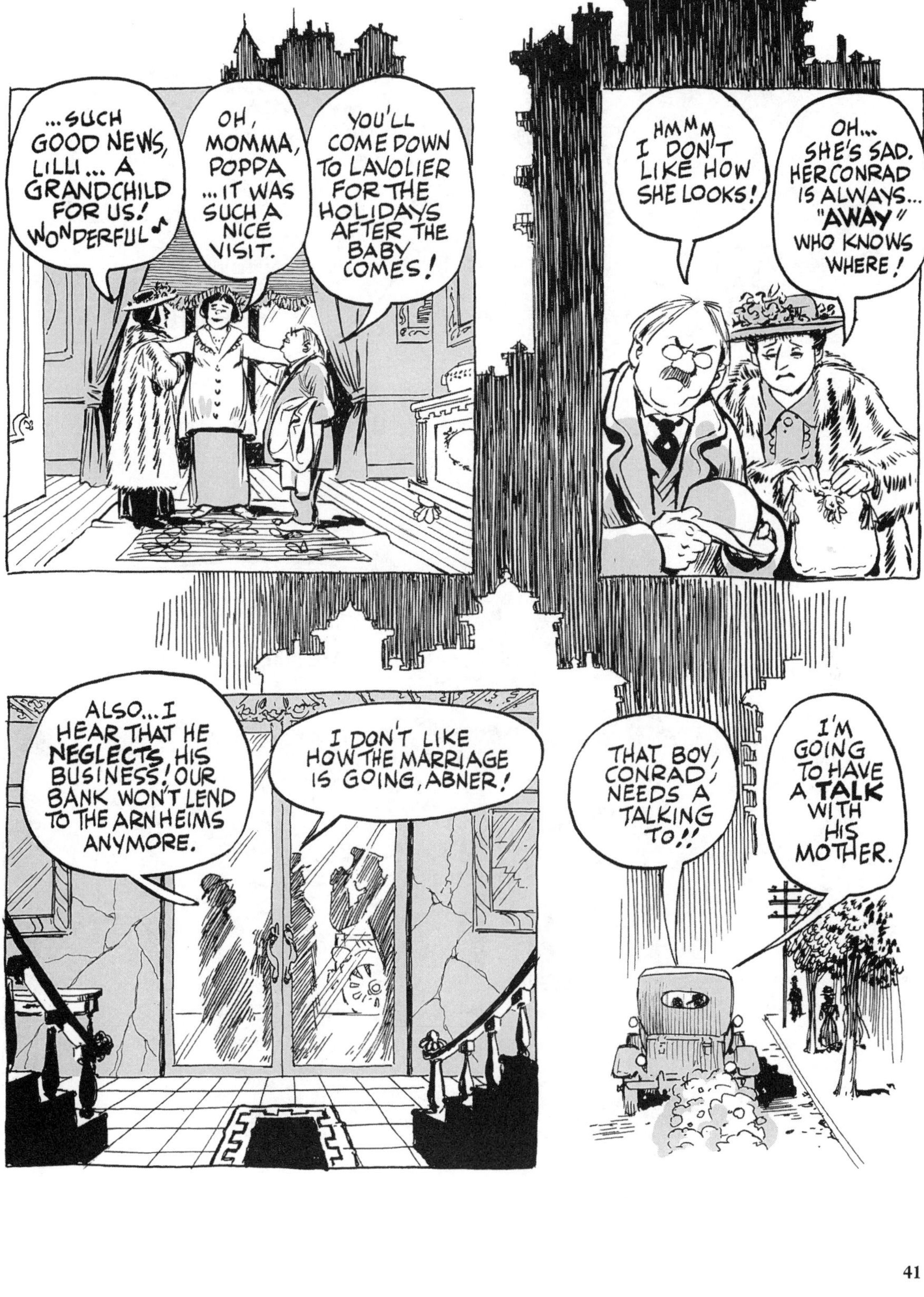
...SUCH GOOD NEWS, LILLI... A GRANDCHILD FOR US! WONDERFUL
OH, MOMMA, POPPA ...IT WAS SUCH A NICE VISIT.
YOU'LL COME DOWN TO LAVOLIER FOR THE HOLIDAYS AFTER THE BABY COMES!
HMMM I DON'T LIKE HOW SHE LOOKS!
OH... SHE'S SAD. HER CONRAD IS ALWAYS... "AWAY" WHO KNOWS WHERE!
ALSO...I HEAR THAT HE NEGLECTS HIS BUSINESS! OUR BANK WON'T LEND TO THE ARNHEIMS ANYMORE.
I DON'T LIKE HOW THE MARRIAGE IS GOING, ABNER!
THAT BOY, CONRAD, NEEDS A TALKING TO!!
I'M GOING TO HAVE A TALK WITH HIS MOTHER.

But the visit with Conrad's mother was fruitless as well as frustrating. The Ober family's values were quite different from those of the Arnheims.

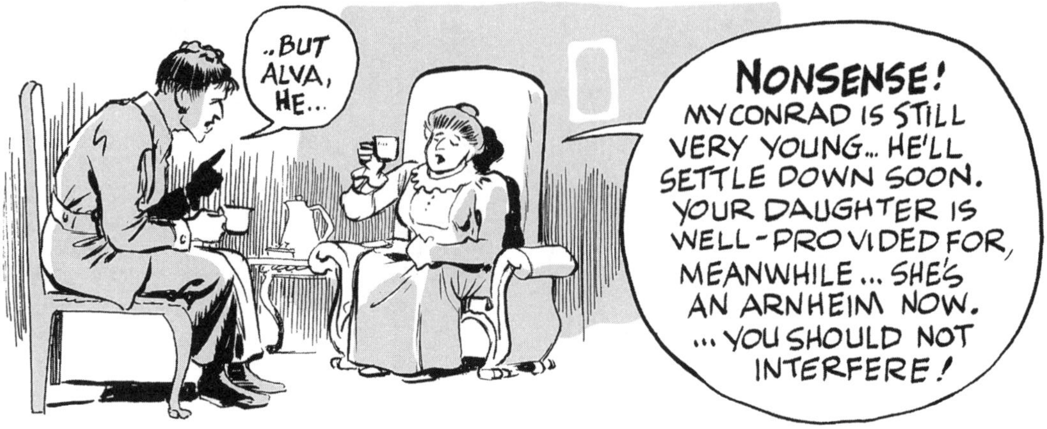
..BUT ALVA, HE...
NONSENSE! MY CONRAD IS STILL VERY YOUNG... HE'LL SETTLE DOWN SOON. YOUR DAUGHTER IS WELL-PROVIDED FOR, MEANWHILE... SHE'S AN ARNHEIM NOW. ...YOU SHOULD NOT INTERFERE!

So the Obers returned to Lavolier, where their bank was having a problem with the Arnheim Company loan.

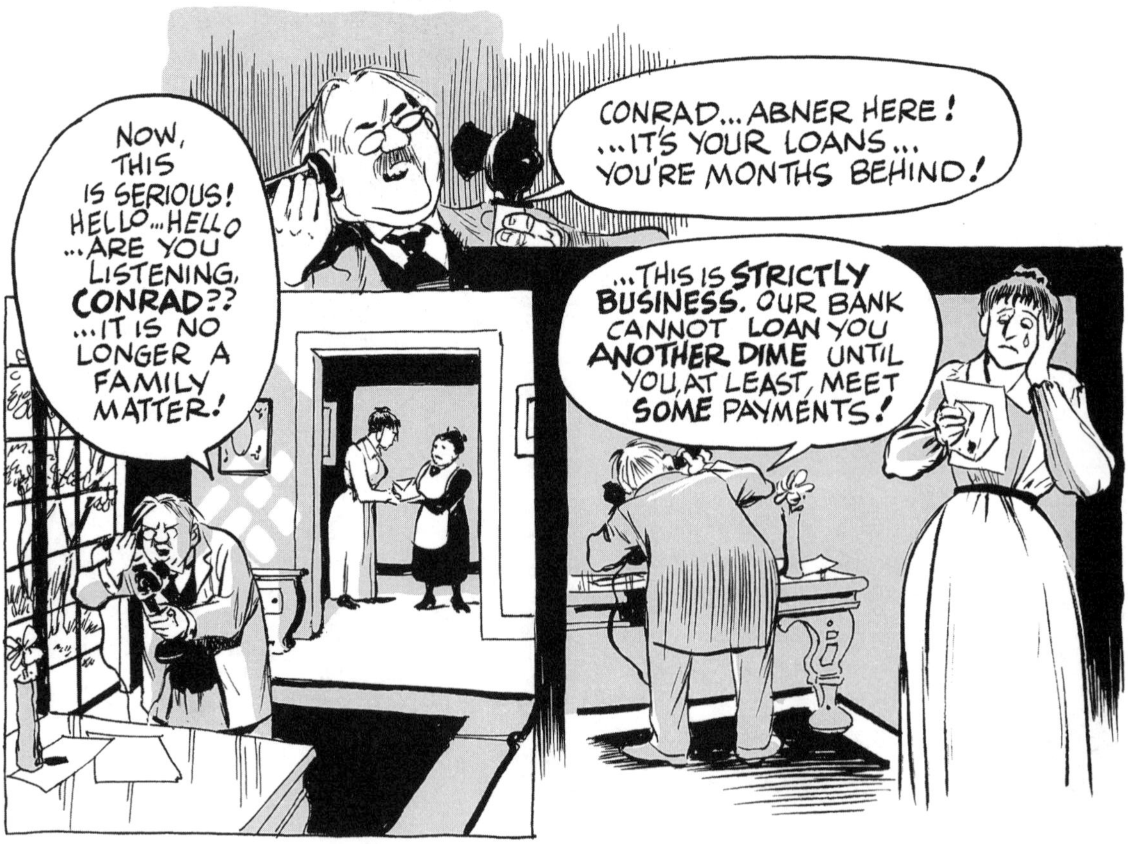
CONRAD...ABNER HERE! ...IT'S YOUR LOANS... YOU'RE MONTHS BEHIND!
...THIS IS STRICTLY BUSINESS. OUR BANK CANNOT LOAN YOU ANOTHER DIME UNTIL YOU, AT LEAST, MEET SOME PAYMENTS!
NOW, THIS IS SERIOUS! HELLO...HELLO ...ARE YOU LISTENING, CONRAD?? ...IT IS NO LONGER A FAMILY MATTER!

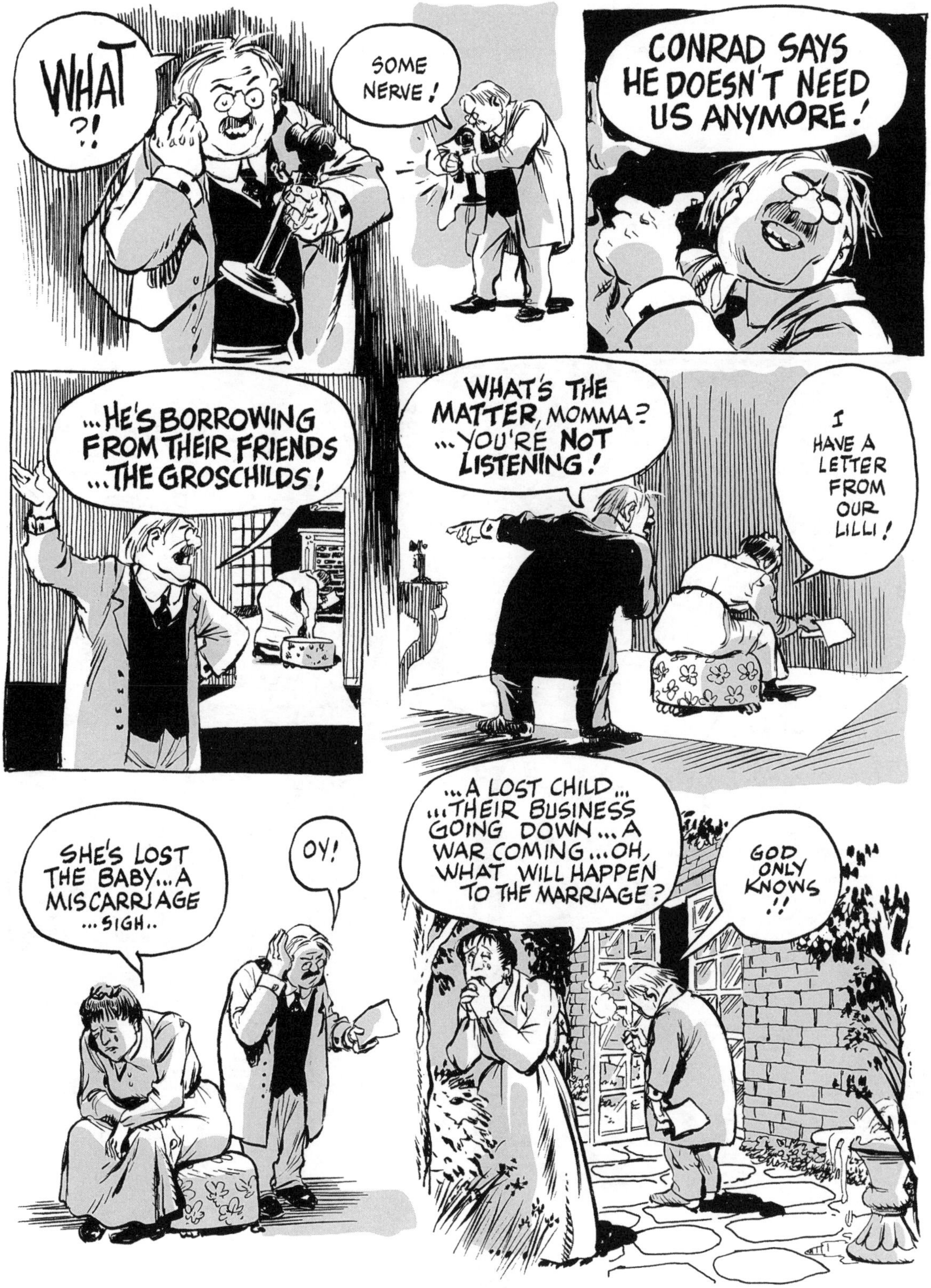
WHAT ?!
SOME NERVE!
CONRAD SAYS HE DOESN'T NEED US ANYMORE!
...HE'S BORROWING FROM THEIR FRIENDS ...THE GROSCHILDS!
WHAT'S THE MATTER, MOMMA? ...YOU'RE NOT LISTENING!
I HAVE A LETTER FROM OUR LILLI!
SHE'S LOST THE BABY...A MISCARRIAGE ...SIGH..
OY!
...A LOST CHILD... ...THEIR BUSINESS GOING DOWN...A WAR COMING...OH, WHAT WILL HAPPEN TO THE MARRIAGE?
GOD ONLY KNOWS !!

Europe was aflame. The war that was set in motion by an assassination in Serbia seemed so very far away that it was hardly noticed by the Arnheims except, of course, it put a stop to the annual continental tour.

Except for the severe drop in their export sales, the Arnheim Corset Company kept afloat.

But the war eventually spread to America.

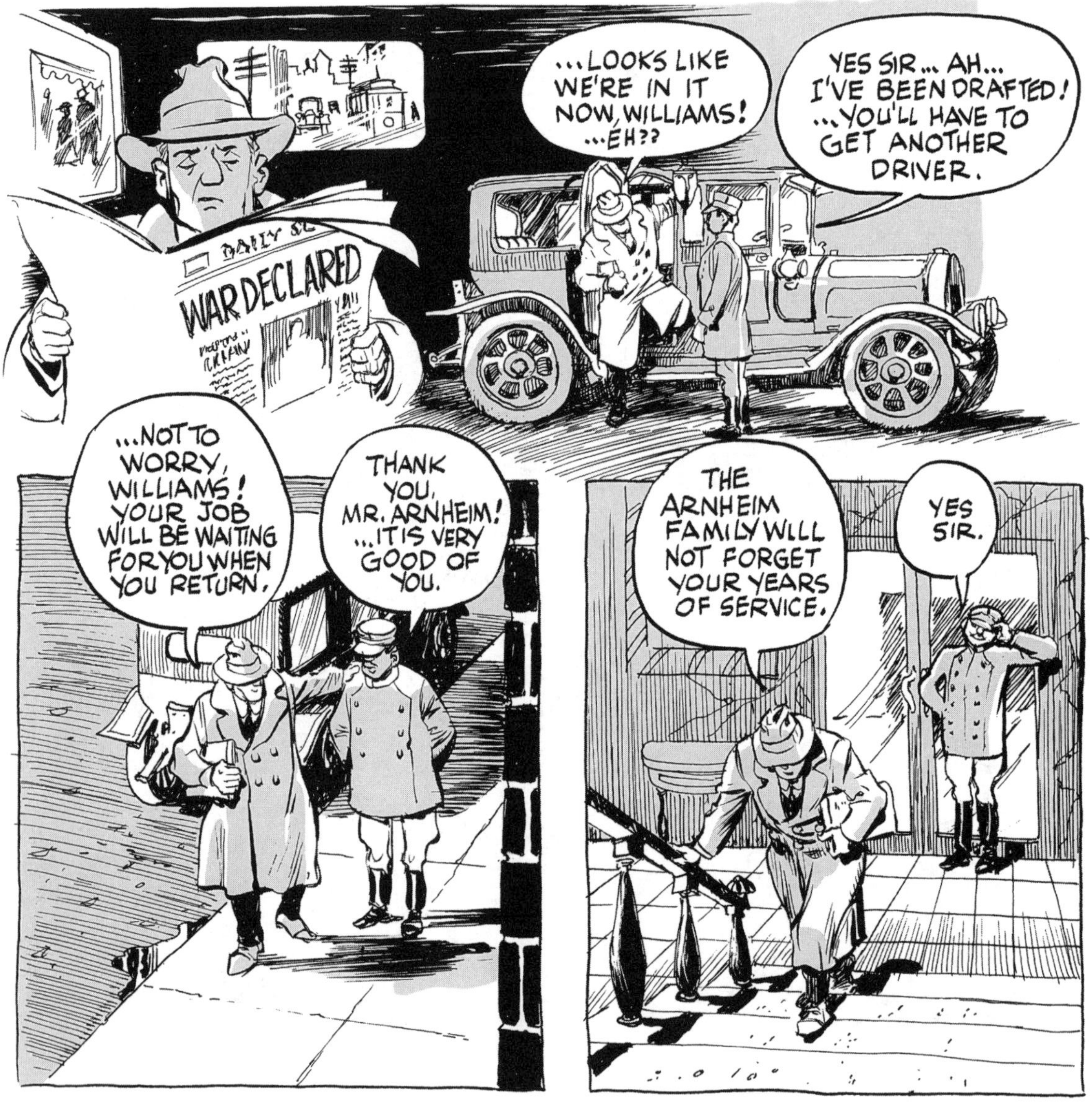

WAR DECLARED
...LOOKS LIKE WE'RE IN IT NOW, WILLIAMS! ...EH??
YES SIR... AH... I'VE BEEN DRAFTED! ...YOU'LL HAVE TO GET ANOTHER DRIVER.
...NOT TO WORRY, WILLIAMS! YOUR JOB WILL BE WAITING FOR YOU WHEN YOU RETURN.
THANK YOU, MR. ARNHEIM! ...IT IS VERY GOOD OF YOU.
THE ARNHEIM FAMILY WILL NOT FORGET YOUR YEARS OF SERVICE.
YES SIR.

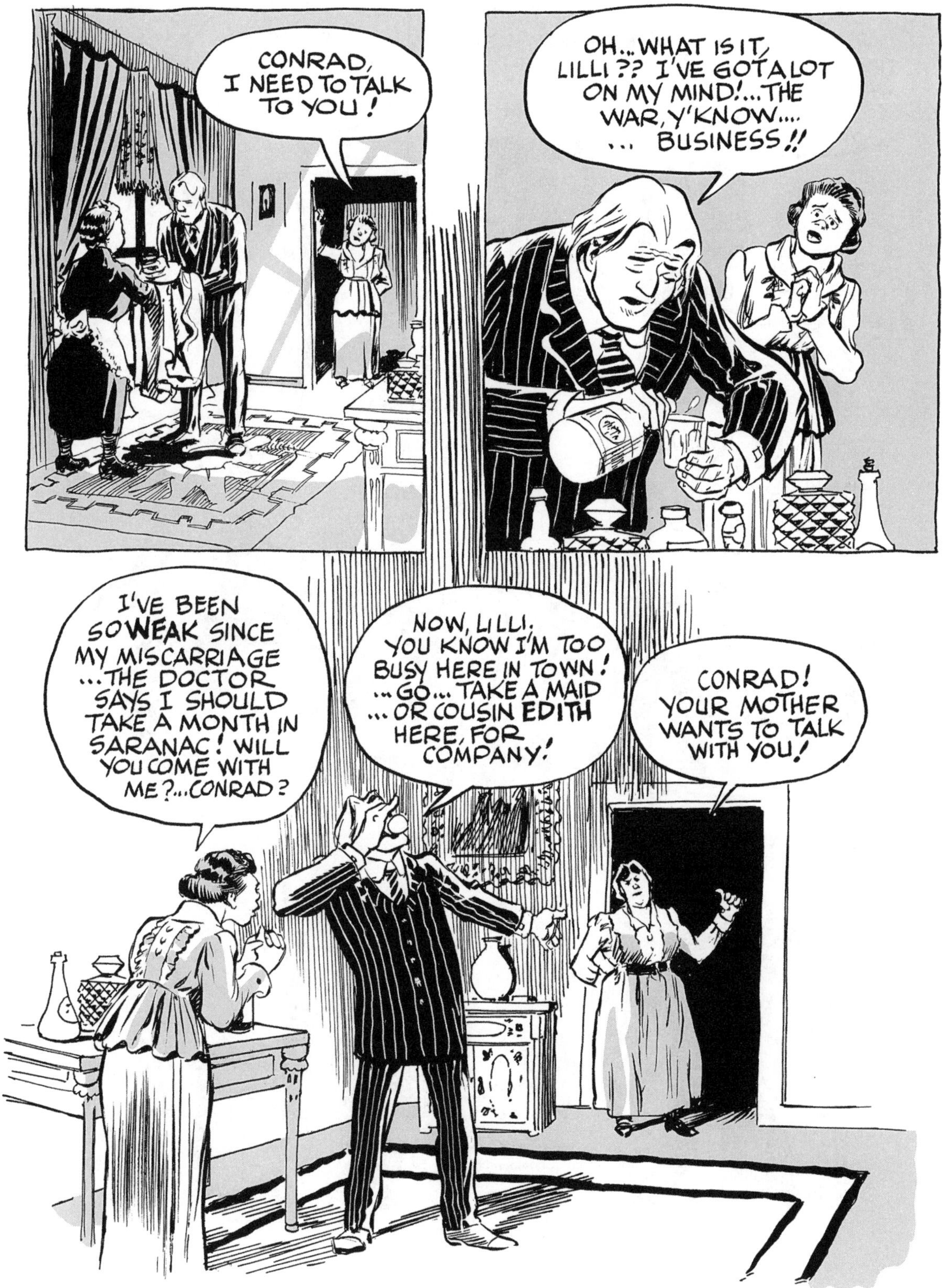
CONRAD, I NEED TO TALK TO YOU!
OH... WHAT IS IT, LILLI?? I'VE GOT A LOT ON MY MIND!... THE WAR, Y'KNOW.... ... BUSINESS!!
I'VE BEEN SO WEAK SINCE MY MISCARRIAGE ...THE DOCTOR SAYS I SHOULD TAKE A MONTH IN SARANAC! WILL YOU COME WITH ME?... CONRAD?
NOW, LILLI. YOU KNOW I'M TOO BUSY HERE IN TOWN! ...GO... TAKE A MAID ...OR COUSIN EDITH HERE, FOR COMPANY!
CONRAD! YOUR MOTHER WANTS TO TALK WITH YOU!

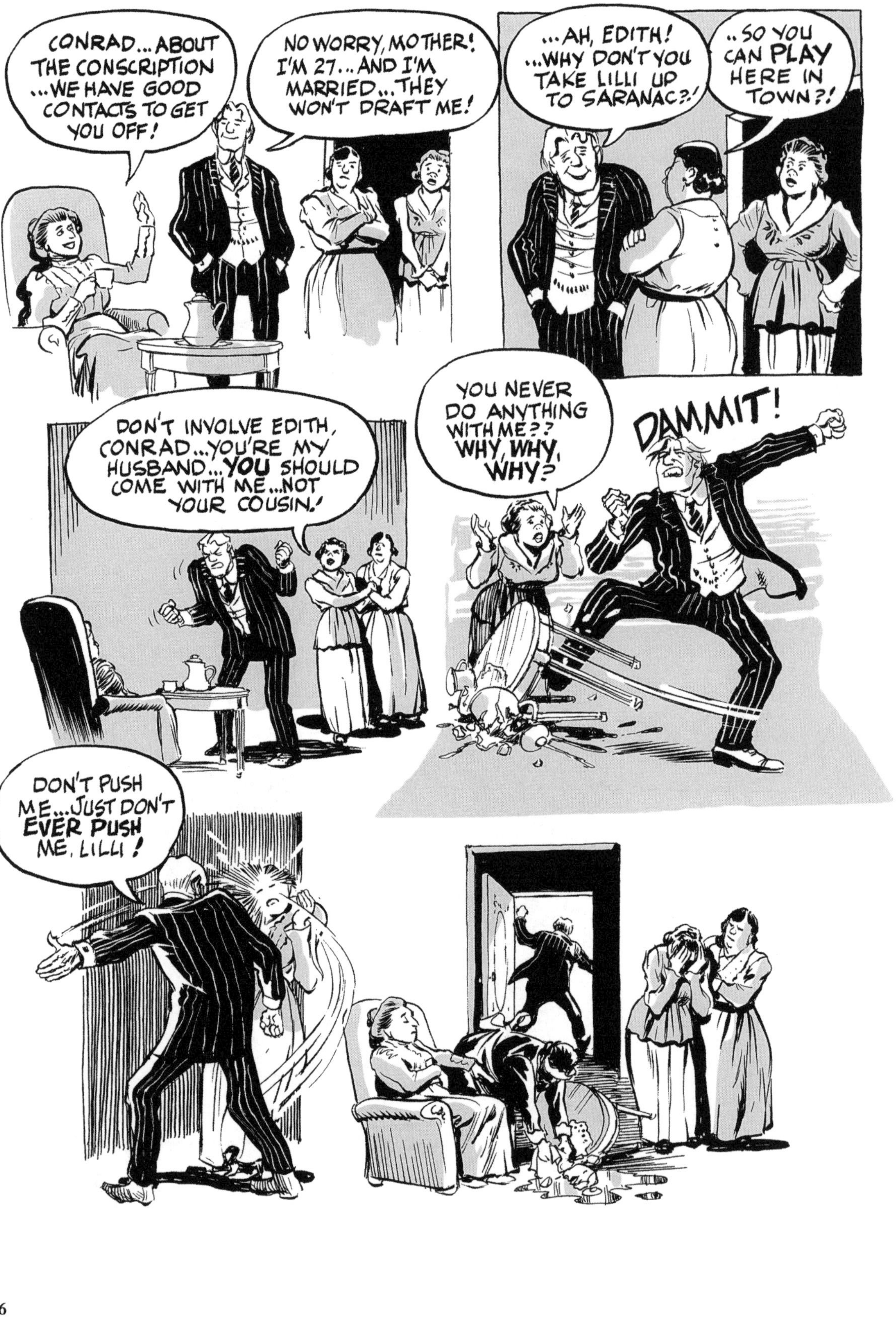
CONRAD... ABOUT THE CONSCRIPTION ...WE HAVE GOOD CONTACTS TO GET YOU OFF!
NO WORRY, MOTHER! I'M 27... AND I'M MARRIED... THEY WON'T DRAFT ME!
...AH, EDITH! ...WHY DON'T YOU TAKE LILLI UP TO SARANAC?!
..SO YOU CAN PLAY HERE IN TOWN?!
DON'T INVOLVE EDITH, CONRAD...YOU'RE MY HUSBAND...YOU SHOULD COME WITH ME...NOT YOUR COUSIN!
YOU NEVER DO ANYTHING WITH ME?? WHY, WHY, WHY?
DAMMIT!
DON'T PUSH ME...JUST DON'T EVER PUSH ME, LILLI!

America's entrance into the First World War accelerated the fortunes of many companies, but it did just the opposite for the Arnheim interests. Conrad succeeded in avoiding military service, concentrated on his social life, and paid little attention to the company's business except for the mandatory quarterly board meetings.

By the end of the war, the Arnheim Corset Company was foundering.

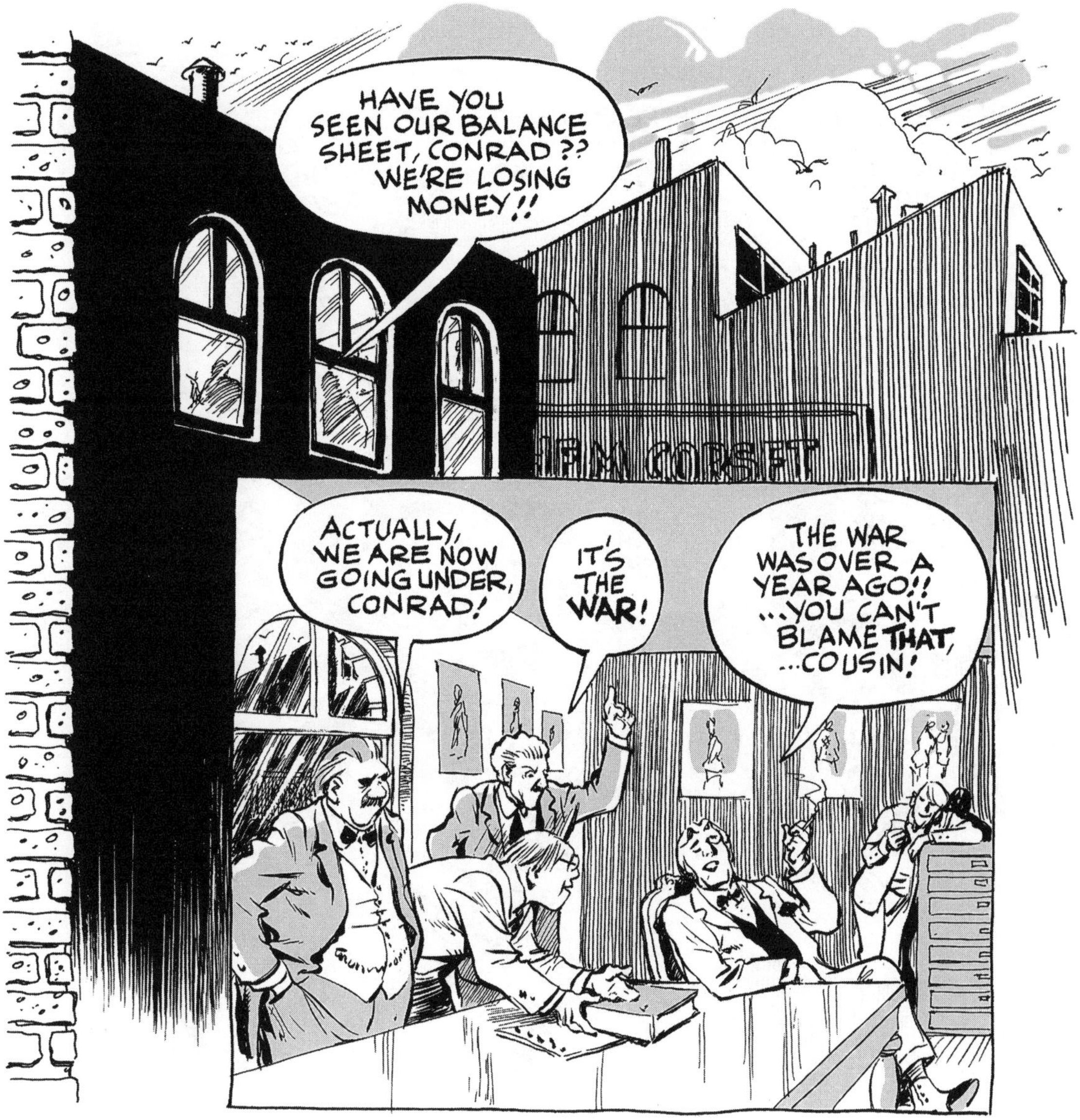

HAVE YOU SEEN OUR BALANCE SHEET, CONRAD ?? WE'RE LOSING MONEY !!
ACTUALLY, WE ARE NOW GOING UNDER, CONRAD!
IT'S THE WAR!
THE WAR WAS OVER A YEAR AGO!! ...YOU CAN'T BLAME THAT, ...COUSIN!

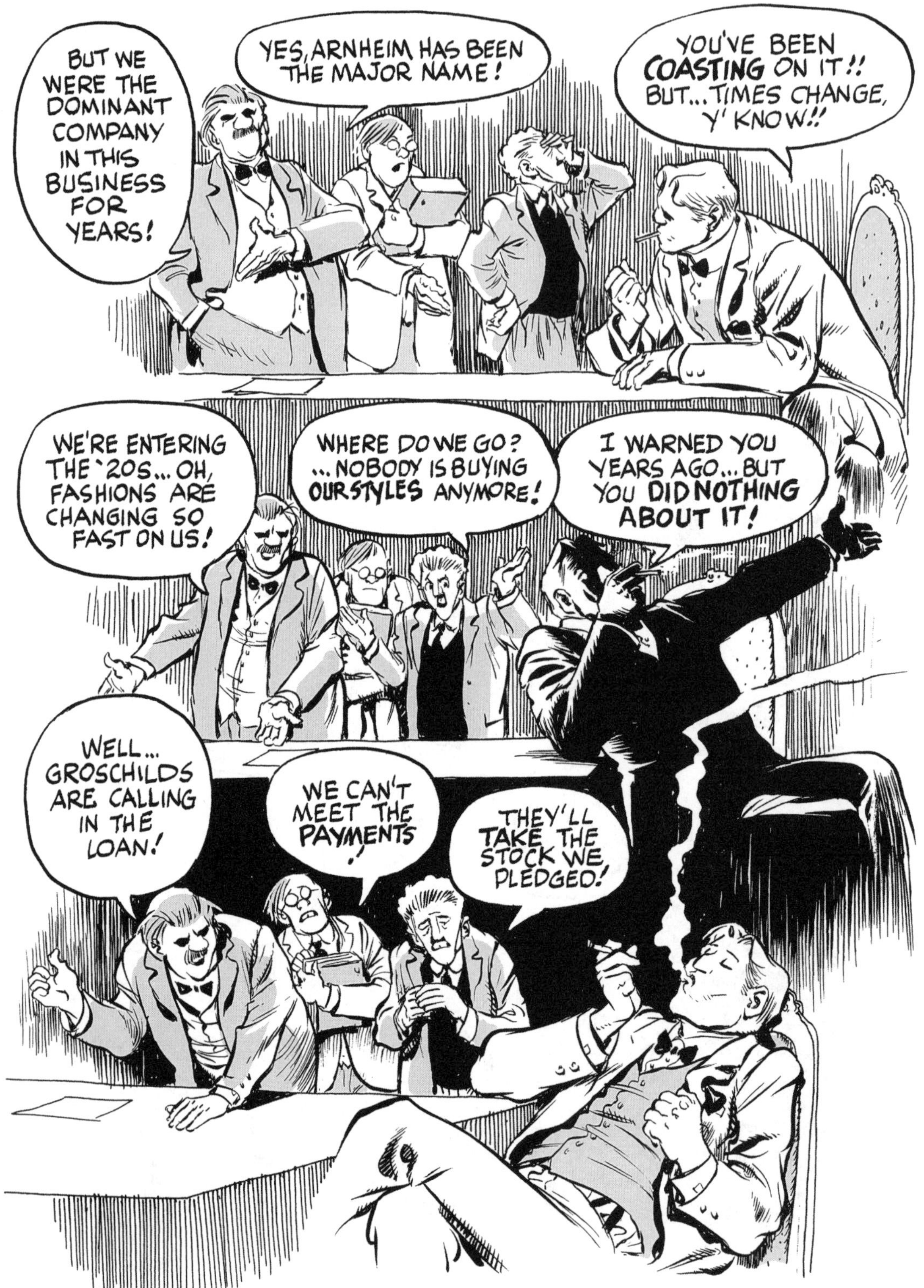
BUT WE WERE THE DOMINANT COMPANY IN THIS BUSINESS FOR YEARS!
YES, ARNHEIM HAS BEEN THE MAJOR NAME!
YOU'VE BEEN COASTING ON IT!! BUT... TIMES CHANGE, Y' KNOW!!
WE'RE ENTERING THE `20s... OH, FASHIONS ARE CHANGING SO FAST ON US!
WHERE DO WE GO? ...NOBODY IS BUYING OUR STYLES ANYMORE!
I WARNED YOU YEARS AGO... BUT YOU DID NOTHING ABOUT IT!
WELL... GROSCHILDS ARE CALLING IN THE LOAN!
WE CAN'T MEET THE PAYMENTS!
THEY'LL TAKE THE STOCK WE PLEDGED!

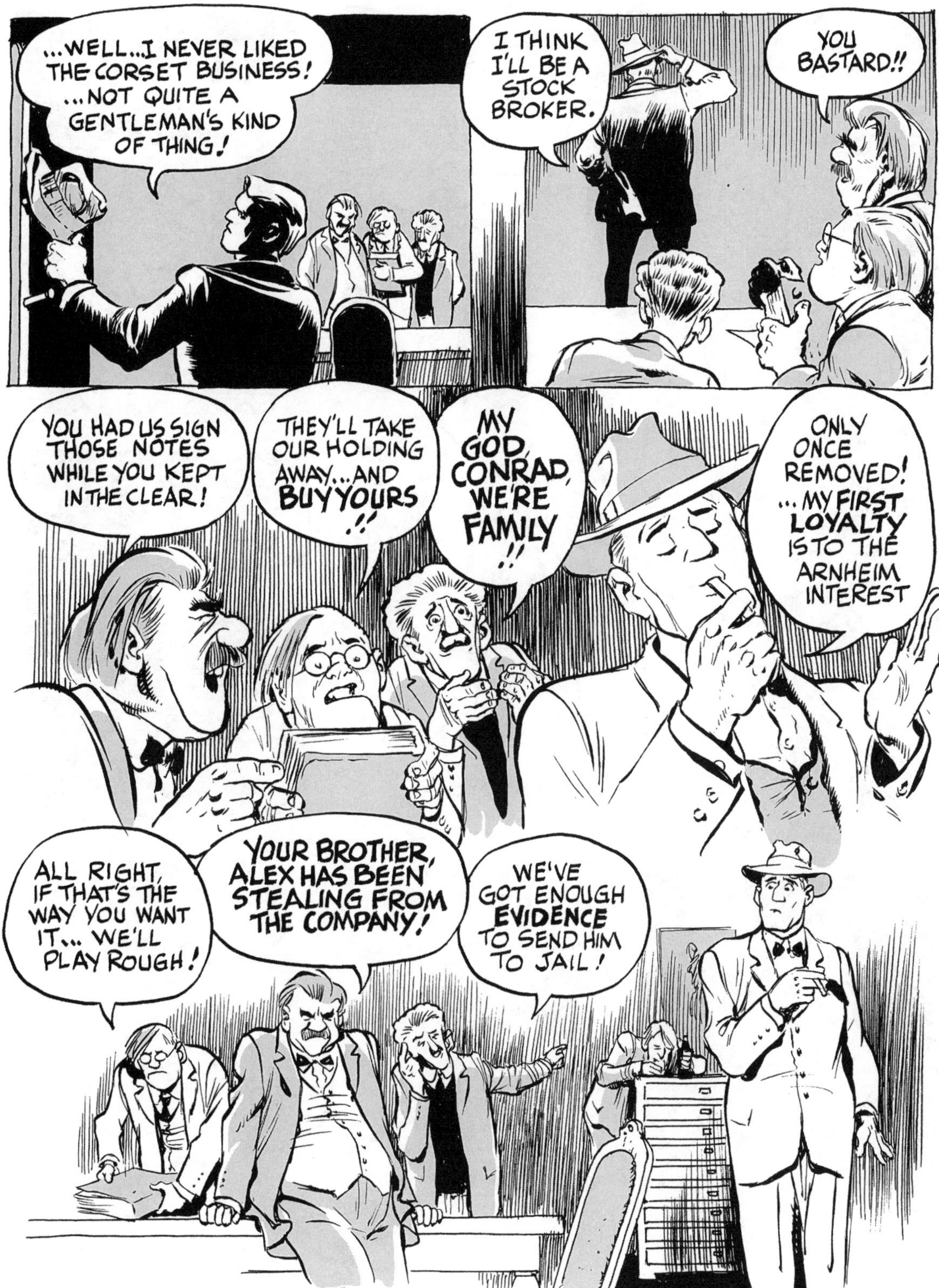
...WELL...I NEVER LIKED THE CORSET BUSINESS! ...NOT QUITE A GENTLEMAN'S KIND OF THING!
I THINK I'LL BE A STOCK BROKER.
YOU BASTARD!!
YOU HAD US SIGN THOSE NOTES WHILE YOU KEPT IN THE CLEAR!
THEY'LL TAKE OUR HOLDING AWAY...AND BUY YOURS!!
MY GOD, CONRAD, WE'RE FAMILY!!
ONLY ONCE REMOVED! ...MY FIRST LOYALTY IS TO THE ARNHEIM INTEREST
ALL RIGHT, IF THAT'S THE WAY YOU WANT IT... WE'LL PLAY ROUGH!
YOUR BROTHER, ALEX HAS BEEN STEALING FROM THE COMPANY!
WE'VE GOT ENOUGH EVIDENCE TO SEND HIM TO JAIL!

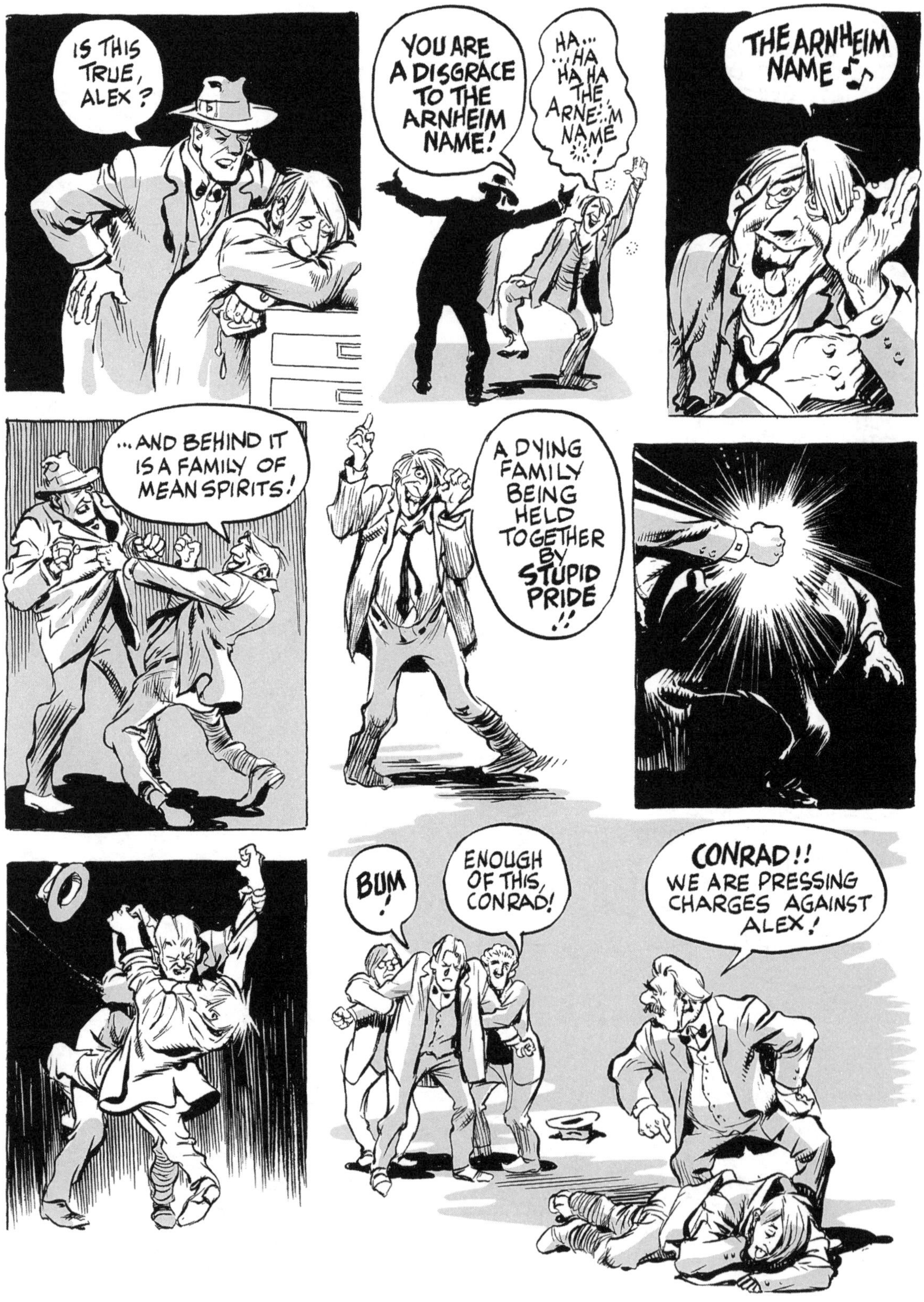
IS THIS TRUE, ALEX ?
YOU ARE A DISGRACE TO THE ARNHEIM NAME!
HA... ...HA HA HA THE ARNE..M NAME
THE ARNHEIM NAME ♫
...AND BEHIND IT IS A FAMILY OF MEAN SPIRITS!
A DYING FAMILY BEING HELD TOGETHER BY STUPID PRIDE !!
BUM !
ENOUGH OF THIS, CONRAD!
CONRAD!! WE ARE PRESSING CHARGES AGAINST ALEX!

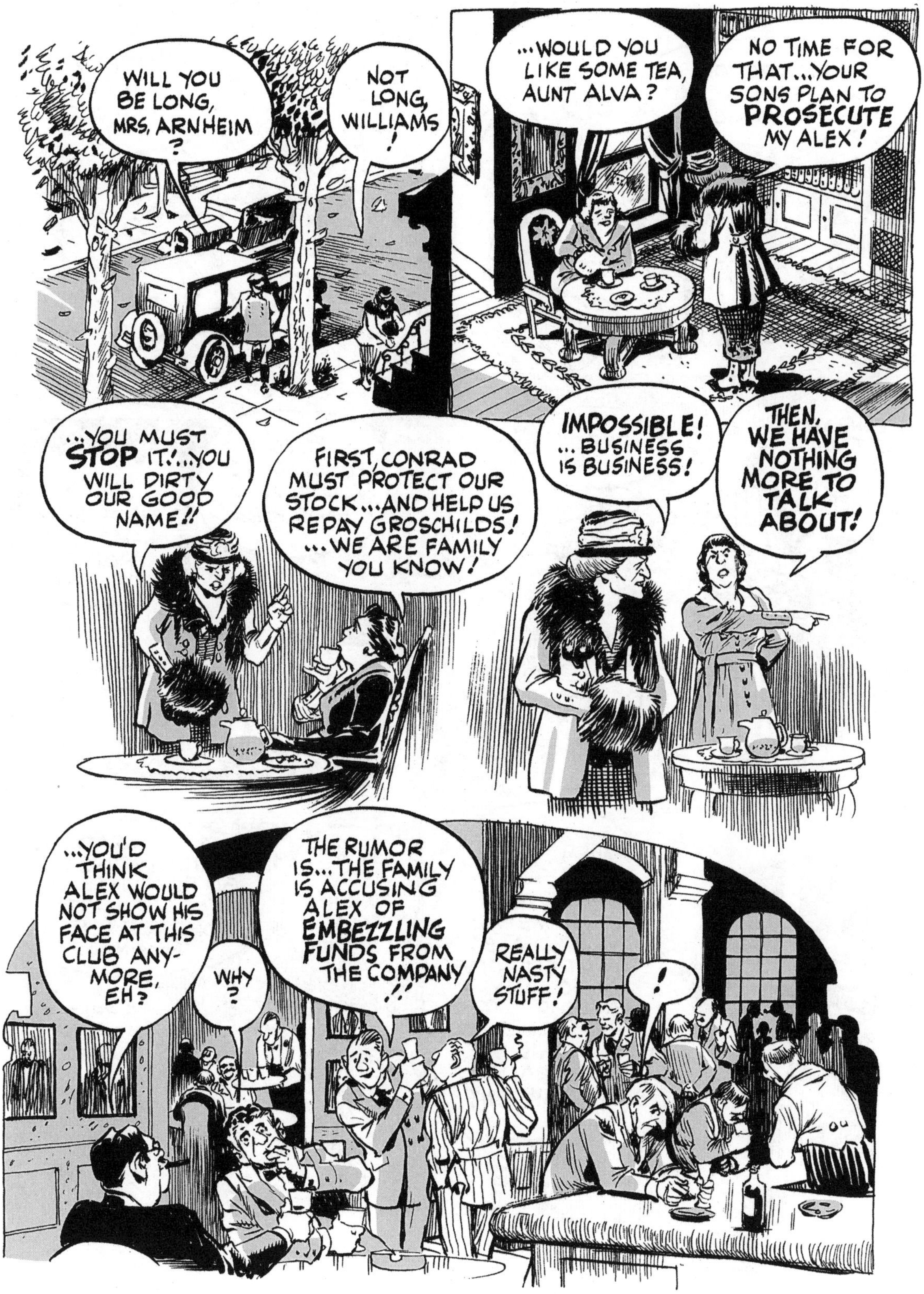
WILL YOU BE LONG, MRS. ARNHEIM?
NOT LONG, WILLIAMS!
...WOULD YOU LIKE SOME TEA, AUNT ALVA?
NO TIME FOR THAT...YOUR SONS PLAN TO PROSECUTE MY ALEX!
...YOU MUST STOP IT!...YOU WILL DIRTY OUR GOOD NAME!!
FIRST, CONRAD MUST PROTECT OUR STOCK...AND HELP US REPAY GROSCHILDS! ...WE ARE FAMILY YOU KNOW!
IMPOSSIBLE! ...BUSINESS IS BUSINESS!
THEN, WE HAVE NOTHING MORE TO TALK ABOUT!
...YOU'D THINK ALEX WOULD NOT SHOW HIS FACE AT THIS CLUB ANY-MORE, EH?
WHY?
THE RUMOR IS...THE FAMILY IS ACCUSING ALEX OF EMBEZZLING FUNDS FROM THE COMPANY!!
REALLY NASTY STUFF!
!

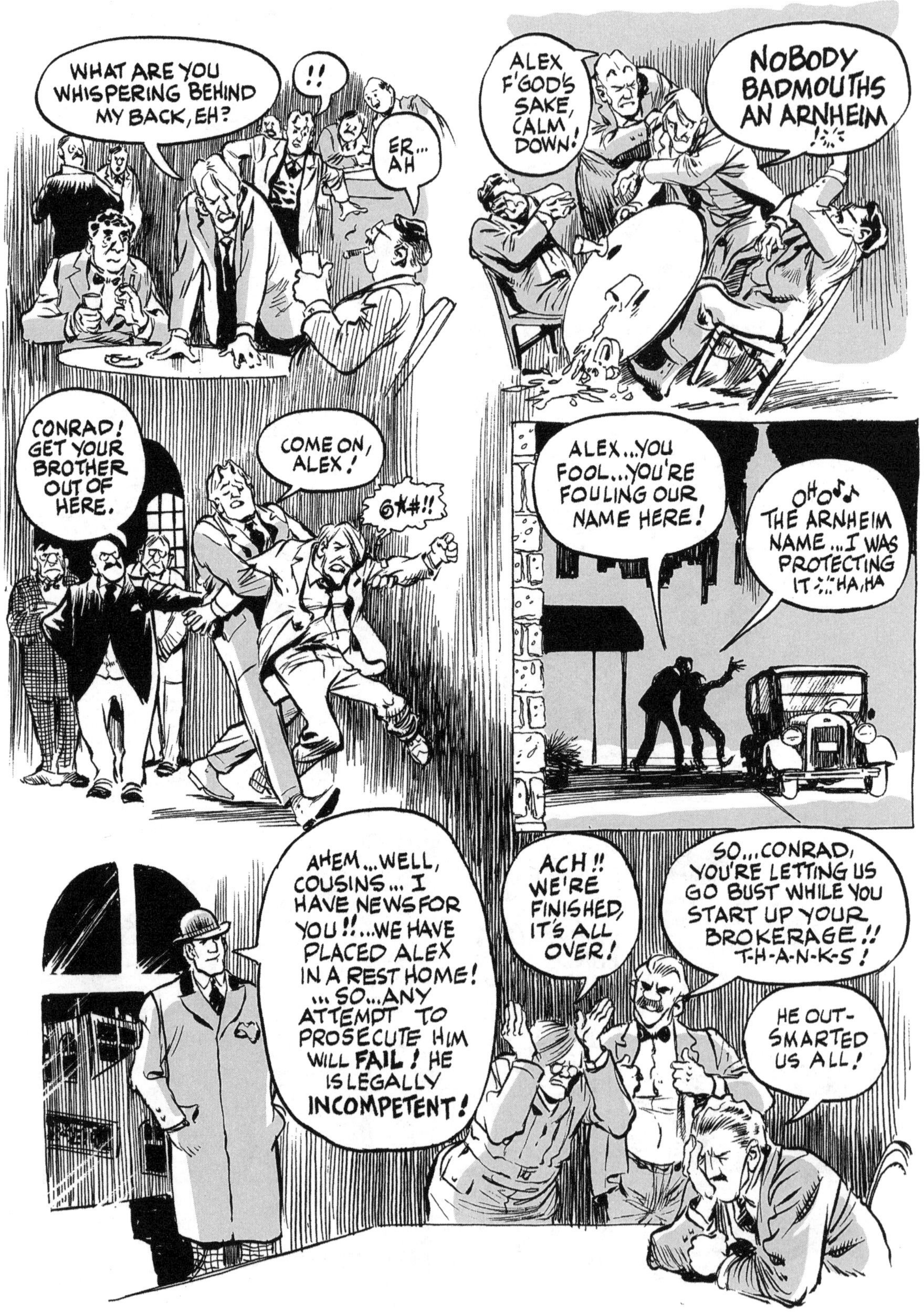

WHAT ARE YOU WHISPERING BEHIND MY BACK, EH?
!!
ER... AH
ALEX F'GOD'S SAKE, CALM DOWN!
NOBODY BADMOUTHS AN ARNHEIM
CONRAD! GET YOUR BROTHER OUT OF HERE.
COME ON, ALEX!
ALEX...YOU FOOL...YOU'RE FOULING OUR NAME HERE!
OHO THE ARNHEIM NAME...I WAS PROTECTING IT HA, HA
AHEM...WELL, COUSINS... I HAVE NEWS FOR YOU!!...WE HAVE PLACED ALEX IN A REST HOME! ...SO...ANY ATTEMPT TO PROSECUTE HIM WILL FAIL! HE IS LEGALLY INCOMPETENT!
ACH!! WE'RE FINISHED, IT'S ALL OVER!
SO...CONRAD, YOU'RE LETTING US GO BUST WHILE YOU START UP YOUR BROKERAGE!! T-H-A-N-K-S!
HE OUT-SMARTED US ALL!

Within a month of the Arnheim Corset Company failure, Conrad Arnheim bought a seat on the New York Stock Exchange and opened a brokerage firm on Park Avenue. It thrived from the start.

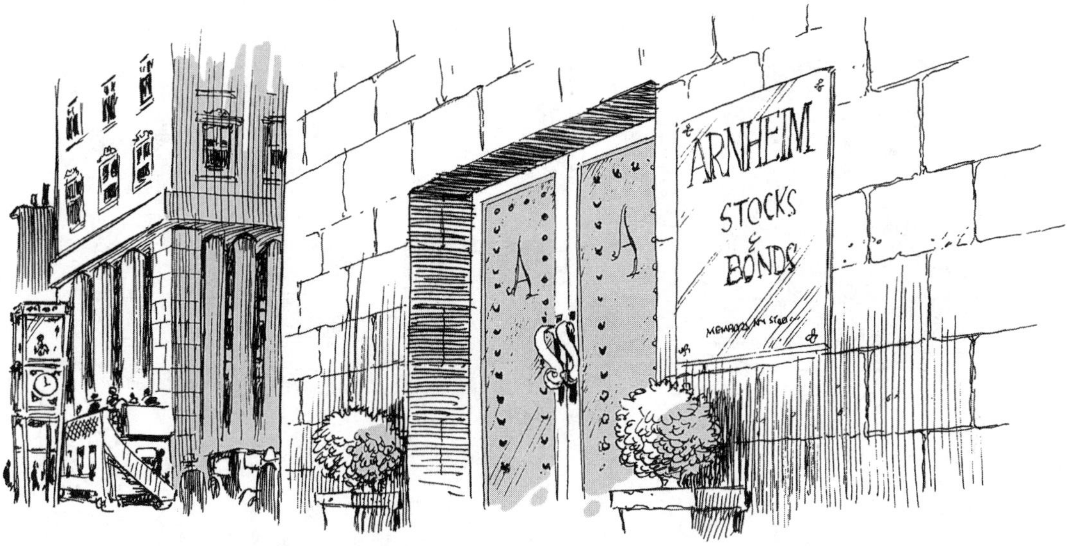
ARNHEIM
STOCKS & BONDS

His patronage came from his family's connections and social contacts. The Arnheim name still meant something. After all, who better to entrust one's money to than "one of us." At any rate, the stock market was booming and Conrad could do no wrong.

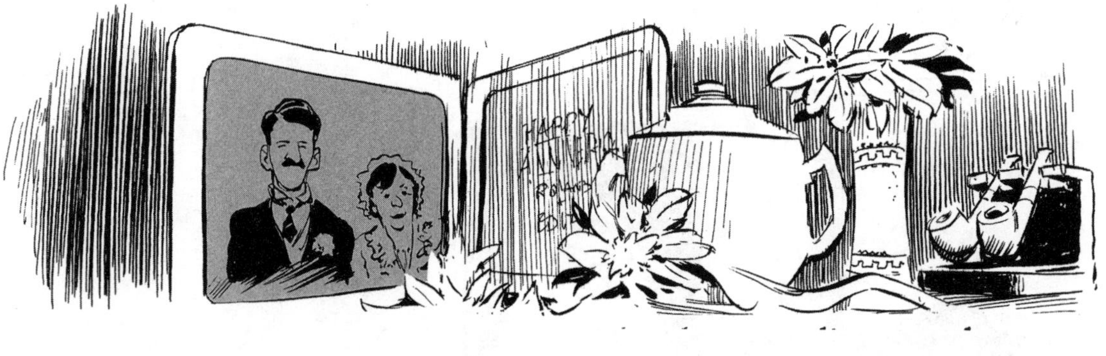
HAPPY

The infection of financial decay seemed to be spreading to other areas of the Arnheim family. Conrad's cousin Edith Arnheim married Roland Sydney, scion of the famed Sydney Clothing Store family. It was a good marriage socially but an unfortunate choice financially. The Sydney stores went bankrupt soon after the marriage of the young couple, leaving Roland unemployed and broke. His had little beyond his family name.

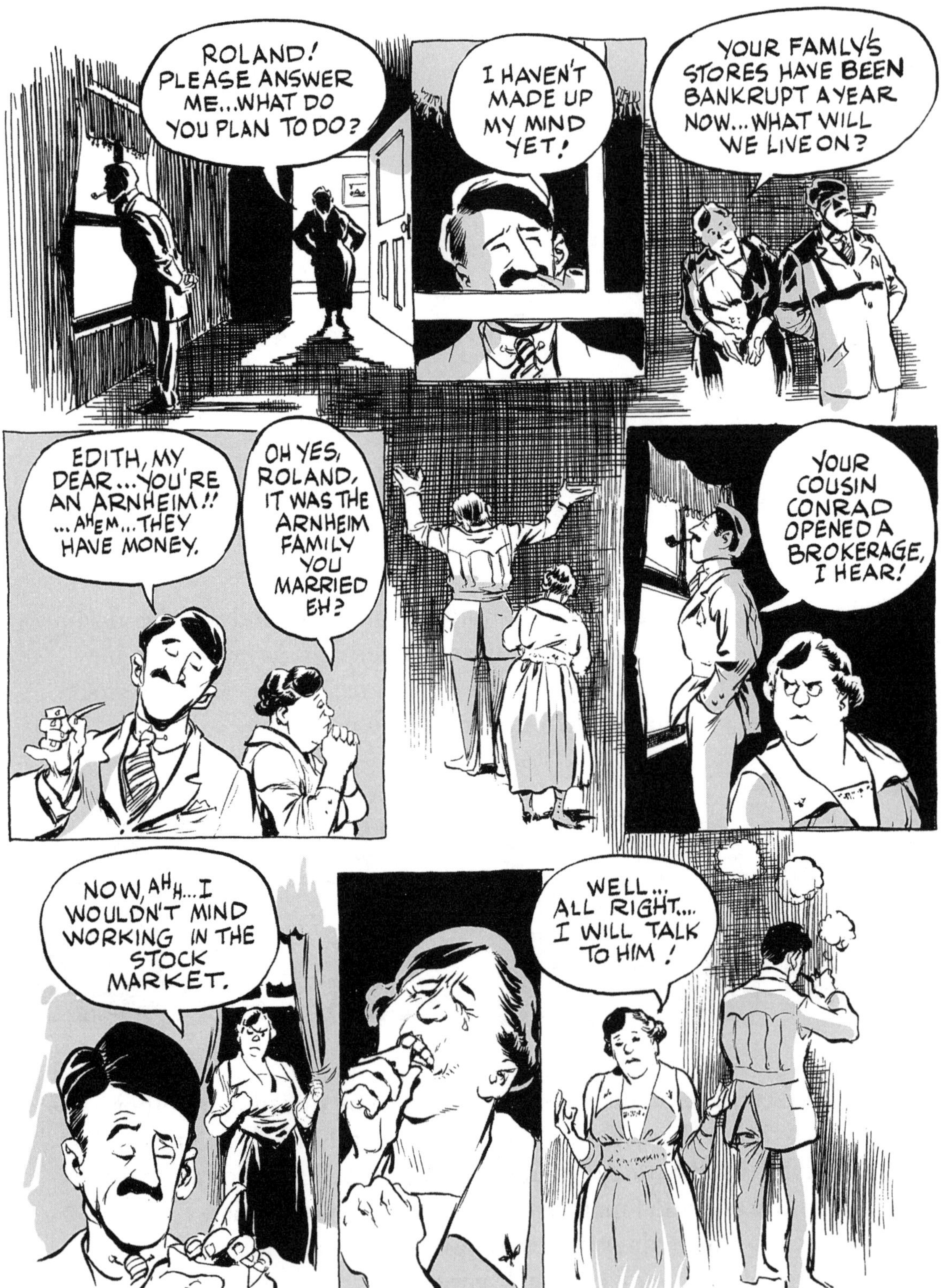
ROLAND! PLEASE ANSWER ME...WHAT DO YOU PLAN TO DO?
I HAVEN'T MADE UP MY MIND YET!
YOUR FAMLY'S STORES HAVE BEEN BANKRUPT A YEAR NOW... WHAT WILL WE LIVE ON?
EDITH, MY DEAR... YOU'RE AN ARNHEIM!! ...AHEM... THEY HAVE MONEY.
OH YES, ROLAND, IT WAS THE ARNHEIM FAMILY YOU MARRIED EH?
YOUR COUSIN CONRAD OPENED A BROKERAGE, I HEAR!
NOW, AHH...I WOULDN'T MIND WORKING IN THE STOCK MARKET.
WELL... ALL RIGHT.... I WILL TALK TO HIM!

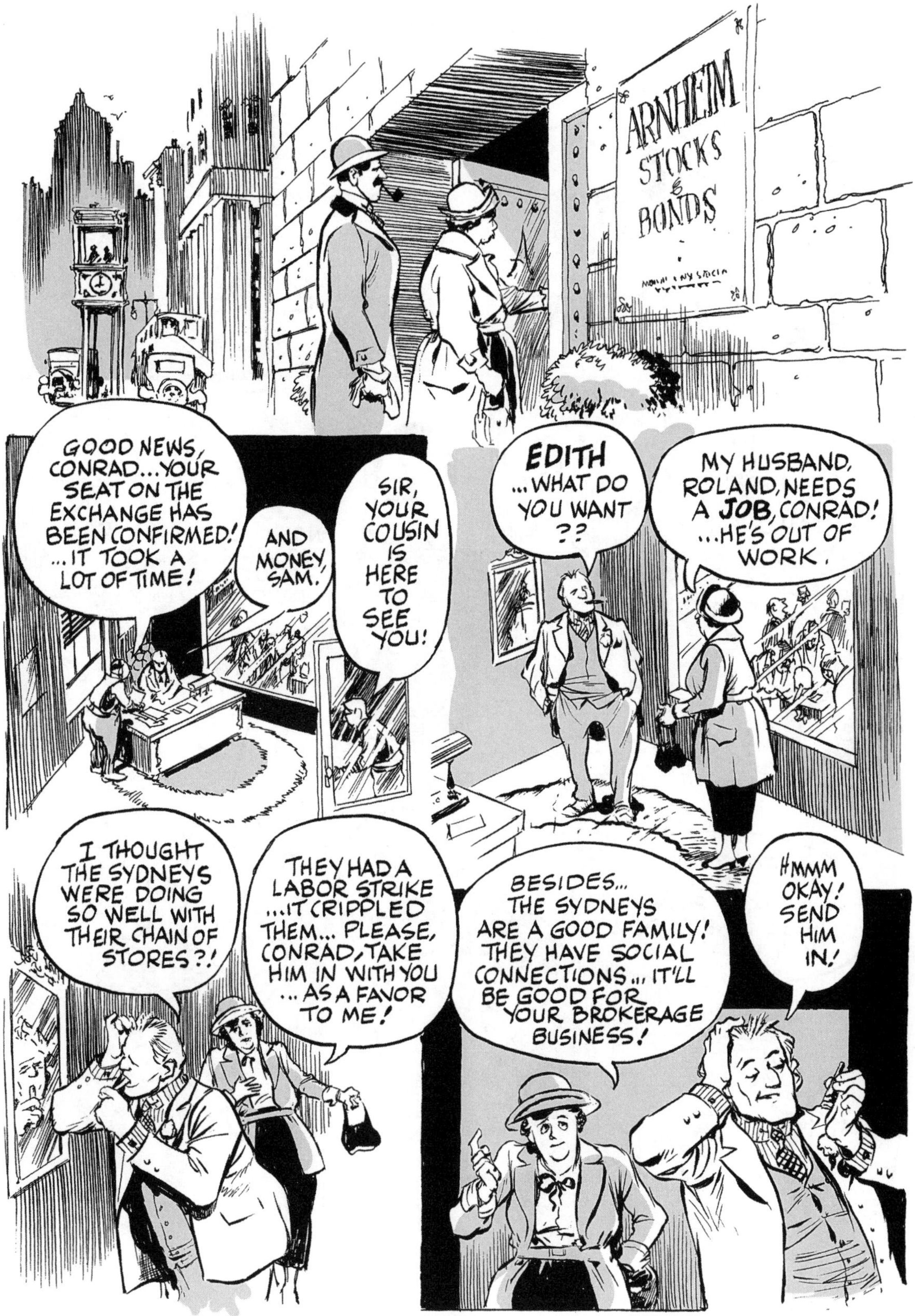
ARNHEIM STOCKS & BONDS
GOOD NEWS, CONRAD... YOUR SEAT ON THE EXCHANGE HAS BEEN CONFIRMED! ...IT TOOK A LOT OF TIME!
AND MONEY, SAM.
SIR, YOUR COUSIN IS HERE TO SEE YOU!
EDITH ...WHAT DO YOU WANT ??
MY HUSBAND, ROLAND, NEEDS A JOB, CONRAD! ...HE'S OUT OF WORK.
I THOUGHT THE SYDNEYS WERE DOING SO WELL WITH THEIR CHAIN OF STORES?!
THEY HAD A LABOR STRIKE ...IT CRIPPLED THEM... PLEASE, CONRAD, TAKE HIM IN WITH YOU ...AS A FAVOR TO ME!
BESIDES... THE SYDNEYS ARE A GOOD FAMILY! THEY HAVE SOCIAL CONNECTIONS... IT'LL BE GOOD FOR YOUR BROKERAGE BUSINESS!
HMMM OKAY! SEND HIM IN!

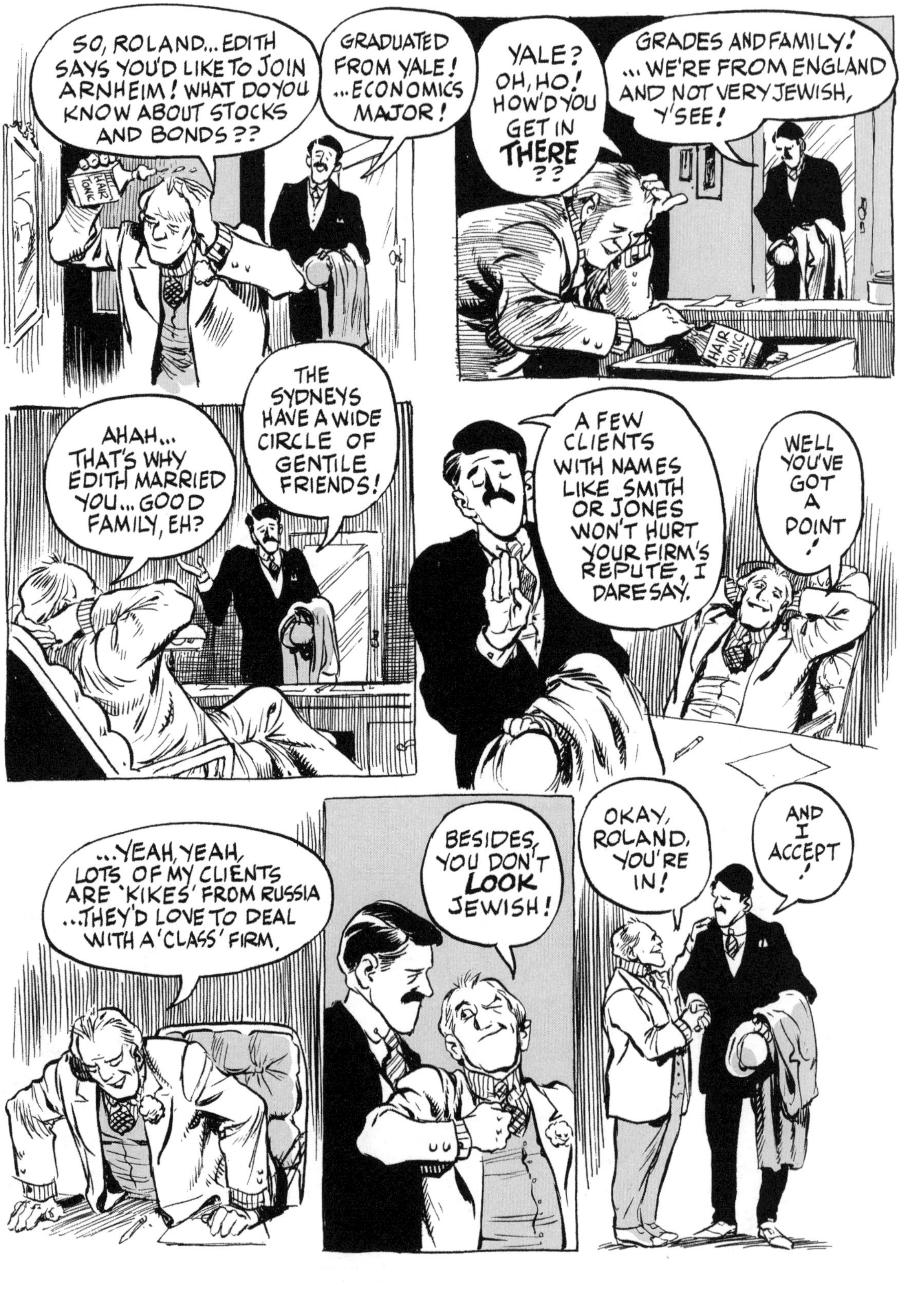
SO, ROLAND... EDITH SAYS YOU'D LIKE TO JOIN ARNHEIM! WHAT DO YOU KNOW ABOUT STOCKS AND BONDS??
HAIR TONIC
GRADUATED FROM YALE! ...ECONOMICS MAJOR!
YALE? OH, HO! HOW'D YOU GET IN THERE??
GRADES AND FAMILY! ...WE'RE FROM ENGLAND AND NOT VERY JEWISH, Y'SEE!
HAIR TONIC
AHAH... THAT'S WHY EDITH MARRIED YOU... GOOD FAMILY, EH?
THE SYDNEYS HAVE A WIDE CIRCLE OF GENTILE FRIENDS!
A FEW CLIENTS WITH NAMES LIKE SMITH OR JONES WON'T HURT YOUR FIRM'S REPUTE, I DARESAY.
WELL YOU'VE GOT A POINT!
...YEAH, YEAH, LOTS OF MY CLIENTS ARE 'KIKES' FROM RUSSIA ...THEY'D LOVE TO DEAL WITH A 'CLASS' FIRM.
BESIDES, YOU DON'T LOOK JEWISH!
OKAY, ROLAND, YOU'RE IN!
AND I ACCEPT!

The boom years and the growth of the brokerage business reinforced the Arnheim name and Conrad's leadership.

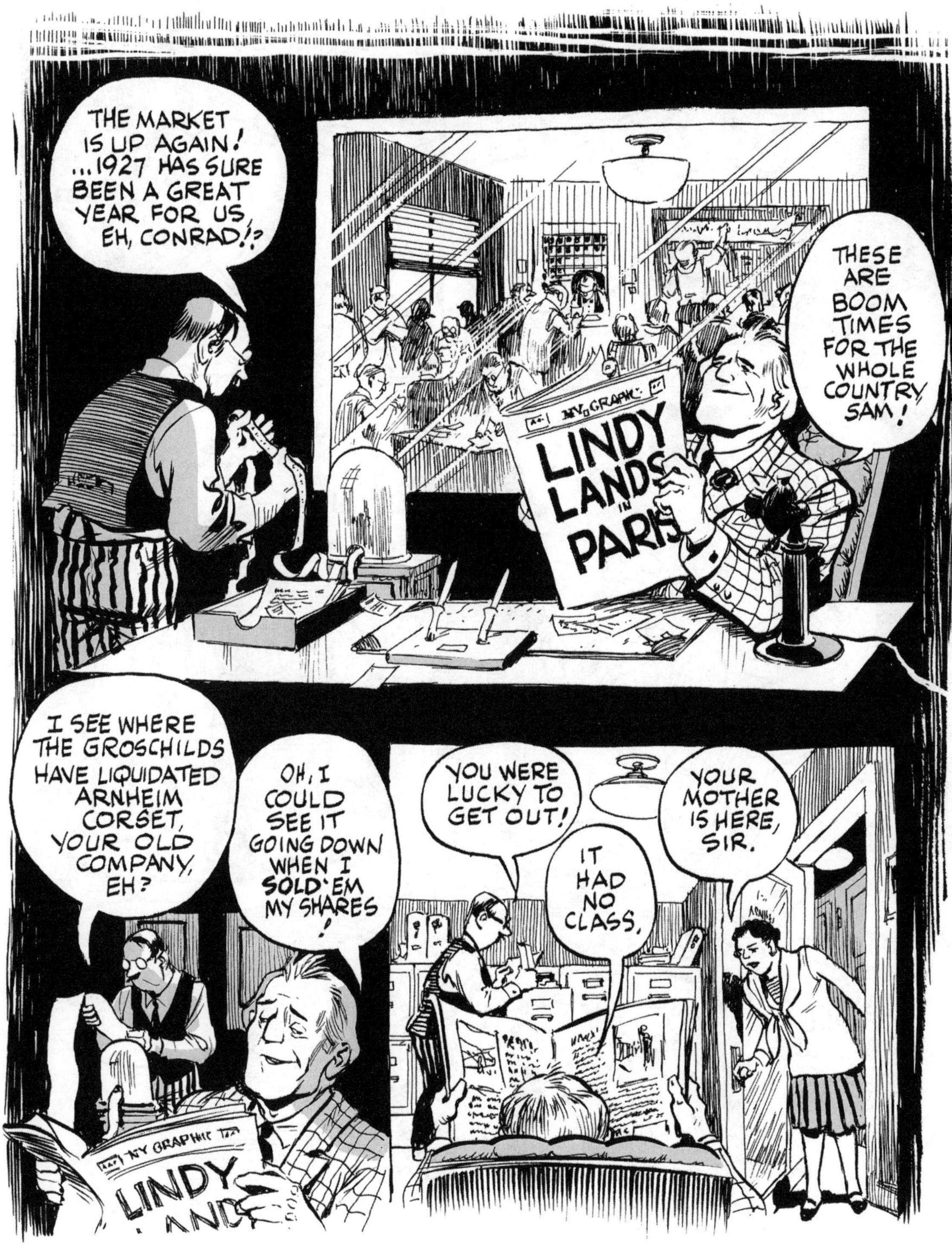
THE MARKET IS UP AGAIN! ...1927 HAS SURE BEEN A GREAT YEAR FOR US, EH, CONRAD!?
THESE ARE BOOM TIMES FOR THE WHOLE COUNTRY, SAM!
NY GRAPHIC
LINDY LANDS IN PARIS
I SEE WHERE THE GROSCHILDS HAVE LIQUIDATED ARNHEIM CORSET, YOUR OLD COMPANY, EH?
OH, I COULD SEE IT GOING DOWN WHEN I **SOLD** 'EM MY SHARES!
YOU WERE LUCKY TO GET OUT!
IT HAD NO CLASS.
YOUR MOTHER IS HERE, SIR.
NY GRAPHIC
LINDY

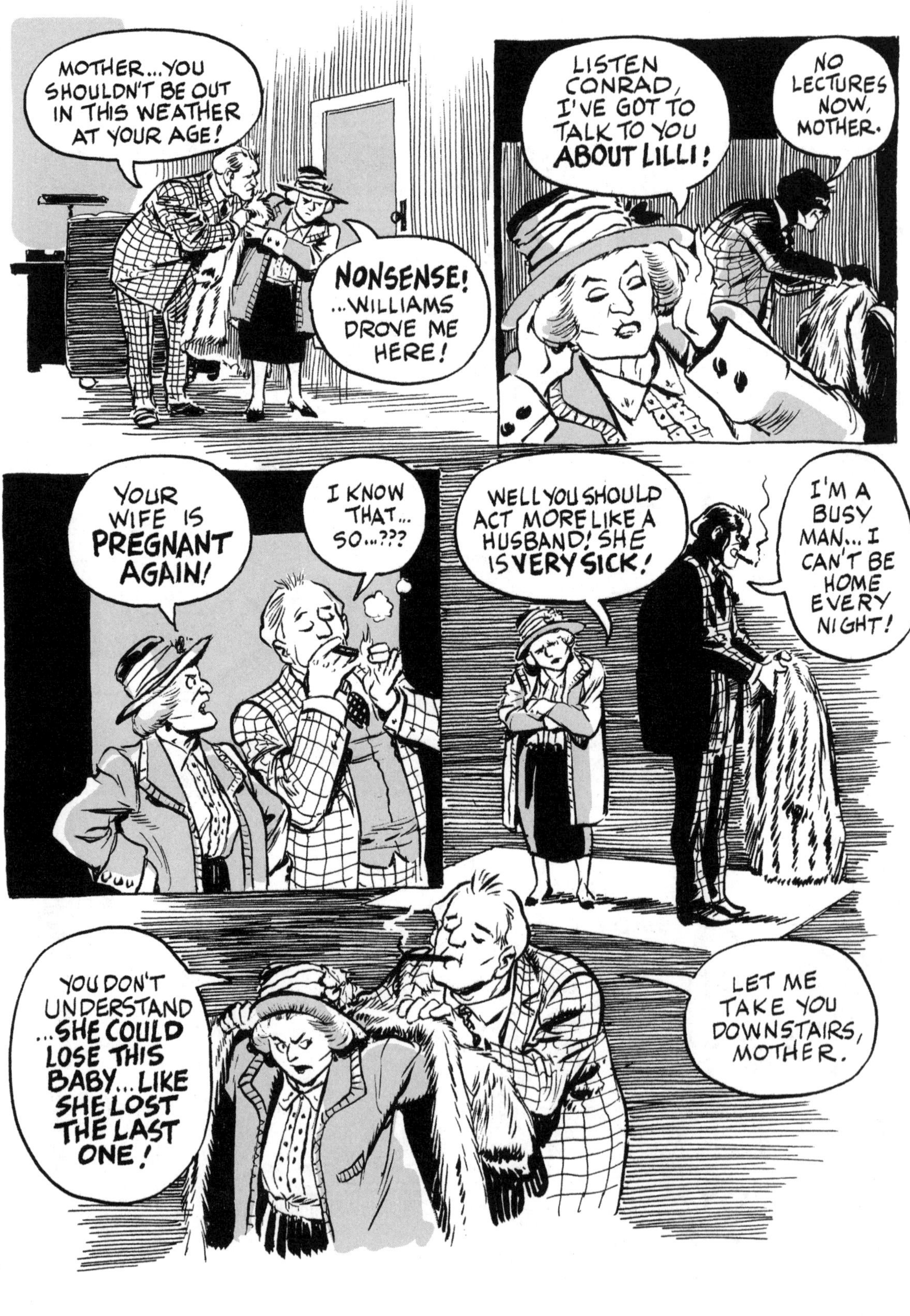
MOTHER...YOU SHOULDN'T BE OUT IN THIS WEATHER AT YOUR AGE!
NONSENSE! ...WILLIAMS DROVE ME HERE!
LISTEN CONRAD, I'VE GOT TO TALK TO YOU ABOUT LILLI!
NO LECTURES NOW, MOTHER.
YOUR WIFE IS PREGNANT AGAIN!
I KNOW THAT... SO...???
WELL YOU SHOULD ACT MORE LIKE A HUSBAND! SHE IS VERY SICK!
I'M A BUSY MAN... I CAN'T BE HOME EVERY NIGHT!
YOU DON'T UNDERSTAND ...SHE COULD LOSE THIS BABY... LIKE SHE LOST THE LAST ONE!
LET ME TAKE YOU DOWNSTAIRS, MOTHER.

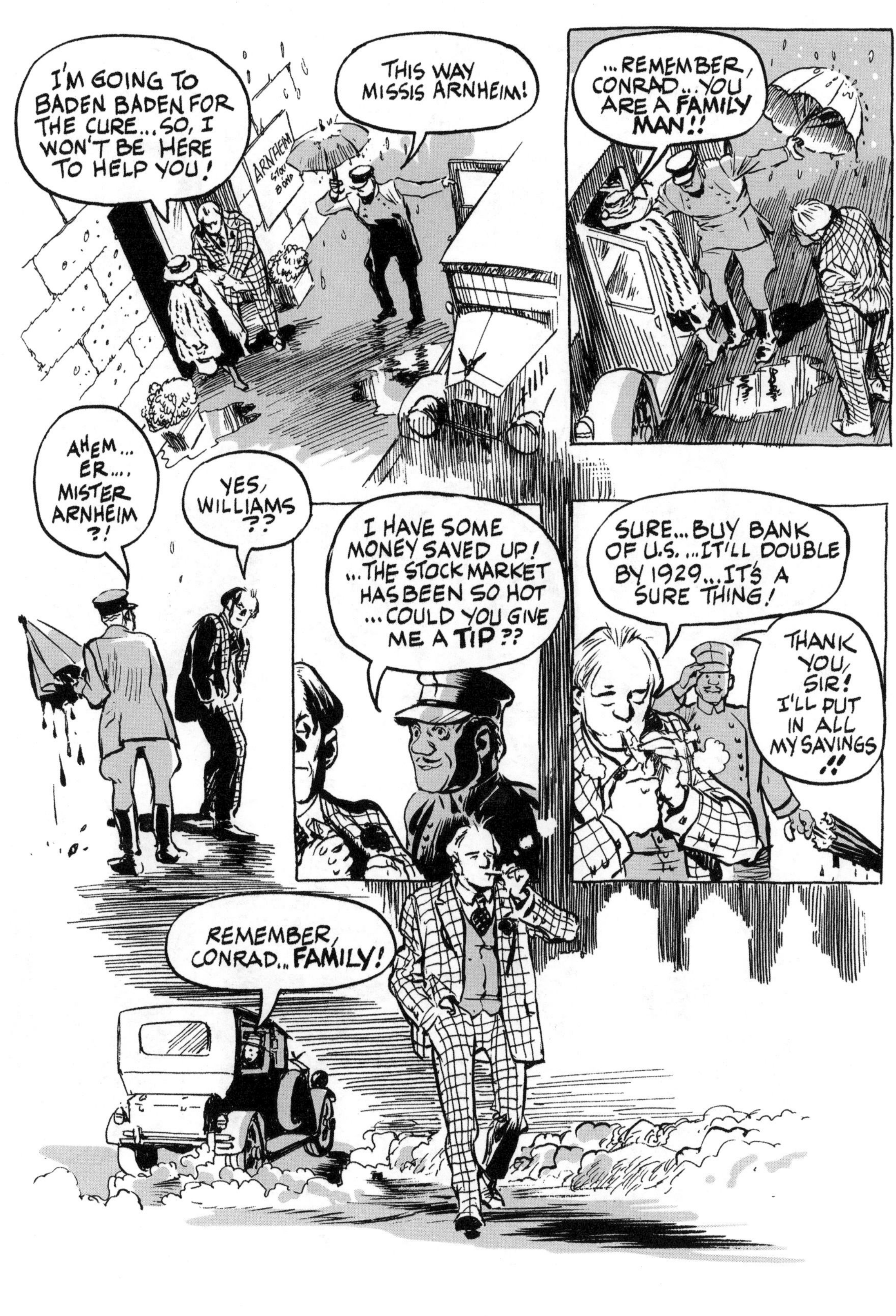
I'M GOING TO BADEN BADEN FOR THE CURE... SO, I WON'T BE HERE TO HELP YOU!
ARNHEIM
THIS WAY MISSIS ARNHEIM!
...REMEMBER, CONRAD... YOU ARE A FAMILY MAN!!
AHEM... ER.... MISTER ARNHEIM ?!
YES, WILLIAMS ??
I HAVE SOME MONEY SAVED UP! ...THE STOCK MARKET HAS BEEN SO HOT ...COULD YOU GIVE ME A TIP??
SURE... BUY BANK OF U.S. ...IT'LL DOUBLE BY 1929... IT'S A SURE THING!
THANK YOU, SIR! I'LL PUT IN ALL MY SAVINGS !!
REMEMBER, CONRAD.. FAMILY!

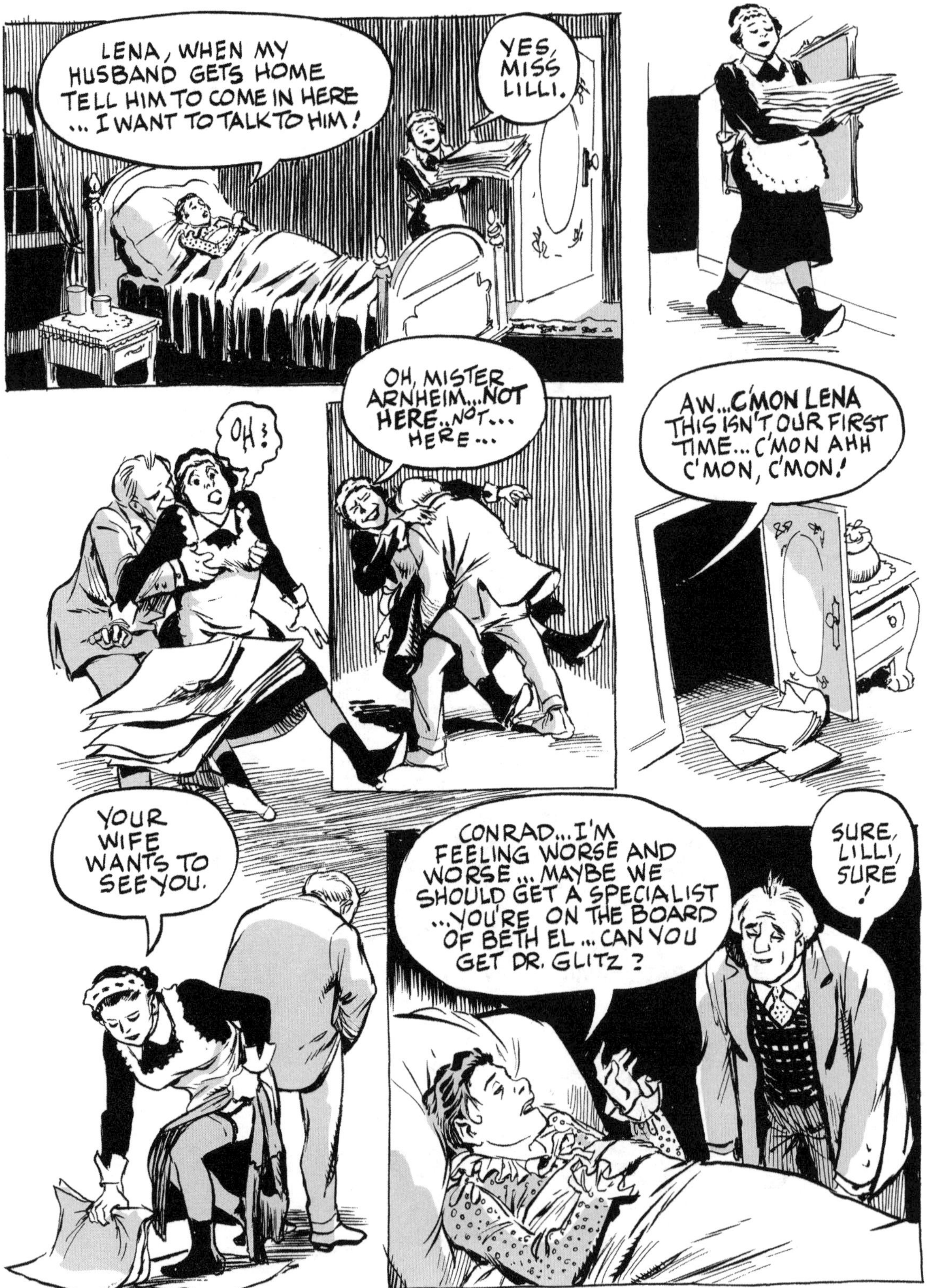

LENA, WHEN MY HUSBAND GETS HOME TELL HIM TO COME IN HERE ... I WANT TO TALK TO HIM!
YES, MISS LILLI.
OH!
OH, MISTER ARNHEIM...NOT HERE..NOT... HERE...
AW...C'MON LENA THIS ISN'T OUR FIRST TIME... C'MON AHH C'MON, C'MON!
YOUR WIFE WANTS TO SEE YOU.
CONRAD...I'M FEELING WORSE AND WORSE... MAYBE WE SHOULD GET A SPECIALIST ...YOU'RE ON THE BOARD OF BETH EL... CAN YOU GET DR. GLITZ?
SURE, LILLI, SURE!

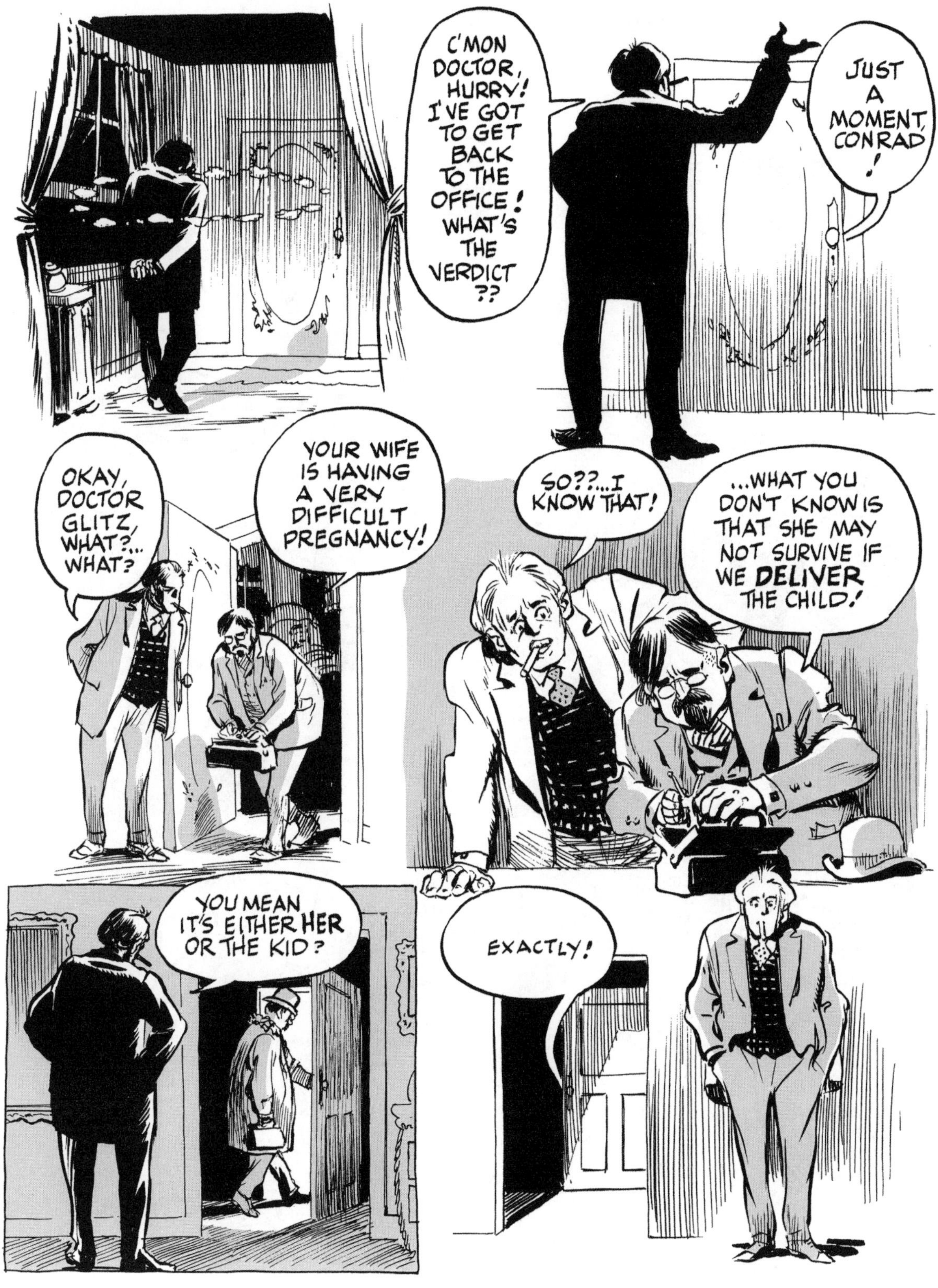
C'MON DOCTOR, HURRY! I'VE GOT TO GET BACK TO THE OFFICE! WHAT'S THE VERDICT ??
JUST A MOMENT, CONRAD!
OKAY, DOCTOR GLITZ, WHAT?... WHAT?
YOUR WIFE IS HAVING A VERY DIFFICULT PREGNANCY!
SO??...I KNOW THAT!
...WHAT YOU DON'T KNOW IS THAT SHE MAY NOT SURVIVE IF WE DELIVER THE CHILD!
YOU MEAN IT'S EITHER HER OR THE KID?
EXACTLY!

The news of Lilli's difficulty brought Alva home from the spa in Switzerland.

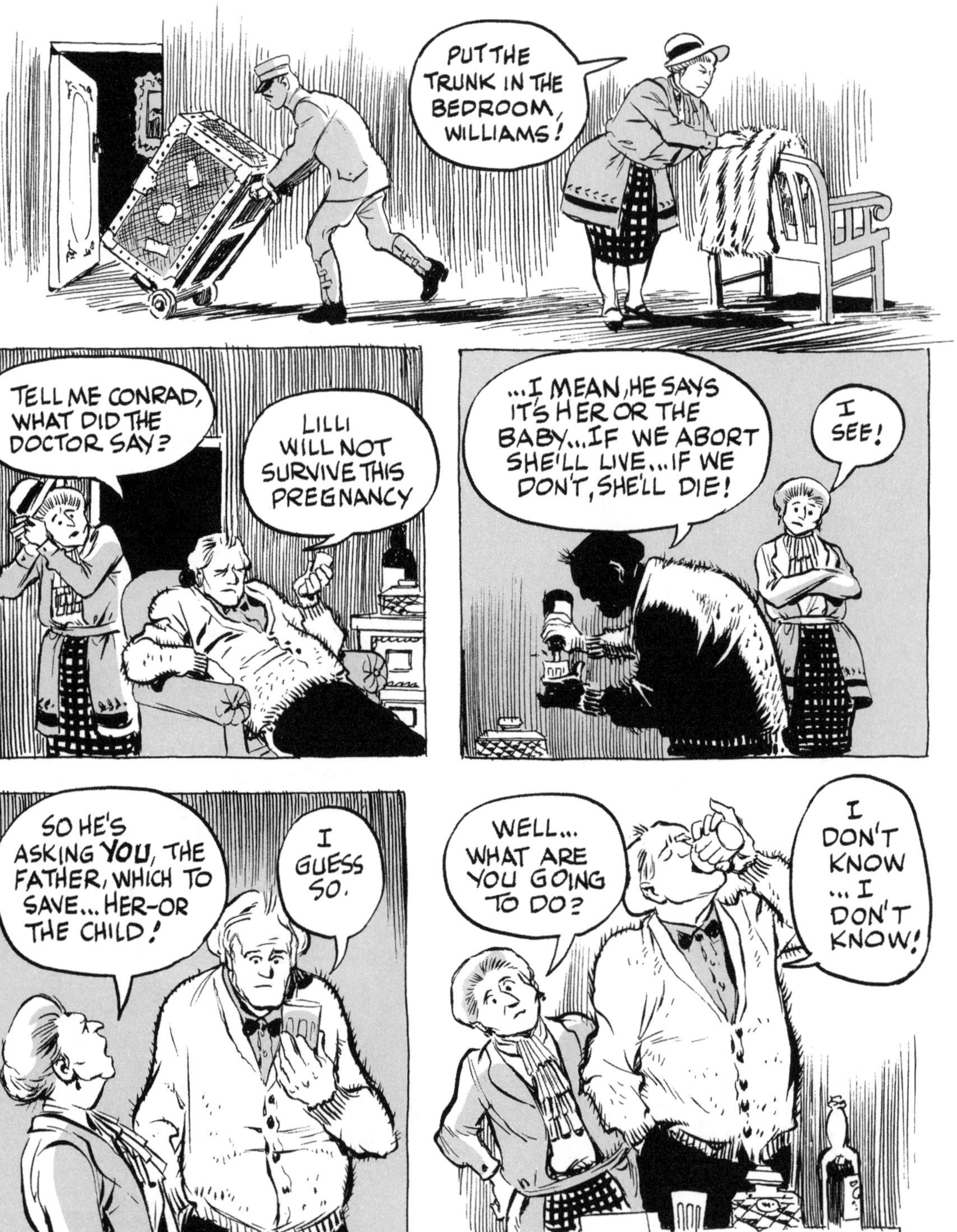
PUT THE TRUNK IN THE BEDROOM, WILLIAMS!
TELL ME CONRAD, WHAT DID THE DOCTOR SAY?
LILLI WILL NOT SURVIVE THIS PREGNANCY
...I MEAN, HE SAYS IT'S HER OR THE BABY...IF WE ABORT SHE'LL LIVE...IF WE DON'T, SHE'LL DIE!
I SEE!
SO HE'S ASKING **YOU**, THE FATHER, WHICH TO SAVE... HER-OR THE CHILD!
I GUESS SO.
WELL... WHAT ARE YOU GOING TO DO?
I DON'T KNOW ...I DON'T KNOW!

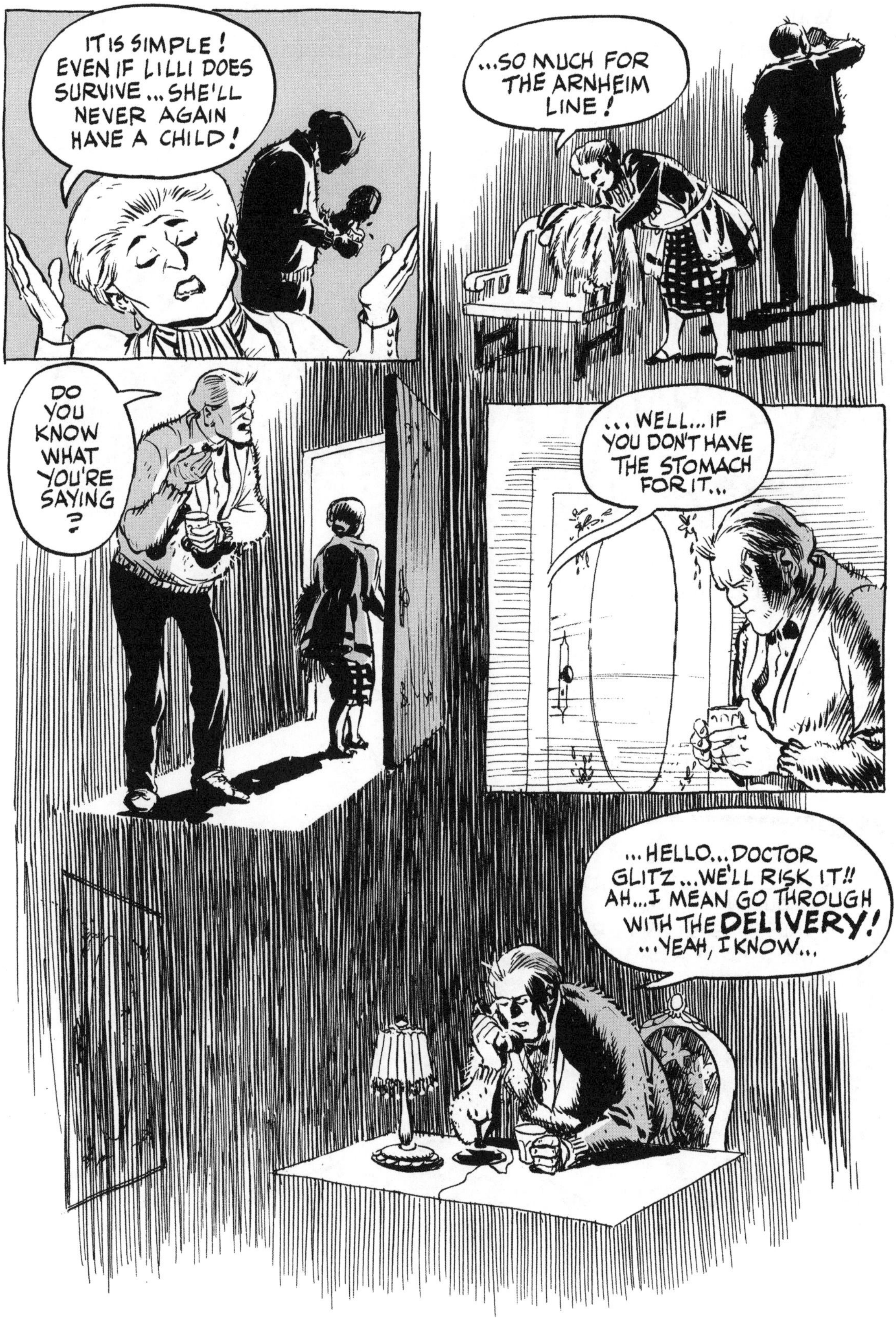
IT IS SIMPLE! EVEN IF LILLI DOES SURVIVE... SHE'LL NEVER AGAIN HAVE A CHILD!
...SO MUCH FOR THE ARNHEIM LINE!
DO YOU KNOW WHAT YOU'RE SAYING?
...WELL...IF YOU DON'T HAVE THE STOMACH FOR IT...
...HELLO...DOCTOR GLITZ...WE'LL RISK IT!! AH...I MEAN GO THROUGH WITH THE DELIVERY! ...YEAH, I KNOW...

As the doctor feared, Lilli died in childbirth. The Obers, who spent her last days with their daughter, remained after the funeral for an Arnheim and Ober family discussion.

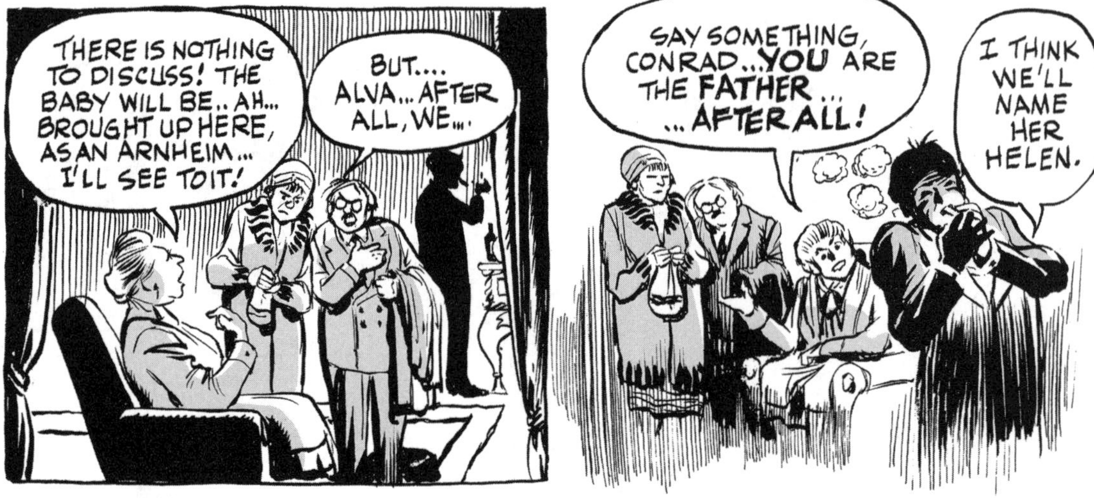
THERE IS NOTHING TO DISCUSS! THE BABY WILL BE.. AH... BROUGHT UP HERE, AS AN ARNHEIM... I'LL SEE TO IT!
BUT.... ALVA... AFTER ALL, WE....
SAY SOMETHING, CONRAD... YOU ARE THE FATHER ... ... AFTER ALL!
I THINK WE'LL NAME HER HELEN.

Of course, the Arnheim family prevailed. The Obers returned home and Alva took charge of Helen's care. With her usual determination, she devoted full time and energy to the matter, which left Conrad plenty of freedom to pursue his social life.

But a few months later . . .

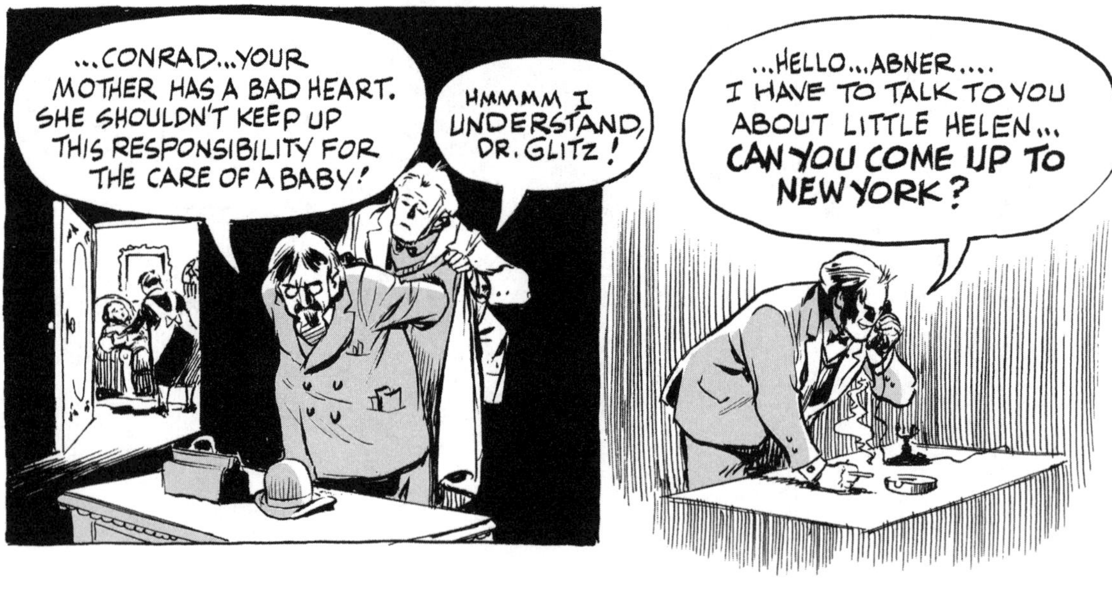
...CONRAD...YOUR MOTHER HAS A BAD HEART. SHE SHOULDN'T KEEP UP THIS RESPONSIBILITY FOR THE CARE OF A BABY!
HMMMM I UNDERSTAND, DR. GLITZ!
...HELLO...ABNER.... I HAVE TO TALK TO YOU ABOUT LITTLE HELEN... CAN YOU COME UP TO NEW YORK?

It was not difficult to convince the Obers. They were more than willing to take the child and bring her up in Lavolier. They arrived within the week.

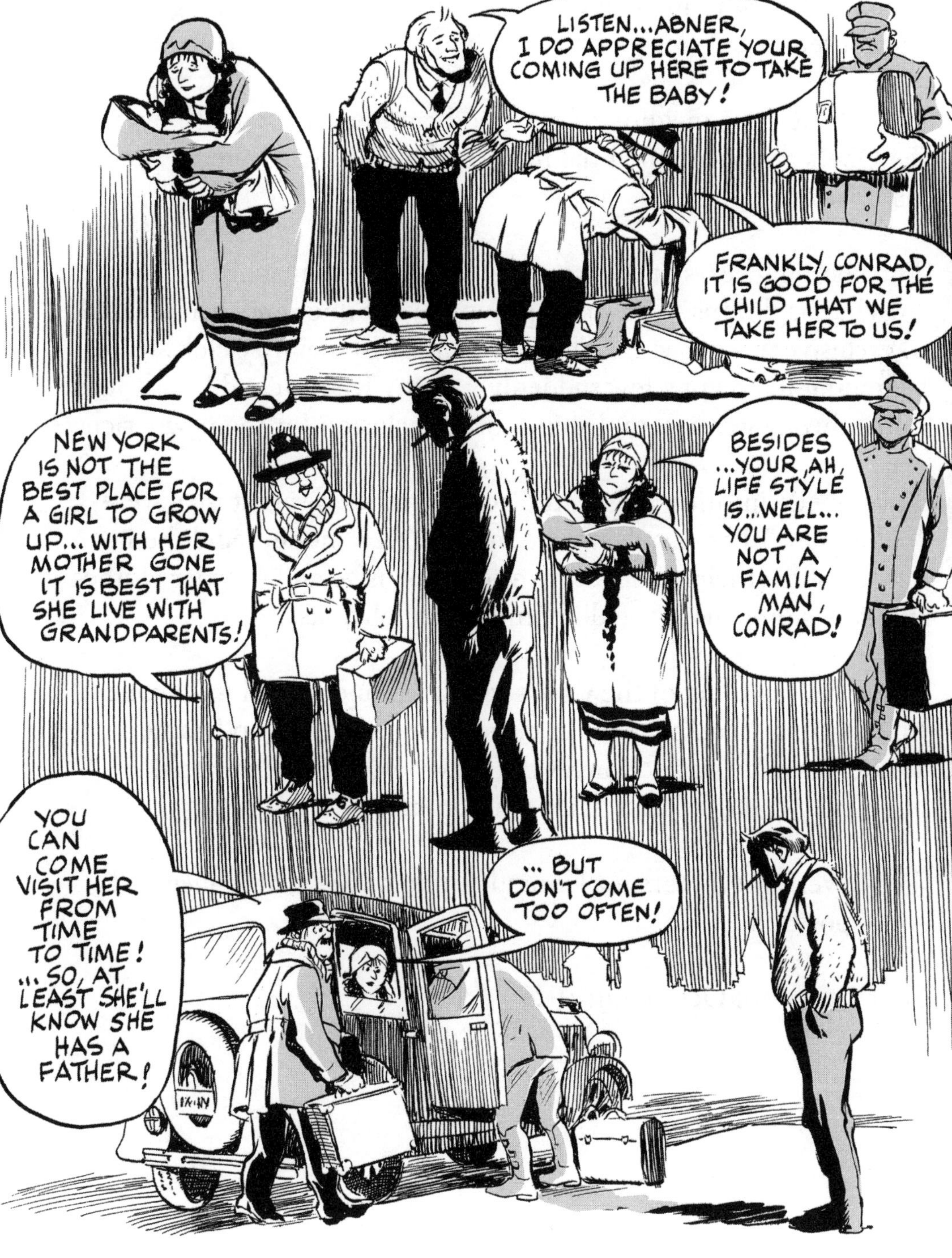
LISTEN...ABNER, I DO APPRECIATE YOUR COMING UP HERE TO TAKE THE BABY!
FRANKLY, CONRAD, IT IS GOOD FOR THE CHILD THAT WE TAKE HER TO US!
NEW YORK IS NOT THE BEST PLACE FOR A GIRL TO GROW UP... WITH HER MOTHER GONE IT IS BEST THAT SHE LIVE WITH GRANDPARENTS!
BESIDES ...YOUR, AH, LIFE STYLE IS...WELL... YOU ARE NOT A FAMILY MAN, CONRAD!
YOU CAN COME VISIT HER FROM TIME TO TIME! ...SO, AT LEAST SHE'LL KNOW SHE HAS A FATHER!
... BUT DON'T COME TOO OFTEN!

This turn of events seemed to finally separate the Ober and the Arnheim families.

Lilli's child was with the Obers. The question of whether she would be brought up as an Ober or an Arnheim was no longer of any consequence.

The alliance, the melding of two good families that would elevate the Obers and strengthen the financial base of the Arnheims, never materialized.

The booming years of the Roaring Twenties was making millionaires by the dozens. The social group that, at one time, had seemed so exclusive was growing. The German Jewish country clubs were beginning to accept a few suddenly wealthy Russian and Polish Jews. Philanthropy was accomplishing social inclusion for the newly rich.

The only delineation left for the good families was that they were "old money." The invaders were merely "new money" and their need to show their affluence by more expensive and showier clothes and goods only made the difference more obvious.

The social standing of the Obers remained unchanged in Lavolier. In New York, the Arnheims managed to keep their good name. While marriage was no longer the only way to a higher social level, big money could still buy status and protect it.

These were good years for Conrad Arnheim. He had money and social position.

So it went until October of 1929.

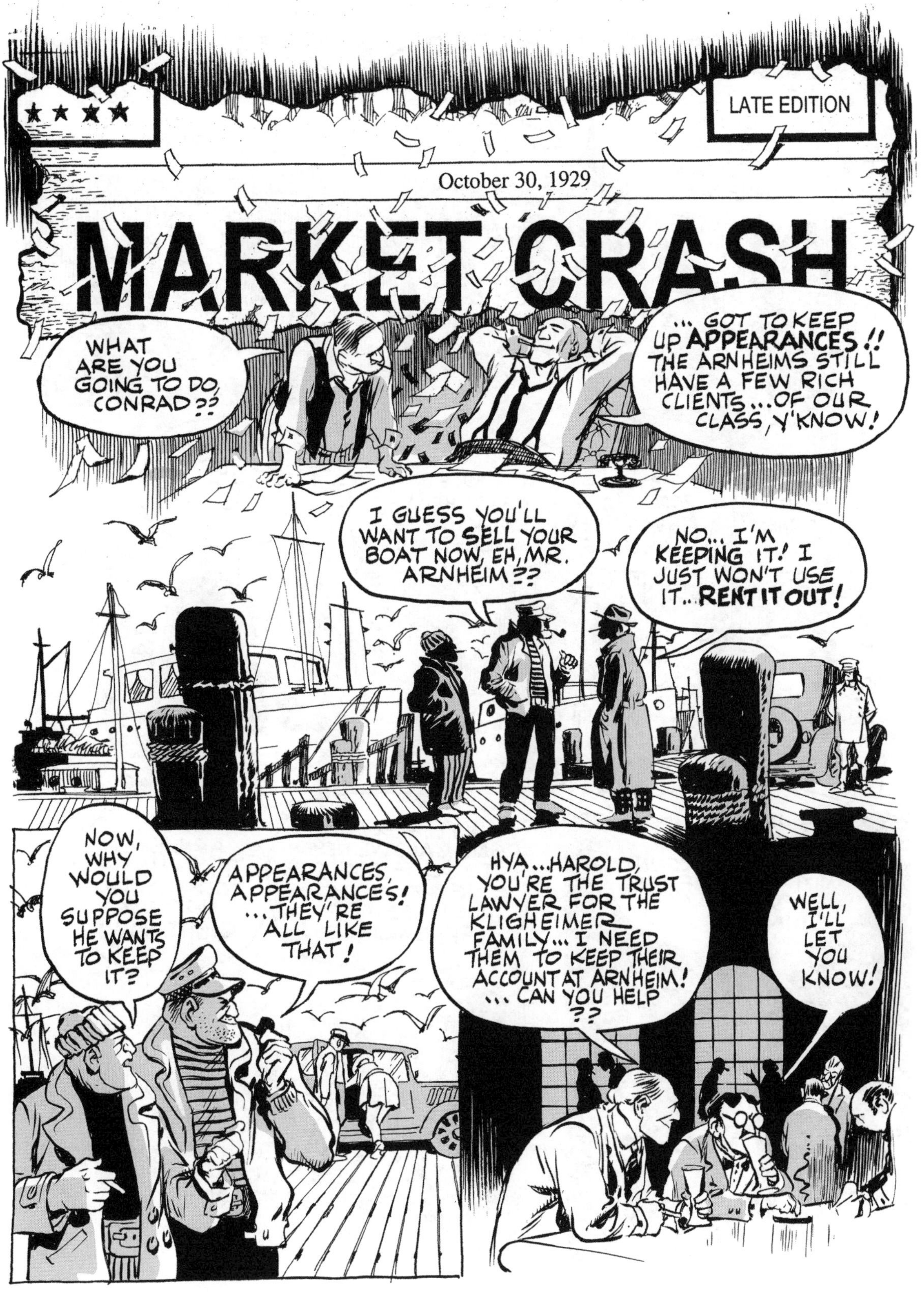
LATE EDITION
October 30, 1929
MARKET CRASH
WHAT ARE YOU GOING TO DO, CONRAD??
... GOT TO KEEP UP APPEARANCES!! THE ARNHEIMS STILL HAVE A FEW RICH CLIENTS... OF OUR CLASS, Y'KNOW!
I GUESS YOU'LL WANT TO SELL YOUR BOAT NOW, EH, MR. ARNHEIM??
NO... I'M KEEPING IT! I JUST WON'T USE IT... RENT IT OUT!
NOW, WHY WOULD YOU SUPPOSE HE WANTS TO KEEP IT?
APPEARANCES, APPEARANCES! ...THEY'RE ALL LIKE THAT!
HYA...HAROLD, YOU'RE THE TRUST LAWYER FOR THE KLIGHEIMER FAMILY... I NEED THEM TO KEEP THEIR ACCOUNT AT ARNHEIM! ... CAN YOU HELP??
WELL, I'LL LET YOU KNOW!

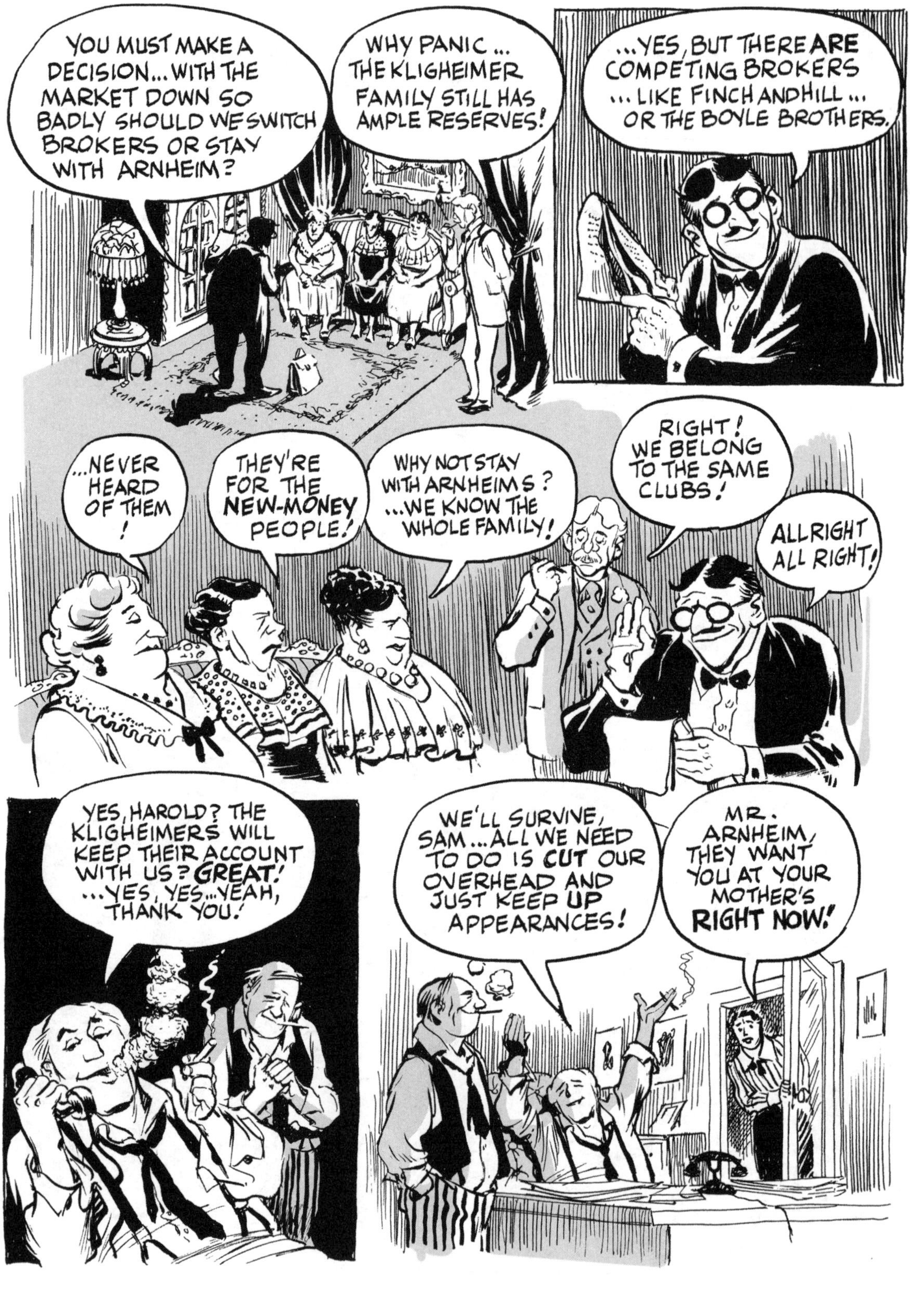
YOU MUST MAKE A DECISION... WITH THE MARKET DOWN SO BADLY SHOULD WE SWITCH BROKERS OR STAY WITH ARNHEIM?
WHY PANIC ... THE KLIGHEIMER FAMILY STILL HAS AMPLE RESERVES!
...YES, BUT THERE ARE COMPETING BROKERS ... LIKE FINCH AND HILL ... OR THE BOYLE BROTHERS.
...NEVER HEARD OF THEM!
THEY'RE FOR THE NEW-MONEY PEOPLE!
WHY NOT STAY WITH ARNHEIMS? ...WE KNOW THE WHOLE FAMILY!
RIGHT! WE BELONG TO THE SAME CLUBS!
ALL RIGHT ALL RIGHT!
YES, HAROLD? THE KLIGHEIMERS WILL KEEP THEIR ACCOUNT WITH US? GREAT! ...YES, YES...YEAH, THANK YOU!
WE'LL SURVIVE, SAM... ALL WE NEED TO DO IS CUT OUR OVERHEAD AND JUST KEEP UP APPEARANCES!
MR. ARNHEIM, THEY WANT YOU AT YOUR MOTHER'S RIGHT NOW!

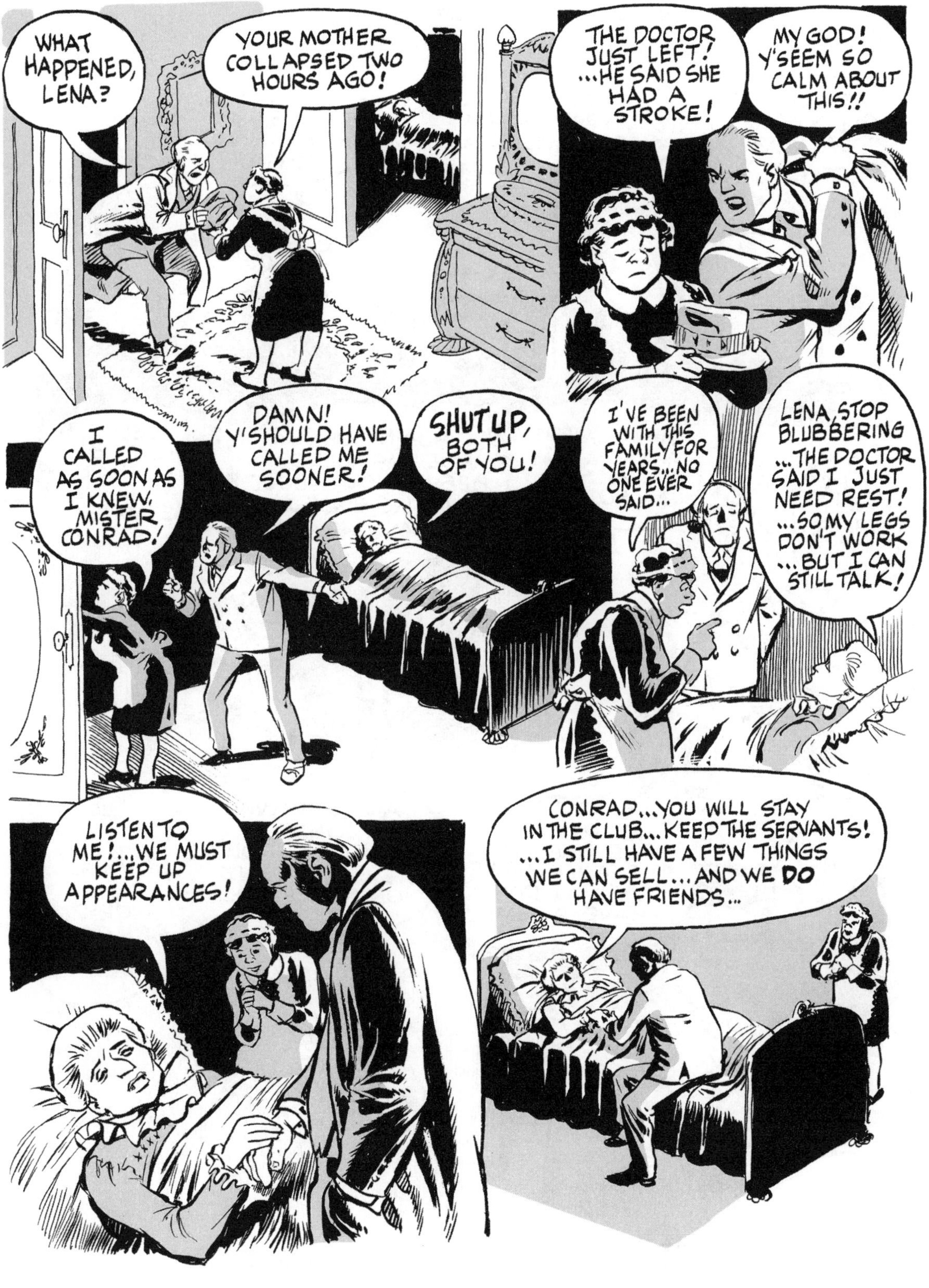
WHAT HAPPENED, LENA?
YOUR MOTHER COLLAPSED TWO HOURS AGO!
THE DOCTOR JUST LEFT! ...HE SAID SHE HAD A STROKE!
MY GOD! Y'SEEM SO CALM ABOUT THIS!!
I CALLED AS SOON AS I KNEW, MISTER CONRAD!
DAMN! Y'SHOULD HAVE CALLED ME SOONER!
SHUT UP, BOTH OF YOU!
I'VE BEEN WITH THIS FAMILY FOR YEARS... NO ONE EVER SAID...
LENA, STOP BLUBBERING ...THE DOCTOR SAID I JUST NEED REST! ...SO MY LEGS DON'T WORK ...BUT I CAN STILL TALK!
LISTEN TO ME!... WE MUST KEEP UP APPEARANCES!
CONRAD... YOU WILL STAY IN THE CLUB... KEEP THE SERVANTS! ...I STILL HAVE A FEW THINGS WE CAN SELL... AND WE DO HAVE FRIENDS...

And indeed, appearances *were* kept up!

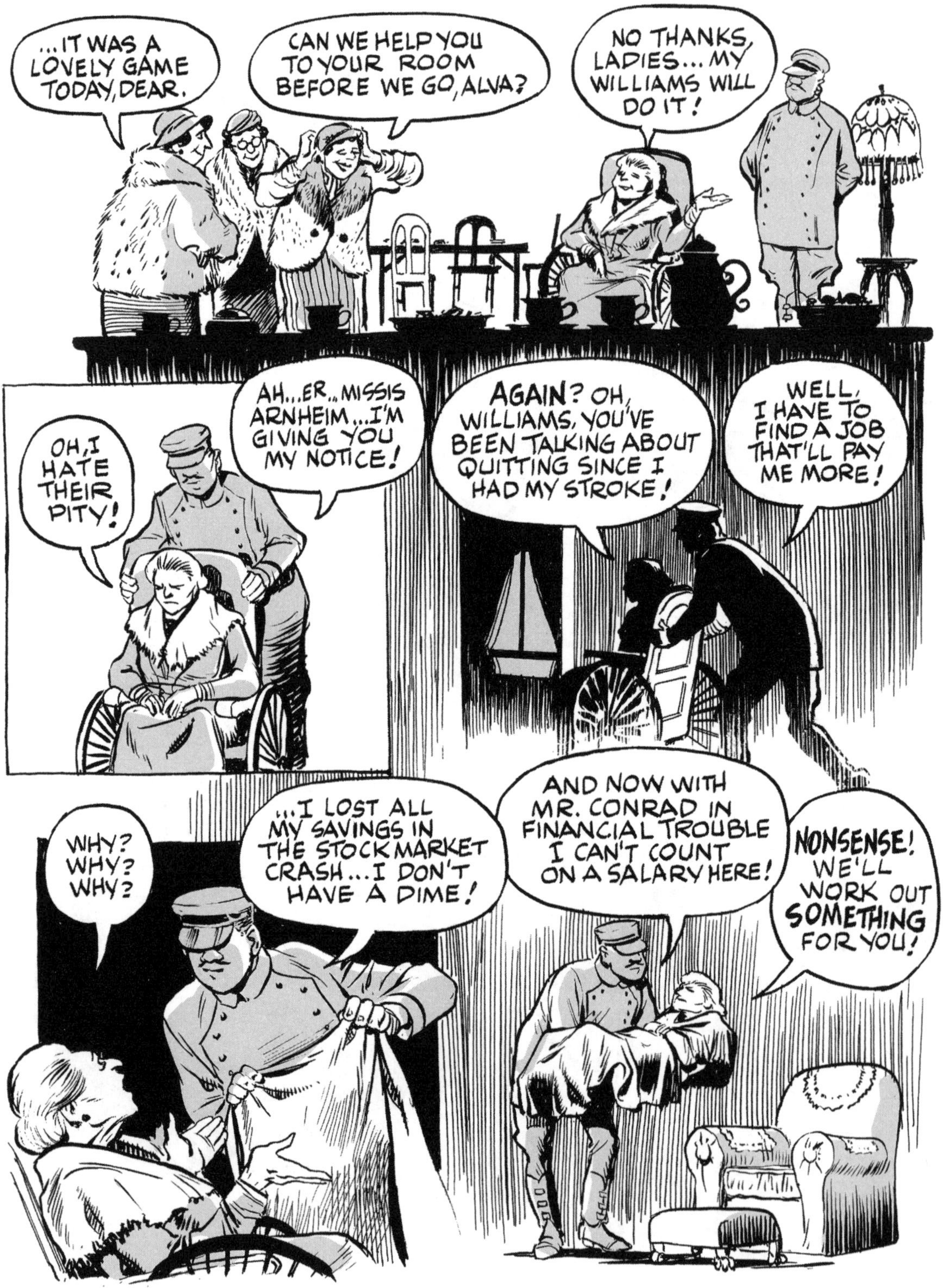
...IT WAS A LOVELY GAME TODAY, DEAR.
CAN WE HELP YOU TO YOUR ROOM BEFORE WE GO, ALVA?
NO THANKS, LADIES... MY WILLIAMS WILL DO IT!
OH, I HATE THEIR PITY!
AH...ER...MISSIS ARNHEIM...I'M GIVING YOU MY NOTICE!
AGAIN? OH, WILLIAMS, YOU'VE BEEN TALKING ABOUT QUITTING SINCE I HAD MY STROKE!
WELL, I HAVE TO FIND A JOB THAT'LL PAY ME MORE!
WHY? WHY? WHY?
...I LOST ALL MY SAVINGS IN THE STOCK MARKET CRASH...I DON'T HAVE A DIME!
AND NOW WITH MR. CONRAD IN FINANCIAL TROUBLE I CAN'T COUNT ON A SALARY HERE!
NONSENSE! WE'LL WORK OUT SOMETHING FOR YOU!

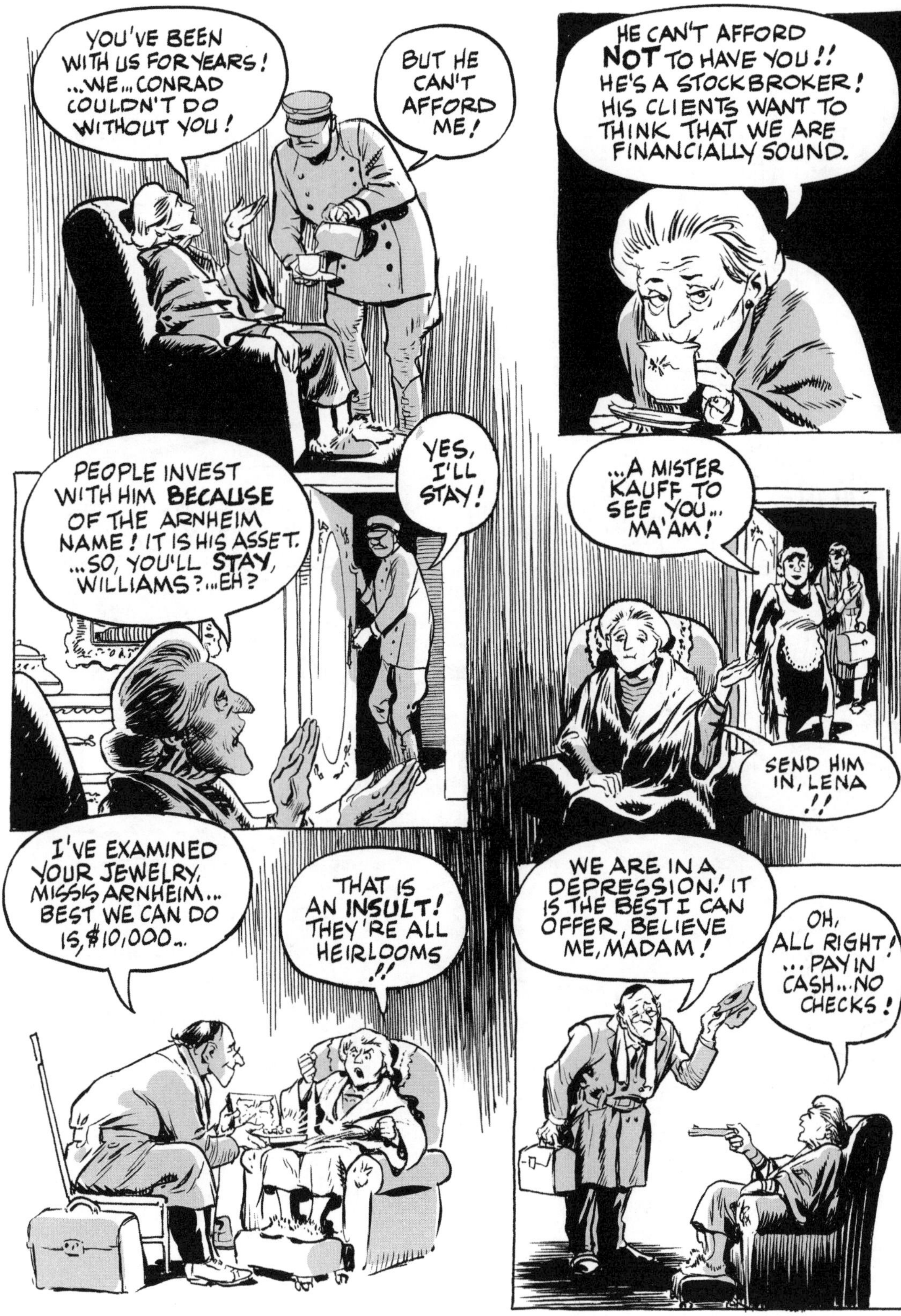
YOU'VE BEEN WITH US FOR YEARS! ...WE... CONRAD COULDN'T DO WITHOUT YOU!
BUT HE CAN'T AFFORD ME!
HE CAN'T AFFORD NOT TO HAVE YOU!! HE'S A STOCKBROKER! HIS CLIENTS WANT TO THINK THAT WE ARE FINANCIALLY SOUND.
PEOPLE INVEST WITH HIM BECAUSE OF THE ARNHEIM NAME! IT IS HIS ASSET. ...SO, YOU'LL STAY, WILLIAMS?...EH?
YES, I'LL STAY!
...A MISTER KAUFF TO SEE YOU... MA'AM!
SEND HIM IN, LENA!!
I'VE EXAMINED YOUR JEWELRY, MISSIS ARNHEIM... BEST WE CAN DO IS, $10,000...
THAT IS AN INSULT! THEY'RE ALL HEIRLOOMS!!
WE ARE IN A DEPRESSION! IT IS THE BEST I CAN OFFER, BELIEVE ME, MADAM!
OH, ALL RIGHT! ...PAY IN CASH...NO CHECKS!

But the frayed outer edges of the family still had to be dealt with . . .

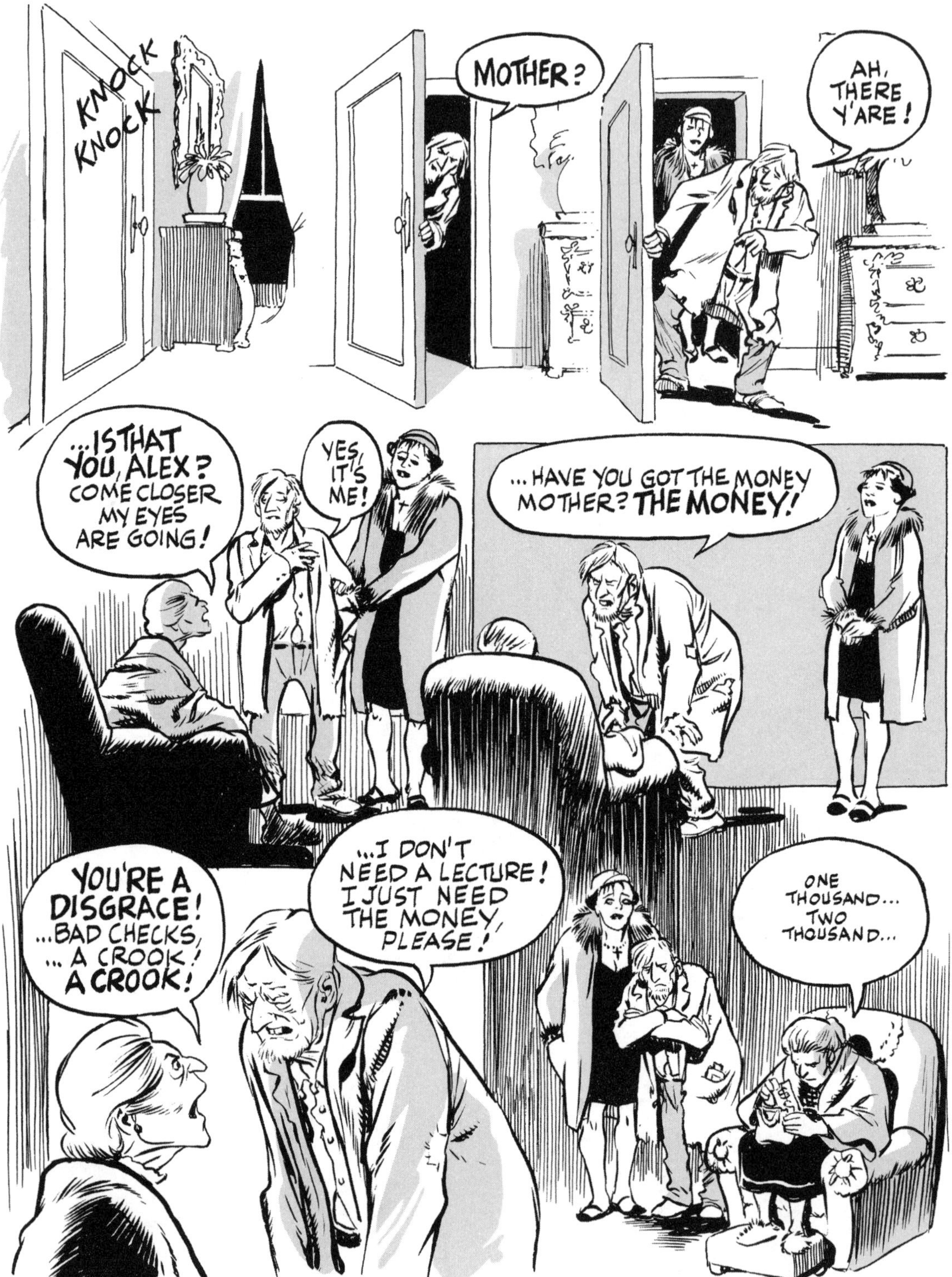
KNOCK KNOCK
MOTHER?
AH, THERE Y'ARE!
...IS THAT YOU, ALEX? COME CLOSER MY EYES ARE GOING!
YES, IT'S ME!
...HAVE YOU GOT THE MONEY MOTHER? THE MONEY!
YOU'RE A DISGRACE! ...BAD CHECKS, ... A CROOK! A CROOK!
...I DON'T NEED A LECTURE! I JUST NEED THE MONEY, PLEASE!
ONE THOUSAND... TWO THOUSAND...

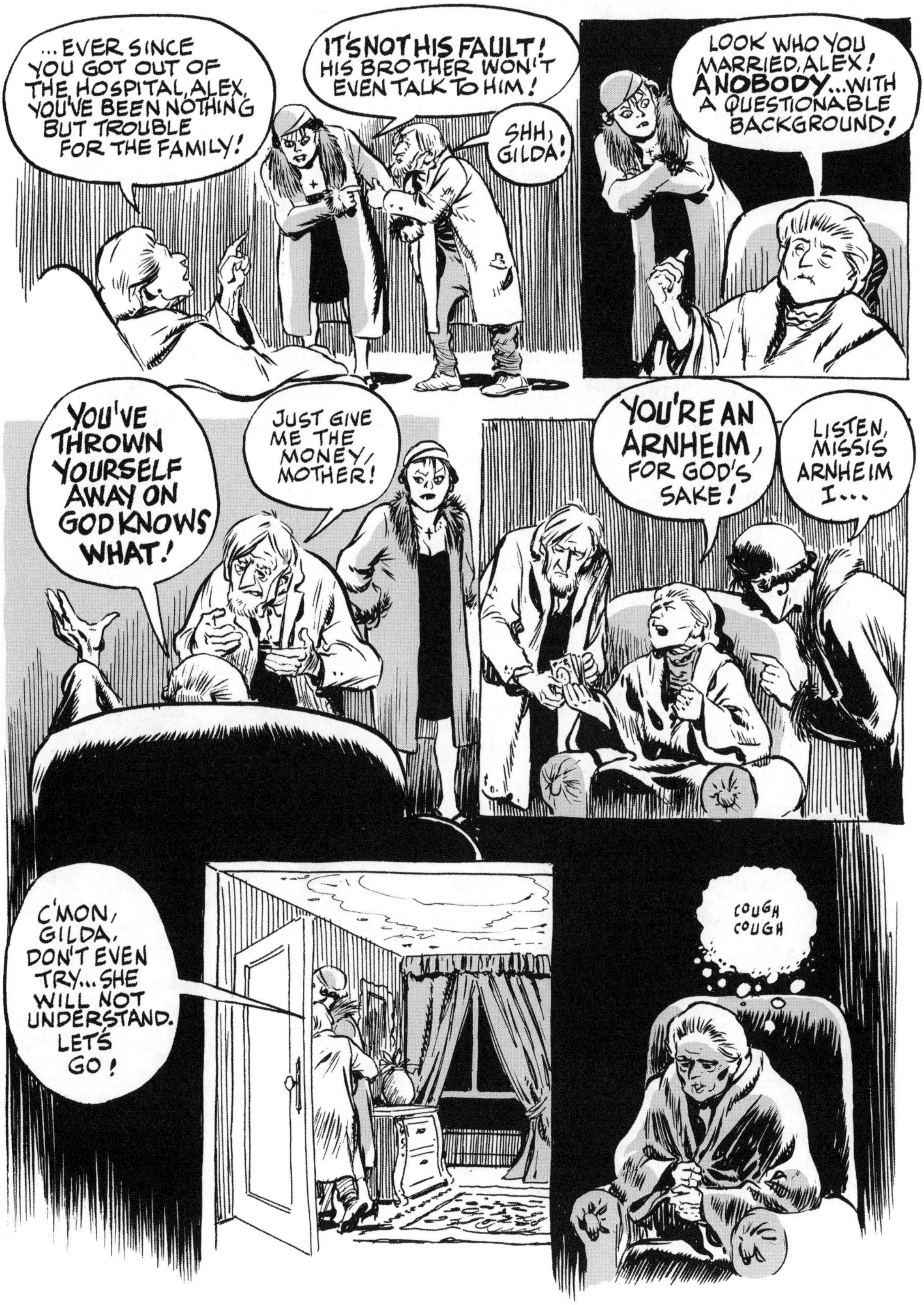
...EVER SINCE YOU GOT OUT OF THE HOSPITAL, ALEX, YOU'VE BEEN NOTHING BUT TROUBLE FOR THE FAMILY!
IT'S NOT HIS FAULT! HIS BROTHER WON'T EVEN TALK TO HIM!
SHH, GILDA!
LOOK WHO YOU MARRIED, ALEX! A NOBODY...WITH A QUESTIONABLE BACKGROUND!
YOU'VE THROWN YOURSELF AWAY ON GOD KNOWS WHAT!
JUST GIVE ME THE MONEY, MOTHER!
YOU'RE AN ARNHEIM, FOR GOD'S SAKE!
LISTEN, MISSIS ARNHEIM I...
C'MON, GILDA, DON'T EVEN TRY...SHE WILL NOT UNDERSTAND. LET'S GO!
COUGH COUGH

Along with the early German Jews who wandered westward, Oskar Krause found his way into a small Nebraska town named Cranston. There he learned how to make clay cooking pots. By the time of the Civil War he had built a small but thriving business making and selling ceramic ware. Soon he set up a factory and became a leading citizen in Cranston. By the time he died in 1890 Krause Ceramics was a large thriving company. Oskar was survived by his young gentile wife and a son, David, who took over when she died five years later.

For a while, Krause Ceramics had a virtual monopoly in the area. But as railroads pushed west providing access to the amply capitalized eastern factories, their competition soon overwhelmed the Krause Company and drove it into insolvency. By then, David was part of the Cranston social set and considered a "good catch." In an effort to shore up his finances, he married the daughter of a substantial Jewish grain broker. She soon died. David then married Edna Wein, a local girl from a modest family. He soon squandered the money left to him by his former wife and died broke in 1914, leaving Edna and their infant daughter with little more than the Krause name. His daughter's name was Eva.

Eva was an exceptionally beautiful child. She was adored by her mother, who showed her off at every opportunity. Edna entered Eva in every fair and beauty contest. Sheltered from the usual teenage contacts by a hovering mother, the girl seemed to have few social relations. There was an occasional flirtation, but aside from an attempted rape by a football player, Eva grew up an untouched beauty.

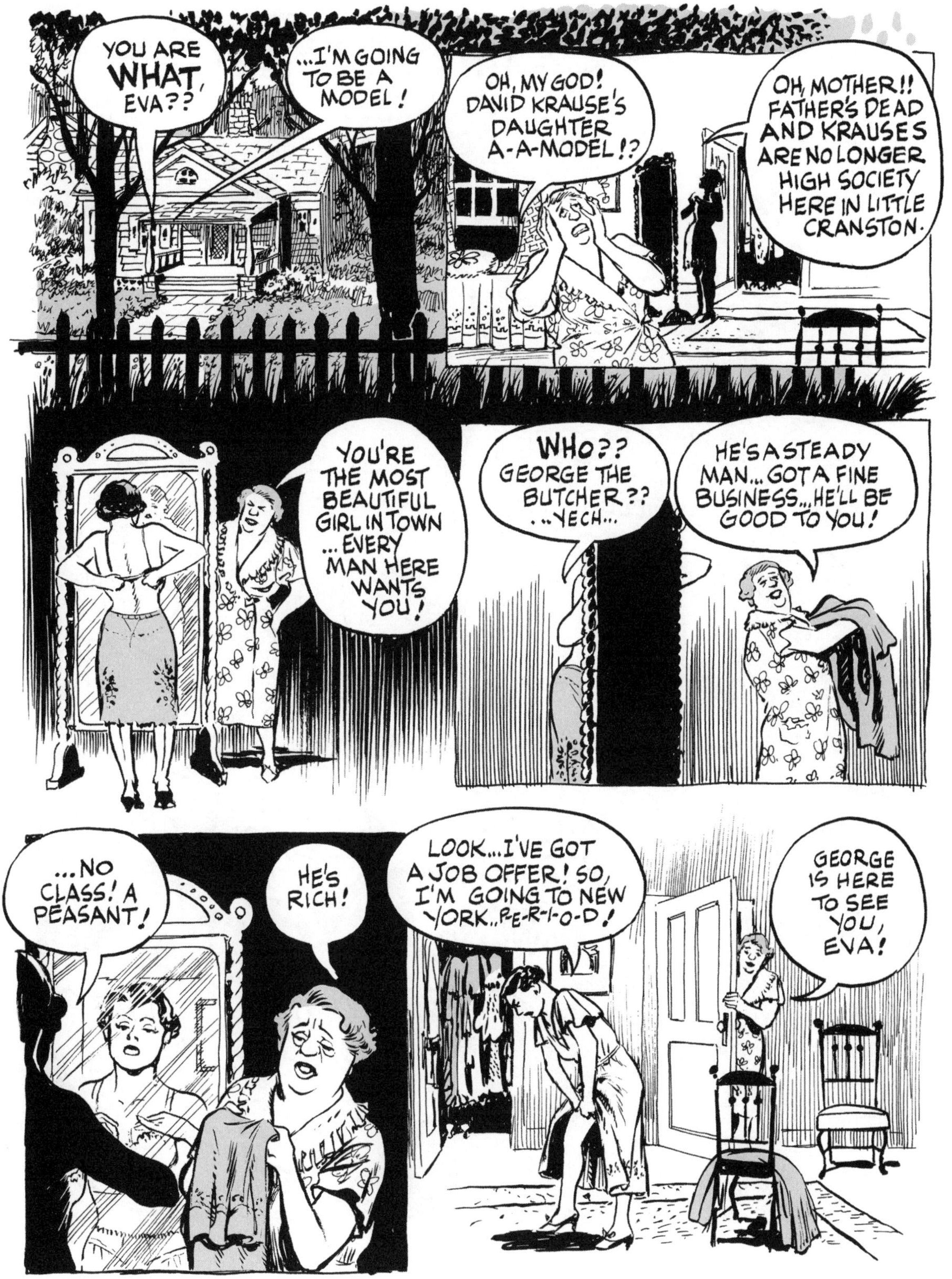
YOU ARE WHAT, EVA??
...I'M GOING TO BE A MODEL!
OH, MY GOD! DAVID KRAUSE'S DAUGHTER A-A-MODEL!?
OH, MOTHER!! FATHER'S DEAD AND KRAUSES ARE NO LONGER HIGH SOCIETY HERE IN LITTLE CRANSTON.
YOU'RE THE MOST BEAUTIFUL GIRL IN TOWN ... EVERY MAN HERE WANTS YOU!
WHO?? GEORGE THE BUTCHER?? ...YECH...
HE'S A STEADY MAN... GOT A FINE BUSINESS... HE'LL BE GOOD TO YOU!
...NO CLASS! A PEASANT!
HE'S RICH!
LOOK... I'VE GOT A JOB OFFER! SO, I'M GOING TO NEW YORK.. P-E-R-I-O-D!
GEORGE IS HERE TO SEE YOU, EVA!

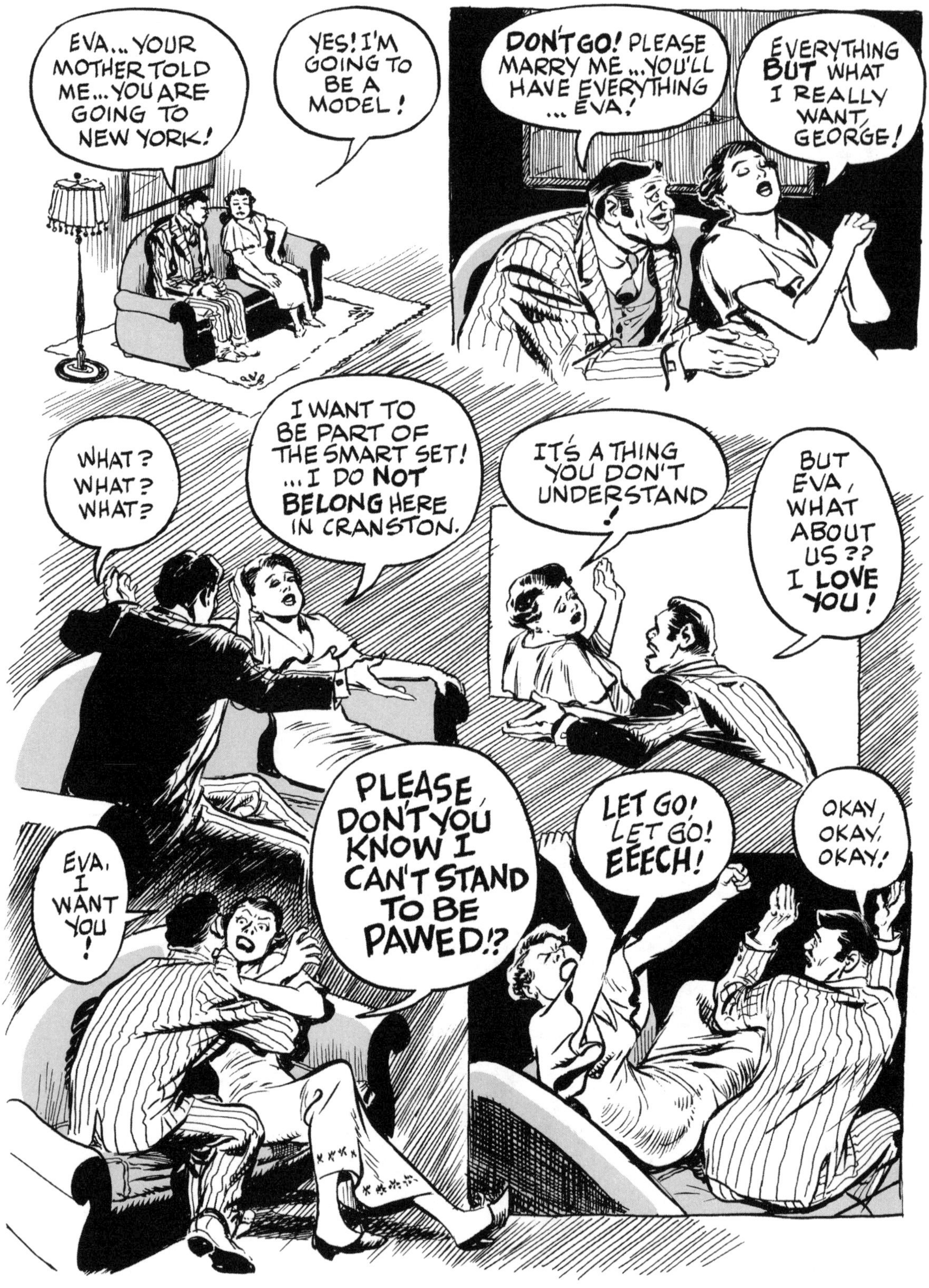
EVA... YOUR MOTHER TOLD ME... YOU ARE GOING TO NEW YORK!
YES! I'M GOING TO BE A MODEL!
DON'T GO! PLEASE MARRY ME... YOU'LL HAVE EVERYTHING ... EVA!
EVERYTHING BUT WHAT I REALLY WANT, GEORGE!
WHAT? WHAT? WHAT?
I WANT TO BE PART OF THE SMART SET! ...I DO NOT BELONG HERE IN CRANSTON.
IT'S A THING YOU DON'T UNDERSTAND!
BUT EVA, WHAT ABOUT US?? I LOVE YOU!
EVA, I WANT YOU!
PLEASE, DON'T YOU KNOW I CAN'T STAND TO BE PAWED!?
LET GO! LET GO! EEECH!
OKAY, OKAY, OKAY!

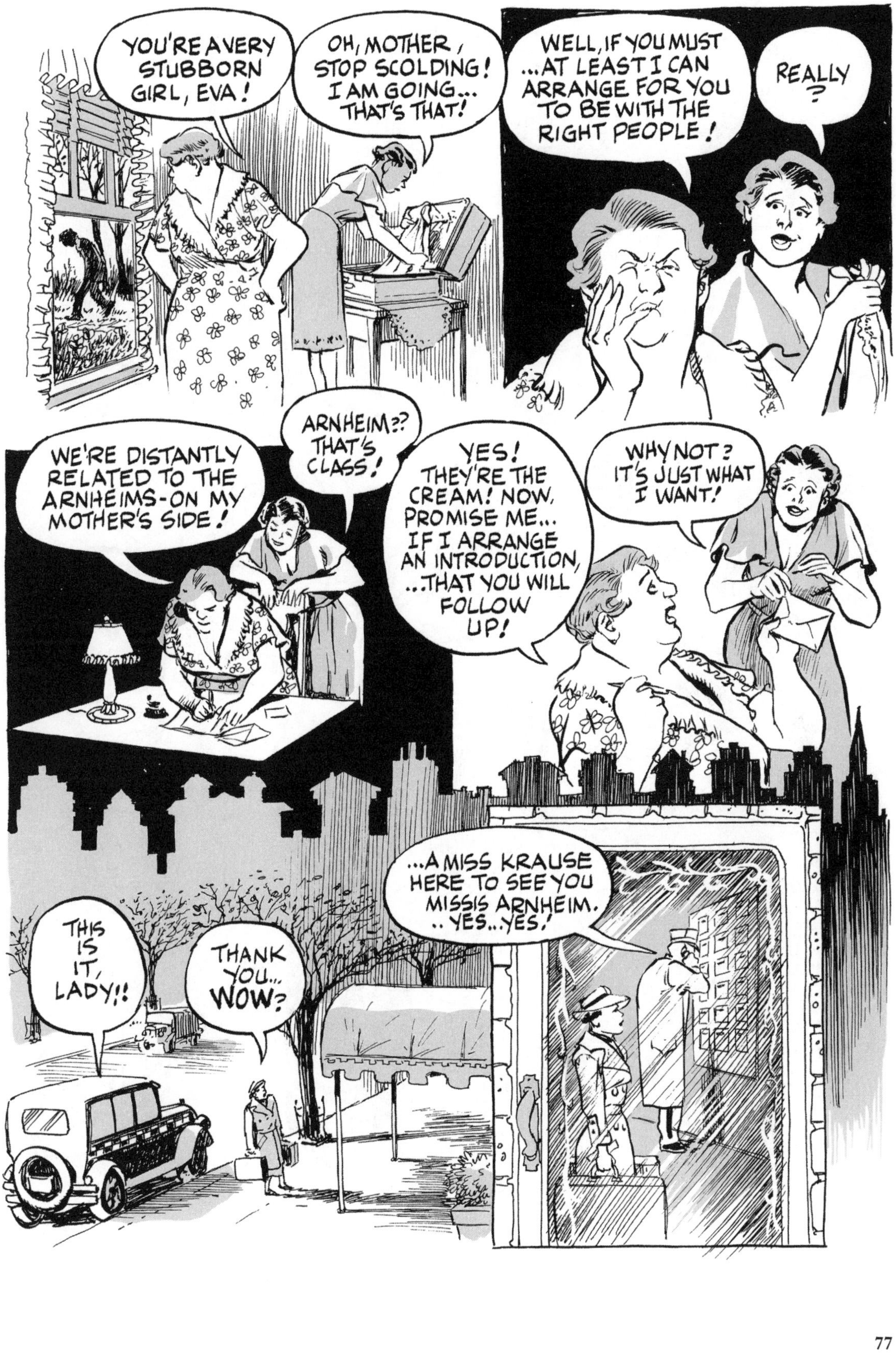
YOU'RE A VERY STUBBORN GIRL, EVA!
OH, MOTHER, STOP SCOLDING! I AM GOING... THAT'S THAT!
WELL, IF YOU MUST ...AT LEAST I CAN ARRANGE FOR YOU TO BE WITH THE RIGHT PEOPLE!
REALLY?
WE'RE DISTANTLY RELATED TO THE ARNHEIMS-ON MY MOTHER'S SIDE!
ARNHEIM?? THAT'S CLASS!
YES! THEY'RE THE CREAM! NOW, PROMISE ME... IF I ARRANGE AN INTRODUCTION, ...THAT YOU WILL FOLLOW UP!
WHY NOT? IT'S JUST WHAT I WANT!
THIS IS IT, LADY!!
THANK YOU... WOW?
...A MISS KRAUSE HERE TO SEE YOU MISSIS ARNHEIM. .. YES...YES!

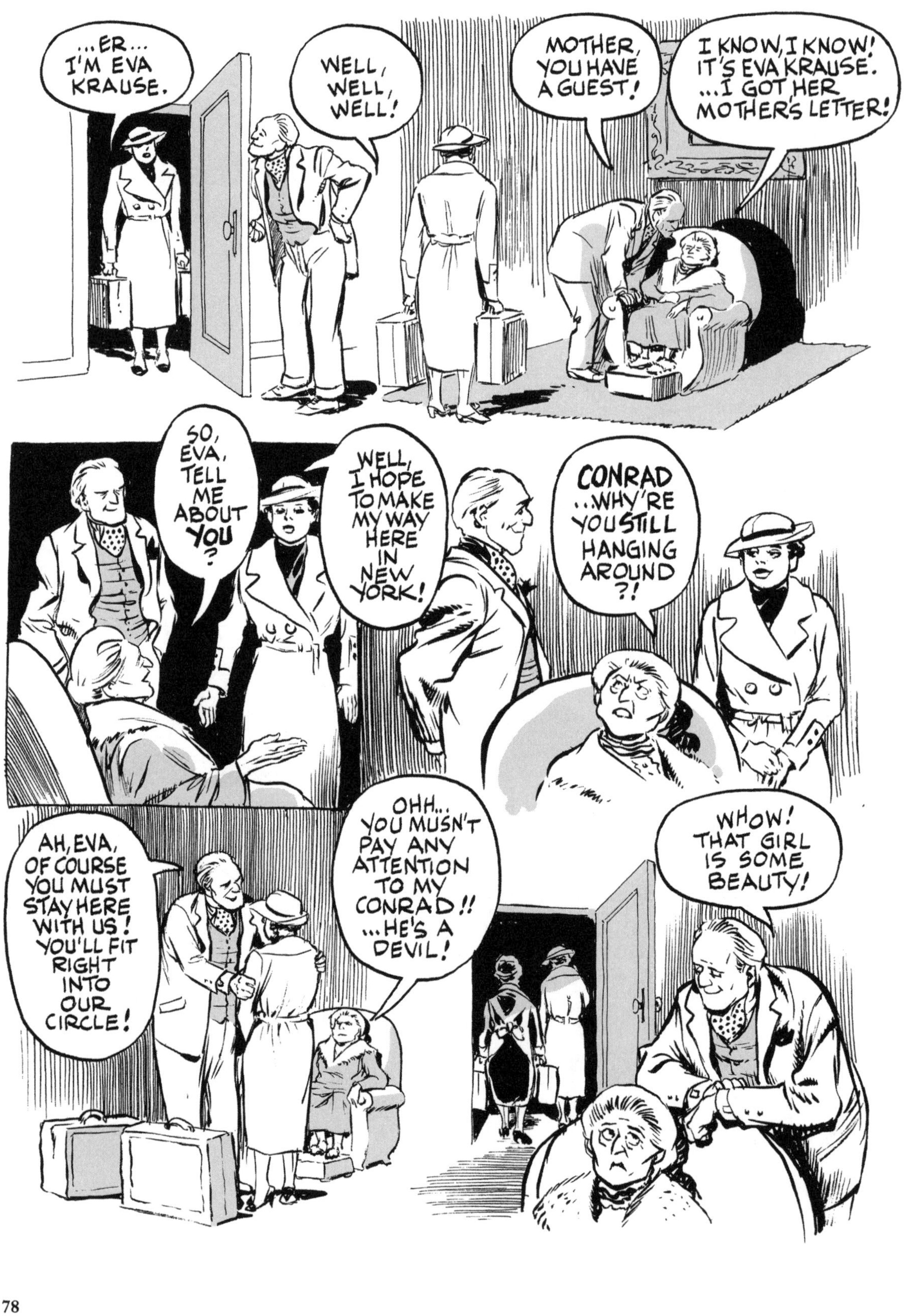
...ER... I'M EVA KRAUSE.
WELL, WELL, WELL!
MOTHER, YOU HAVE A GUEST!
I KNOW, I KNOW! IT'S EVA KRAUSE. ...I GOT HER MOTHER'S LETTER!
SO, EVA, TELL ME ABOUT YOU?
WELL, I HOPE TO MAKE MY WAY HERE IN NEW YORK!
CONRAD ...WHY'RE YOU STILL HANGING AROUND?!
AH, EVA, OF COURSE YOU MUST STAY HERE WITH US! YOU'LL FIT RIGHT INTO OUR CIRCLE!
OHH... YOU MUSN'T PAY ANY ATTENTION TO MY CONRAD!! ...HE'S A DEVIL!
WHOW! THAT GIRL IS SOME BEAUTY!

Back in Cranston, the news from New York set the town's society abuzz. Edna Wein Krause's daughter was moving in the Arnheim crowd, and the rumors of her glittering social life were supported by her letters. Edna Wein Krause had reason to be proud. It was a social triumph.

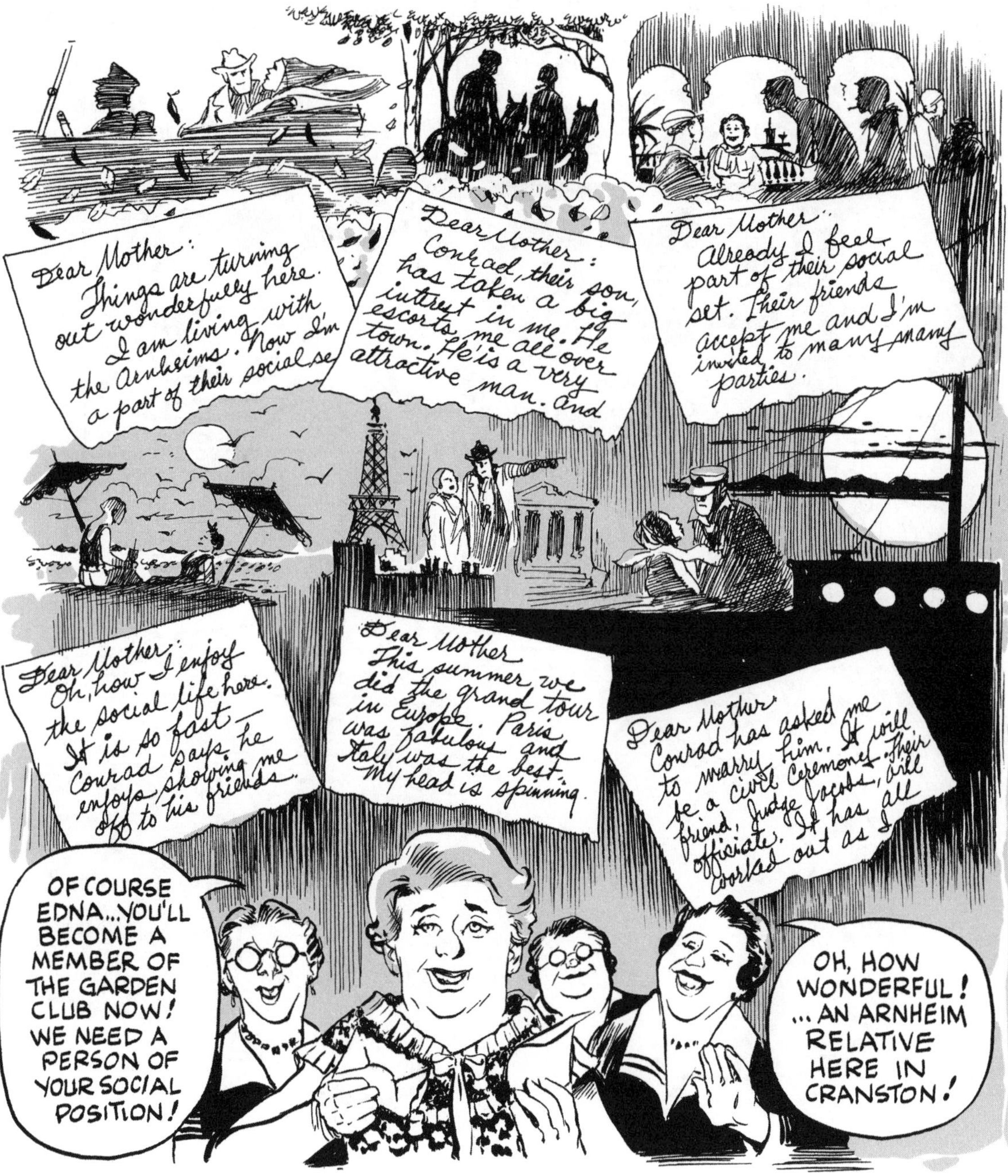

Dear Mother: Things are turning out wonderfully here. I am living with the Arnheims. Now I'm a part of their social se
Dear Mother: Conrad, their son, has taken a big interest in me. He escorts me all over town. He is a very attractive man. And
Dear Mother: Already I feel part of their social set. Their friends accept me and I'm invited to many many parties.
Dear Mother: Oh, how I enjoy the social life here. It is so fast— Conrad says he enjoys showing me off to his friends.
Dear Mother This summer we did the grand tour in Europe. Paris was fabulous and Italy was the best. My head is spinning.
Dear Mother: Conrad has asked me to marry him. It will be a civil ceremony. Their friend, Judge Jacobs, will officiate. It has all worked out as I
OF COURSE EDNA...YOU'LL BECOME A MEMBER OF THE GARDEN CLUB NOW! WE NEED A PERSON OF YOUR SOCIAL POSITION!
OH, HOW WONDERFUL! ...AN ARNHEIM RELATIVE HERE IN CRANSTON!

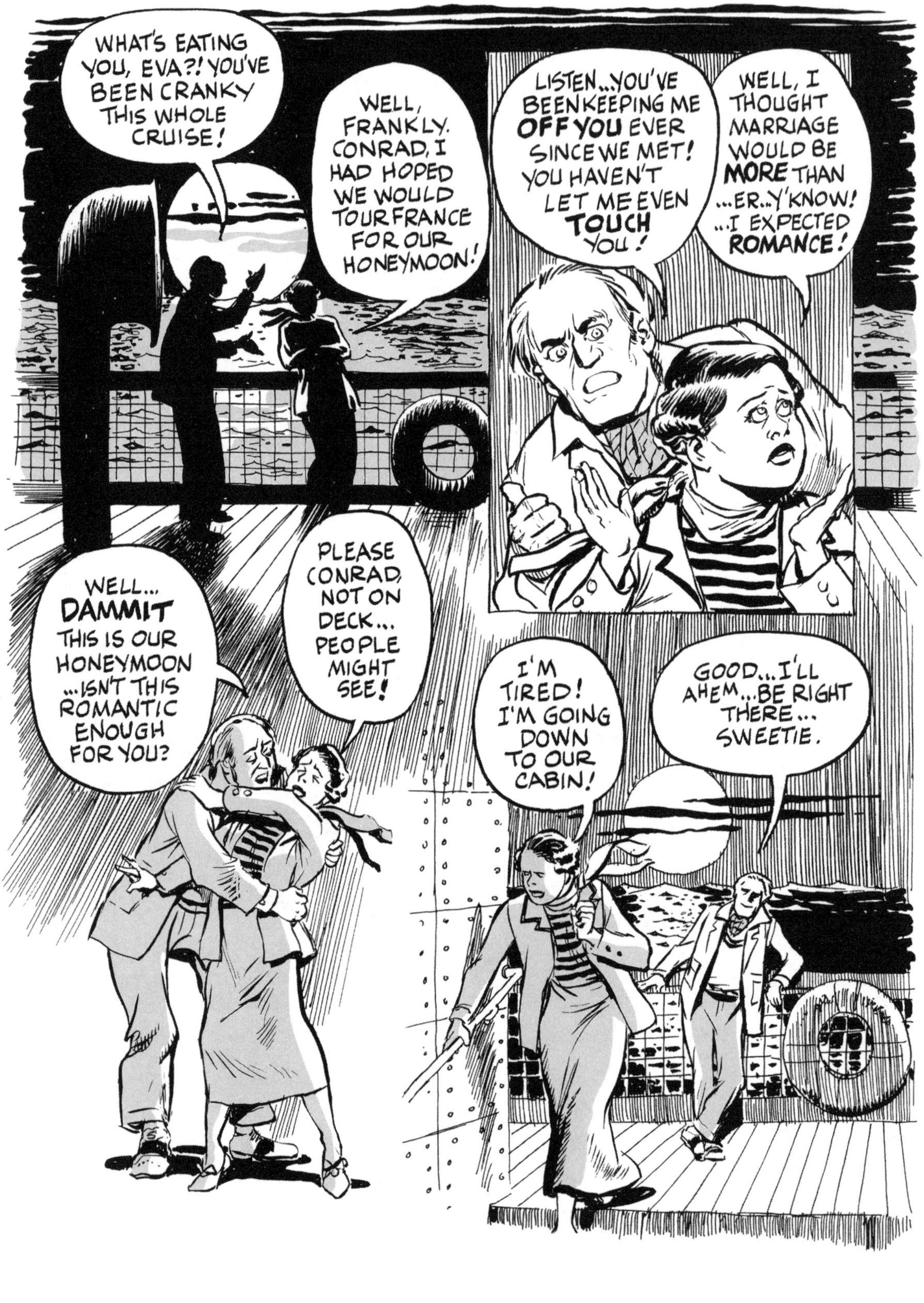
WHAT'S EATING YOU, EVA?! YOU'VE BEEN CRANKY THIS WHOLE CRUISE!
WELL, FRANKLY. CONRAD, I HAD HOPED WE WOULD TOUR FRANCE FOR OUR HONEYMOON!
LISTEN...YOU'VE BEEN KEEPING ME OFF YOU EVER SINCE WE MET! YOU HAVEN'T LET ME EVEN TOUCH YOU!
WELL, I THOUGHT MARRIAGE WOULD BE MORE THAN ...ER..Y'KNOW! ...I EXPECTED ROMANCE!
WELL... DAMMIT THIS IS OUR HONEYMOON ...ISN'T THIS ROMANTIC ENOUGH FOR YOU?
PLEASE CONRAD, NOT ON DECK... PEOPLE MIGHT SEE!
I'M TIRED! I'M GOING DOWN TO OUR CABIN!
GOOD...I'LL AHEM...BE RIGHT THERE... SWEETIE.

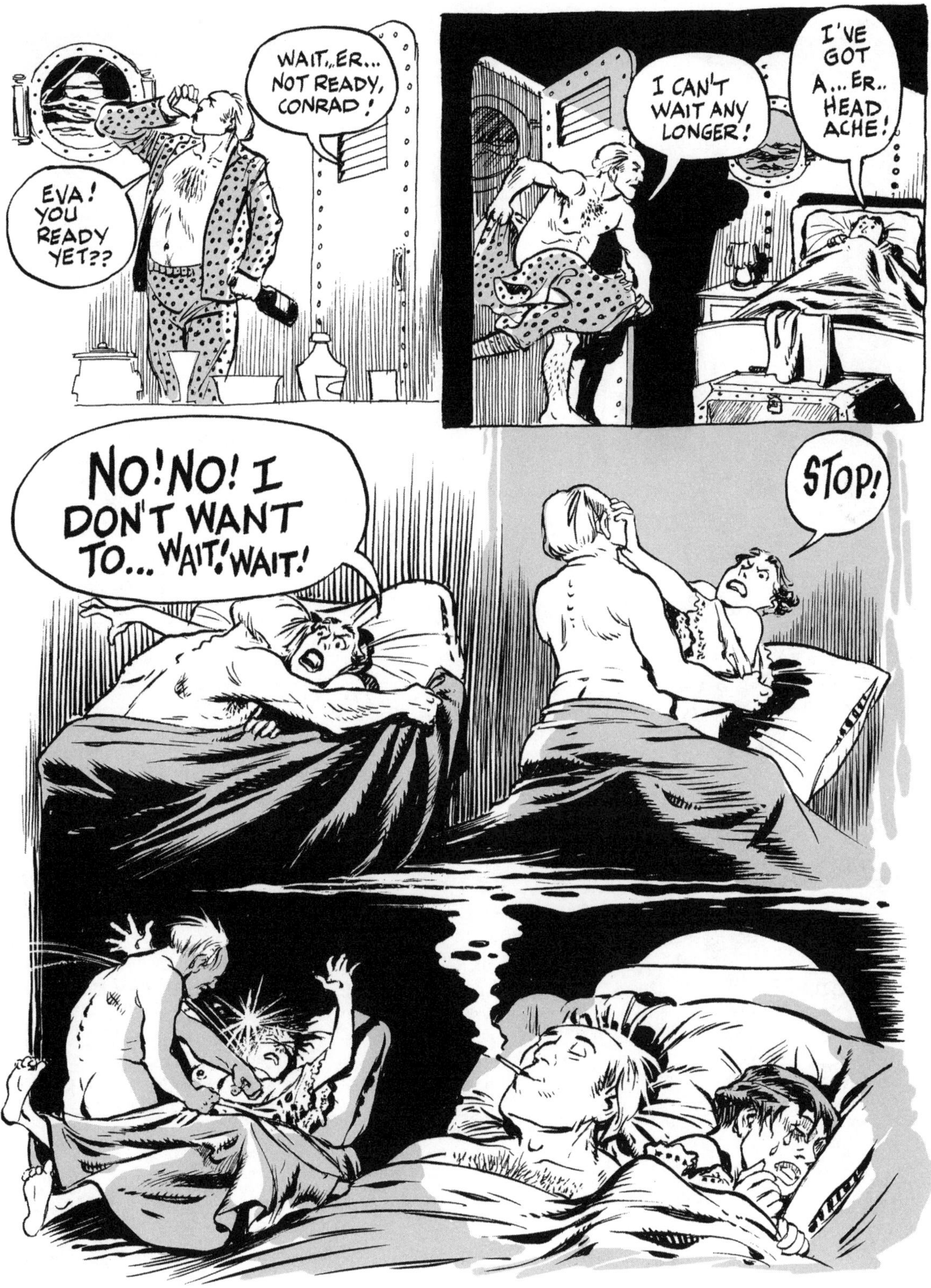
EVA! YOU READY YET??
WAIT,..ER... NOT READY, CONRAD!
I CAN'T WAIT ANY LONGER!
I'VE GOT A... ER.. HEAD ACHE!
NO! NO! I DON'T WANT TO... WAIT! WAIT!
STOP!

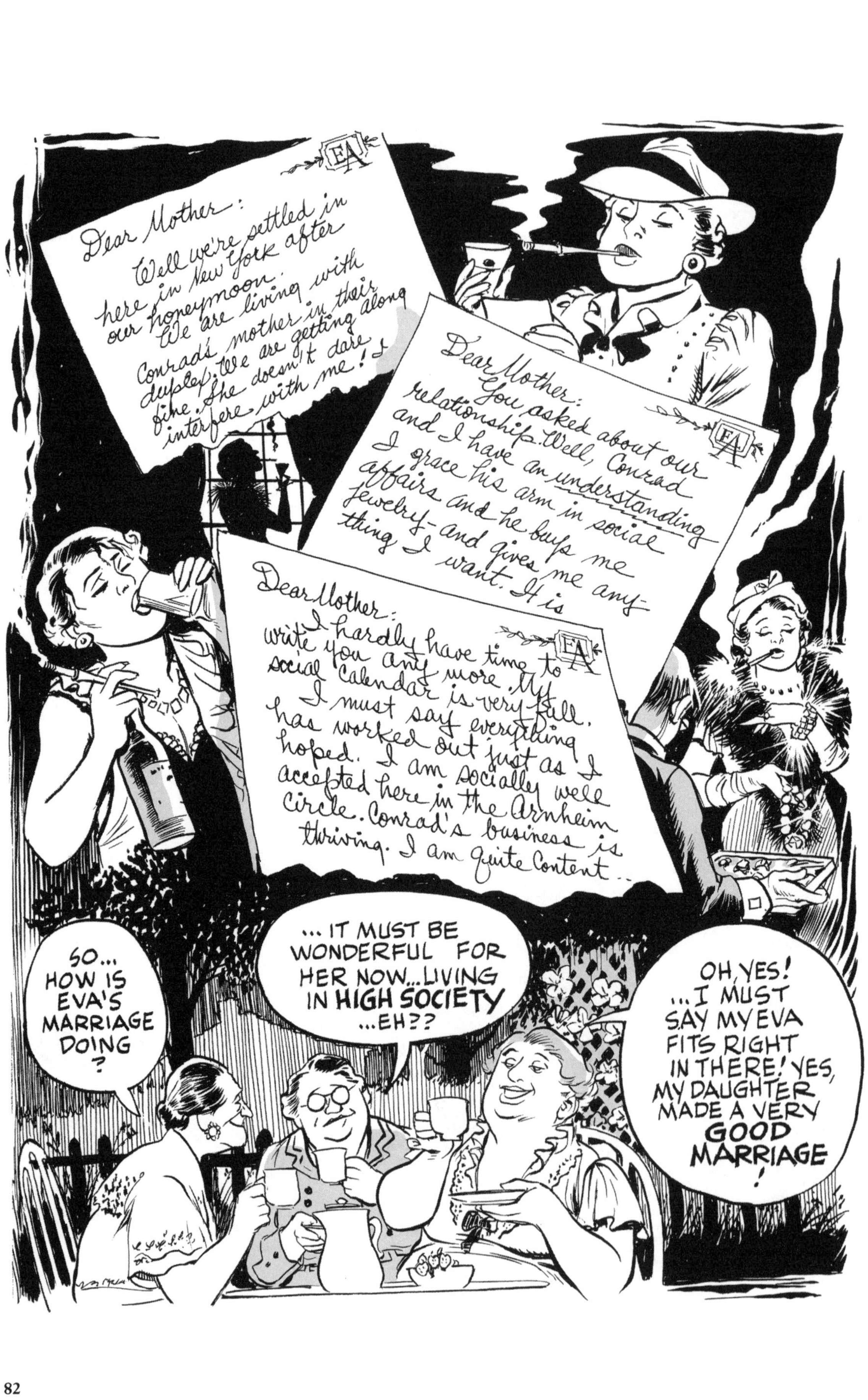
Dear Mother: Well we're settled in here in New York after our honeymoon. We are living with Conrad's mother in their duplex. We are getting along fine. She doesn't dare interfere with me! I
Dear Mother: You asked about our relationship. Well, Conrad and I have an understanding. I grace his arm in social affairs and he buys me jewelry—and gives me anything I want. It is
Dear Mother: I hardly have time to write you any more. My social calendar is very full. I must say everything has worked out just as I hoped. I am socially well accepted here in the Arnheim circle. Conrad's business is thriving. I am quite content...
SO... HOW IS EVA'S MARRIAGE DOING ?
... IT MUST BE WONDERFUL FOR HER NOW... LIVING IN HIGH SOCIETY ...EH??
OH, YES! ...I MUST SAY MY EVA FITS RIGHT IN THERE! YES, MY DAUGHTER MADE A VERY GOOD MARRIAGE !

All her life Alva Straus Arnheim never had a moment of doubt about the way things were and the way they ought to be in their society. Her marriage to Isidore was exactly as she was taught to expect. There was plenty of money, and her husband's success provided status and stability. The uncertain feeling of being Jewish in a Christian world had dissipated after years of living so securely in America. There was no question about this in the minds of anyone in the social enclave that the Arnheims dominated. Her energy and instinct for control enabled her to maintain a certain leadership during the long years of her widowhood. The family had become a kind of royality whose position needed constant vigilance and protection.

Strength of character or manipulation were the ways to deal with unsettling events or to monitor the wayward.

But the aging matriarch finally succumbed to the effects of the stroke she had suffered years before.

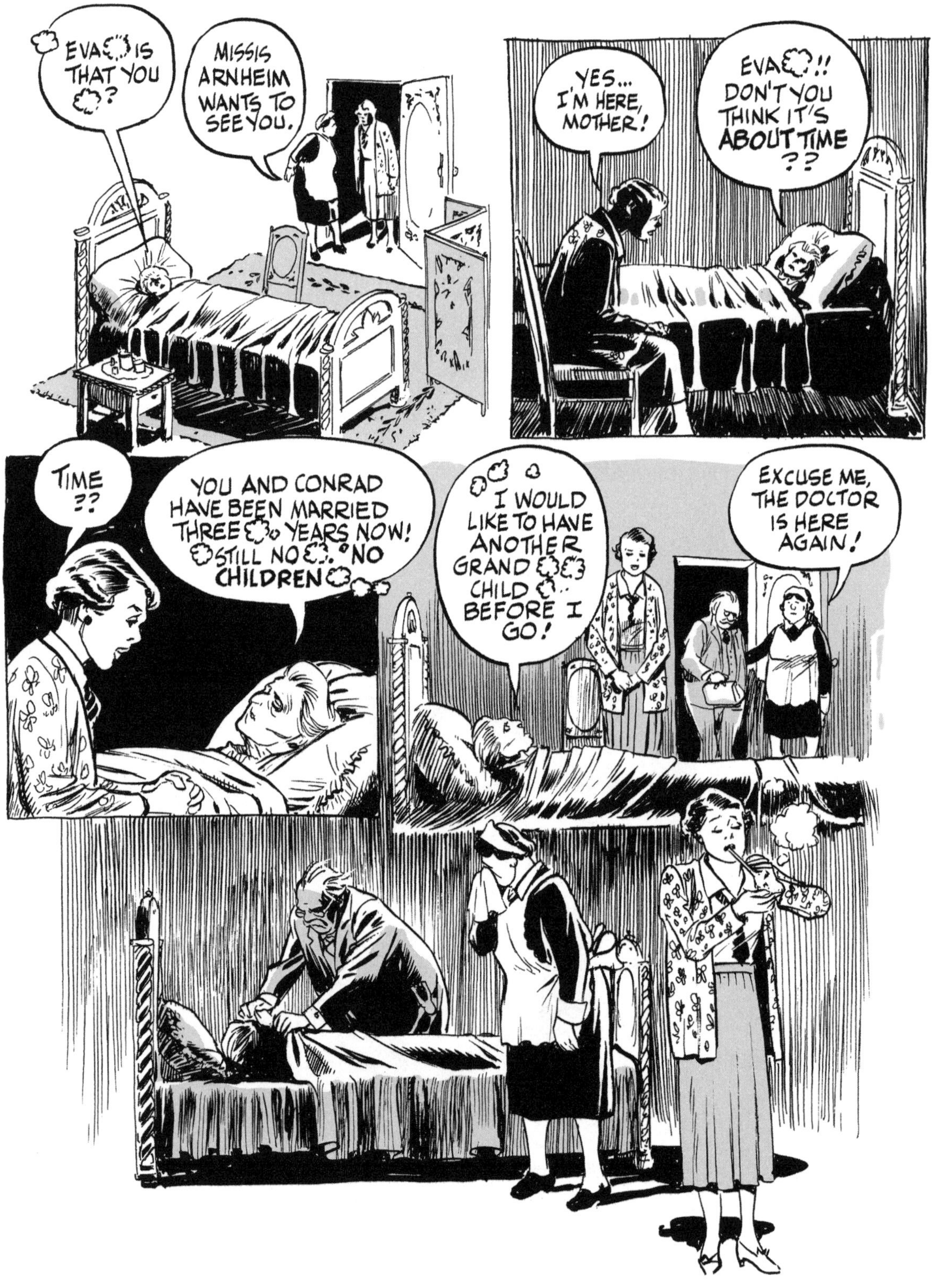
EVA IS THAT YOU ?
MISSIS ARNHEIM WANTS TO SEE YOU.
YES... I'M HERE, MOTHER!
EVA !! DON'T YOU THINK IT'S ABOUT TIME ??
TIME ??
YOU AND CONRAD HAVE BEEN MARRIED THREE YEARS NOW! STILL NO . NO CHILDREN
I WOULD LIKE TO HAVE ANOTHER GRAND CHILD BEFORE I GO!
EXCUSE ME, THE DOCTOR IS HERE AGAIN!

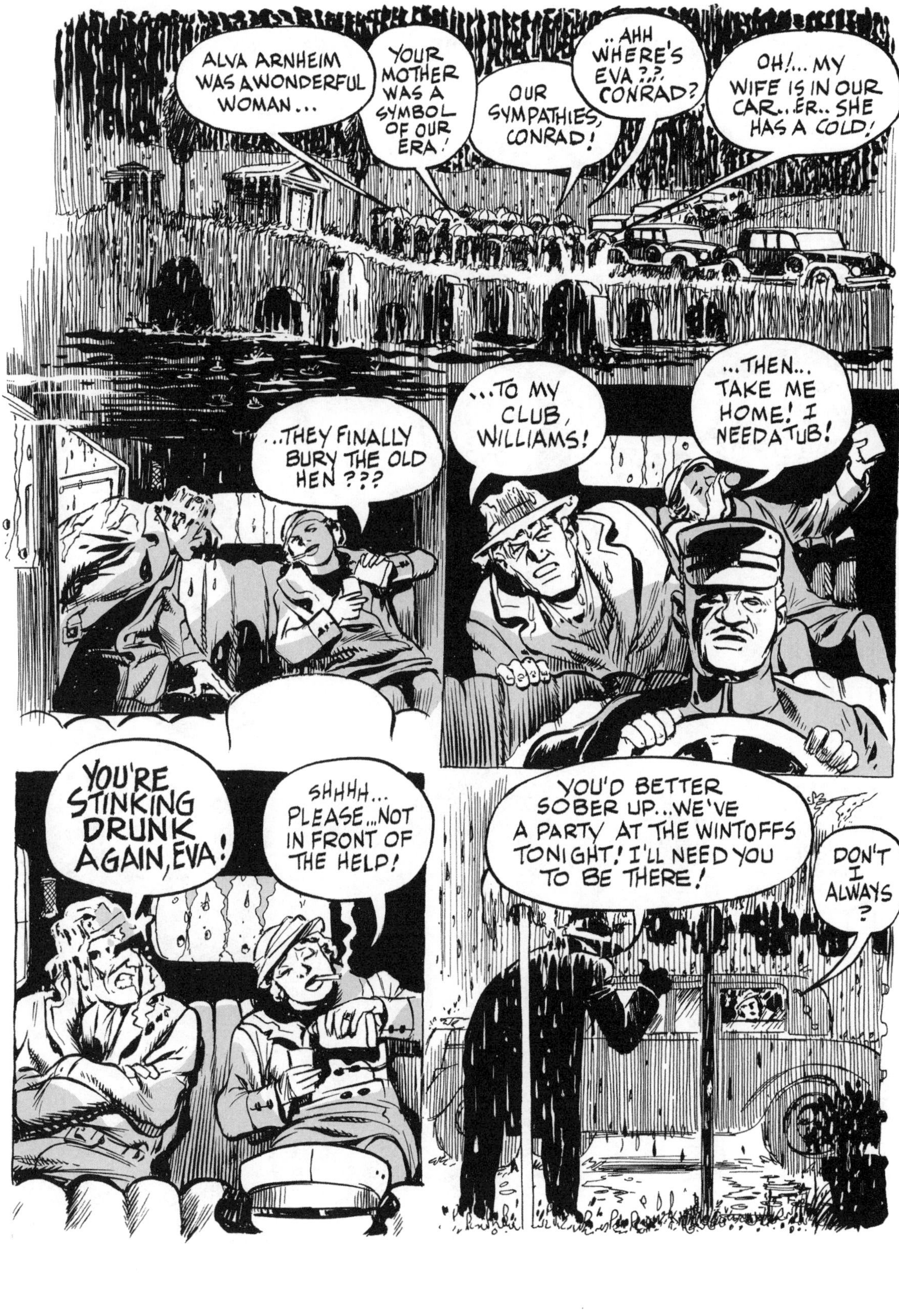
ALVA ARNHEIM WAS A WONDERFUL WOMAN...
YOUR MOTHER WAS A SYMBOL OF OUR ERA!
OUR SYMPATHIES, CONRAD!
..AHH WHERE'S EVA ??. CONRAD?
OH!... MY WIFE IS IN OUR CAR..ER.. SHE HAS A COLD!
...THEY FINALLY BURY THE OLD HEN ???
...TO MY CLUB, WILLIAMS!
...THEN... TAKE ME HOME! I NEEDA TUB!
YOU'RE STINKING DRUNK AGAIN, EVA!
SHHHH... PLEASE...NOT IN FRONT OF THE HELP!
YOU'D BETTER SOBER UP...WE'VE A PARTY AT THE WINTOFFS TONIGHT! I'LL NEED YOU TO BE THERE!
DON'T I ALWAYS ?

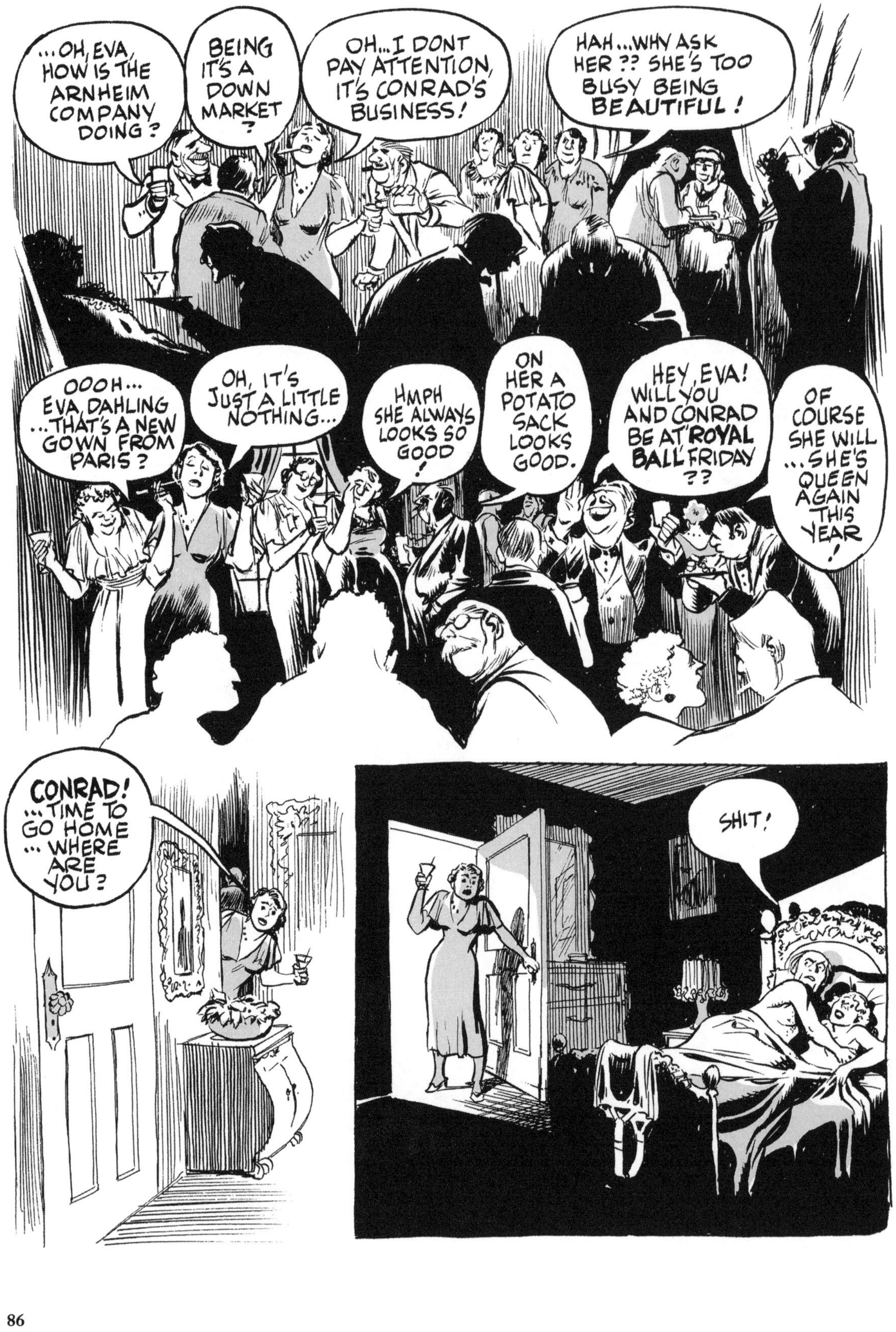
...OH, EVA, HOW IS THE ARNHEIM COMPANY DOING?
BEING IT'S A DOWN MARKET ?
OH...I DONT PAY ATTENTION, IT'S CONRAD'S BUSINESS!
HAH...WHY ASK HER?? SHE'S TOO BUSY BEING BEAUTIFUL!
OOOH... EVA DAHLING ...THAT'S A NEW GOWN FROM PARIS?
OH, IT'S JUST A LITTLE NOTHING...
HMPH SHE ALWAYS LOOKS SO GOOD!
ON HER A POTATO SACK LOOKS GOOD.
HEY, EVA! WILL YOU AND CONRAD BE AT 'ROYAL BALL' FRIDAY??
OF COURSE SHE WILL ...SHE'S QUEEN AGAIN THIS YEAR!
CONRAD! ...TIME TO GO HOME ...WHERE ARE YOU?
SHIT!

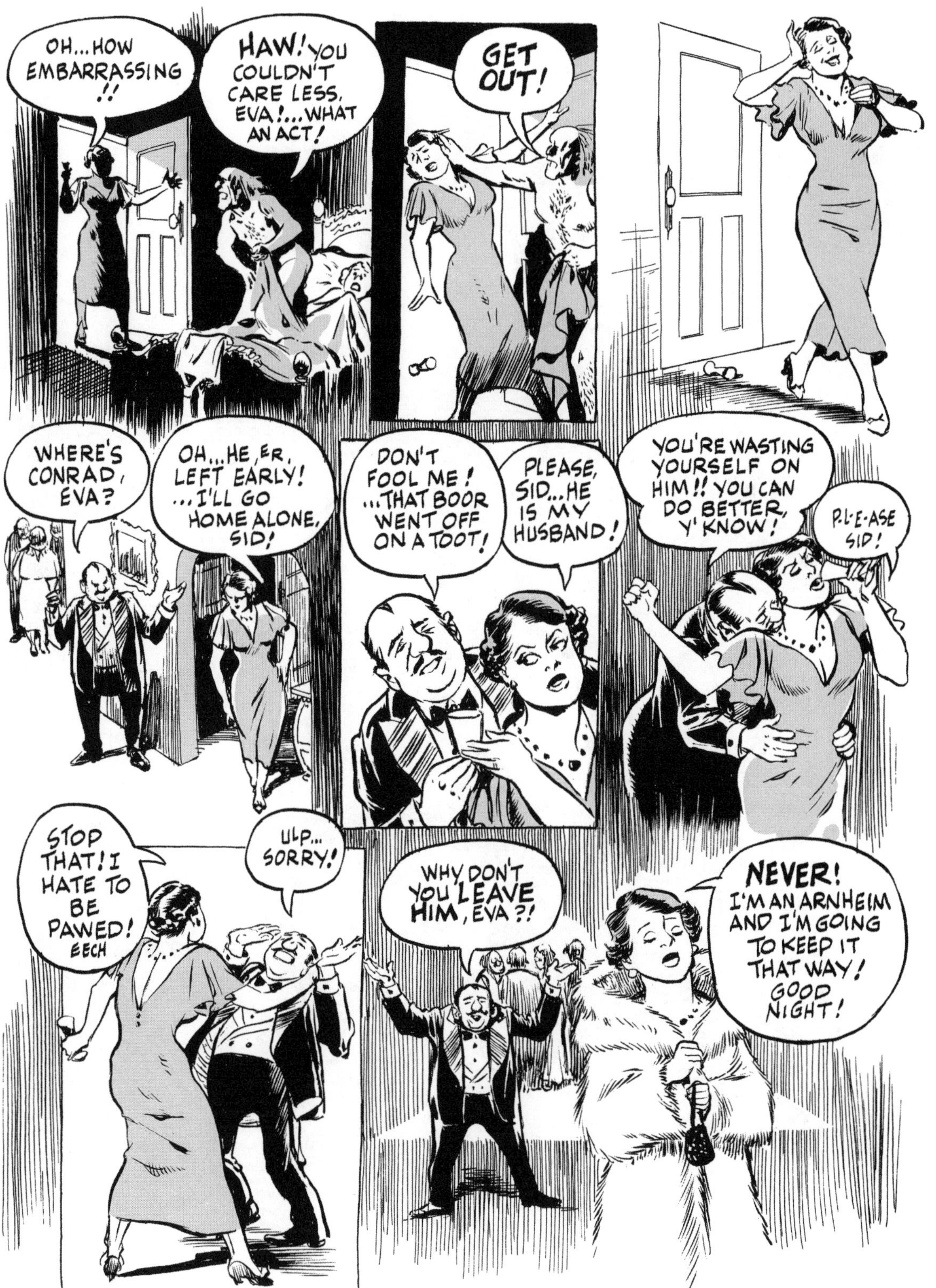
OH...HOW EMBARRASSING !!
HAW! YOU COULDN'T CARE LESS, EVA!...WHAT AN ACT!
GET OUT!
WHERE'S CONRAD, EVA?
OH...HE, ER, LEFT EARLY! ...I'LL GO HOME ALONE, SID!
DON'T FOOL ME! ...THAT BOOR WENT OFF ON A TOOT!
PLEASE, SID...HE IS MY HUSBAND!
YOU'RE WASTING YOURSELF ON HIM!! YOU CAN DO BETTER, Y'KNOW!
P-L-E-ASE SID!
STOP THAT! I HATE TO BE PAWED! EECH
ULP... SORRY!
WHY DON'T YOU LEAVE HIM, EVA?!
NEVER! I'M AN ARNHEIM AND I'M GOING TO KEEP IT THAT WAY! GOOD NIGHT!

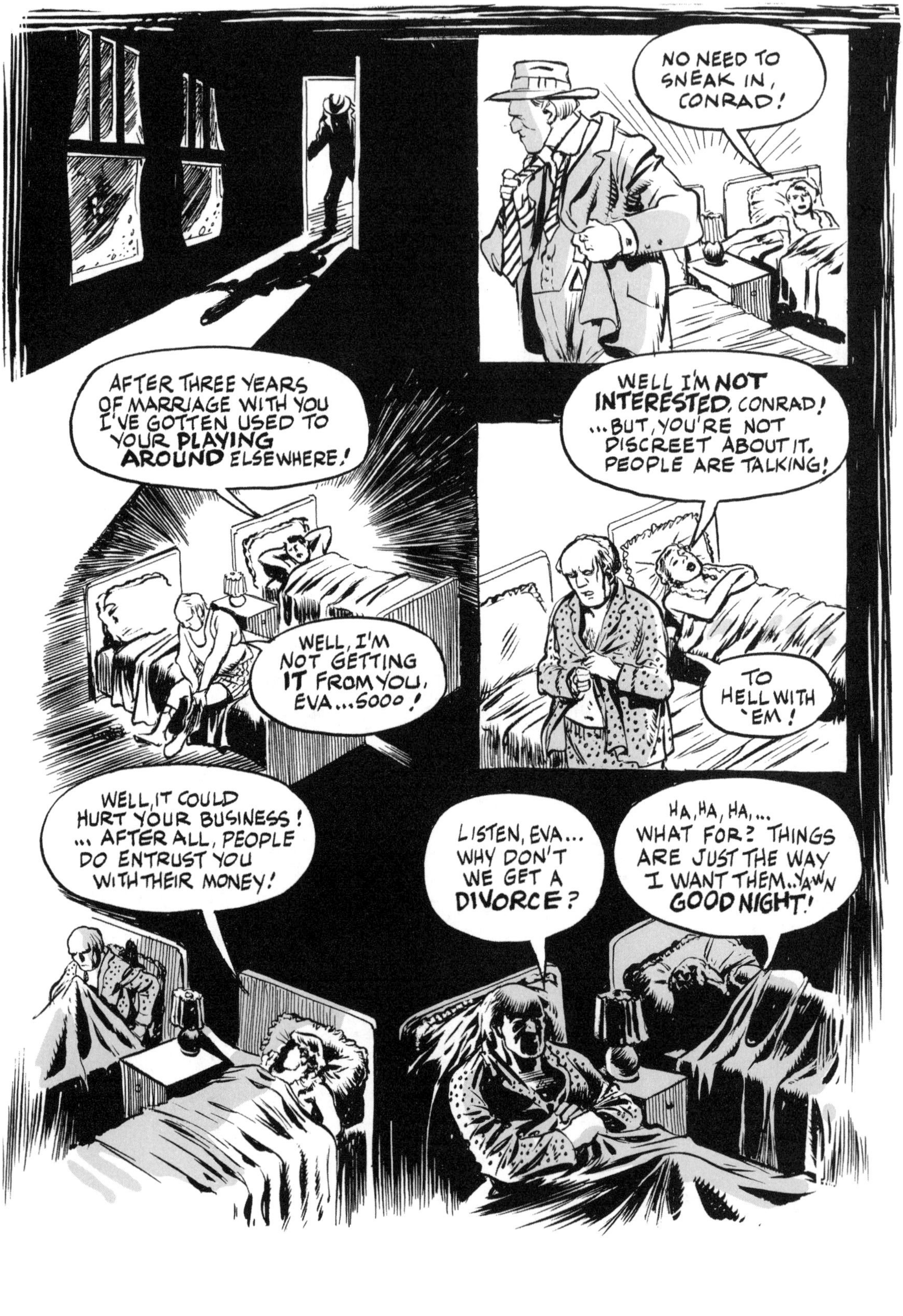
NO NEED TO SNEAK IN, CONRAD!
AFTER THREE YEARS OF MARRIAGE WITH YOU I'VE GOTTEN USED TO YOUR **PLAYING AROUND** ELSEWHERE!
WELL, I'M NOT GETTING **IT** FROM YOU, EVA...SOOO!
WELL I'M **NOT INTERESTED**, CONRAD! ...BUT, YOU'RE NOT DISCREET ABOUT IT. PEOPLE ARE TALKING!
TO HELL WITH 'EM!
WELL, IT COULD HURT YOUR BUSINESS! ... AFTER ALL, PEOPLE DO ENTRUST YOU WITH THEIR MONEY!
LISTEN, EVA... WHY DON'T WE GET A **DIVORCE**?
HA, HA, HA, ... WHAT FOR? THINGS ARE JUST THE WAY I WANT THEM..YAWN **GOOD NIGHT**!

While Conrad's business was doing well, something was nagging him . . . family! Strangely, with the death of his mother, a sense of family preservation began to occupy his mind.

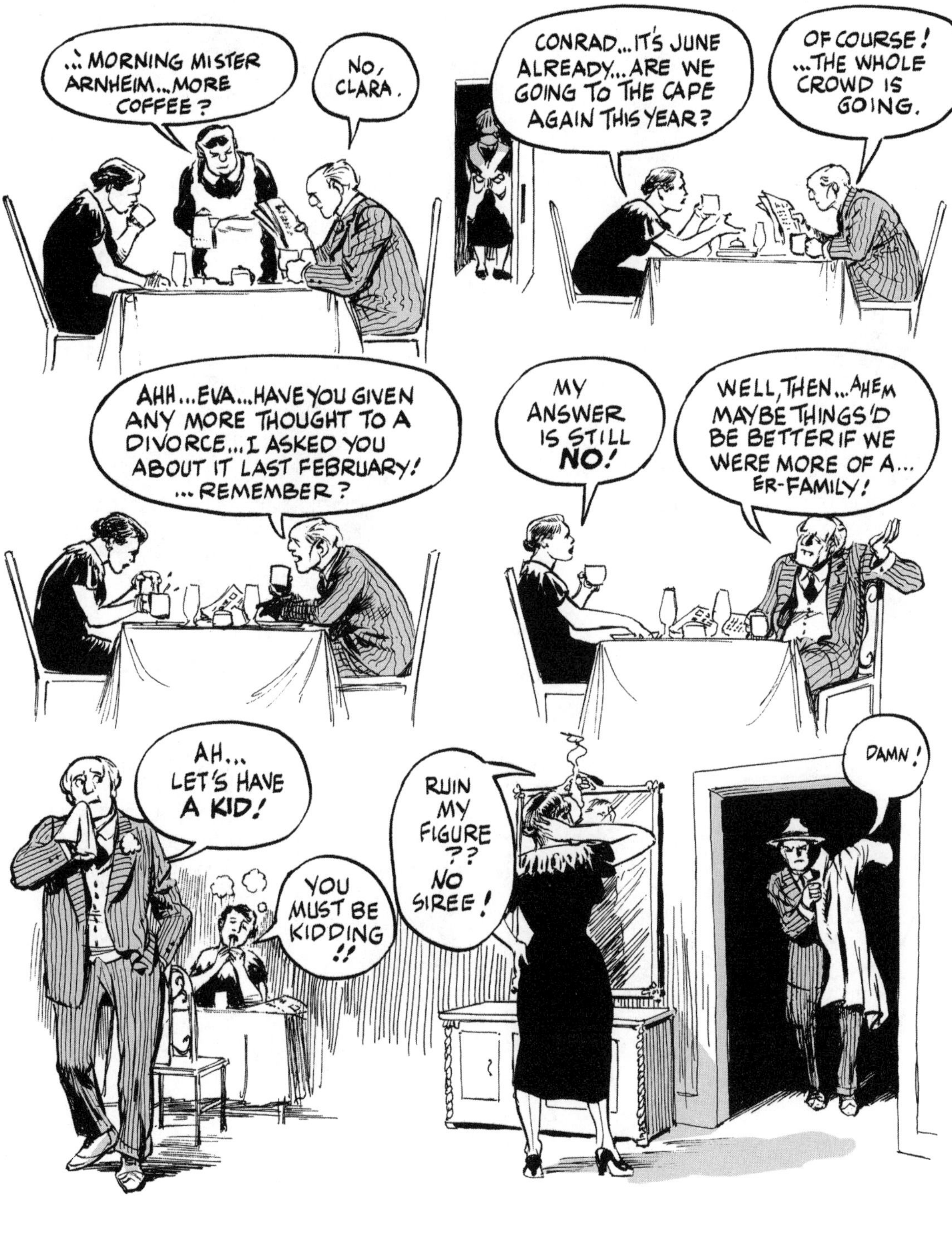
... MORNING MISTER ARNHEIM... MORE COFFEE?
NO, CLARA.
CONRAD... IT'S JUNE ALREADY... ARE WE GOING TO THE CAPE AGAIN THIS YEAR?
OF COURSE! ...THE WHOLE CROWD IS GOING.
AHH... EVA... HAVE YOU GIVEN ANY MORE THOUGHT TO A DIVORCE... I ASKED YOU ABOUT IT LAST FEBRUARY! ... REMEMBER?
MY ANSWER IS STILL NO!
WELL, THEN... AHEM MAYBE THINGS'D BE BETTER IF WE WERE MORE OF A... ER-FAMILY!
AH... LET'S HAVE A KID!
YOU MUST BE KIDDING!!
RUIN MY FIGURE?? NO SIREE!
DAMN!

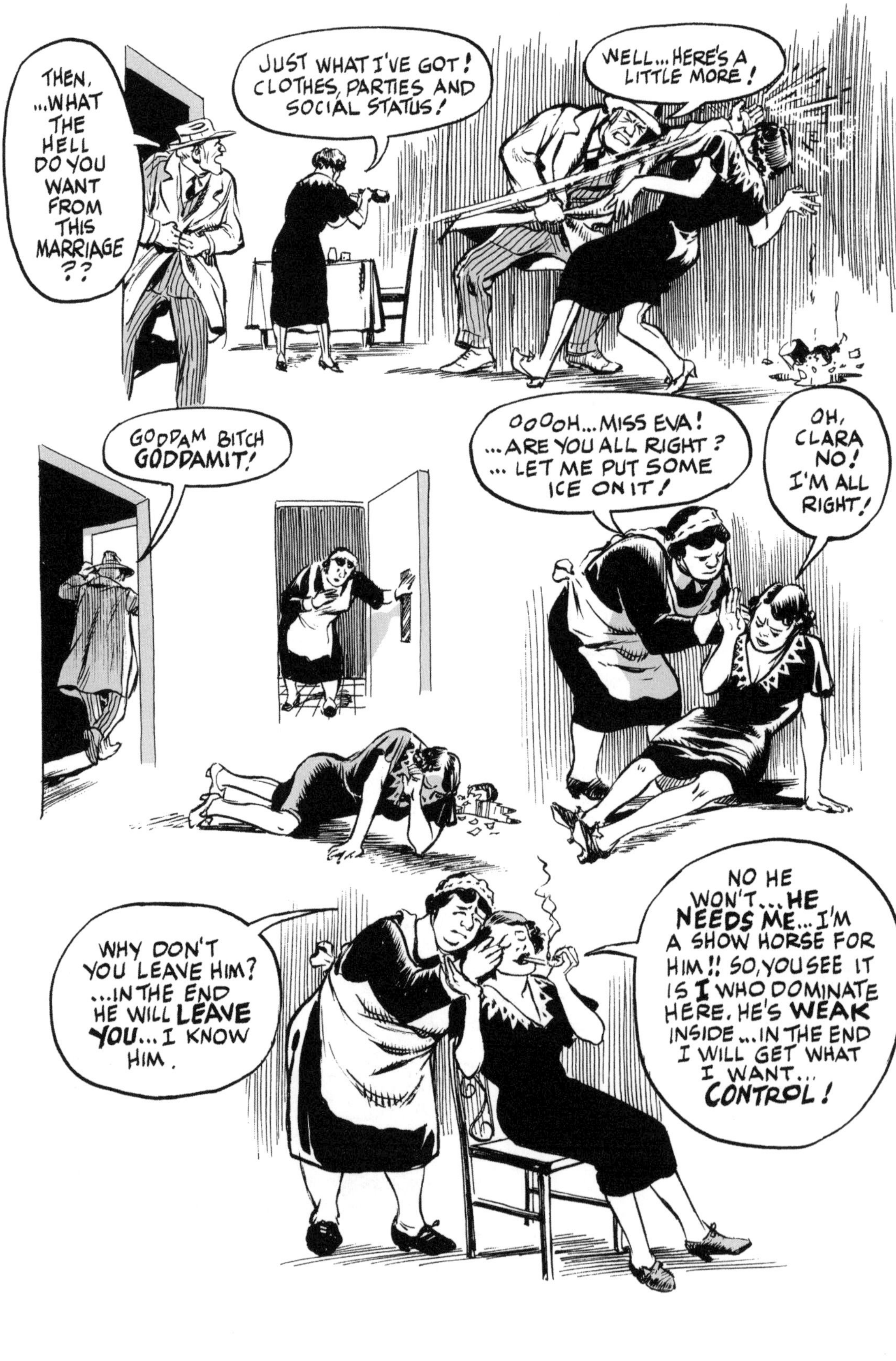
THEN, ...WHAT THE HELL DO YOU WANT FROM THIS MARRIAGE ??
JUST WHAT I'VE GOT! CLOTHES, PARTIES AND SOCIAL STATUS!
WELL... HERE'S A LITTLE MORE!
GODDAM BITCH GODDAMIT!
OOOOH... MISS EVA! ...ARE YOU ALL RIGHT? ...LET ME PUT SOME ICE ON IT!
OH, CLARA NO! I'M ALL RIGHT!
WHY DON'T YOU LEAVE HIM? ...IN THE END HE WILL LEAVE YOU... I KNOW HIM.
NO HE WON'T... HE NEEDS ME... I'M A SHOW HORSE FOR HIM!! SO, YOU SEE IT IS I WHO DOMINATE HERE. HE'S WEAK INSIDE... IN THE END I WILL GET WHAT I WANT... CONTROL!

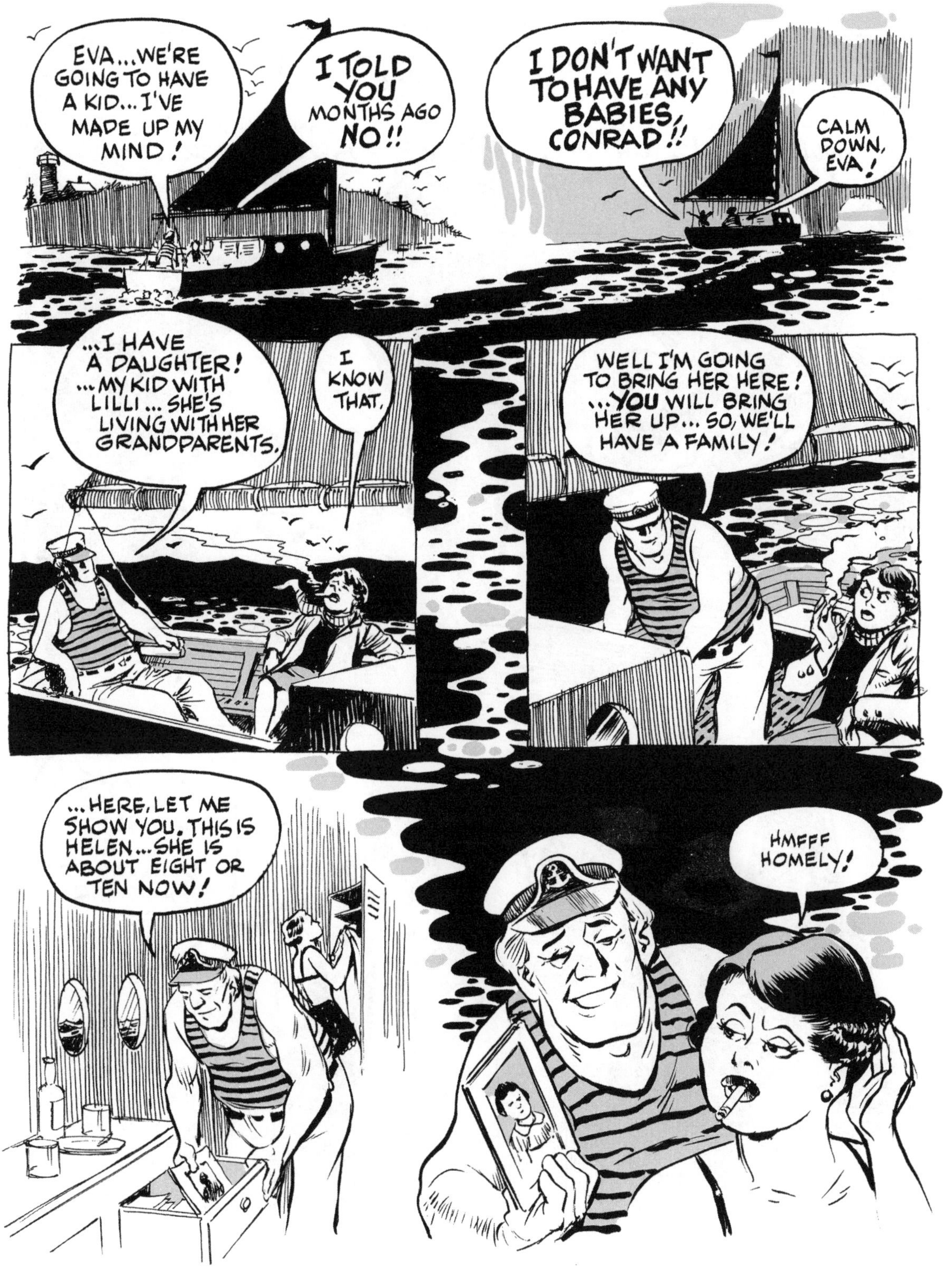

EVA... WE'RE GOING TO HAVE A KID... I'VE MADE UP MY MIND!
I TOLD YOU MONTHS AGO NO!!
I DON'T WANT TO HAVE ANY BABIES, CONRAD!!
CALM DOWN, EVA!
...I HAVE A DAUGHTER! ...MY KID WITH LILLI... SHE'S LIVING WITH HER GRANDPARENTS.
I KNOW THAT.
WELL I'M GOING TO BRING HER HERE! ...YOU WILL BRING HER UP... SO, WE'LL HAVE A FAMILY!
...HERE, LET ME SHOW YOU. THIS IS HELEN... SHE IS ABOUT EIGHT OR TEN NOW!
HMFFF HOMELY!

A month later . . .

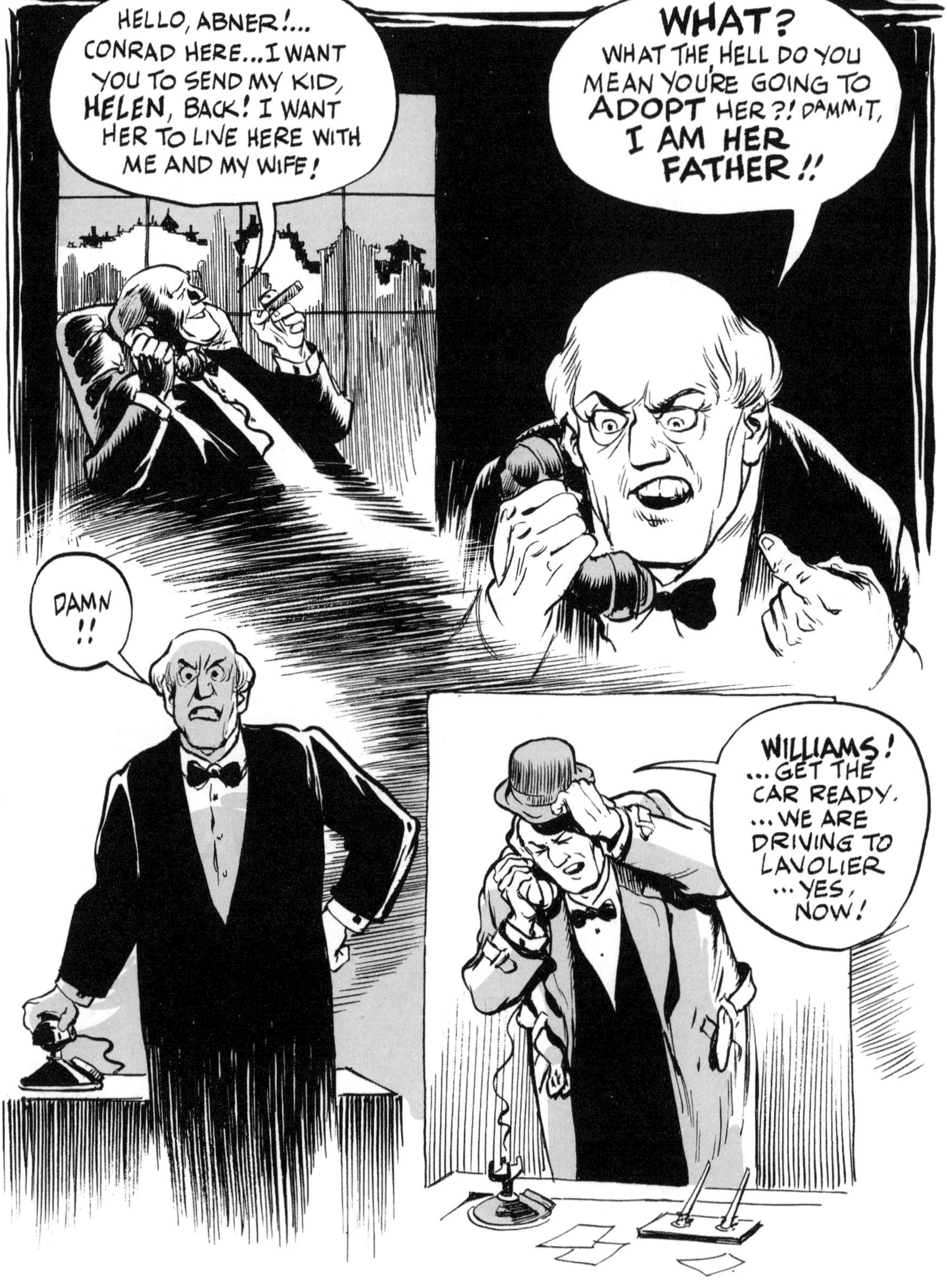
HELLO, ABNER!... CONRAD HERE...I WANT YOU TO SEND MY KID, HELEN, BACK! I WANT HER TO LIVE HERE WITH ME AND MY WIFE!
WHAT? WHAT THE HELL DO YOU MEAN YOU'RE GOING TO ADOPT HER?! DAMMIT, I AM HER FATHER!!
DAMN!!
WILLIAMS! ...GET THE CAR READY. ...WE ARE DRIVING TO LAVOLIER ...YES, NOW!

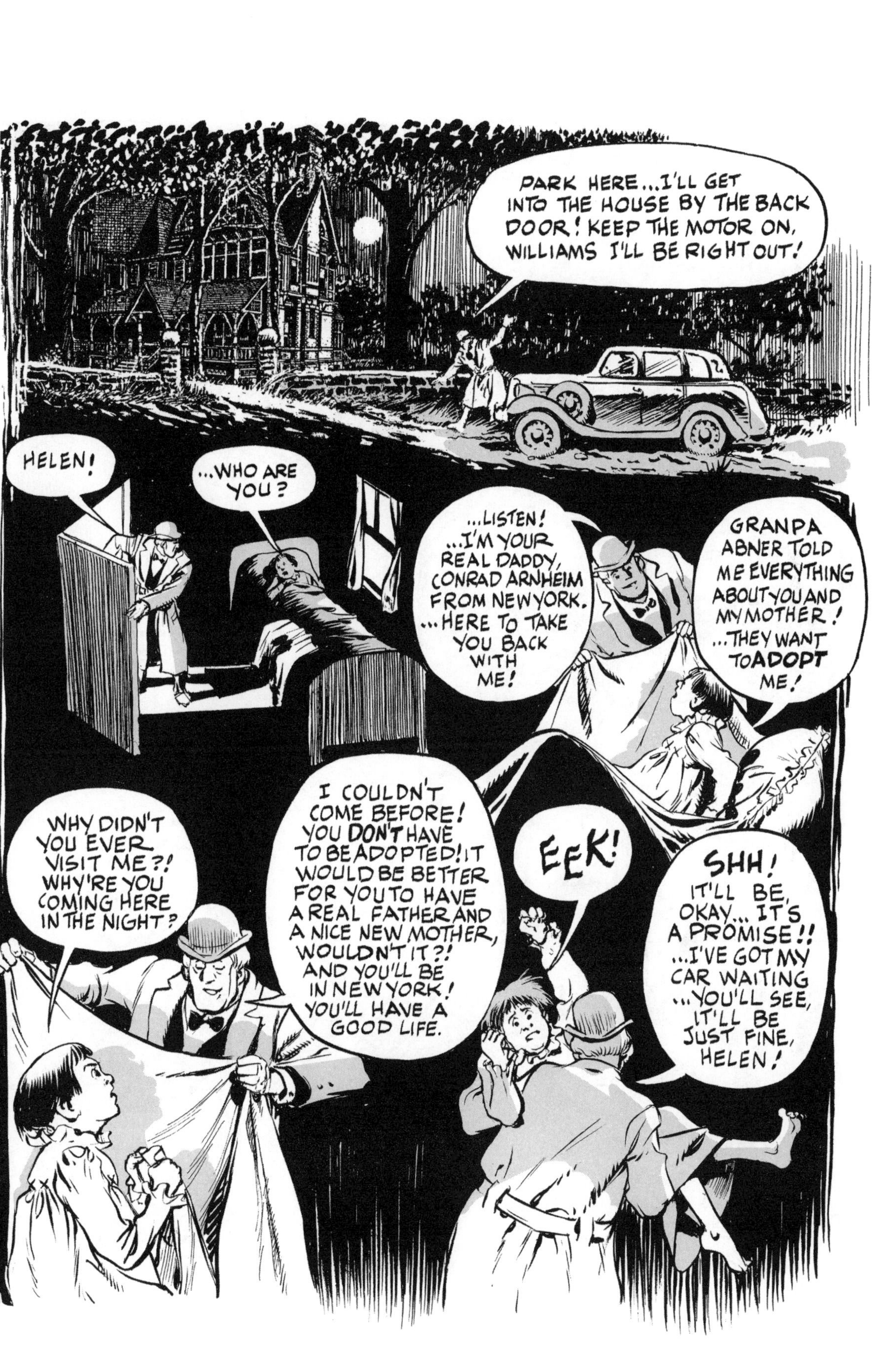
PARK HERE...I'LL GET INTO THE HOUSE BY THE BACK DOOR! KEEP THE MOTOR ON, WILLIAMS I'LL BE RIGHT OUT!
HELEN!
...WHO ARE YOU?
...LISTEN! ...I'M YOUR REAL DADDY, CONRAD ARNHEIM FROM NEW YORK. ...HERE TO TAKE YOU BACK WITH ME!
GRANPA ABNER TOLD ME EVERYTHING ABOUT YOU AND MY MOTHER! ...THEY WANT TO ADOPT ME!
WHY DIDN'T YOU EVER VISIT ME?! WHY'RE YOU COMING HERE IN THE NIGHT?
I COULDN'T COME BEFORE! YOU DON'T HAVE TO BE ADOPTED! IT WOULD BE BETTER FOR YOU TO HAVE A REAL FATHER AND A NICE NEW MOTHER, WOULDN'T IT?! AND YOU'LL BE IN NEW YORK! YOU'LL HAVE A GOOD LIFE.
EEK!
SHH! IT'LL BE, OKAY... IT'S A PROMISE!! ...I'VE GOT MY CAR WAITING ...YOU'LL SEE, IT'LL BE JUST FINE, HELEN!

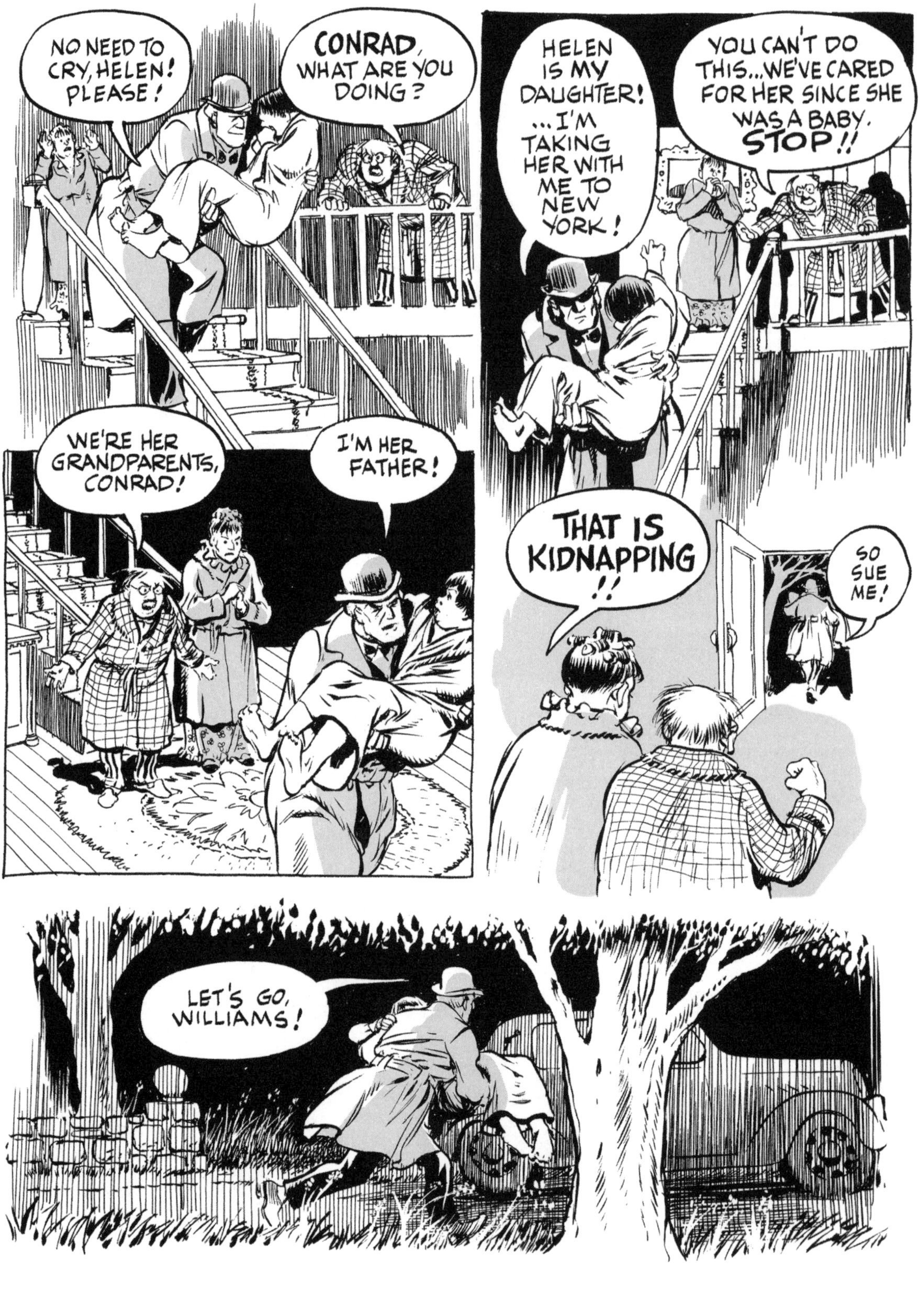
NO NEED TO CRY, HELEN! PLEASE!
CONRAD, WHAT ARE YOU DOING?
HELEN IS MY DAUGHTER! ...I'M TAKING HER WITH ME TO NEW YORK!
YOU CAN'T DO THIS...WE'VE CARED FOR HER SINCE SHE WAS A BABY. STOP!!
WE'RE HER GRANDPARENTS, CONRAD!
I'M HER FATHER!
THAT IS KIDNAPPING!!
SO SUE ME!
LET'S GO, WILLIAMS!

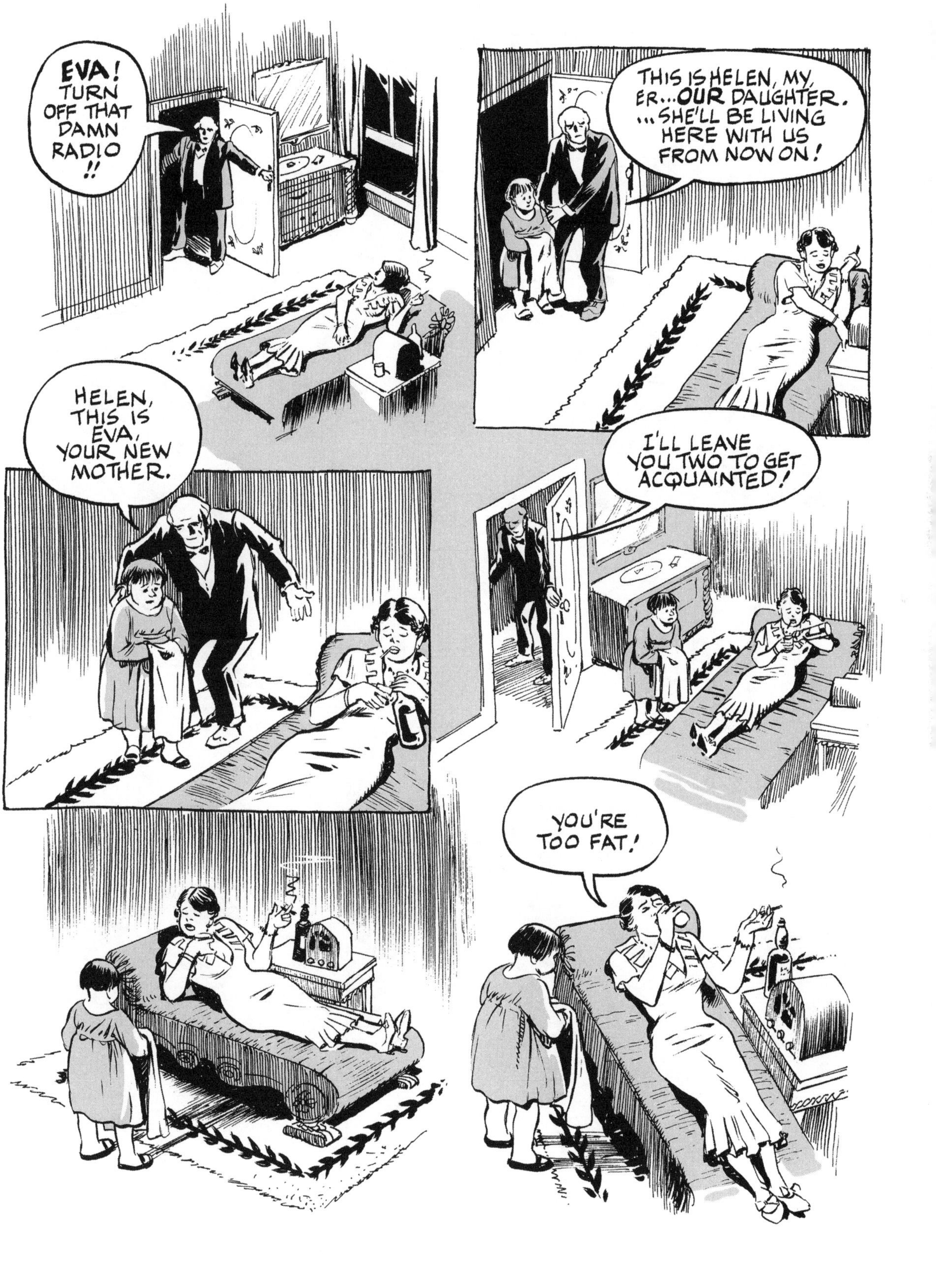
EVA! TURN OFF THAT DAMN RADIO !!
THIS IS HELEN, MY, ER...OUR DAUGHTER. ...SHE'LL BE LIVING HERE WITH US FROM NOW ON!
HELEN, THIS IS EVA, YOUR NEW MOTHER.
I'LL LEAVE YOU TWO TO GET ACQUAINTED!
YOU'RE TOO FAT!

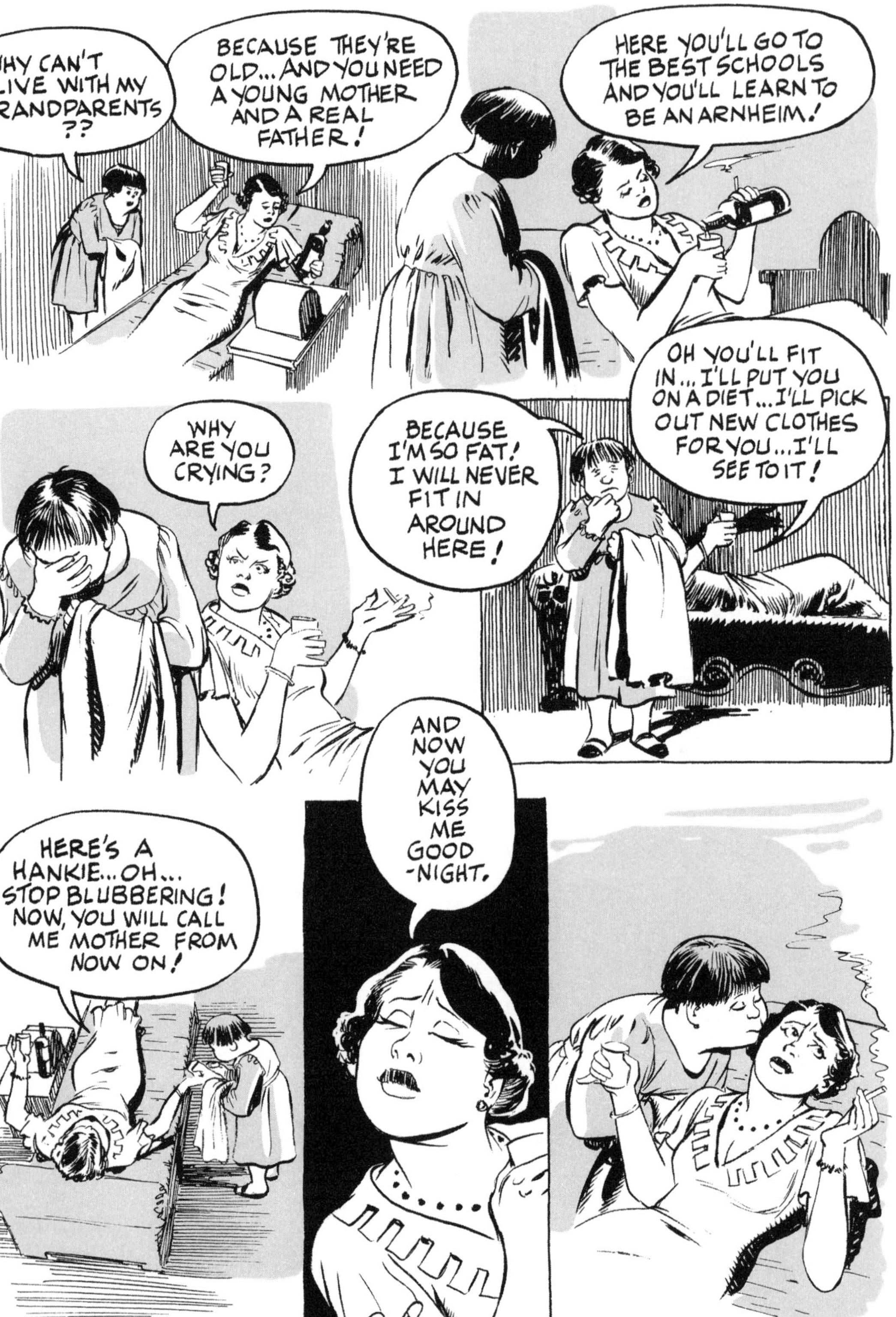
WHY CAN'T I LIVE WITH MY GRANDPARENTS ??
BECAUSE THEY'RE OLD... AND YOU NEED A YOUNG MOTHER AND A REAL FATHER!
HERE YOU'LL GO TO THE BEST SCHOOLS AND YOU'LL LEARN TO BE AN ARNHEIM!
WHY ARE YOU CRYING?
BECAUSE I'M SO FAT! I WILL NEVER FIT IN AROUND HERE!
OH YOU'LL FIT IN... I'LL PUT YOU ON A DIET... I'LL PICK OUT NEW CLOTHES FOR YOU... I'LL SEE TO IT!
HERE'S A HANKIE... OH... STOP BLUBBERING! NOW, YOU WILL CALL ME MOTHER FROM NOW ON!
AND NOW YOU MAY KISS ME GOOD-NIGHT.

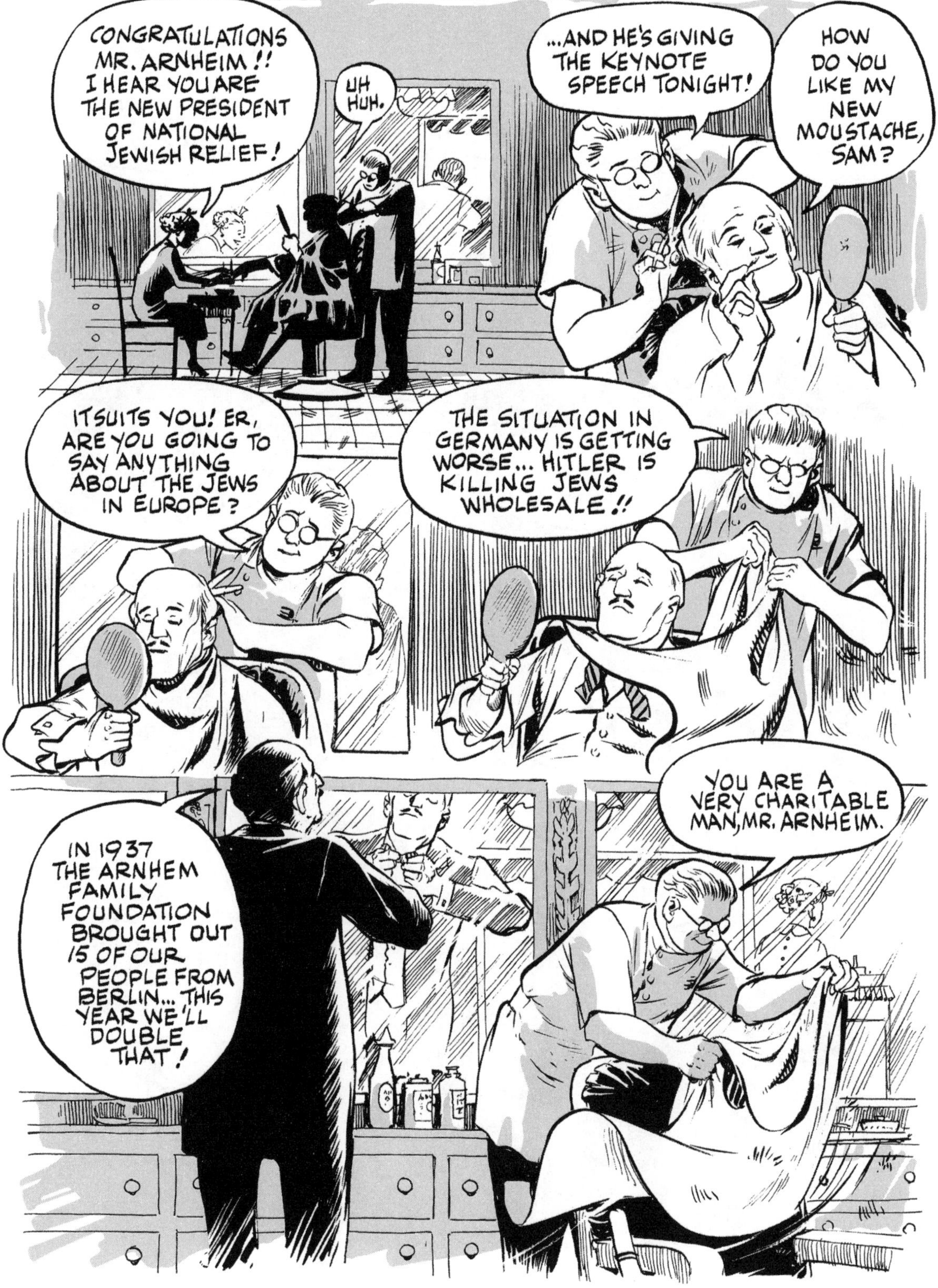
CONGRATULATIONS MR. ARNHEIM!! I HEAR YOU ARE THE NEW PRESIDENT OF NATIONAL JEWISH RELIEF!
UH HUH.
...AND HE'S GIVING THE KEYNOTE SPEECH TONIGHT!
HOW DO YOU LIKE MY NEW MOUSTACHE, SAM?
IT SUITS YOU! ER, ARE YOU GOING TO SAY ANYTHING ABOUT THE JEWS IN EUROPE?
THE SITUATION IN GERMANY IS GETTING WORSE... HITLER IS KILLING JEWS WHOLESALE!!
IN 1937 THE ARNHEM FAMILY FOUNDATION BROUGHT OUT 15 OF OUR PEOPLE FROM BERLIN... THIS YEAR WE'LL DOUBLE THAT!
YOU ARE A VERY CHARITABLE MAN, MR. ARNHEIM.

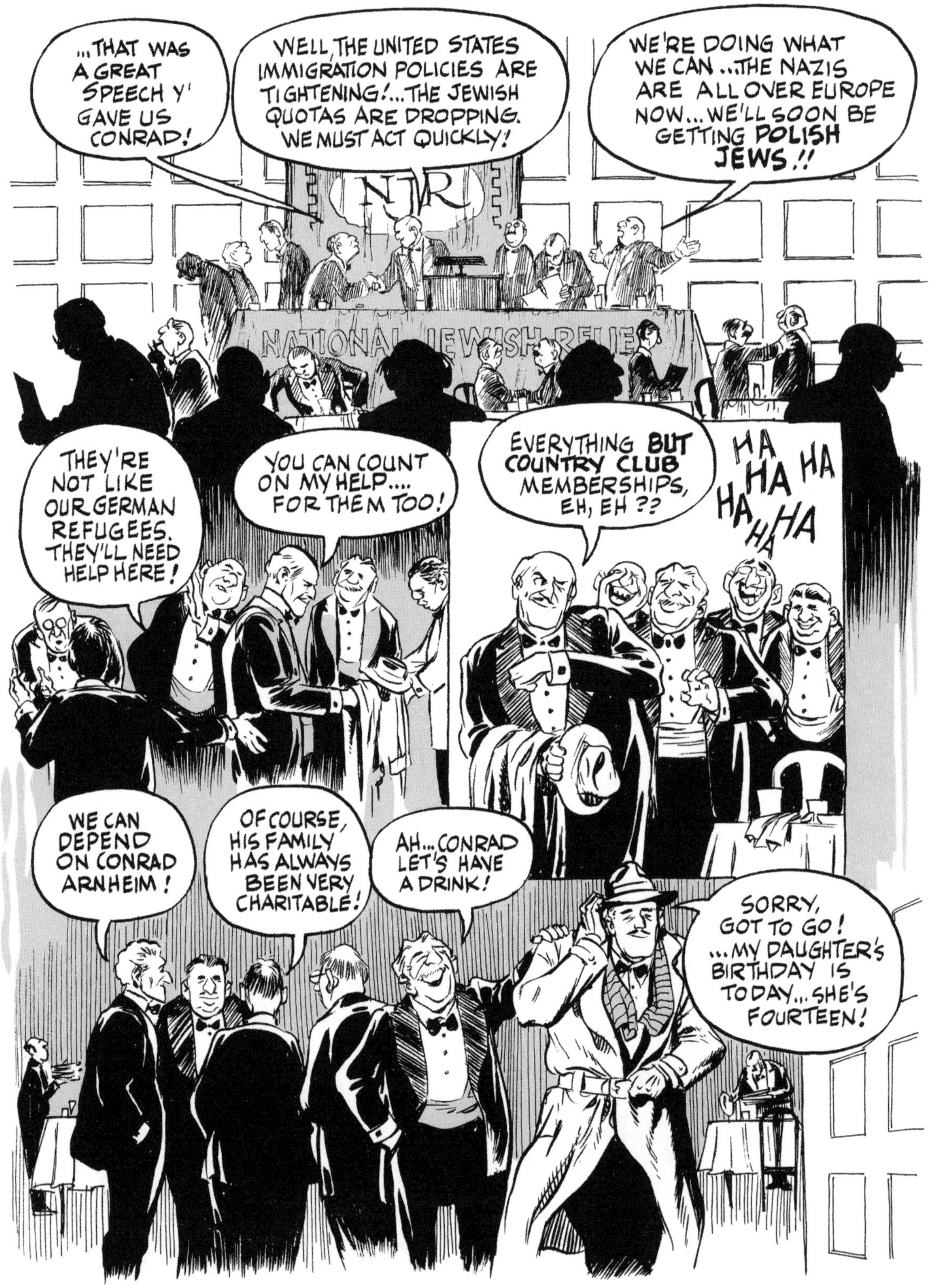

...THAT WAS A GREAT SPEECH Y' GAVE US CONRAD!
WELL, THE UNITED STATES IMMIGRATION POLICIES ARE TIGHTENING!...THE JEWISH QUOTAS ARE DROPPING. WE MUST ACT QUICKLY!
WE'RE DOING WHAT WE CAN ...THE NAZIS ARE ALL OVER EUROPE NOW... WE'LL SOON BE GETTING **POLISH JEWS**!!
NJR
NATIONAL JEWISH RELIE
THEY'RE NOT LIKE OUR GERMAN REFUGEES. THEY'LL NEED HELP HERE!
YOU CAN COUNT ON MY HELP.... FOR THEM TOO!
EVERYTHING **BUT COUNTRY CLUB** MEMBERSHIPS, EH, EH ??
HA HA HA HA HA HA HA
WE CAN DEPEND ON CONRAD ARNHEIM!
OF COURSE, HIS FAMILY HAS ALWAYS BEEN VERY CHARITABLE!
AH... CONRAD LET'S HAVE A DRINK!
SORRY, GOT TO GO! ...MY DAUGHTER'S BIRTHDAY IS TODAY... SHE'S FOURTEEN!

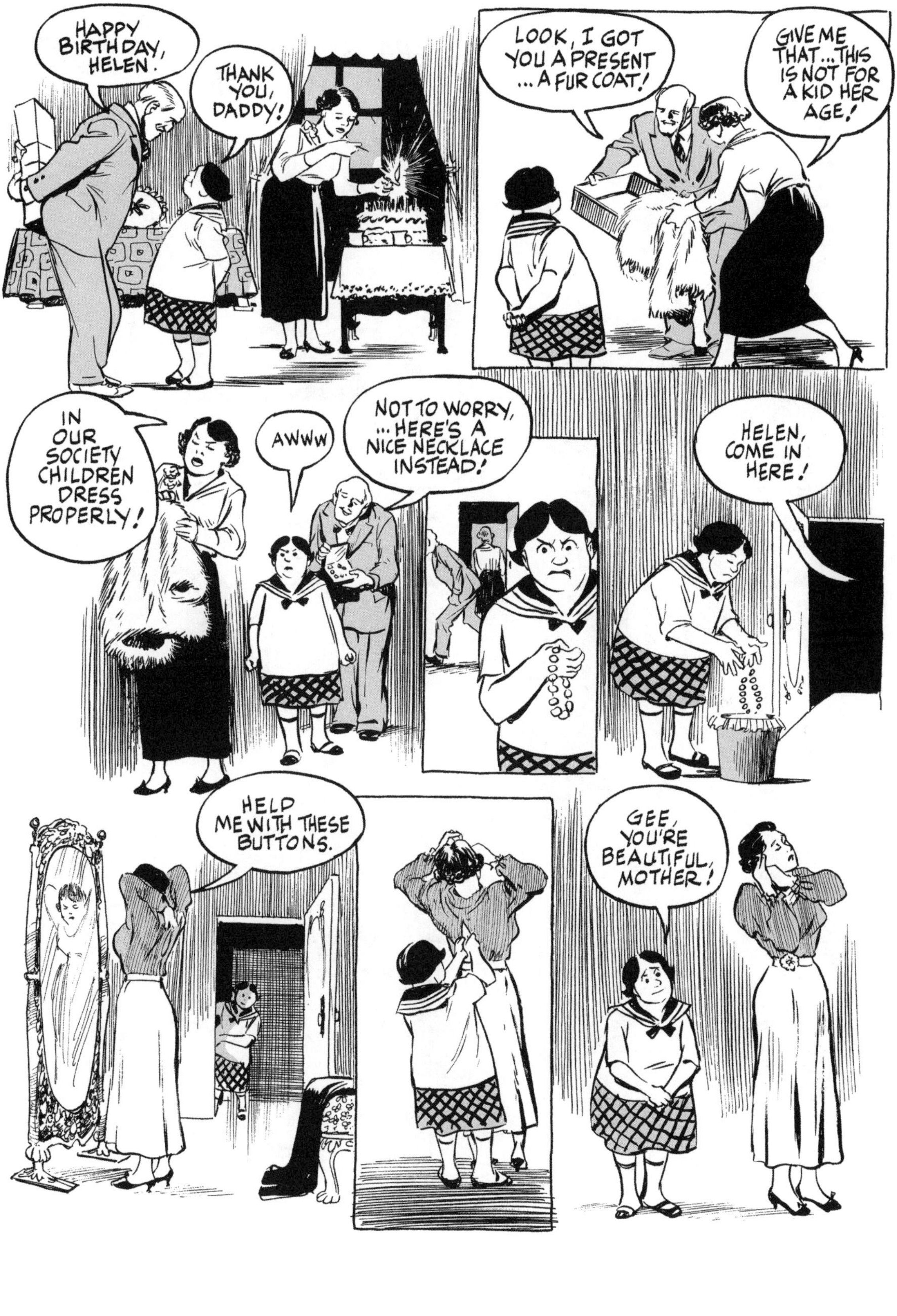
HAPPY BIRTHDAY, HELEN.
THANK YOU, DADDY!
LOOK, I GOT YOU A PRESENT ... A FUR COAT!
GIVE ME THAT... THIS IS NOT FOR A KID HER AGE!
IN OUR SOCIETY CHILDREN DRESS PROPERLY!
AWWW
NOT TO WORRY, ... HERE'S A NICE NECKLACE INSTEAD!
HELEN, COME IN HERE!
HELP ME WITH THESE BUTTONS.
GEE, YOU'RE BEAUTIFUL, MOTHER!

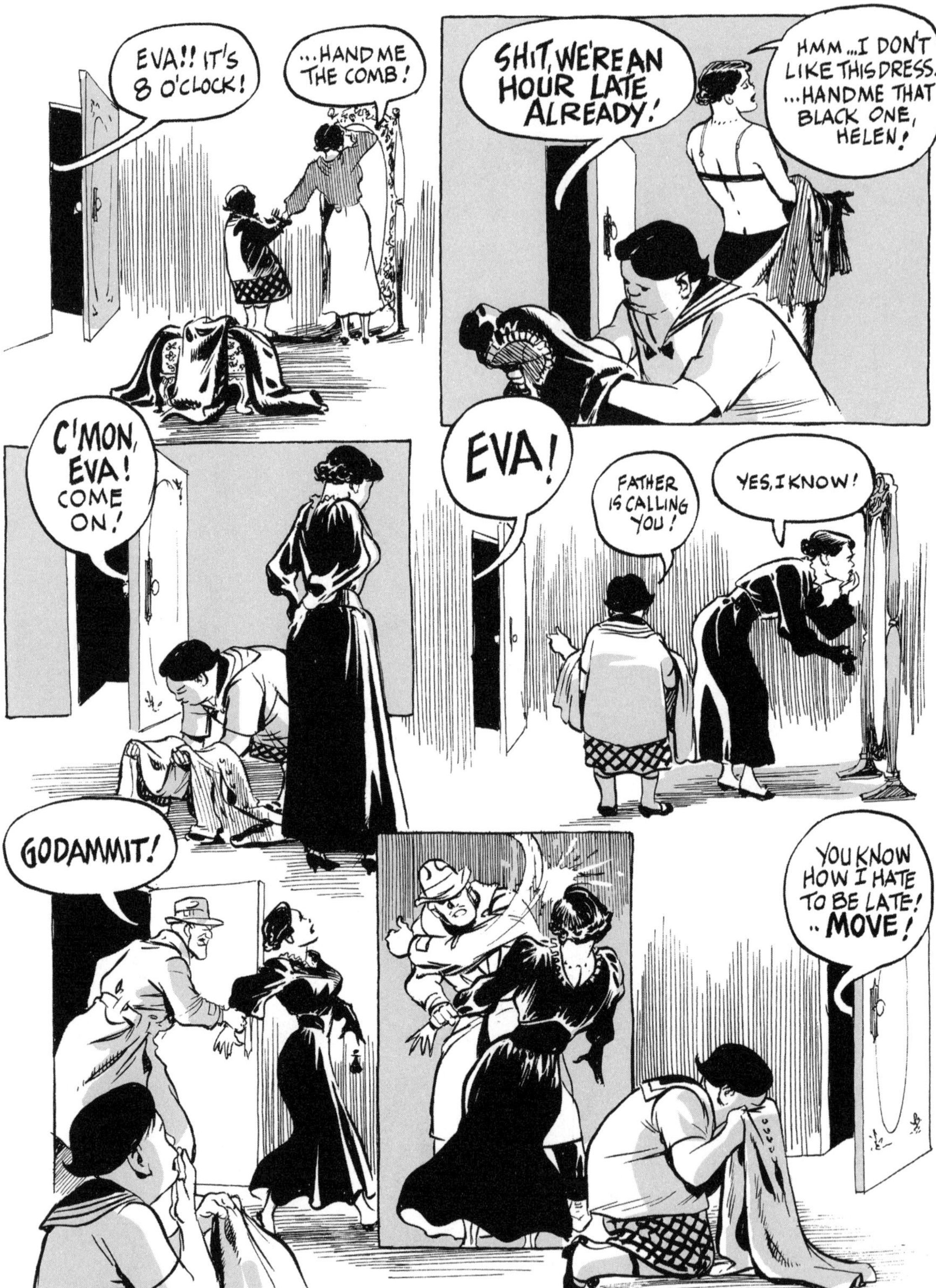
EVA!! IT'S 8 O'CLOCK!
...HAND ME THE COMB!
SHIT, WE'RE AN HOUR LATE ALREADY!
HMM...I DON'T LIKE THIS DRESS. ...HAND ME THAT BLACK ONE, HELEN!
C'MON, EVA! COME ON!
EVA!
FATHER IS CALLING YOU!
YES, I KNOW!
GODAMMIT!
YOU KNOW HOW I HATE TO BE LATE! ..MOVE!

The custody matter did not "go away" as Conrad hoped and expected. No Arnheim had ever been threatened like this.

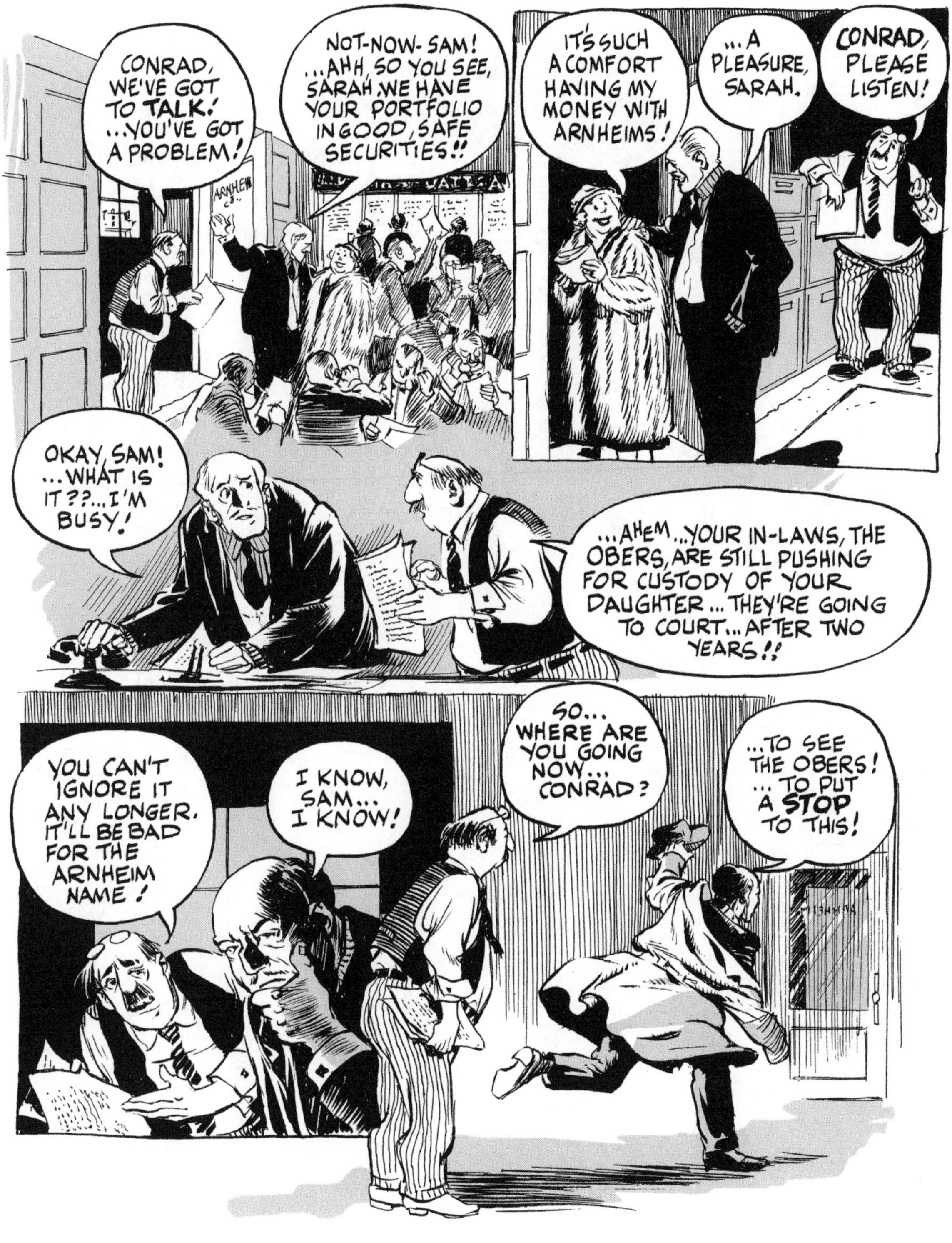
CONRAD, WE'VE GOT TO TALK! ..YOU'VE GOT A PROBLEM!
NOT-NOW- SAM! ...AHH, SO YOU SEE, SARAH WE HAVE YOUR PORTFOLIO IN GOOD, SAFE SECURITIES!!
ARNHEIM
IT'S SUCH A COMFORT HAVING MY MONEY WITH ARNHEIMS!
...A PLEASURE, SARAH.
CONRAD, PLEASE LISTEN!
OKAY, SAM! ...WHAT IS IT??...I'M BUSY!
...AHEM...YOUR IN-LAWS, THE OBERS, ARE STILL PUSHING FOR CUSTODY OF YOUR DAUGHTER... THEY'RE GOING TO COURT...AFTER TWO YEARS!!
YOU CAN'T IGNORE IT ANY LONGER. IT'LL BE BAD FOR THE ARNHEIM NAME!
I KNOW, SAM... I KNOW!
SO... WHERE ARE YOU GOING NOW... CONRAD?
...TO SEE THE OBERS! ... TO PUT A STOP TO THIS!

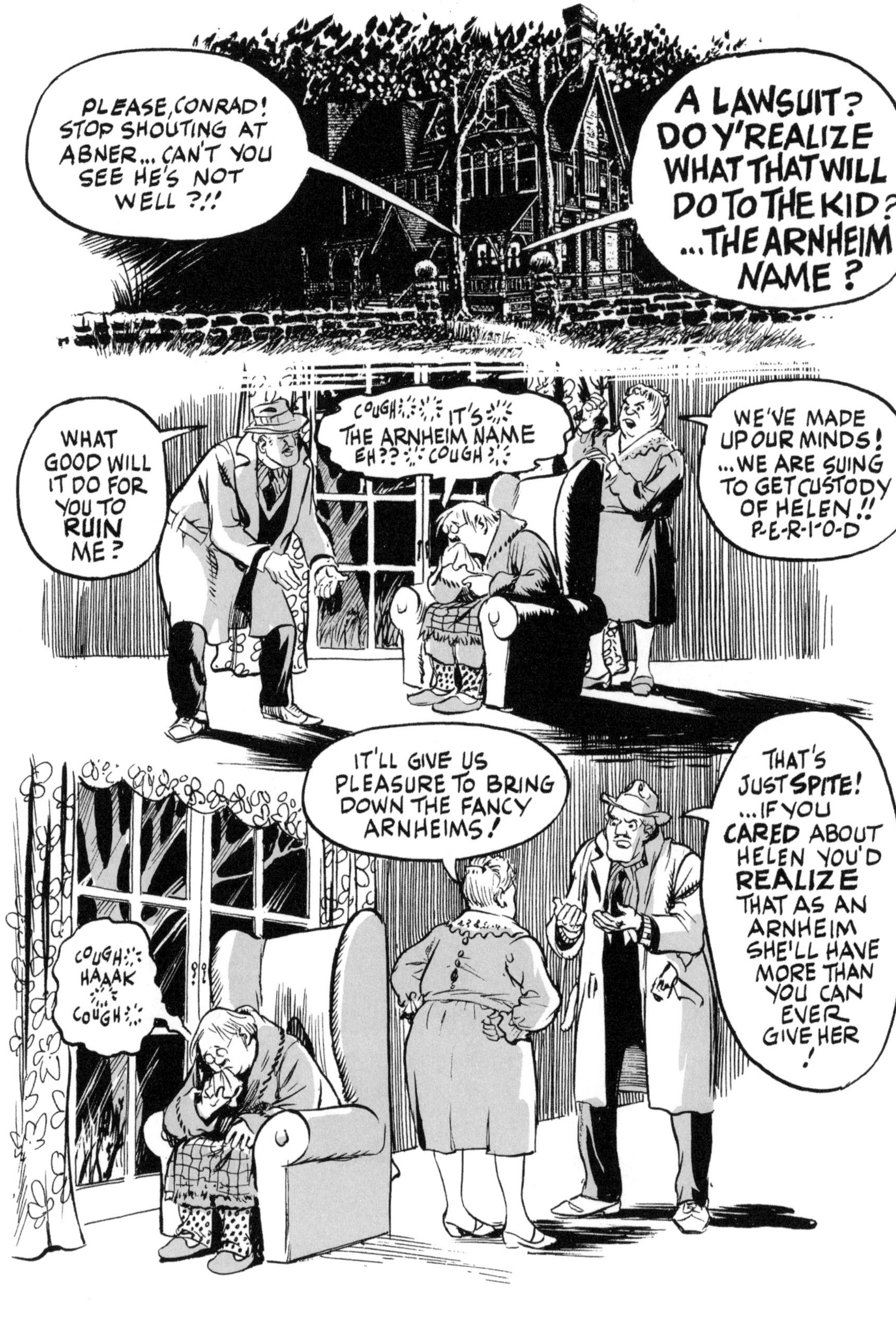
PLEASE, CONRAD! STOP SHOUTING AT ABNER... CAN'T YOU SEE HE'S NOT WELL ?!!
A LAWSUIT? DO Y'REALIZE WHAT THAT WILL DO TO THE KID? ...THE ARNHEIM NAME ?
WHAT GOOD WILL IT DO FOR YOU TO RUIN ME?
COUGH IT'S THE ARNHEIM NAME EH?? COUGH
WE'VE MADE UP OUR MINDS! ...WE ARE SUING TO GET CUSTODY OF HELEN!! P-E-R-I-O-D
IT'LL GIVE US PLEASURE TO BRING DOWN THE FANCY ARNHEIMS!
THAT'S JUST SPITE! ...IF YOU CARED ABOUT HELEN YOU'D REALIZE THAT AS AN ARNHEIM SHE'LL HAVE MORE THAN YOU CAN EVER GIVE HER!
COUGH HAAAK COUGH

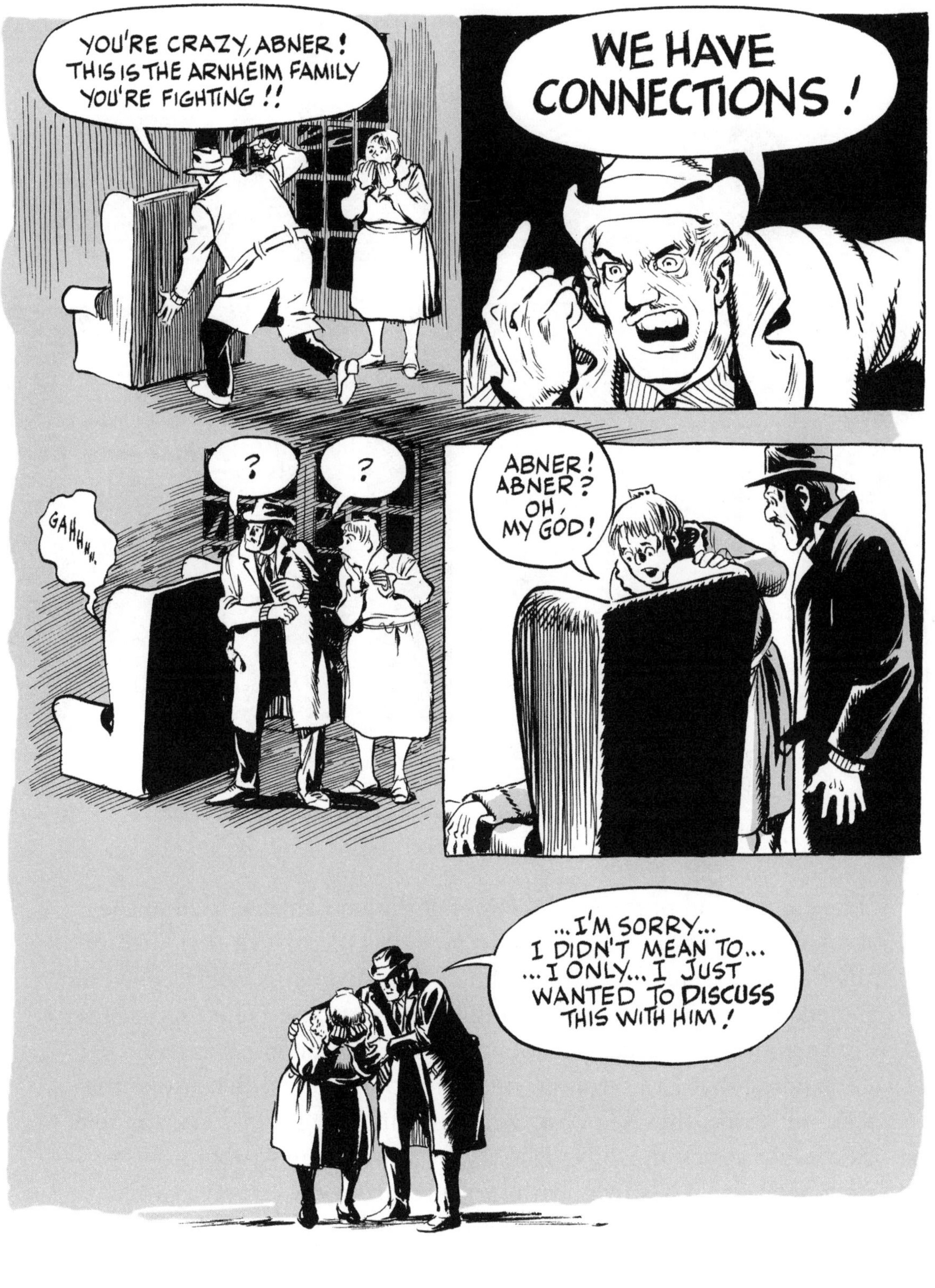
YOU'RE CRAZY, ABNER! THIS IS THE ARNHEIM FAMILY YOU'RE FIGHTING!!
WE HAVE CONNECTIONS!
?
?
GAHHH..
ABNER! ABNER? OH, MY GOD!
...I'M SORRY... I DIDN'T MEAN TO... ...I ONLY... I JUST WANTED TO DISCUSS THIS WITH HIM!

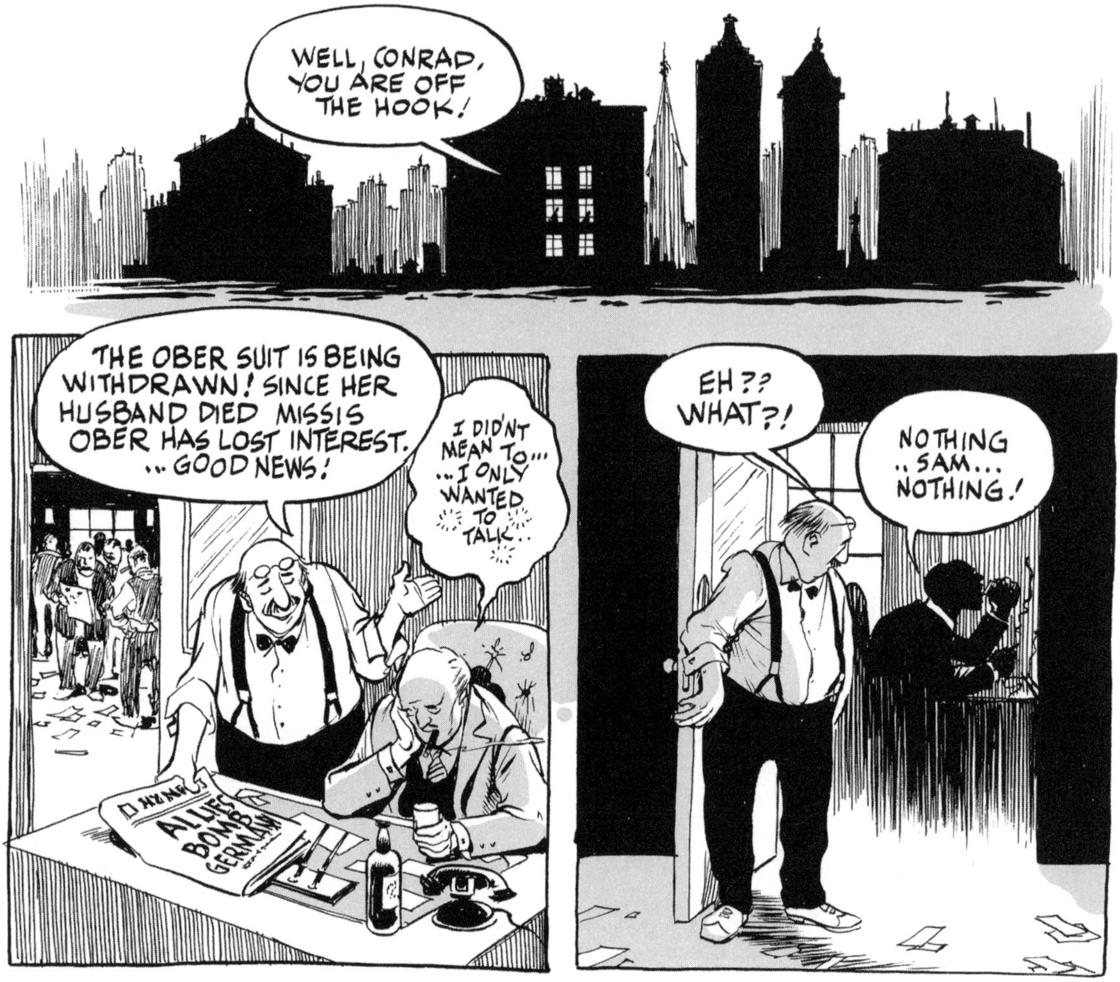
WELL, CONRAD, YOU ARE OFF THE HOOK!
THE OBER SUIT IS BEING WITHDRAWN! SINCE HER HUSBAND DIED MISSIS OBER HAS LOST INTEREST. ..GOOD NEWS!
I DIDN'T MEAN TO... ..I ONLY WANTED TO TALK..
EH?? WHAT?!
NOTHING ..SAM... NOTHING!

The elimination of the Ober claim left Helen firmly settled in the Arnheim household. Eva began to play the role of "Mother," which their friends seemed to expect of her. The Arnheims' social schedule included a lot of "being seen," and for a short time Helen served as a convenient show piece. But soon their social schedule was so demanding that Eva began to find it uncomfortable. Because of the war in Europe, the use of Switzerland, which had long been suitable as the location of finishing schools for most of the Arnheim set, was no longer viable. Canada, with its ski resorts, now served a similar purpose. Eva began to think of this option as a way of relieving herself of Helen's care.

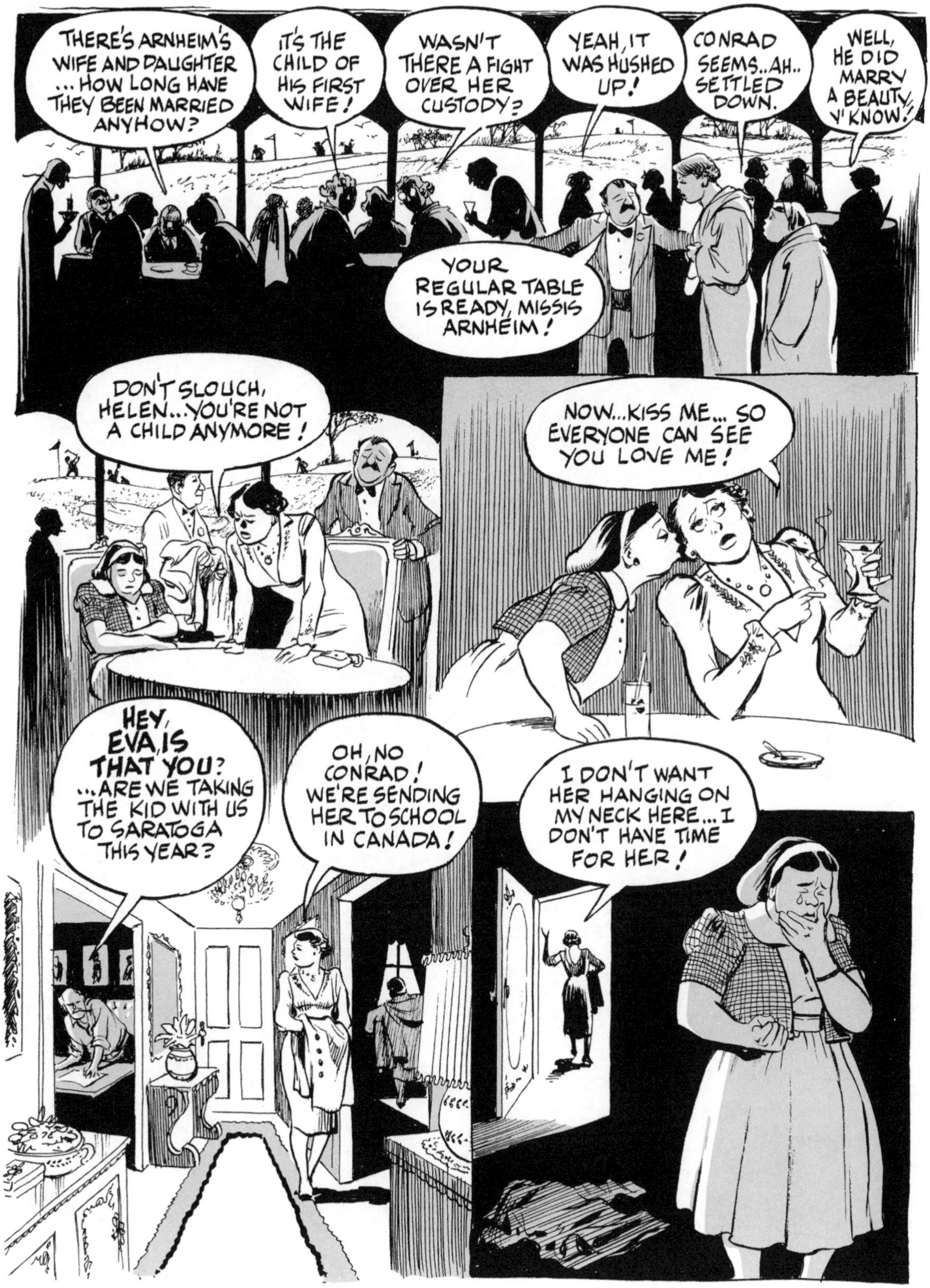

THERE'S ARNHEIM'S WIFE AND DAUGHTER ... HOW LONG HAVE THEY BEEN MARRIED ANYHOW?
IT'S THE CHILD OF HIS FIRST WIFE!
WASN'T THERE A FIGHT OVER HER CUSTODY?
YEAH, IT WAS HUSHED UP!
CONRAD SEEMS..AH.. SETTLED DOWN.
WELL, HE DID MARRY A BEAUTY, Y'KNOW!
YOUR REGULAR TABLE IS READY, MISSIS ARNHEIM!
DON'T SLOUCH, HELEN...YOU'RE NOT A CHILD ANYMORE!
NOW...KISS ME... SO EVERYONE CAN SEE YOU LOVE ME!
HEY, EVA, IS THAT YOU? ...ARE WE TAKING THE KID WITH US TO SARATOGA THIS YEAR?
OH, NO CONRAD! WE'RE SENDING HER TO SCHOOL IN CANADA!
I DON'T WANT HER HANGING ON MY NECK HERE... I DON'T HAVE TIME FOR HER!

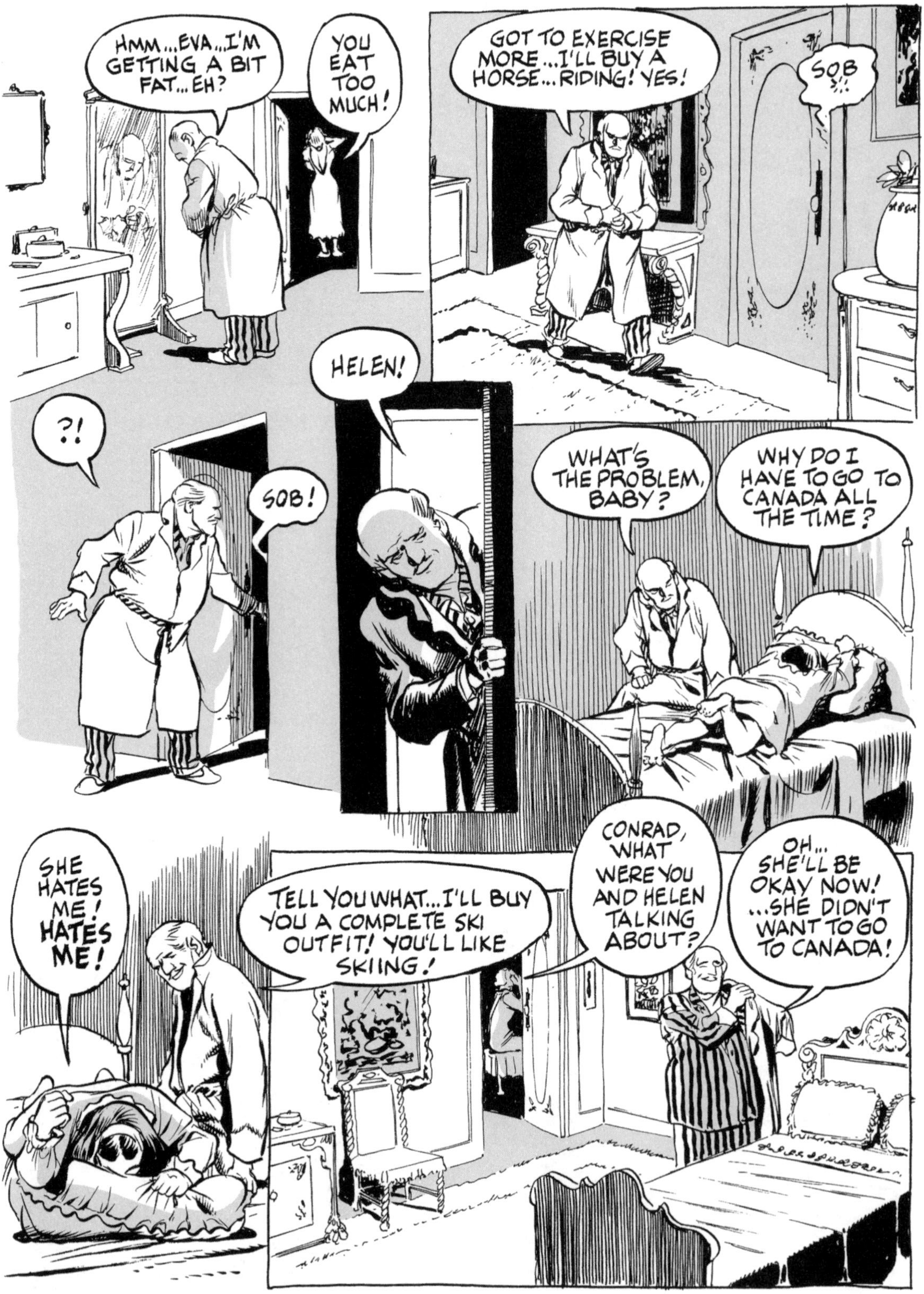
HMM...EVA...I'M GETTING A BIT FAT...EH?
YOU EAT TOO MUCH!
GOT TO EXERCISE MORE...I'LL BUY A HORSE...RIDING! YES!
SOB
HELEN!
?!
SOB!
WHAT'S THE PROBLEM, BABY?
WHY DO I HAVE TO GO TO CANADA ALL THE TIME?
SHE HATES ME! HATES ME!
TELL YOU WHAT...I'LL BUY YOU A COMPLETE SKI OUTFIT! YOU'LL LIKE SKIING!
CONRAD, WHAT WERE YOU AND HELEN TALKING ABOUT?
OH... SHE'LL BE OKAY NOW! ...SHE DIDN'T WANT TO GO TO CANADA!

Helen was now in Canada. It left Conrad and Eva alone again. Their world seemed to settle into its normal orbit. Very little changed in their relationship . . . except . . . one night . . .

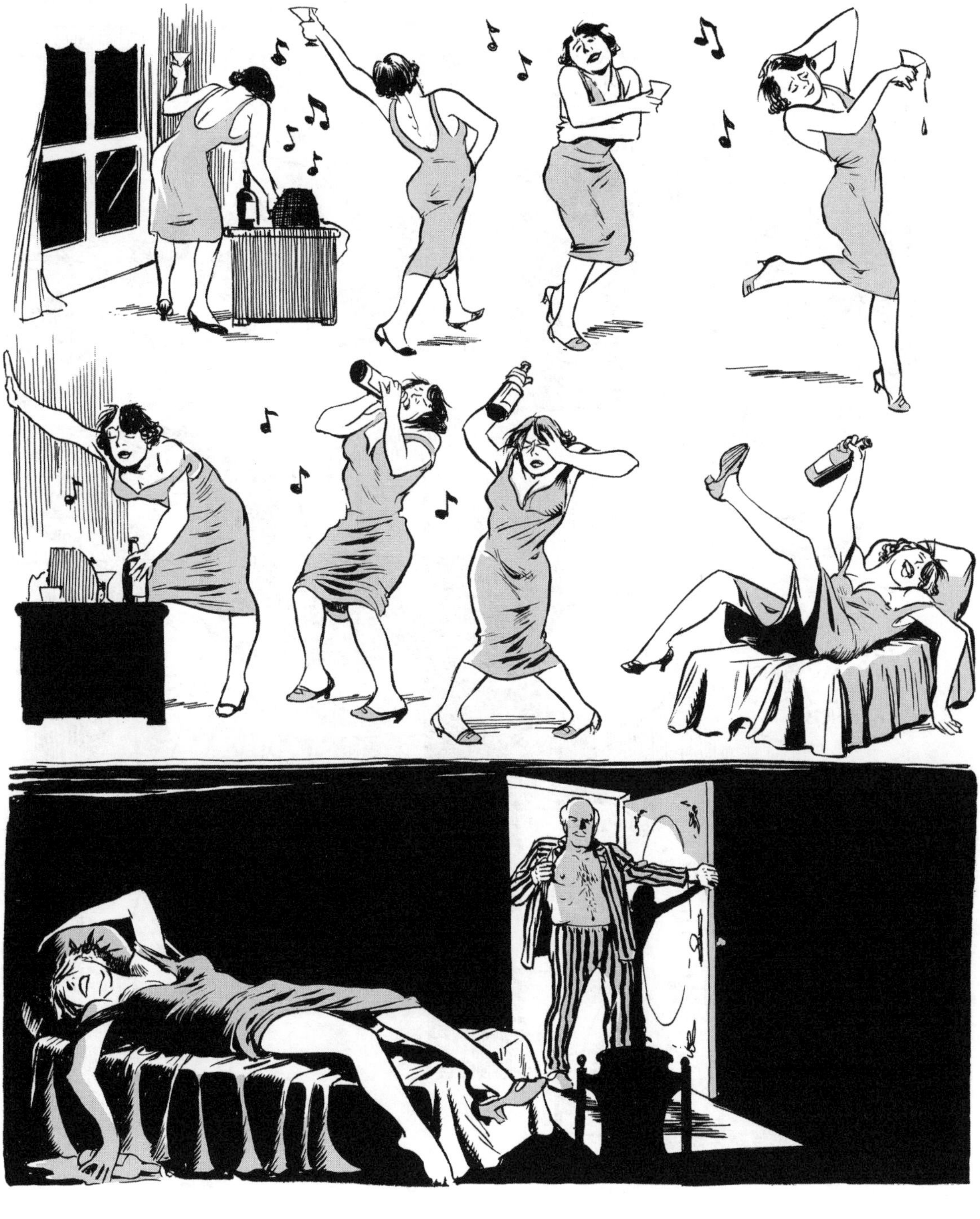

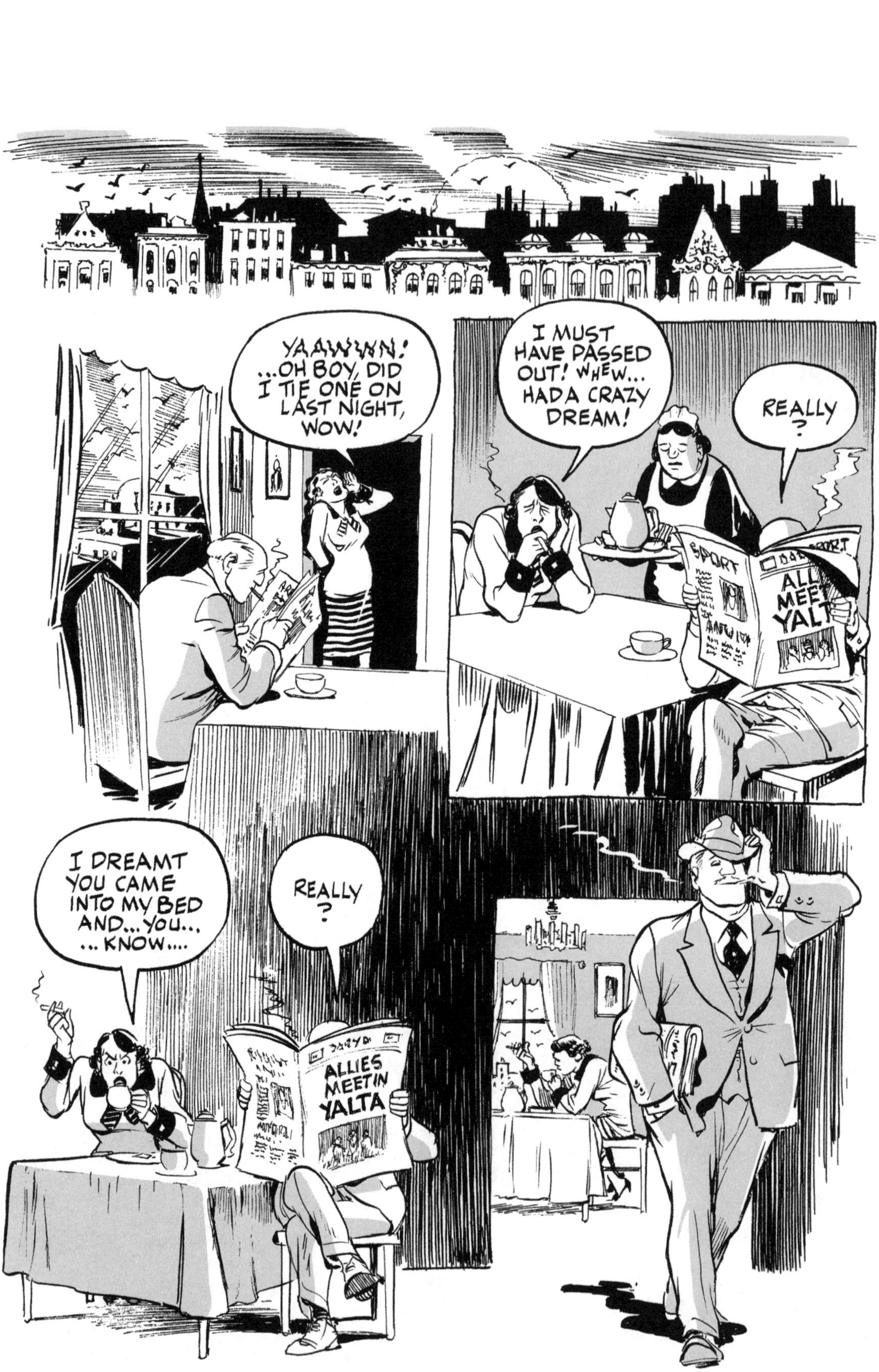

YAAWWN! ...OH BOY, DID I TIE ONE ON LAST NIGHT, WOW!
I MUST HAVE PASSED OUT! WHEW... HAD A CRAZY DREAM!
REALLY?
SPORT
ALL MEET YALTA
I DREAMT YOU CAME INTO MY BED AND... YOU... ...KNOW....
REALLY?
ALLIES MEET IN YALTA

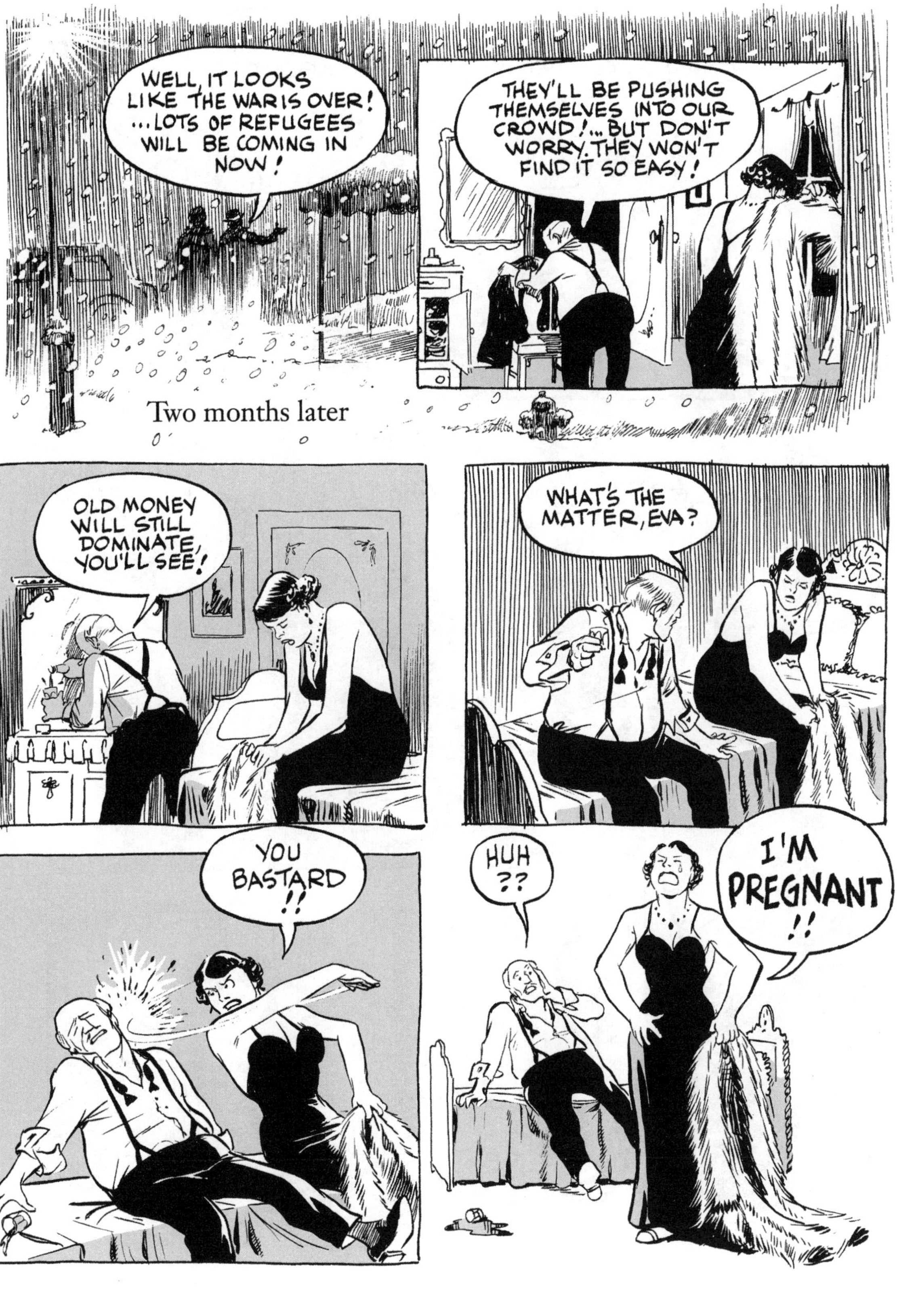
WELL, IT LOOKS LIKE THE WAR IS OVER! ...LOTS OF REFUGEES WILL BE COMING IN NOW!
THEY'LL BE PUSHING THEMSELVES INTO OUR CROWD!... BUT DON'T WORRY. THEY WON'T FIND IT SO EASY!
Two months later
OLD MONEY WILL STILL DOMINATE, YOU'LL SEE!
WHAT'S THE MATTER, EVA?
YOU BASTARD !!
HUH ??
I'M PREGNANT !!

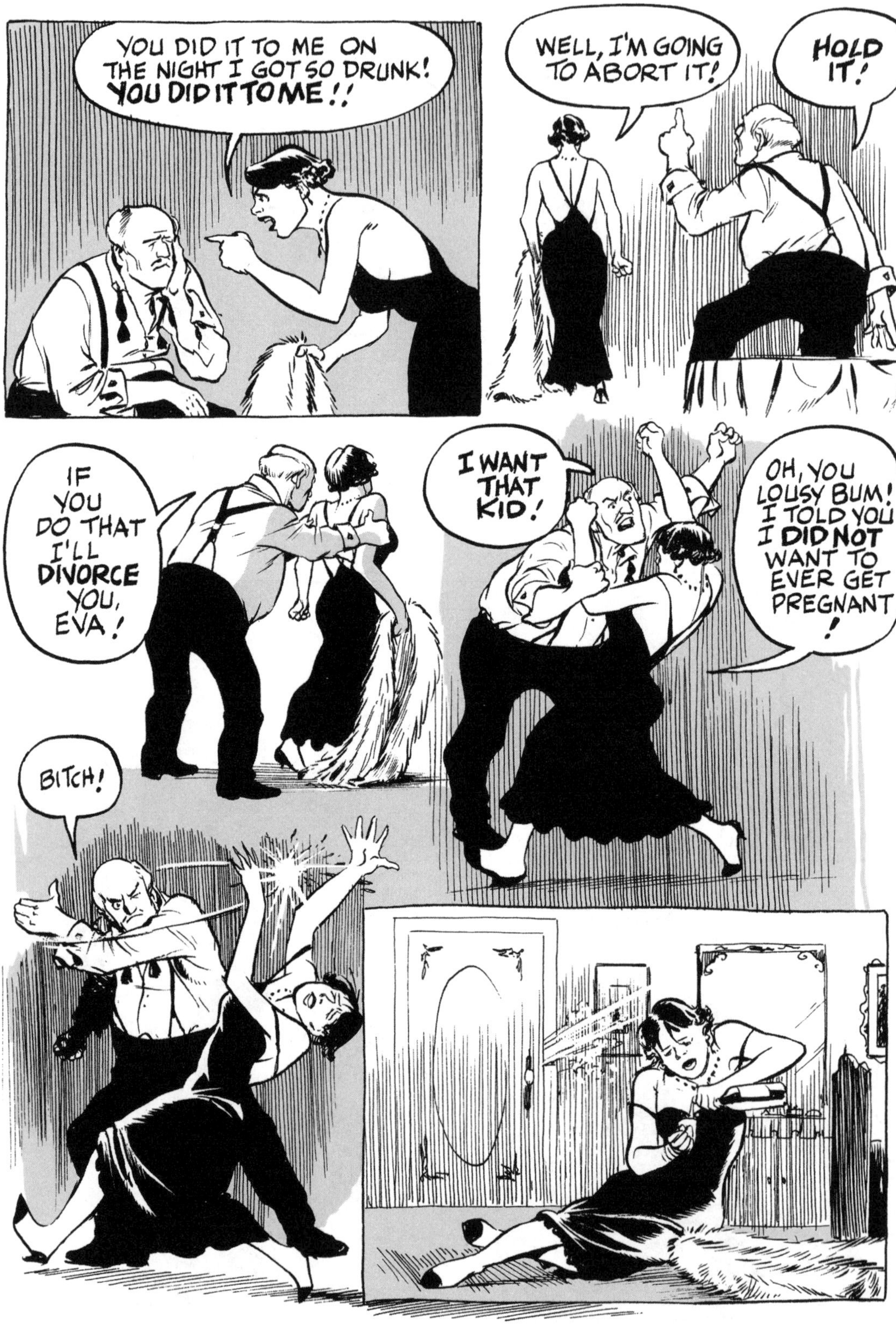
YOU DID IT TO ME ON THE NIGHT I GOT SO DRUNK! YOU DID IT TO ME!!
WELL, I'M GOING TO ABORT IT!
HOLD IT!
IF YOU DO THAT I'LL DIVORCE YOU, EVA!
I WANT THAT KID!
OH, YOU LOUSY BUM! I TOLD YOU I DID NOT WANT TO EVER GET PREGNANT!
BITCH!

Eva's pregnancy was an easy one and to everyone's surprise, she accepted her new role with the confidence of an actress.

Conrad was delighted and immediately used the event as a celebration.

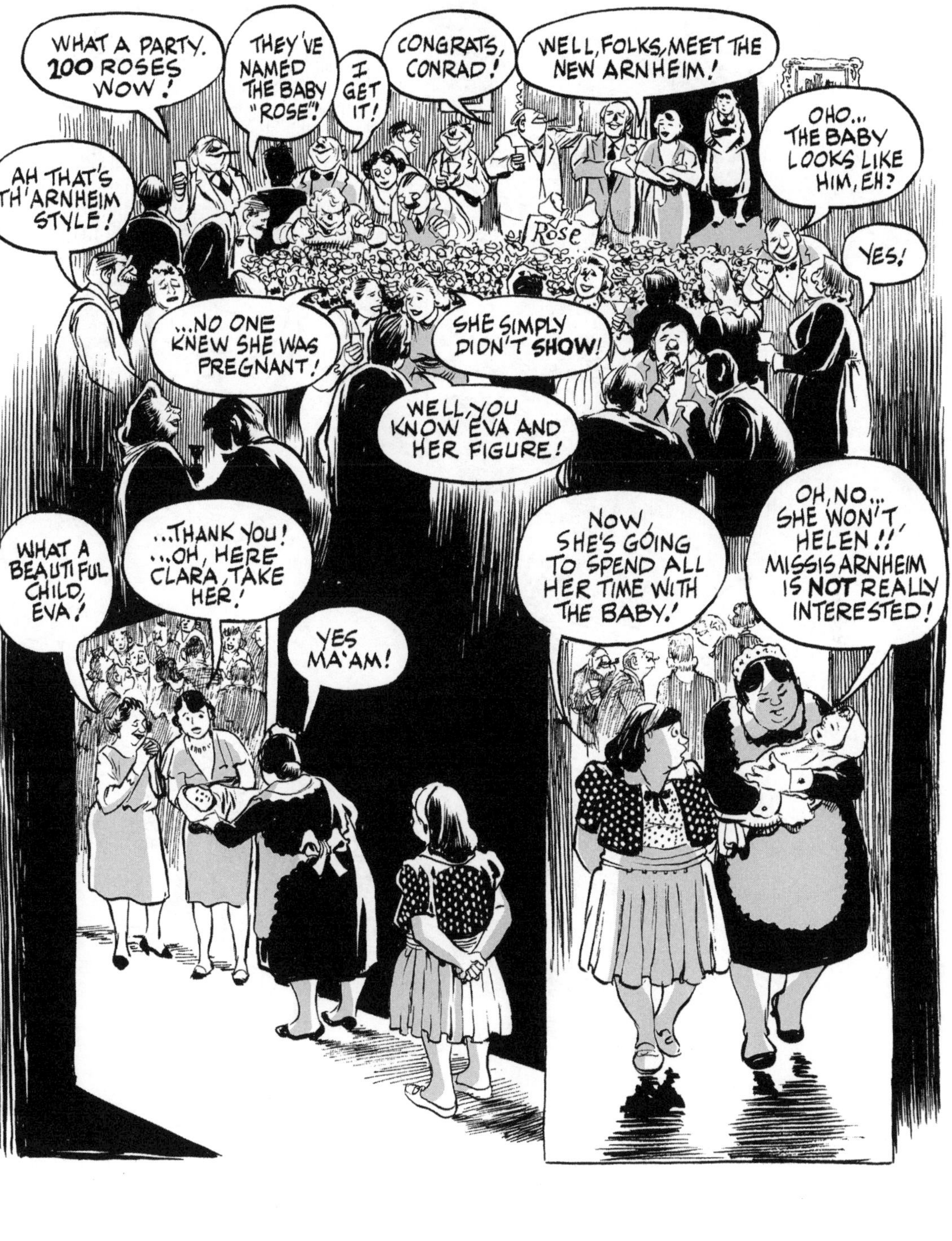

WHAT A PARTY. 200 ROSES WOW!
THEY'VE NAMED THE BABY "ROSE"!
I GET IT!
CONGRATS, CONRAD!
WELL, FOLKS, MEET THE NEW ARNHEIM!
AH THAT'S TH'ARNHEIM STYLE!
OHO... THE BABY LOOKS LIKE HIM, EH?
Rose
YES!
...NO ONE KNEW SHE WAS PREGNANT!
SHE SIMPLY DIDN'T SHOW!
WELL, YOU KNOW EVA AND HER FIGURE!
WHAT A BEAUTIFUL CHILD, EVA!
...THANK YOU! ...OH, HERE CLARA, TAKE HER!
YES MA'AM!
NOW, SHE'S GOING TO SPEND ALL HER TIME WITH THE BABY!
OH, NO... SHE WON'T, HELEN!! MISSIS ARNHEIM IS NOT REALLY INTERESTED!

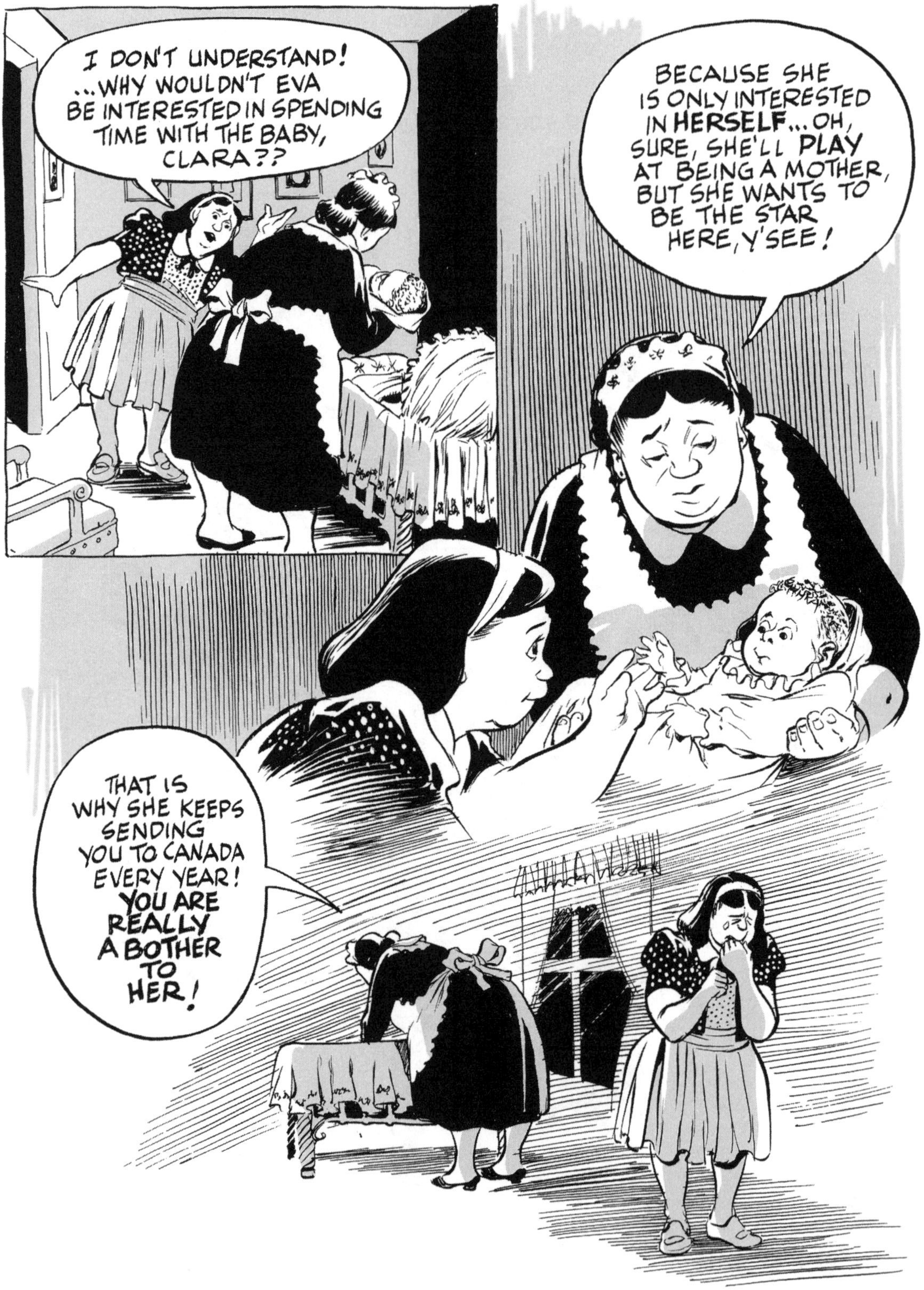
I DON'T UNDERSTAND! ...WHY WOULDN'T EVA BE INTERESTED IN SPENDING TIME WITH THE BABY, CLARA??
BECAUSE SHE IS ONLY INTERESTED IN HERSELF... OH, SURE, SHE'LL PLAY AT BEING A MOTHER, BUT SHE WANTS TO BE THE STAR HERE, Y'SEE!
THAT IS WHY SHE KEEPS SENDING YOU TO CANADA EVERY YEAR! YOU ARE REALLY A BOTHER TO HER!

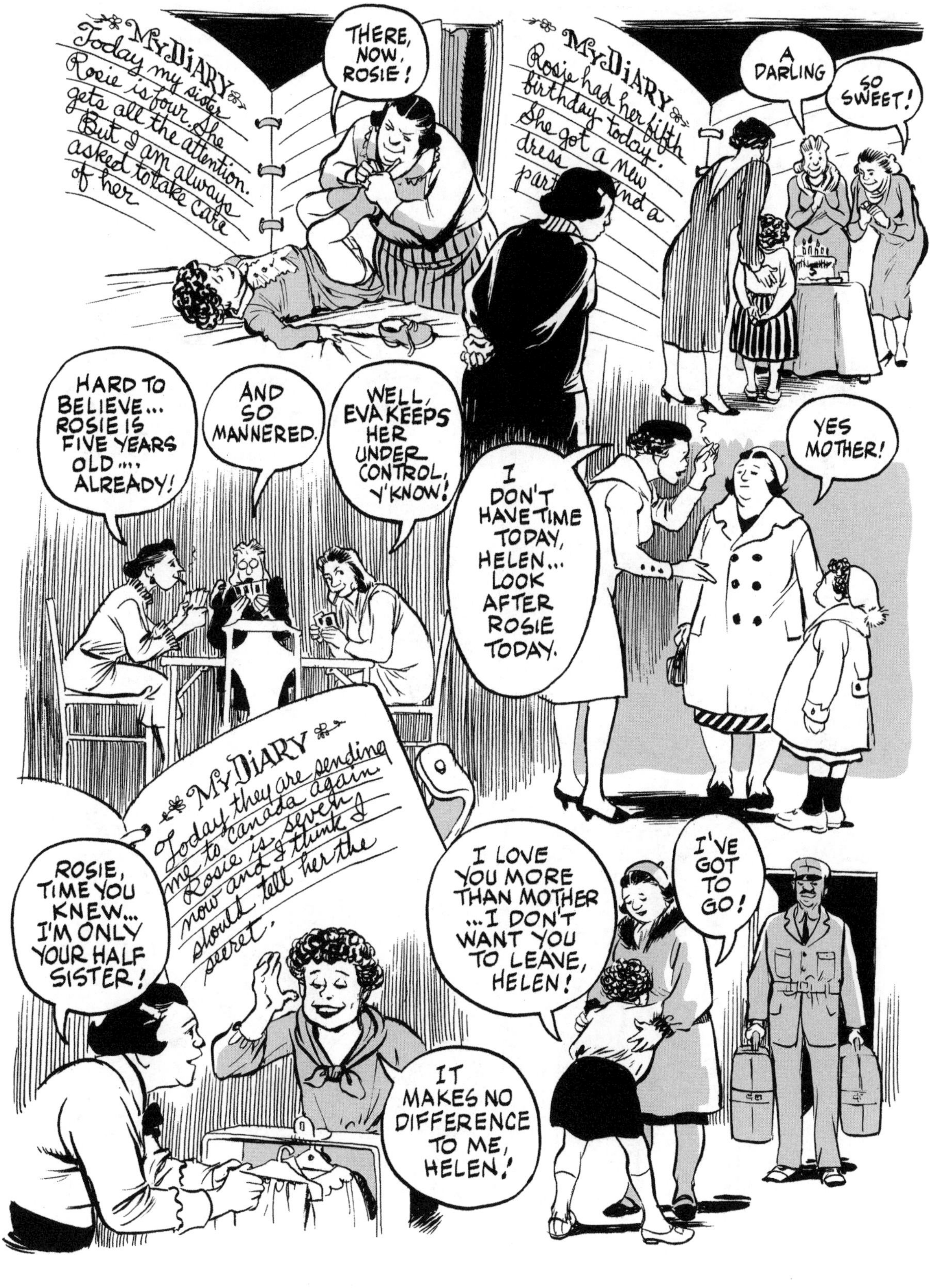
My Diary
Today my sister Rosie is four. She gets all the attention. But I am always asked to take care of her
THERE, NOW, ROSIE!
My Diary
Rosie had her fifth birthday today. She got a new dress and a party
A DARLING
SO SWEET!
HARD TO BELIEVE... ROSIE IS FIVE YEARS OLD.... ALREADY!
AND SO MANNERED.
WELL, EVA KEEPS HER UNDER CONTROL, Y'KNOW!
I DON'T HAVE TIME TODAY, HELEN... LOOK AFTER ROSIE TODAY.
YES MOTHER!
My Diary
Today they are sending me to canada again. Rosie is seven now and I think I should tell her the secret.
ROSIE, TIME YOU KNEW... I'M ONLY YOUR HALF SISTER!
IT MAKES NO DIFFERENCE TO ME, HELEN!
I LOVE YOU MORE THAN MOTHER ...I DON'T WANT YOU TO LEAVE, HELEN!
I'VE GOT TO GO!

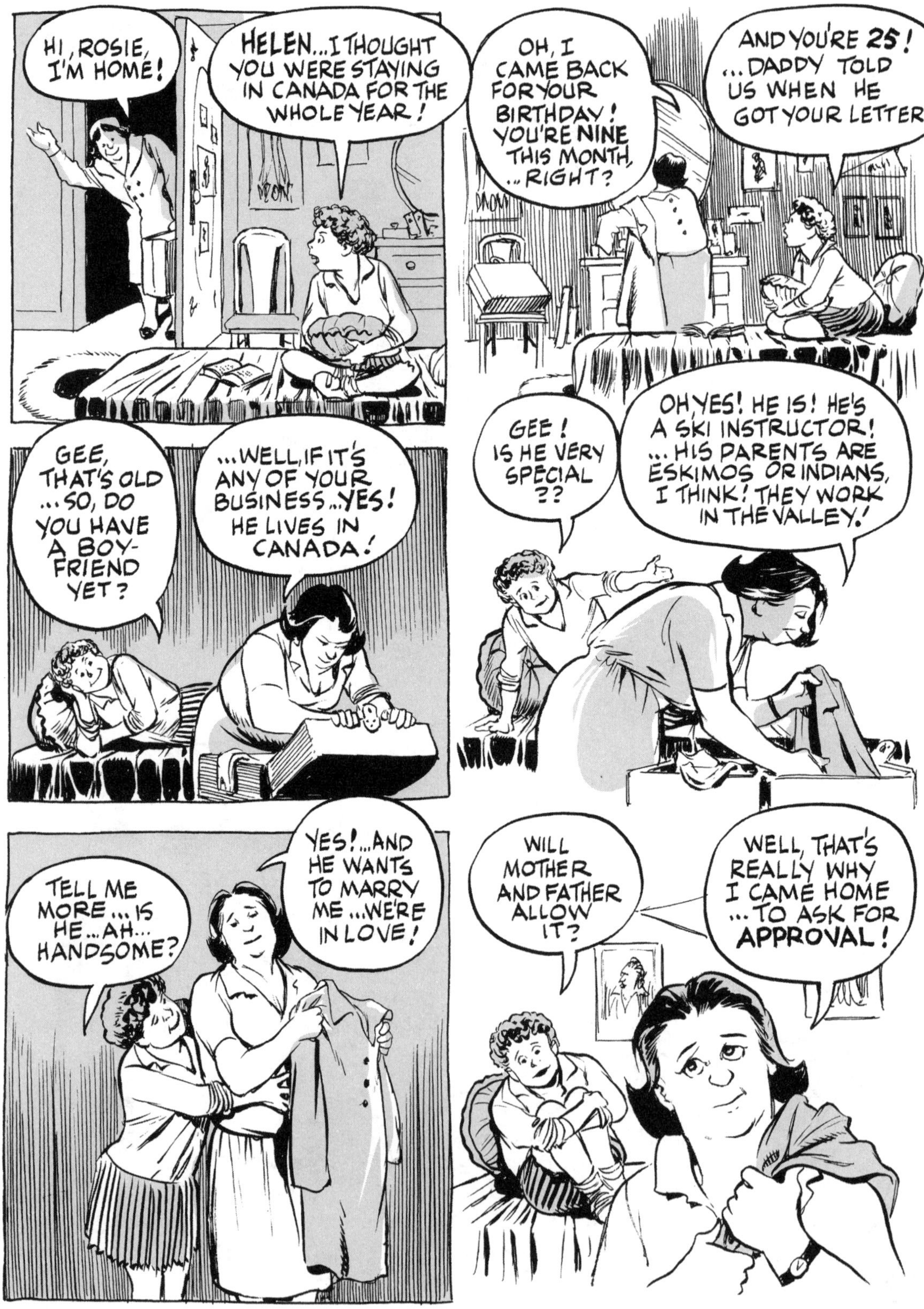
HI, ROSIE, I'M HOME!
HELEN...I THOUGHT YOU WERE STAYING IN CANADA FOR THE WHOLE YEAR!
OH, I CAME BACK FOR YOUR BIRTHDAY! YOU'RE NINE THIS MONTH, ..RIGHT?
AND YOU'RE 25! ...DADDY TOLD US WHEN HE GOT YOUR LETTER.
GEE, THAT'S OLD ...SO, DO YOU HAVE A BOY-FRIEND YET?
...WELL, IF IT'S ANY OF YOUR BUSINESS...YES! HE LIVES IN CANADA!
GEE! IS HE VERY SPECIAL ??
OH YES! HE IS! HE'S A SKI INSTRUCTOR! ...HIS PARENTS ARE ESKIMOS OR INDIANS, I THINK! THEY WORK IN THE VALLEY!
TELL ME MORE... IS HE...AH... HANDSOME?
YES!...AND HE WANTS TO MARRY ME...WE'RE IN LOVE!
WILL MOTHER AND FATHER ALLOW IT?
WELL, THAT'S REALLY WHY I CAME HOME ...TO ASK FOR APPROVAL!

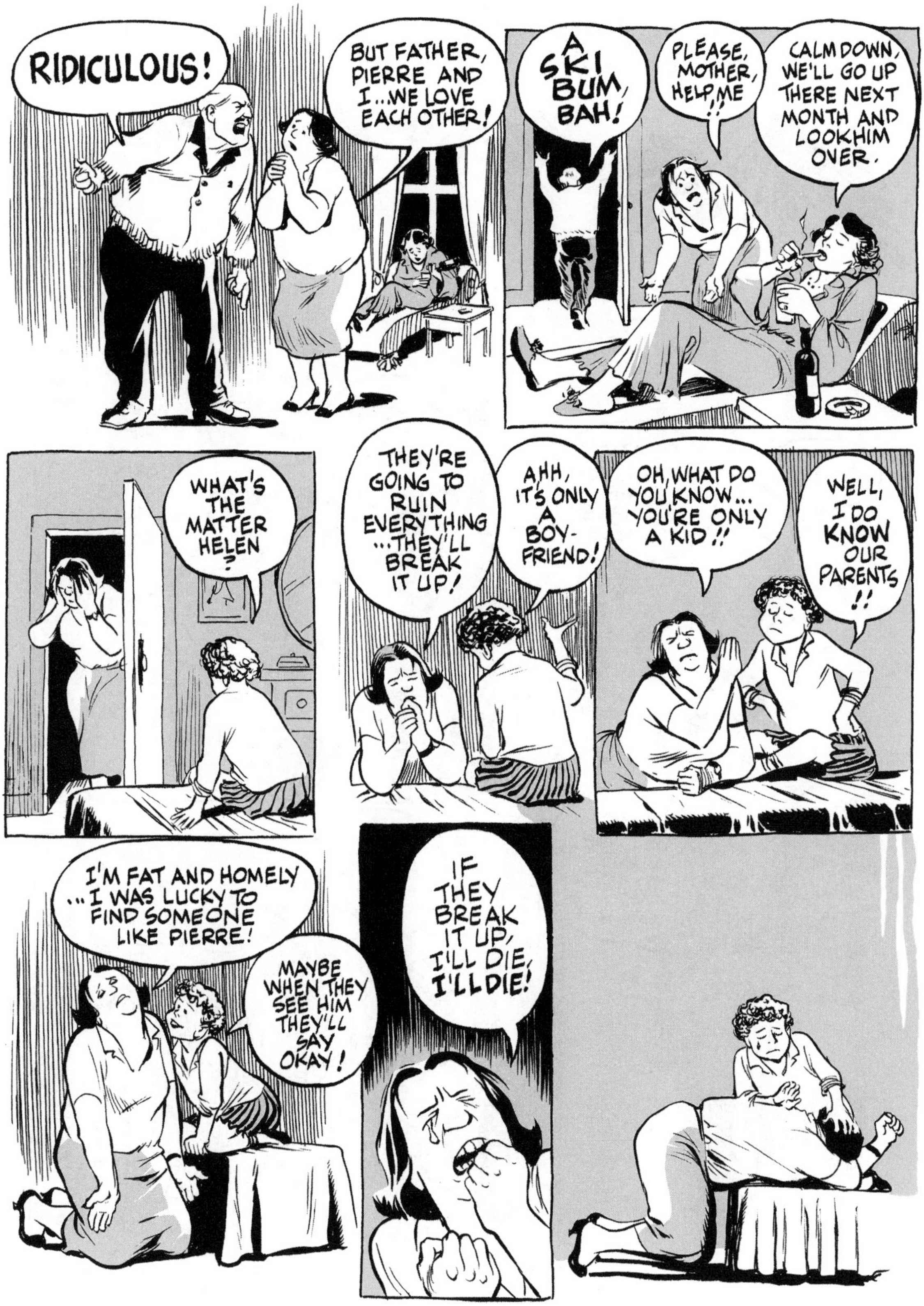
RIDICULOUS!
BUT FATHER, PIERRE AND I...WE LOVE EACH OTHER!
A SKI BUM, BAH!
PLEASE, MOTHER, HELP ME!!
CALM DOWN, WE'LL GO UP THERE NEXT MONTH AND LOOK HIM OVER.
WHAT'S THE MATTER HELEN?
THEY'RE GOING TO RUIN EVERYTHING ...THEY'LL BREAK IT UP!
AHH, IT'S ONLY A BOY-FRIEND!
OH, WHAT DO YOU KNOW... YOU'RE ONLY A KID!!
WELL, I DO KNOW OUR PARENTS!!
I'M FAT AND HOMELY ...I WAS LUCKY TO FIND SOMEONE LIKE PIERRE!
MAYBE WHEN THEY SEE HIM THEY'LL SAY OKAY!
IF THEY BREAK IT UP, I'LL DIE, I'LL DIE!

. . . That January . . .
In Canada . . .

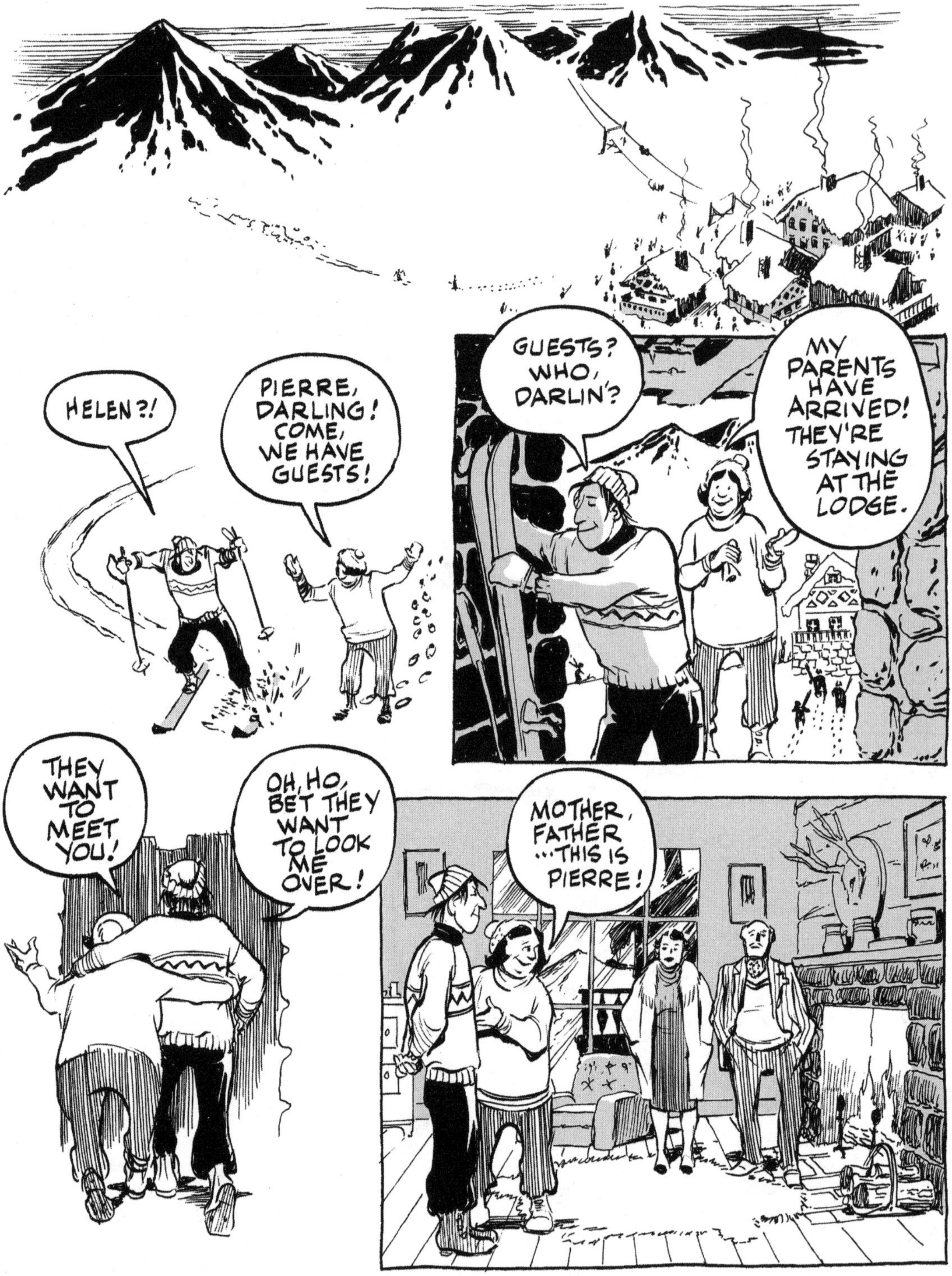
HELEN?!
PIERRE, DARLING! COME, WE HAVE GUESTS!
GUESTS? WHO, DARLIN'?
MY PARENTS HAVE ARRIVED! THEY'RE STAYING AT THE LODGE.
THEY WANT TO MEET YOU!
OH, HO, BET THEY WANT TO LOOK ME OVER!
MOTHER, FATHER ...THIS IS PIERRE!

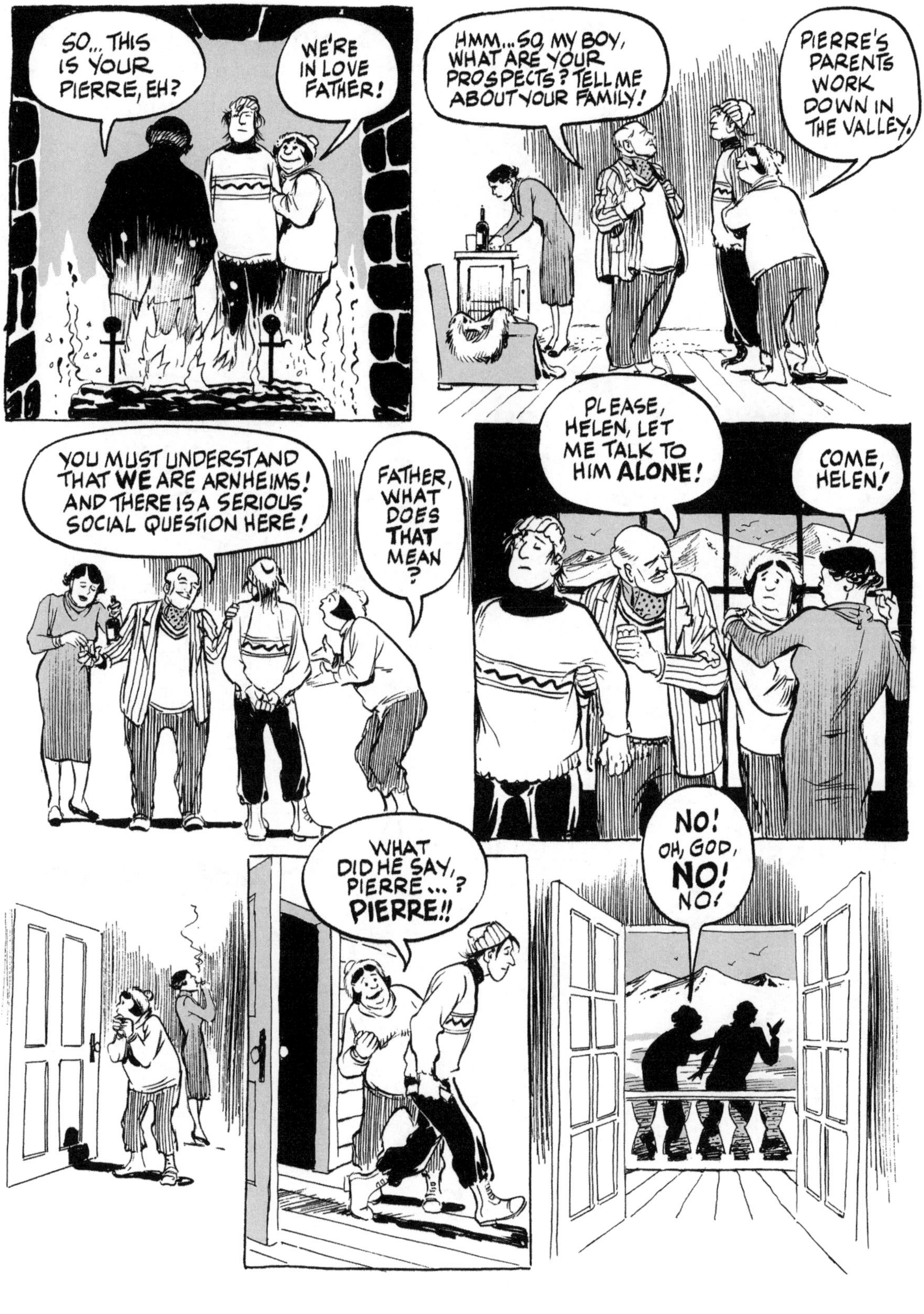
SO... THIS IS YOUR PIERRE, EH?
WE'RE IN LOVE FATHER!
HMM... SO, MY BOY, WHAT ARE YOUR PROSPECTS? TELL ME ABOUT YOUR FAMILY!
PIERRE'S PARENTS WORK DOWN IN THE VALLEY.
YOU MUST UNDERSTAND THAT WE ARE ARNHEIMS! AND THERE IS A SERIOUS SOCIAL QUESTION HERE!
FATHER, WHAT DOES THAT MEAN?
PLEASE, HELEN, LET ME TALK TO HIM ALONE!
COME, HELEN!
WHAT DID HE SAY, PIERRE...? PIERRE!!
NO! OH, GOD, NO! NO!

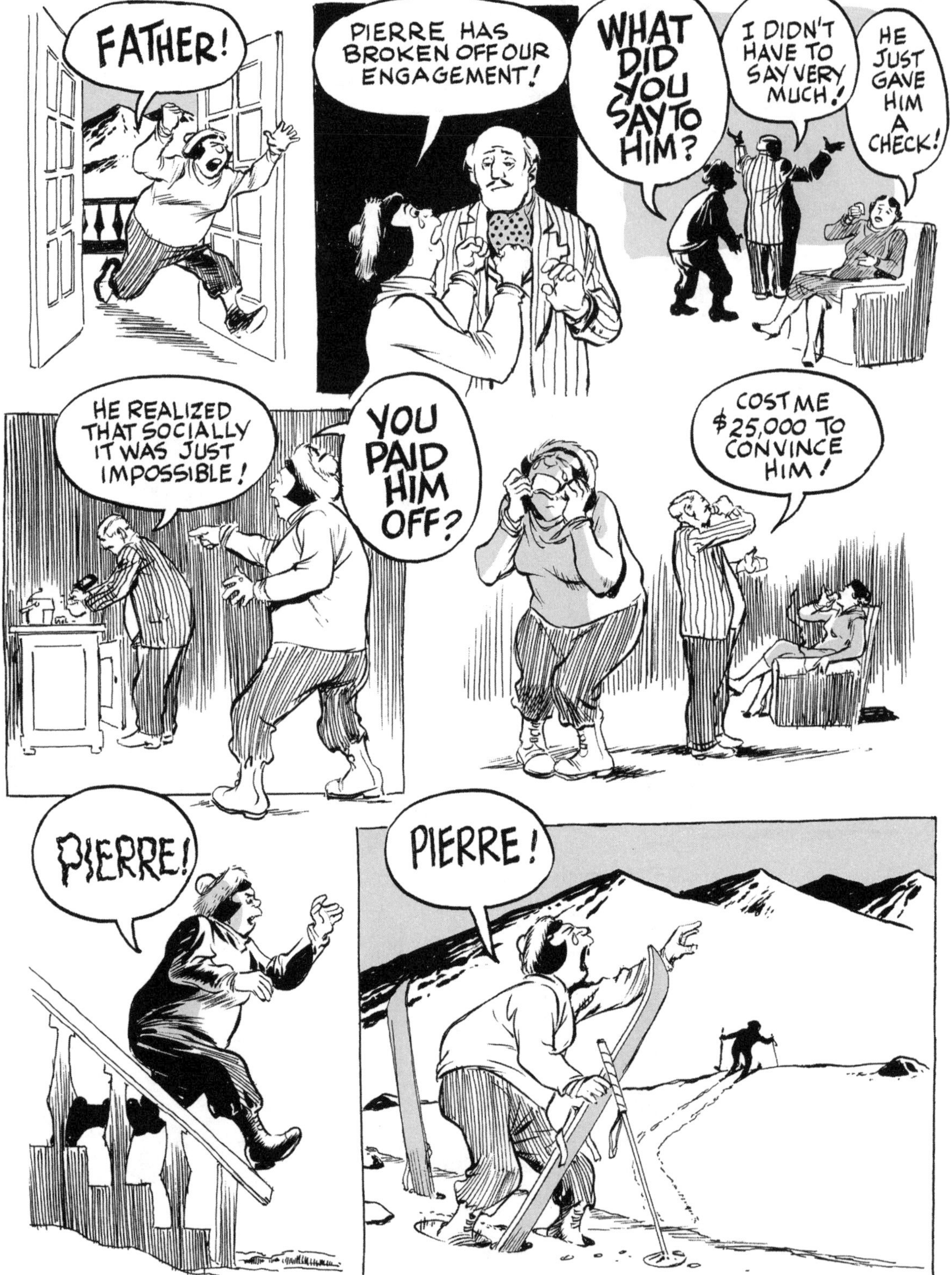
FATHER!
PIERRE HAS BROKEN OFF OUR ENGAGEMENT!
WHAT DID YOU SAY TO HIM?
I DIDN'T HAVE TO SAY VERY MUCH!
HE JUST GAVE HIM A CHECK!
HE REALIZED THAT SOCIALLY IT WAS JUST IMPOSSIBLE!
YOU PAID HIM OFF?
COST ME $25,000 TO CONVINCE HIM!
PIERRE!
PIERRE!

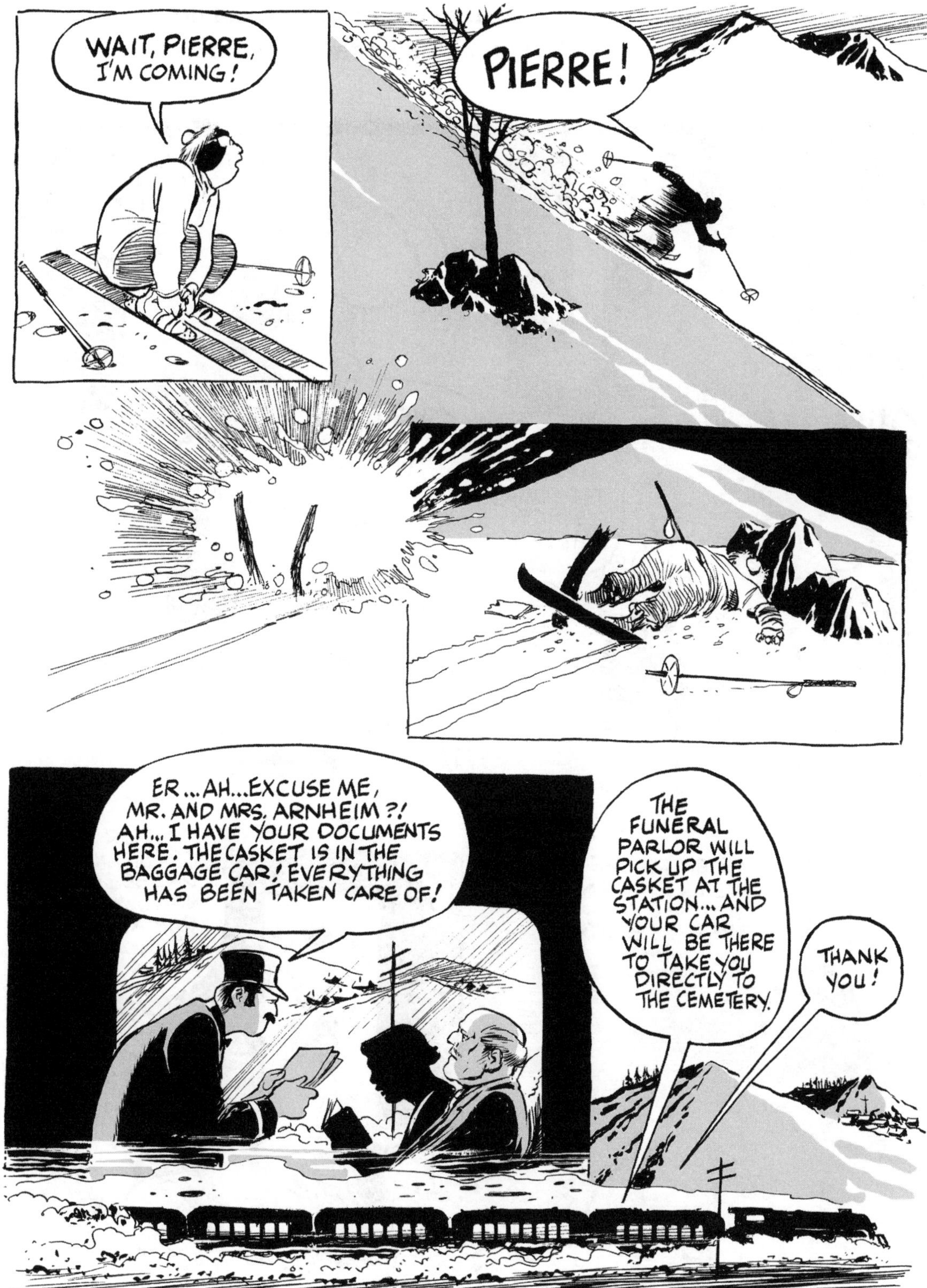
WAIT, PIERRE, I'M COMING!
PIERRE!
ER...AH...EXCUSE ME, MR. AND MRS. ARNHEIM?! AH... I HAVE YOUR DOCUMENTS HERE. THE CASKET IS IN THE BAGGAGE CAR! EVERYTHING HAS BEEN TAKEN CARE OF!
THE FUNERAL PARLOR WILL PICK UP THE CASKET AT THE STATION... AND YOUR CAR WILL BE THERE TO TAKE YOU DIRECTLY TO THE CEMETERY.
THANK YOU!

Outward appearances, so important to the Arnheims, did not change, but the tragedy had an impact upon the dynamics between Conrad and Eva.

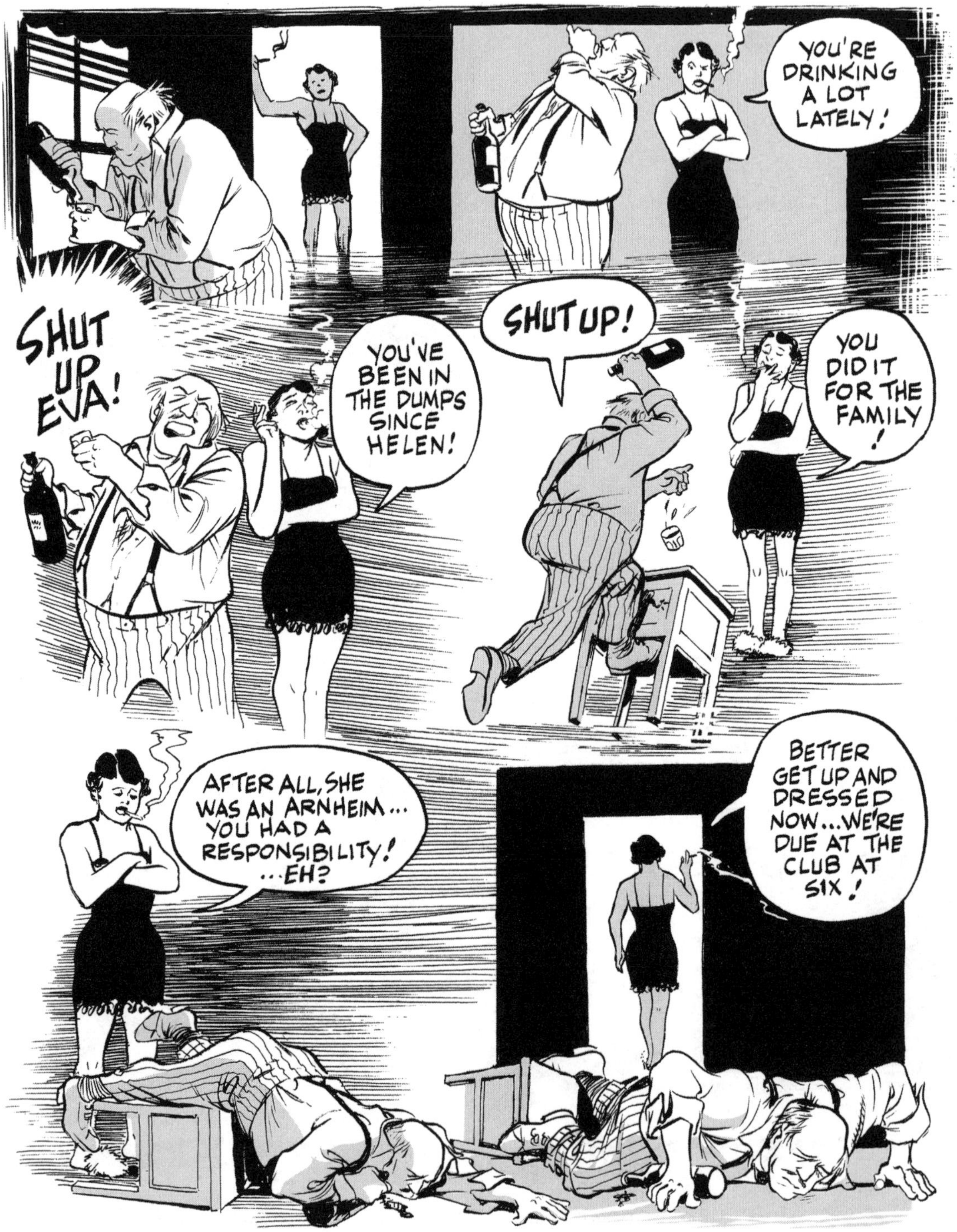
YOU'RE DRINKING A LOT LATELY!
SHUT UP EVA!
YOU'VE BEEN IN THE DUMPS SINCE HELEN!
SHUT UP!
YOU DID IT FOR THE FAMILY!
AFTER ALL, SHE WAS AN ARNHEIM... YOU HAD A RESPONSIBILITY! ...EH?
BETTER GET UP AND DRESSED NOW... WE'RE DUE AT THE CLUB AT SIX!

Eva Arnheim was now consolidating control over the family's social position. With Helen's passing, she was free to concentrate on Rosie.

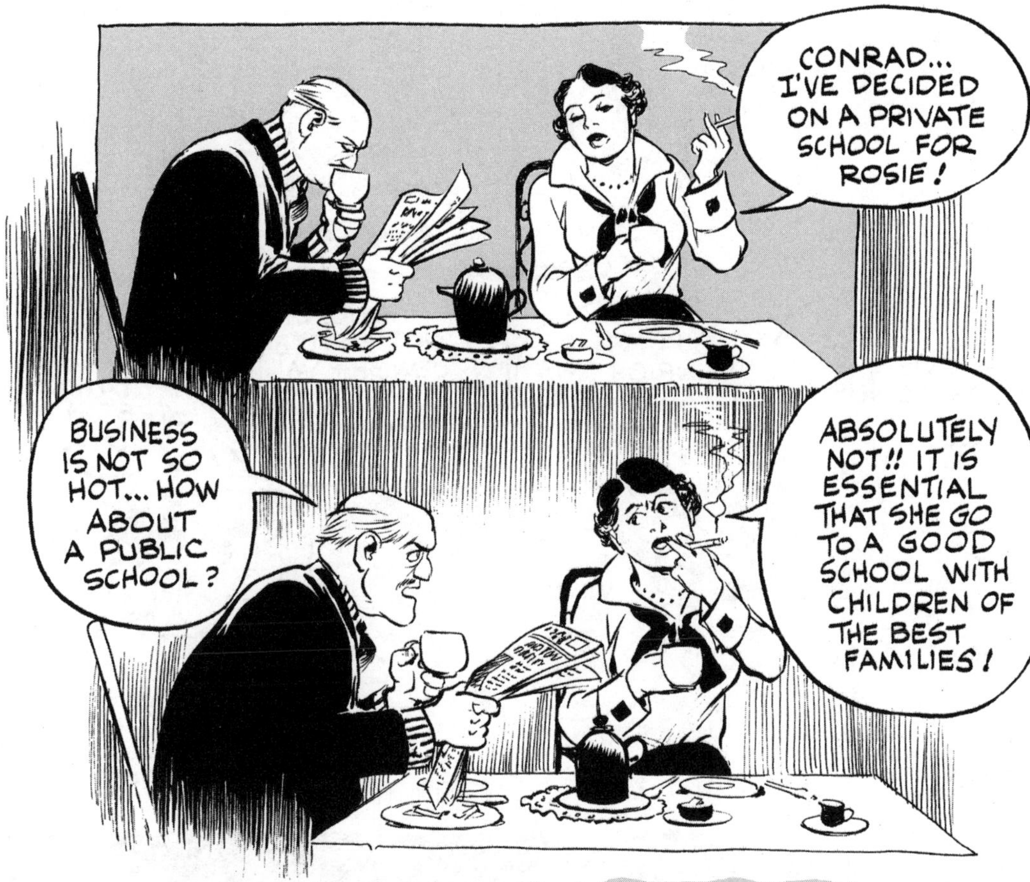
CONRAD... I'VE DECIDED ON A PRIVATE SCHOOL FOR ROSIE!
BUSINESS IS NOT SO HOT... HOW ABOUT A PUBLIC SCHOOL?
ABSOLUTELY NOT!! IT IS ESSENTIAL THAT SHE GO TO A GOOD SCHOOL WITH CHILDREN OF THE BEST FAMILIES!

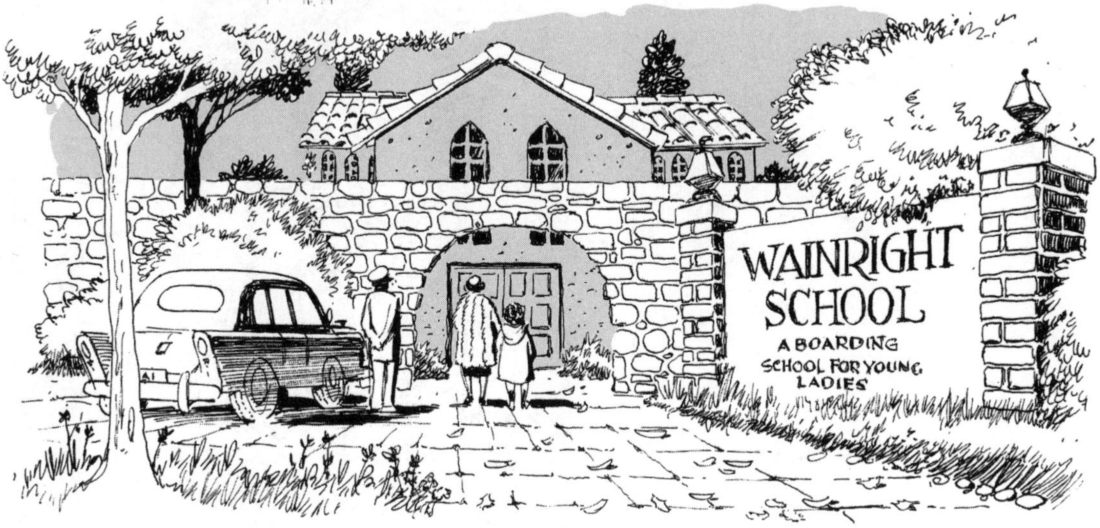
WAINRIGHT SCHOOL
A BOARDING SCHOOL FOR YOUNG LADIES

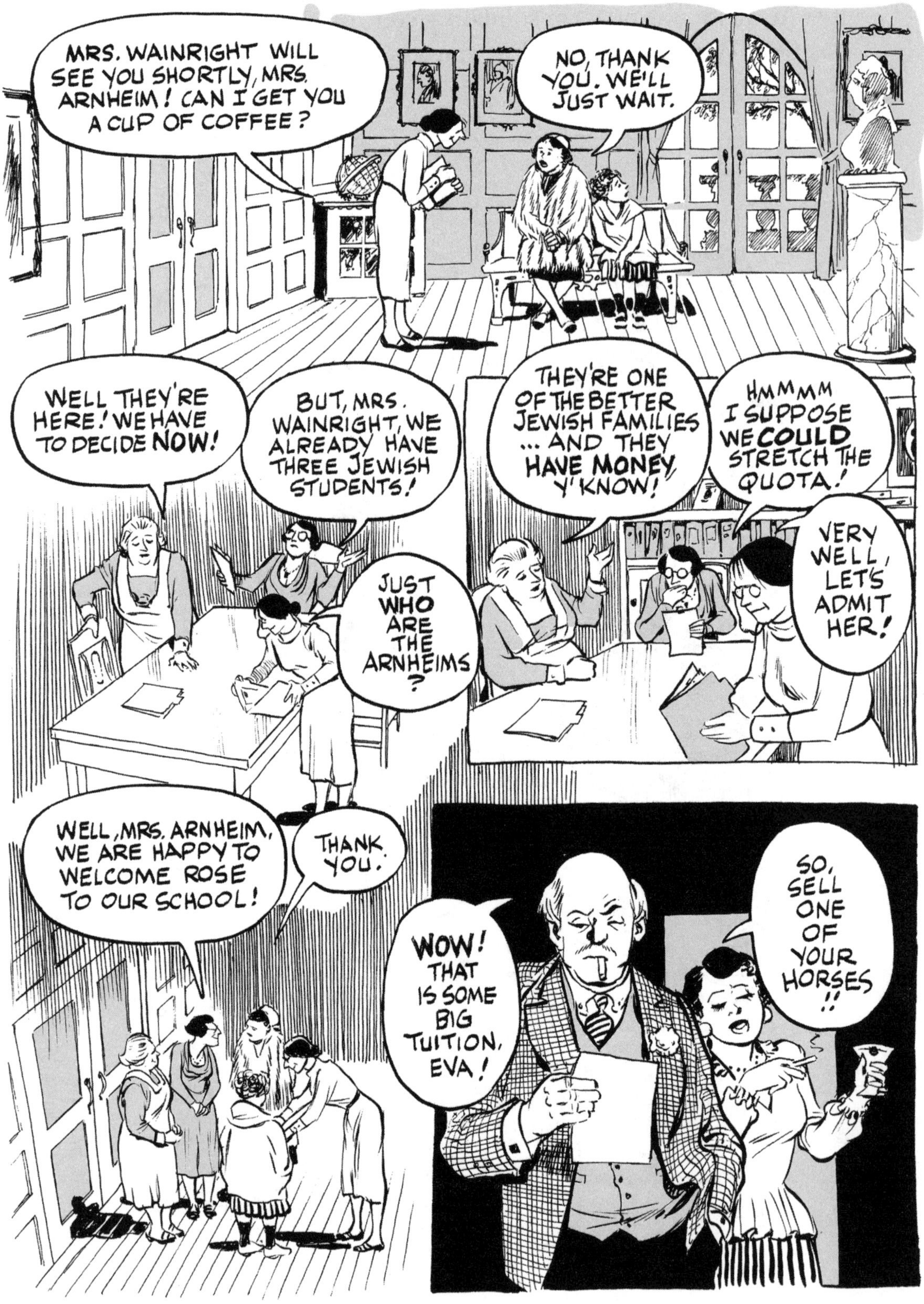
MRS. WAINRIGHT WILL SEE YOU SHORTLY, MRS. ARNHEIM! CAN I GET YOU A CUP OF COFFEE?
NO, THANK YOU. WE'LL JUST WAIT.
WELL THEY'RE HERE! WE HAVE TO DECIDE NOW!
BUT, MRS. WAINRIGHT, WE ALREADY HAVE THREE JEWISH STUDENTS!
JUST WHO ARE THE ARNHEIMS?
THEY'RE ONE OF THE BETTER JEWISH FAMILIES ... AND THEY HAVE MONEY, Y'KNOW!
HMMMM I SUPPOSE WE COULD STRETCH THE QUOTA!
VERY WELL, LET'S ADMIT HER!
WELL, MRS. ARNHEIM, WE ARE HAPPY TO WELCOME ROSE TO OUR SCHOOL!
THANK YOU.
WOW! THAT IS SOME BIG TUITION, EVA!
SO, SELL ONE OF YOUR HORSES!!

The war's end opened a new era in the stock market. Trading was now becoming more sophisticated. There even were days when a million shares were traded. One or two houses were starting mutual funds, and more pension funds were enlarging their stock portfolios.

The Arnheim Company still catered to small holders—widows, retirees and old-line family estates.

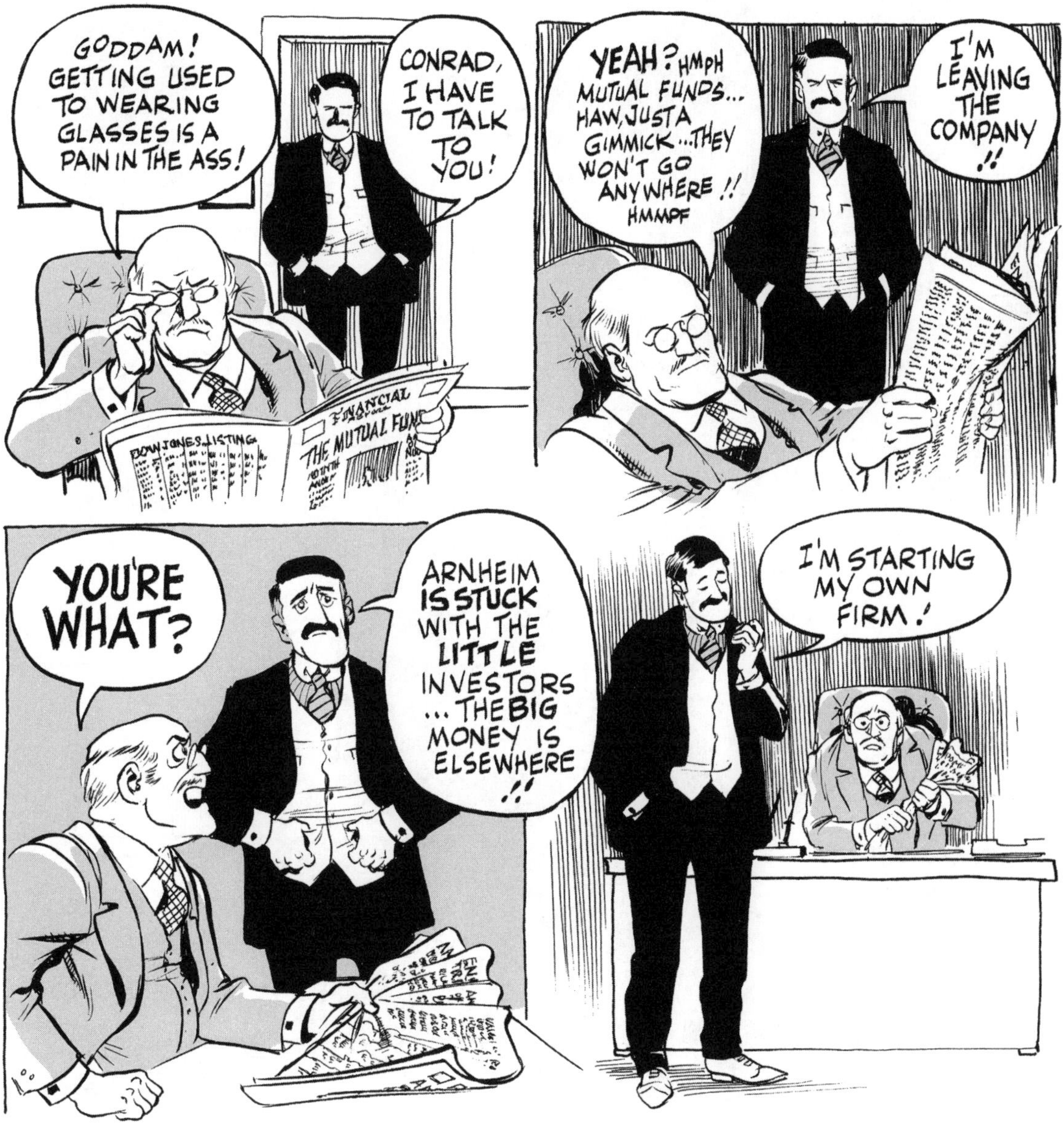

GODDAM! GETTING USED TO WEARING GLASSES IS A PAIN IN THE ASS!
CONRAD, I HAVE TO TALK TO YOU!
FINANCIAL
DOW JONES LISTING
THE MUTUAL FUNDS
YEAH? HMPH MUTUAL FUNDS... HAW, JUST A GIMMICK...THEY WON'T GO ANYWHERE!! HMMPF
I'M LEAVING THE COMPANY!!
YOU'RE WHAT?
ARNHEIM IS STUCK WITH THE LITTLE INVESTORS ...THE BIG MONEY IS ELSEWHERE!!
I'M STARTING MY OWN FIRM!

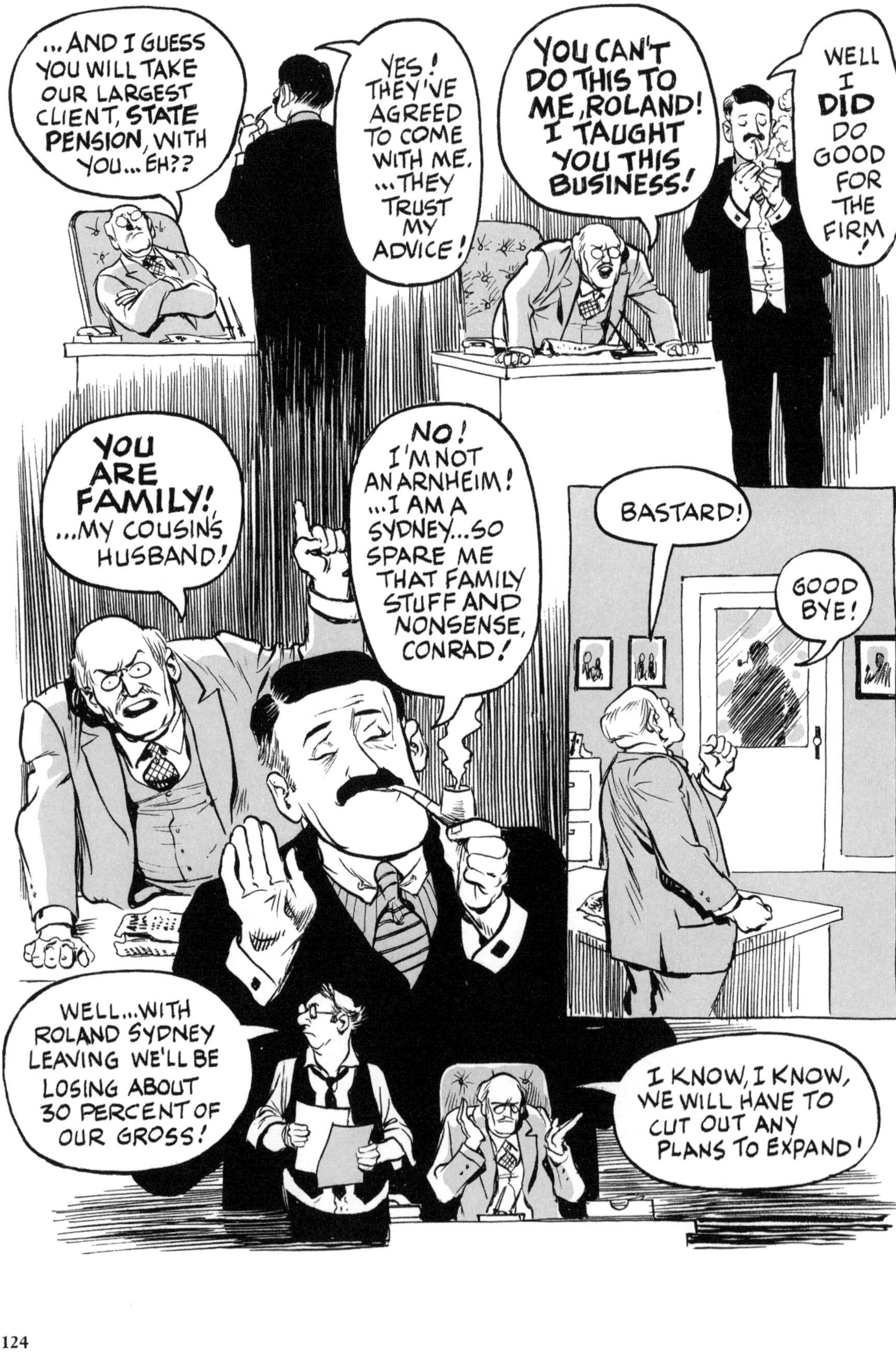
...AND I GUESS YOU WILL TAKE OUR LARGEST CLIENT, STATE PENSION, WITH YOU... EH??
YES! THEY'VE AGREED TO COME WITH ME. ...THEY TRUST MY ADVICE!
YOU CAN'T DO THIS TO ME, ROLAND! I TAUGHT YOU THIS BUSINESS!
WELL I DID DO GOOD FOR THE FIRM!
YOU ARE FAMILY! ...MY COUSIN'S HUSBAND!
NO! I'M NOT AN ARNHEIM! ...I AM A SYDNEY... SO SPARE ME THAT FAMILY STUFF AND NONSENSE, CONRAD!
BASTARD!
GOOD BYE!
WELL... WITH ROLAND SYDNEY LEAVING WE'LL BE LOSING ABOUT 30 PERCENT OF OUR GROSS!
I KNOW, I KNOW, WE WILL HAVE TO CUT OUT ANY PLANS TO EXPAND!

Rosie did well at Wainright, academically. But socially she remained out of the inner circle of student life. Independent and outspoken, she was rarely included socially.

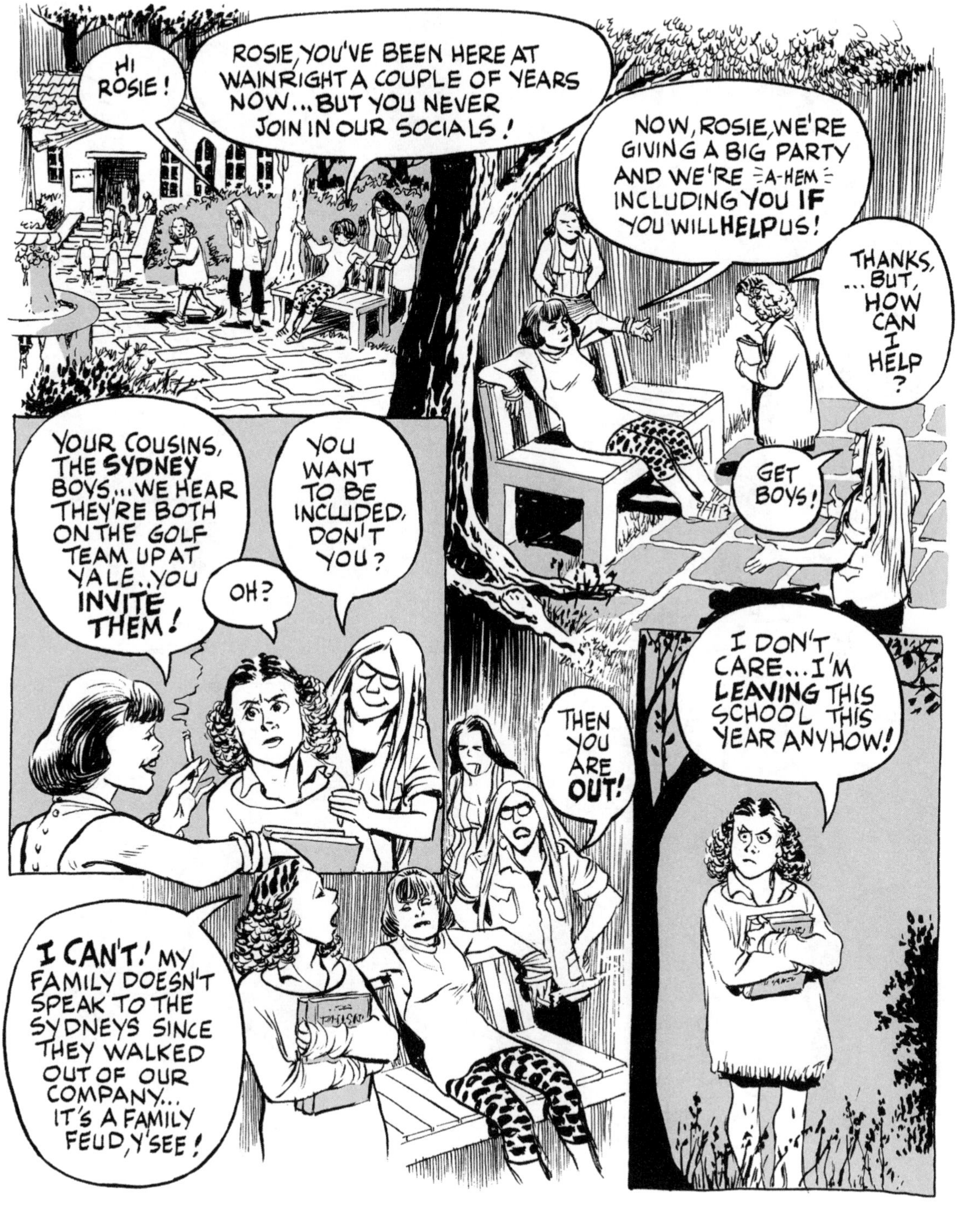
HI ROSIE!
ROSIE, YOU'VE BEEN HERE AT WAINRIGHT A COUPLE OF YEARS NOW... BUT YOU NEVER JOIN IN OUR SOCIALS!
NOW, ROSIE, WE'RE GIVING A BIG PARTY AND WE'RE =A-HEM= INCLUDING YOU IF YOU WILL HELP US!
THANKS, ...BUT, HOW CAN I HELP?
GET BOYS!
YOUR COUSINS, THE SYDNEY BOYS... WE HEAR THEY'RE BOTH ON THE GOLF TEAM UP AT YALE.. YOU INVITE THEM!
OH?
YOU WANT TO BE INCLUDED, DON'T YOU?
I CAN'T! MY FAMILY DOESN'T SPEAK TO THE SYDNEYS SINCE THEY WALKED OUT OF OUR COMPANY... IT'S A FAMILY FEUD, Y'SEE!
THEN YOU ARE OUT!
I DON'T CARE... I'M LEAVING THIS SCHOOL THIS YEAR ANYHOW!

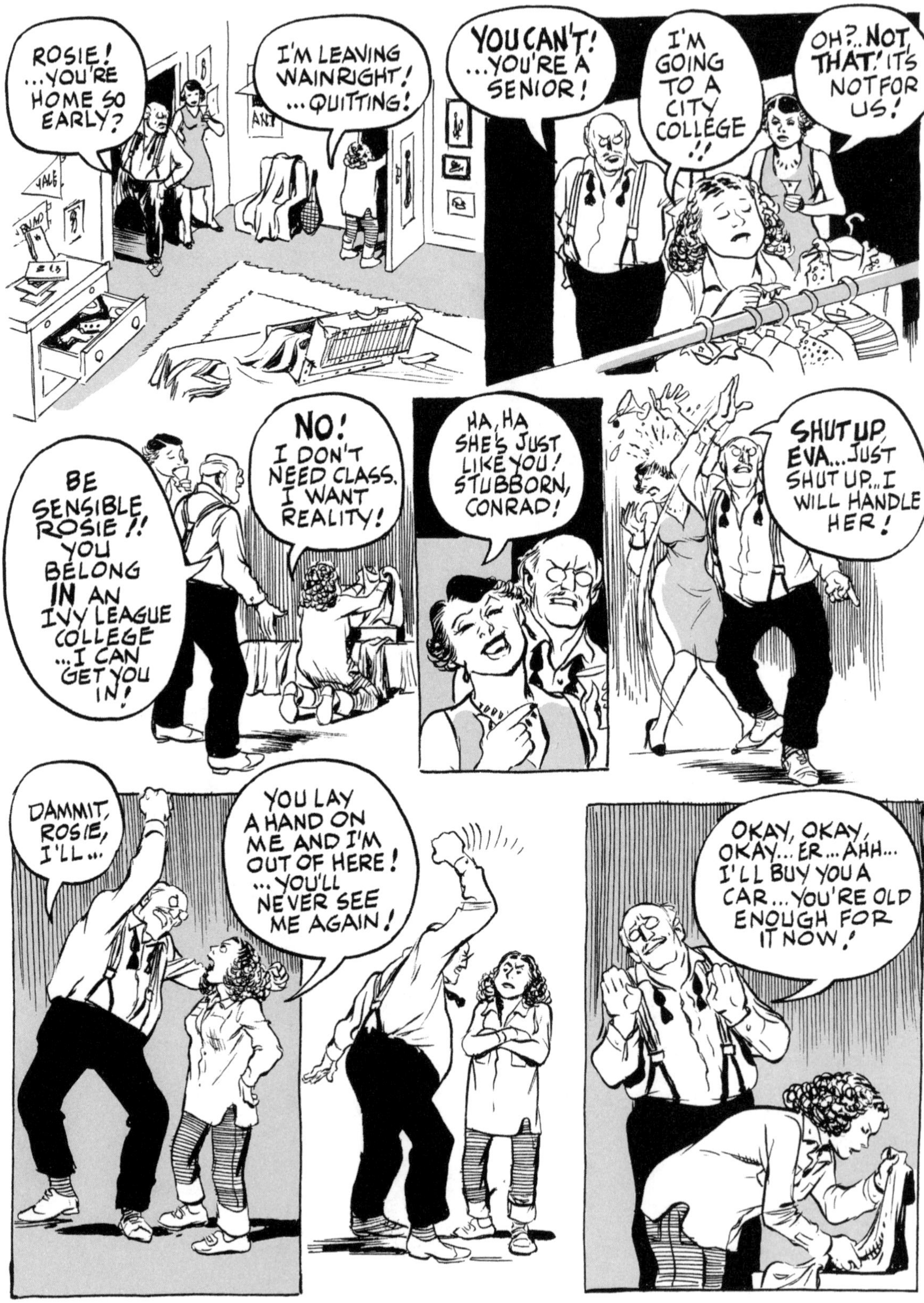
ROSIE! ...YOU'RE HOME SO EARLY?
I'M LEAVING WAINRIGHT! ...QUITTING!
YOU CAN'T! ...YOU'RE A SENIOR!
I'M GOING TO A CITY COLLEGE!!
OH?..NOT THAT! IT'S NOT FOR US!
BE SENSIBLE ROSIE!! YOU BELONG IN AN IVY LEAGUE COLLEGE ...I CAN GET YOU IN!
NO! I DON'T NEED CLASS. I WANT REALITY!
HA, HA SHE'S JUST LIKE YOU! STUBBORN, CONRAD!
SHUT UP EVA...JUST SHUT UP...I WILL HANDLE HER!
DAMMIT, ROSIE, I'LL...
YOU LAY A HAND ON ME AND I'M OUT OF HERE! ...YOU'LL NEVER SEE ME AGAIN!
OKAY, OKAY, OKAY... ER... AHH... I'LL BUY YOU A CAR... YOU'RE OLD ENOUGH FOR IT NOW!

So Rosie remained home but went to the school of her choice.

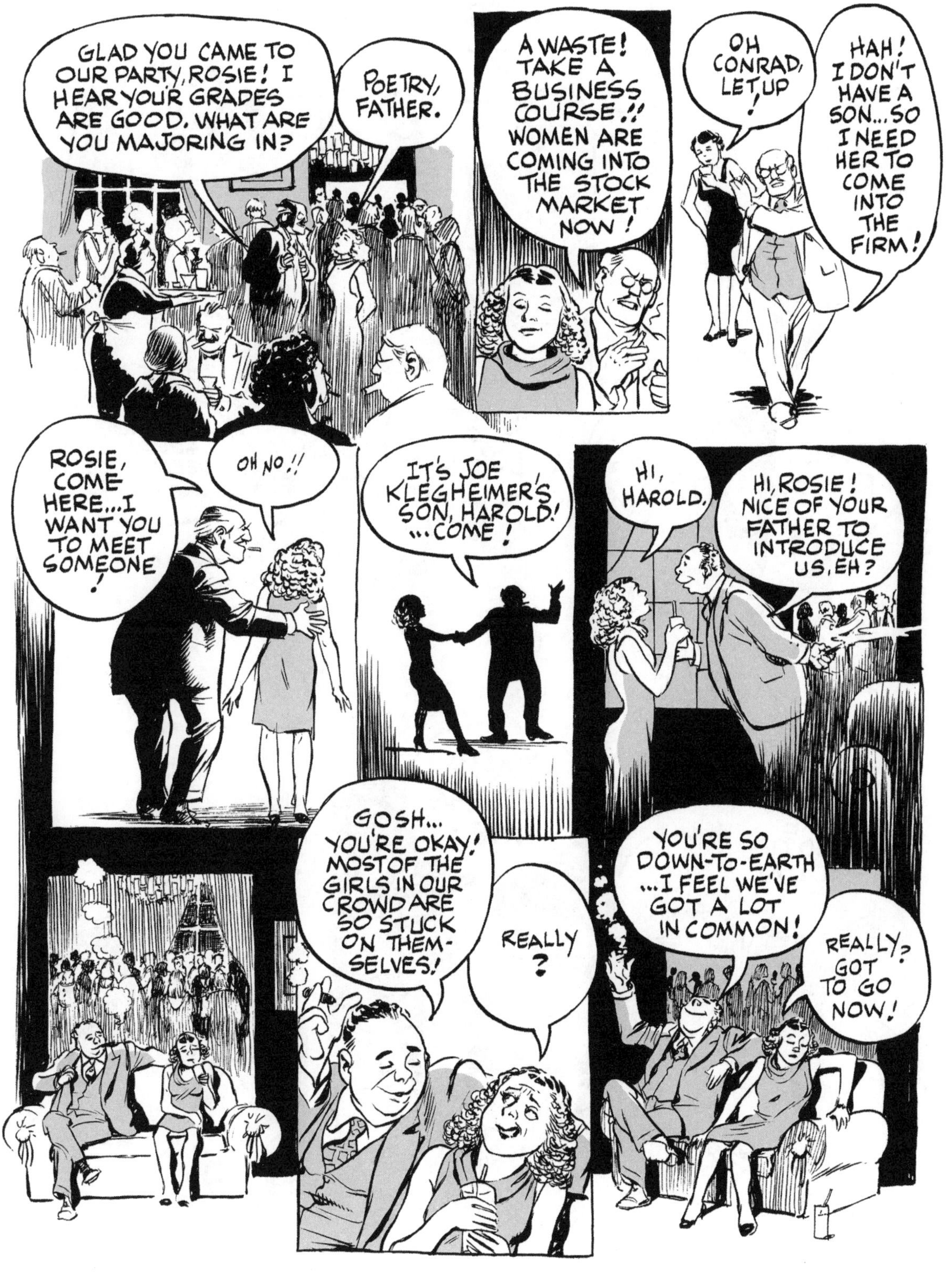
GLAD YOU CAME TO OUR PARTY, ROSIE! I HEAR YOUR GRADES ARE GOOD. WHAT ARE YOU MAJORING IN?
POETRY, FATHER.
A WASTE! TAKE A BUSINESS COURSE!! WOMEN ARE COMING INTO THE STOCK MARKET NOW!
OH CONRAD, LET UP!
HAH! I DON'T HAVE A SON... SO I NEED HER TO COME INTO THE FIRM!
ROSIE, COME HERE... I WANT YOU TO MEET SOMEONE!
OH NO!!
IT'S JOE KLEGHEIMER'S SON, HAROLD! ...COME!
HI, HAROLD.
HI, ROSIE! NICE OF YOUR FATHER TO INTRODUCE US, EH?
GOSH... YOU'RE OKAY! MOST OF THE GIRLS IN OUR CROWD ARE SO STUCK ON THEMSELVES!
REALLY?
YOU'RE SO DOWN-TO-EARTH ...I FEEL WE'VE GOT A LOT IN COMMON!
REALLY? GOT TO GO NOW!

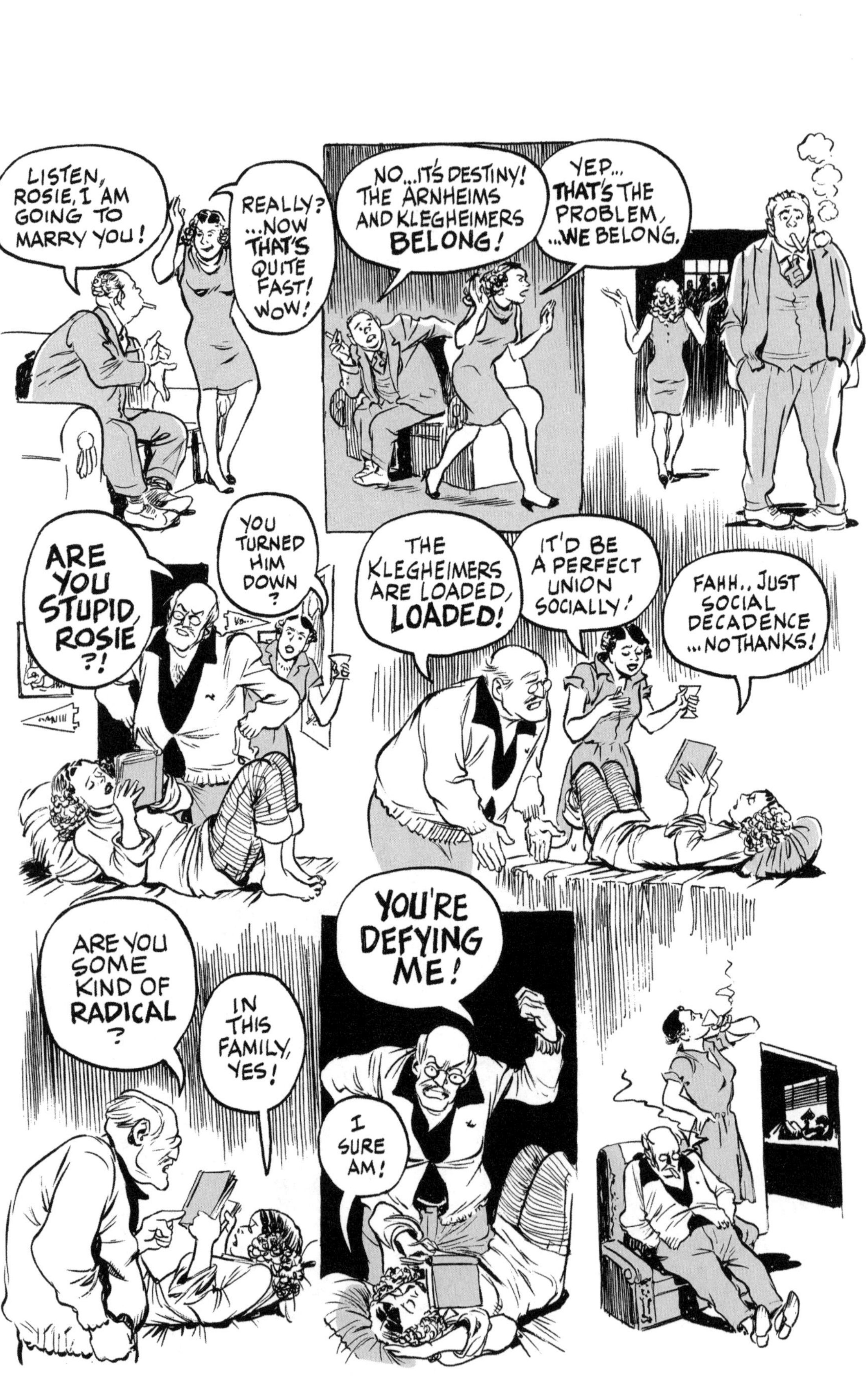
LISTEN, ROSIE, I AM GOING TO MARRY YOU!
REALLY? ...NOW THAT'S QUITE FAST! WOW!
NO...IT'S DESTINY! THE ARNHEIMS AND KLEGHEIMERS BELONG!
YEP... THAT'S THE PROBLEM, ...WE BELONG.
ARE YOU STUPID, ROSIE ?!
YOU TURNED HIM DOWN ?
THE KLEGHEIMERS ARE LOADED, LOADED!
IT'D BE A PERFECT UNION SOCIALLY!
FAHH.. JUST SOCIAL DECADENCE ...NO THANKS!
ARE YOU SOME KIND OF RADICAL ?
IN THIS FAMILY, YES!
YOU'RE DEFYING ME!
I SURE AM!

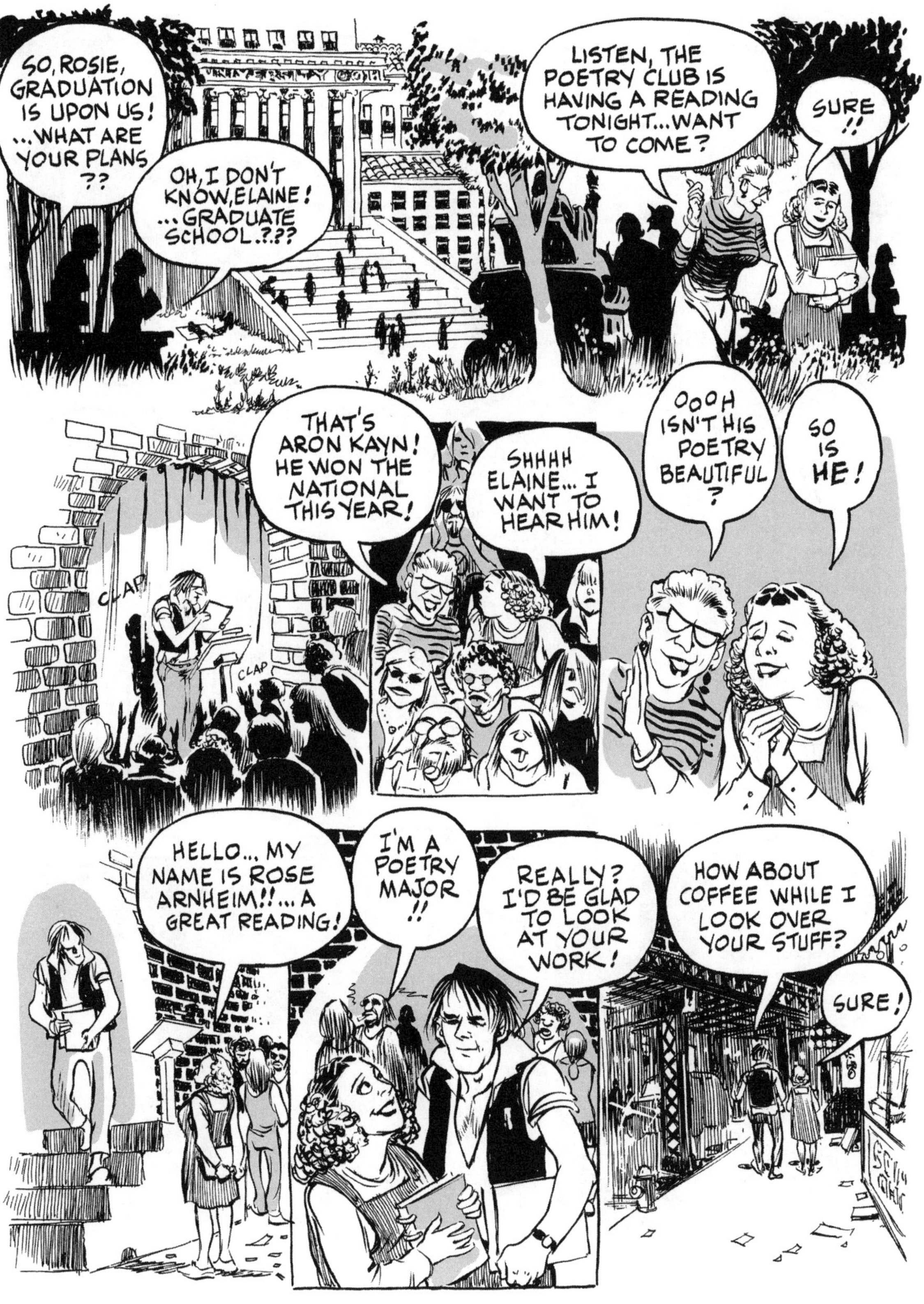

SO, ROSIE, GRADUATION IS UPON US! ...WHAT ARE YOUR PLANS ??
OH, I DON'T KNOW, ELAINE! ...GRADUATE SCHOOL.?.??
LISTEN, THE POETRY CLUB IS HAVING A READING TONIGHT...WANT TO COME?
SURE !!
CLAP
CLAP
THAT'S ARON KAYN! HE WON THE NATIONAL THIS YEAR!
SHHHH ELAINE... I WANT TO HEAR HIM!
OOOH ISN'T HIS POETRY BEAUTIFUL ?
SO IS HE!
HELLO... MY NAME IS ROSE ARNHEIM!!... A GREAT READING!
I'M A POETRY MAJOR !!
REALLY? I'D BE GLAD TO LOOK AT YOUR WORK!
HOW ABOUT COFFEE WHILE I LOOK OVER YOUR STUFF?
SURE!

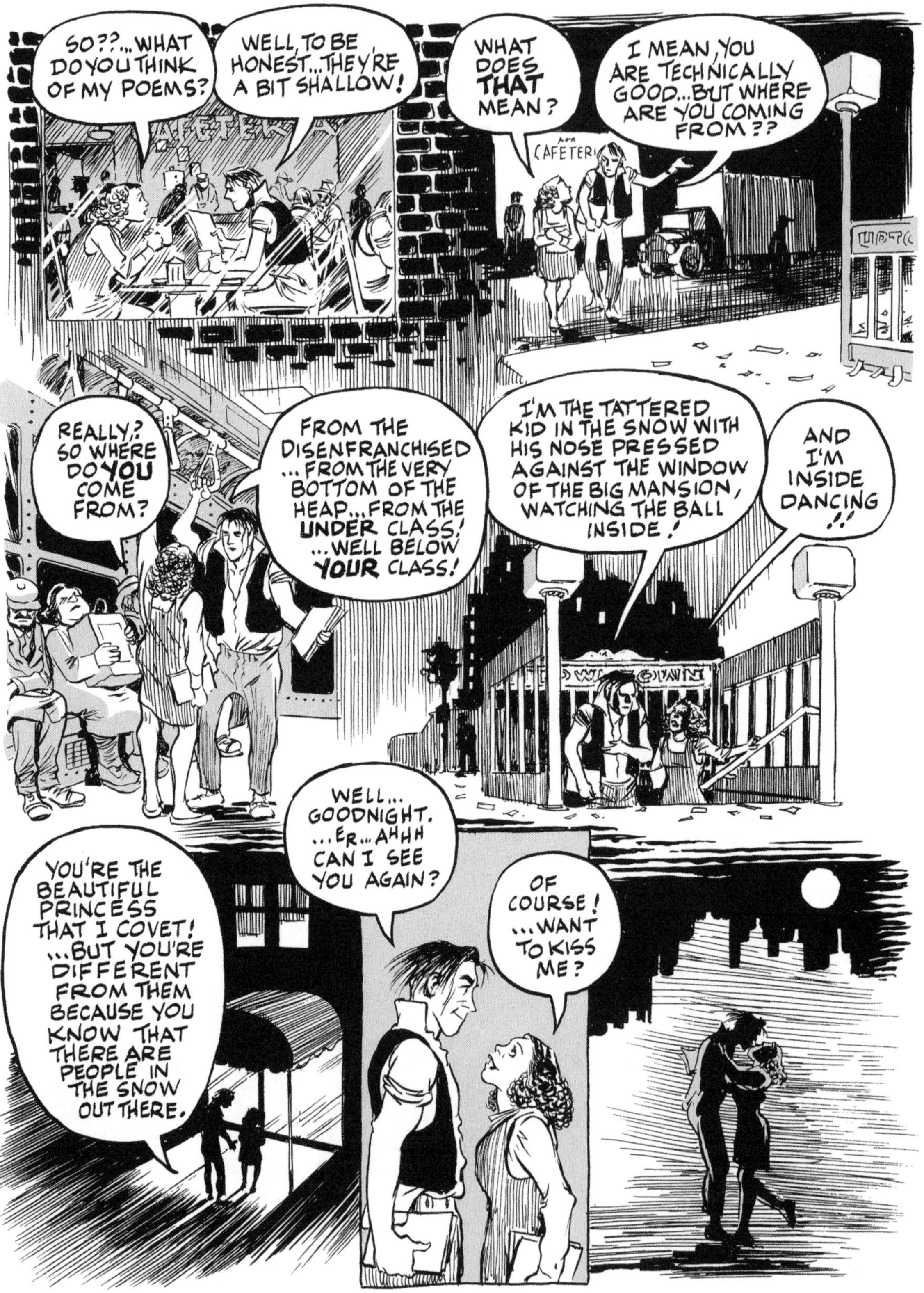
SO??...WHAT DO YOU THINK OF MY POEMS?
WELL, TO BE HONEST...THEY'RE A BIT SHALLOW!
CAFETER
WHAT DOES **THAT** MEAN?
CAFETERI
I MEAN, YOU ARE TECHNICALLY GOOD...BUT WHERE ARE YOU COMING FROM??
REALLY? SO WHERE DO **YOU** COME FROM?
FROM THE DISENFRANCHISED ...FROM THE VERY BOTTOM OF THE HEAP...FROM THE **UNDER** CLASS! ...WELL BELOW **YOUR** CLASS!
I'M THE TATTERED KID IN THE SNOW WITH HIS NOSE PRESSED AGAINST THE WINDOW OF THE BIG MANSION, WATCHING THE BALL INSIDE!
AND I'M INSIDE DANCING!!
YOU'RE THE BEAUTIFUL PRINCESS THAT I COVET! ...BUT YOU'RE DIFFERENT FROM THEM BECAUSE YOU KNOW THAT THERE ARE PEOPLE IN THE SNOW OUT THERE.
WELL... GOODNIGHT. ...ER...AHHH CAN I SEE YOU AGAIN?
OF COURSE! ...WANT TO KISS ME?

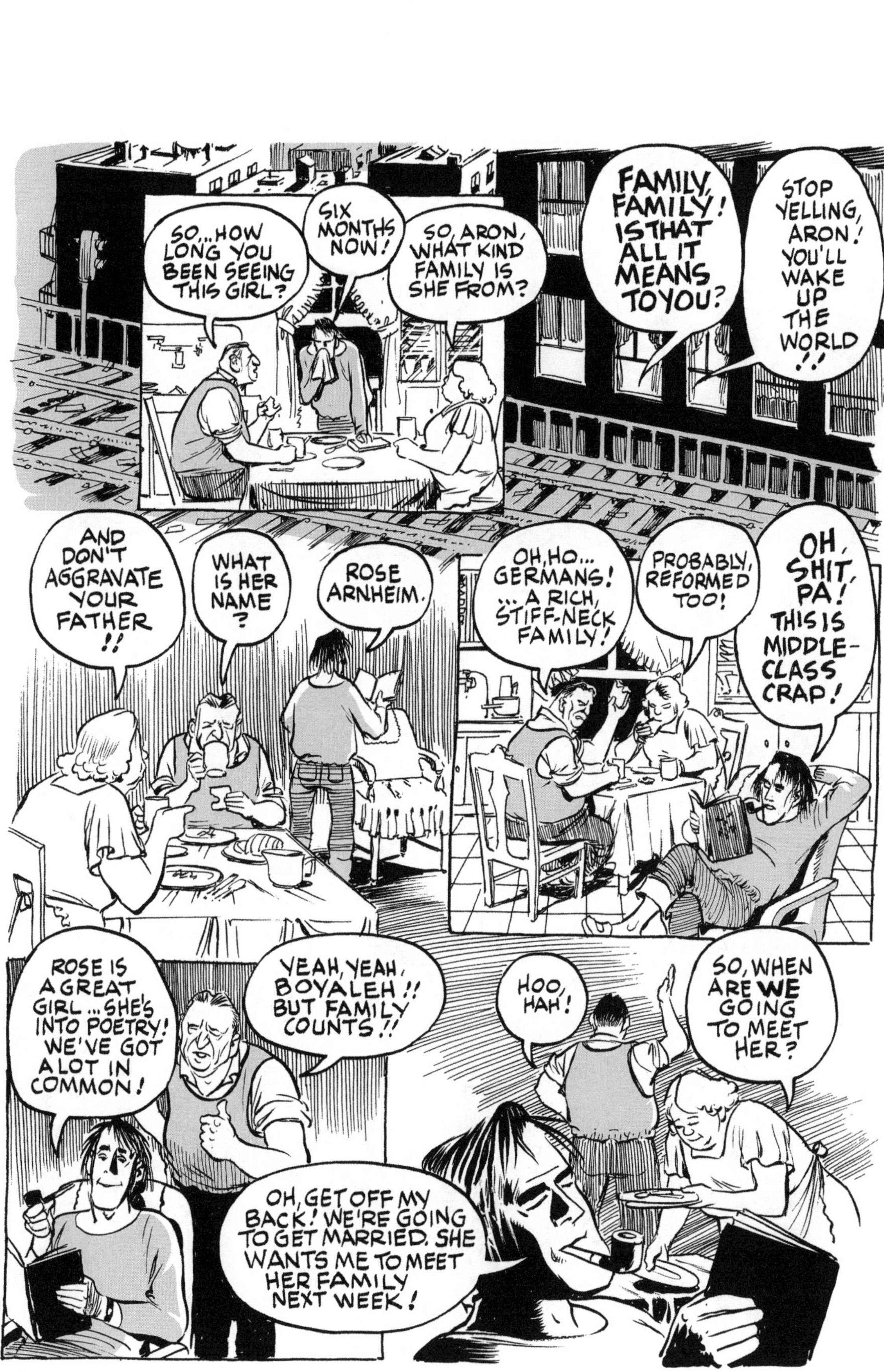
SO...HOW LONG YOU BEEN SEEING THIS GIRL?
SIX MONTHS NOW!
SO, ARON, WHAT KIND FAMILY IS SHE FROM?
FAMILY, FAMILY! IS THAT ALL IT MEANS TO YOU?
STOP YELLING, ARON! YOU'LL WAKE UP THE WORLD!!
AND DON'T AGGRAVATE YOUR FATHER!!
WHAT IS HER NAME?
ROSE ARNHEIM.
OH, HO... GERMANS! ...A RICH, STIFF-NECK FAMILY!
PROBABLY, REFORMED TOO!
OH, SHIT, PA! THIS IS MIDDLE-CLASS CRAP!
ROSE IS A GREAT GIRL ... SHE'S INTO POETRY! WE'VE GOT A LOT IN COMMON!
YEAH, YEAH, BOYALEH!! BUT FAMILY COUNTS!!
HOO, HAH!
SO, WHEN ARE **WE** GOING TO MEET HER?
OH, GET OFF MY BACK! WE'RE GOING TO GET MARRIED. SHE WANTS ME TO MEET HER FAMILY NEXT WEEK!

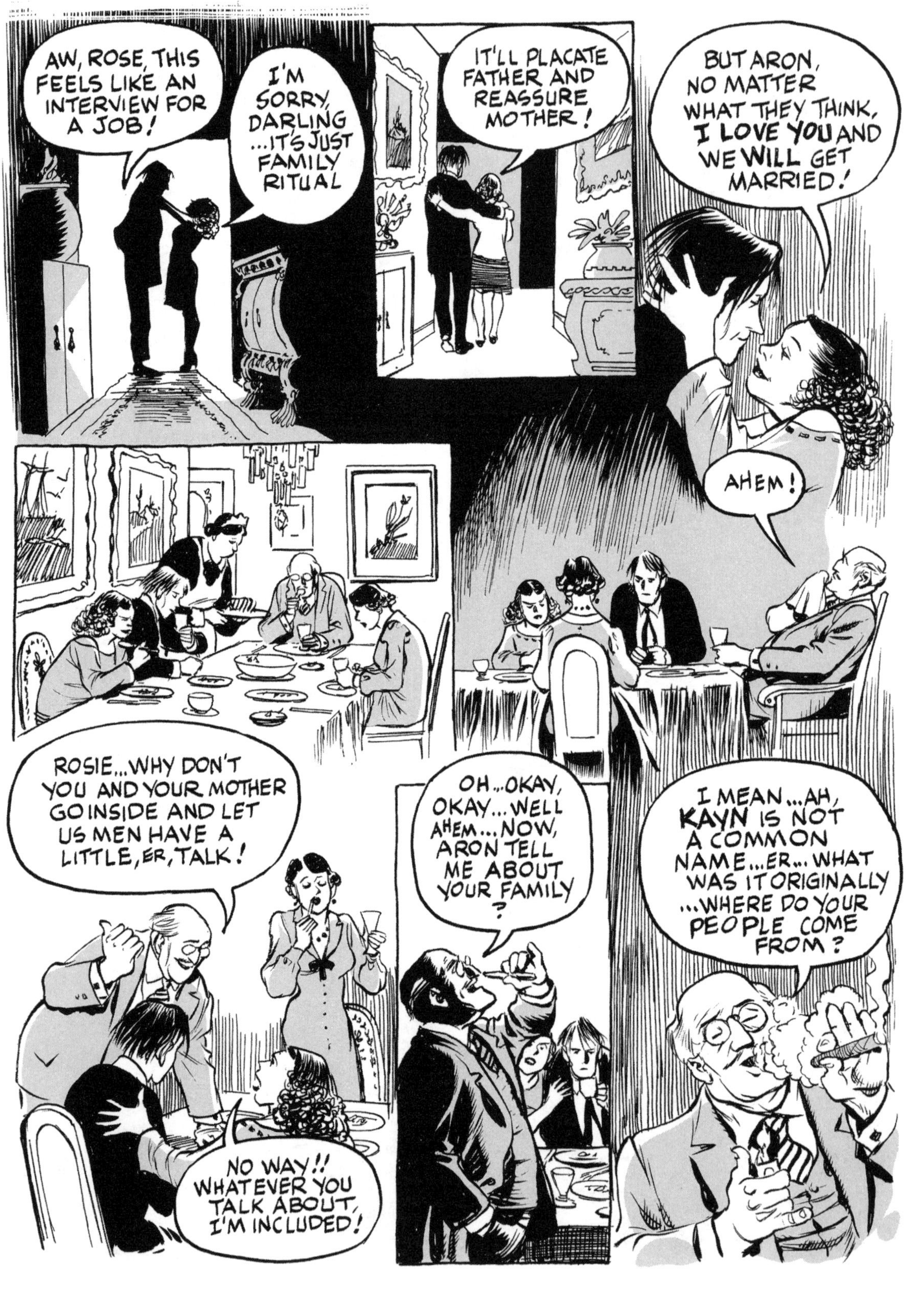
AW, ROSE, THIS FEELS LIKE AN INTERVIEW FOR A JOB!
I'M SORRY, DARLING ...IT'S JUST FAMILY RITUAL
IT'LL PLACATE FATHER AND REASSURE MOTHER!
BUT ARON, NO MATTER WHAT THEY THINK, I LOVE YOU AND WE WILL GET MARRIED!
AHEM!
ROSIE...WHY DON'T YOU AND YOUR MOTHER GO INSIDE AND LET US MEN HAVE A LITTLE, ER, TALK!
NO WAY!! WHATEVER YOU TALK ABOUT, I'M INCLUDED!
OH...OKAY, OKAY...WELL AHEM...NOW, ARON TELL ME ABOUT YOUR FAMILY?
I MEAN...AH, KAYN IS NOT A COMMON NAME...ER...WHAT WAS IT ORIGINALLY ...WHERE DO YOUR PEOPLE COME FROM?

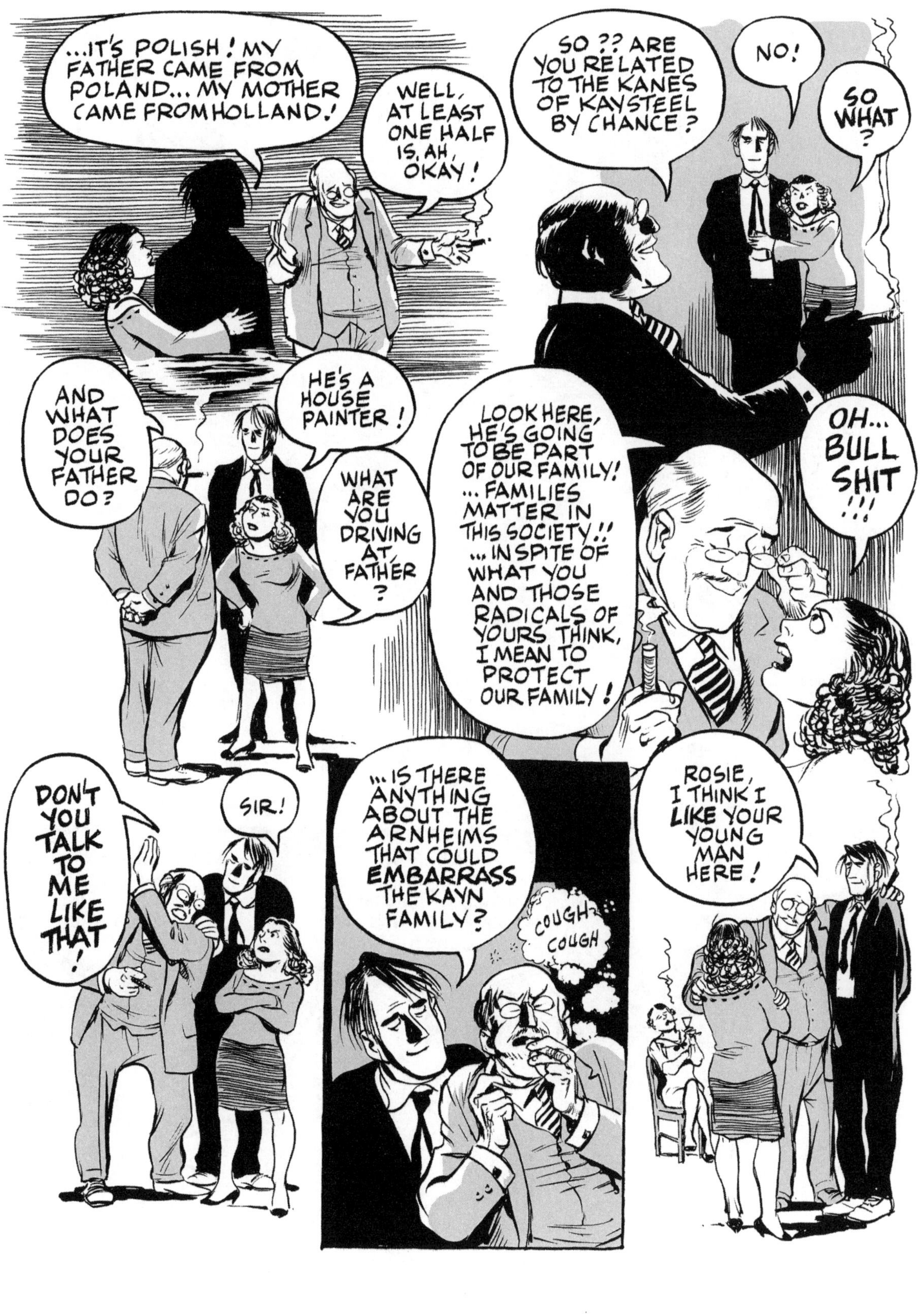
...IT'S POLISH! MY FATHER CAME FROM POLAND... MY MOTHER CAME FROM HOLLAND!
WELL, AT LEAST ONE HALF IS, AH, OKAY!
SO ?? ARE YOU RELATED TO THE KANES OF KAYSTEEL BY CHANCE?
NO!
SO WHAT?
AND WHAT DOES YOUR FATHER DO?
HE'S A HOUSE PAINTER!
WHAT ARE YOU DRIVING AT, FATHER?
LOOK HERE, HE'S GOING TO BE PART OF OUR FAMILY! ...FAMILIES MATTER IN THIS SOCIETY!! ...IN SPITE OF WHAT YOU AND THOSE RADICALS OF YOURS THINK, I MEAN TO PROTECT OUR FAMILY!
OH... BULL SHIT!!!
DON'T YOU TALK TO ME LIKE THAT!
SIR!
...IS THERE ANYTHING ABOUT THE ARNHEIMS THAT COULD EMBARRASS THE KAYN FAMILY?
COUGH COUGH
ROSIE, I THINK I LIKE YOUR YOUNG MAN HERE!

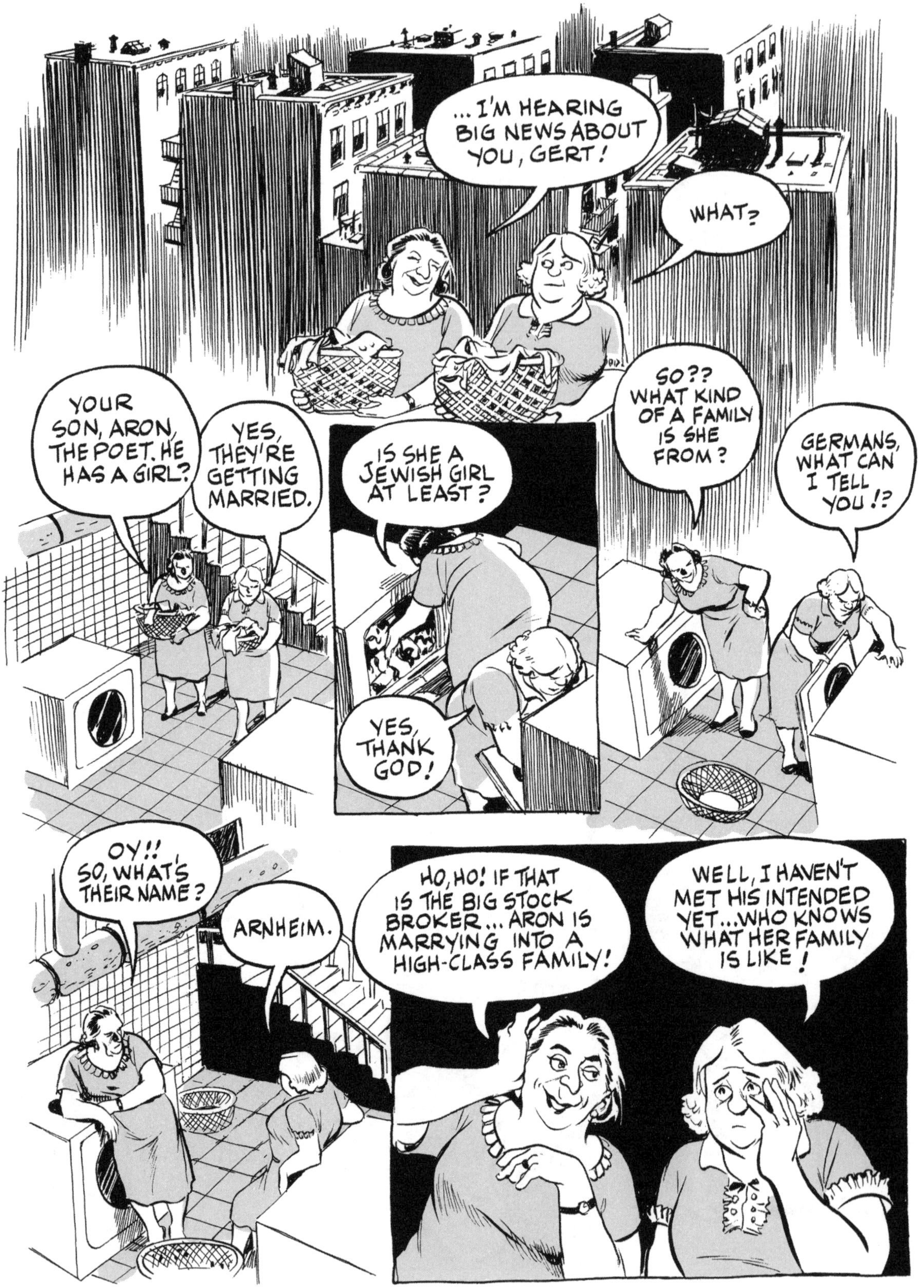
... I'M HEARING BIG NEWS ABOUT YOU, GERT!
WHAT?
YOUR SON, ARON, THE POET. HE HAS A GIRL?
YES, THEY'RE GETTING MARRIED.
IS SHE A JEWISH GIRL AT LEAST?
YES, THANK GOD!
SO?? WHAT KIND OF A FAMILY IS SHE FROM?
GERMANS, WHAT CAN I TELL YOU!?
OY!! SO, WHAT'S THEIR NAME?
ARNHEIM.
HO, HO! IF THAT IS THE BIG STOCK BROKER... ARON IS MARRYING INTO A HIGH-CLASS FAMILY!
WELL, I HAVEN'T MET HIS INTENDED YET... WHO KNOWS WHAT HER FAMILY IS LIKE!

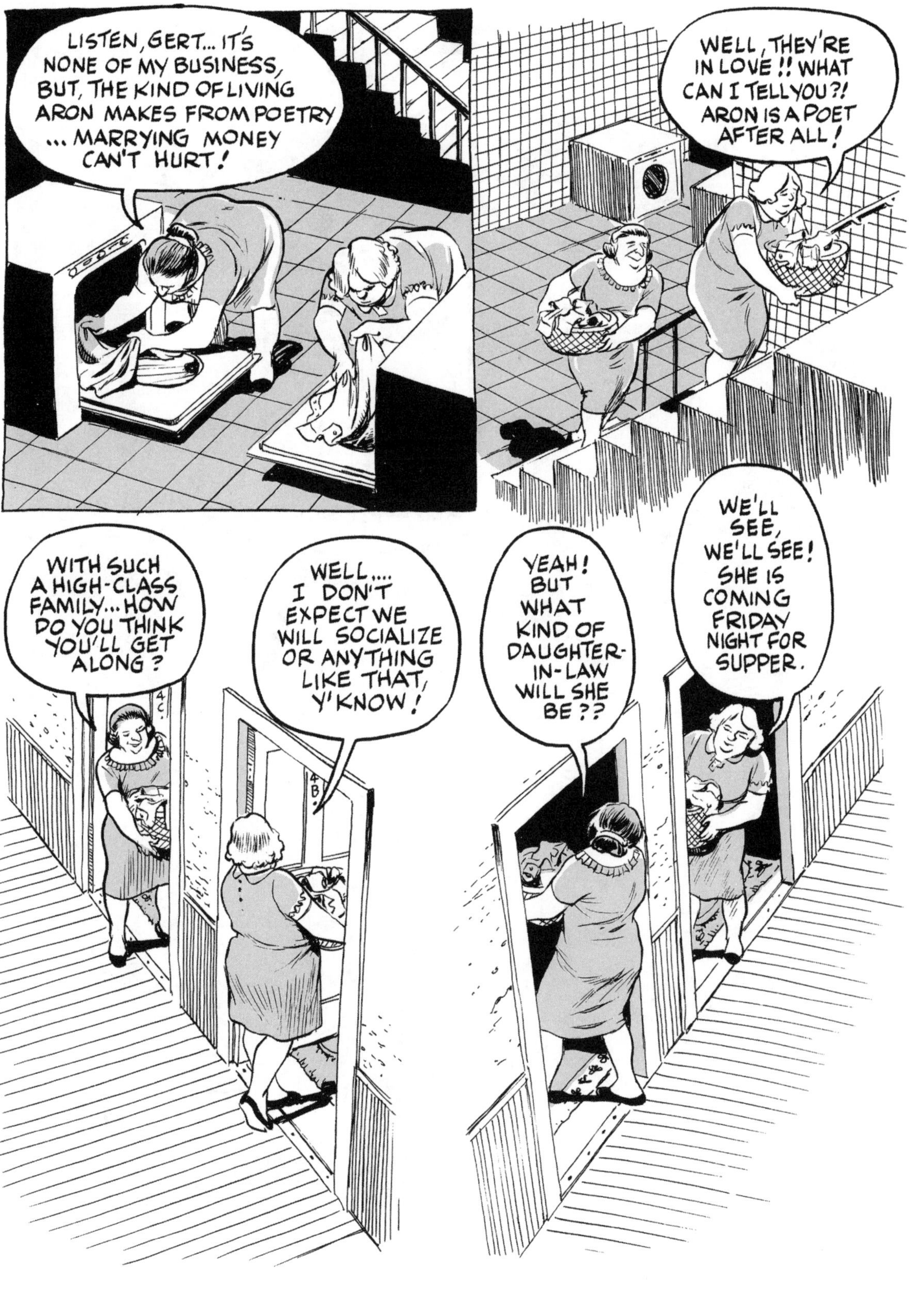

LISTEN, GERT... IT'S NONE OF MY BUSINESS, BUT, THE KIND OF LIVING ARON MAKES FROM POETRY ... MARRYING MONEY CAN'T HURT!
WELL, THEY'RE IN LOVE!! WHAT CAN I TELL YOU?! ARON IS A POET AFTER ALL!
WITH SUCH A HIGH-CLASS FAMILY... HOW DO YOU THINK YOU'LL GET ALONG?
4C
WELL.... I DON'T EXPECT WE WILL SOCIALIZE OR ANYTHING LIKE THAT, Y'KNOW!
4B
YEAH! BUT WHAT KIND OF DAUGHTER-IN-LAW WILL SHE BE??
WE'LL SEE, WE'LL SEE! SHE IS COMING FRIDAY NIGHT FOR SUPPER.

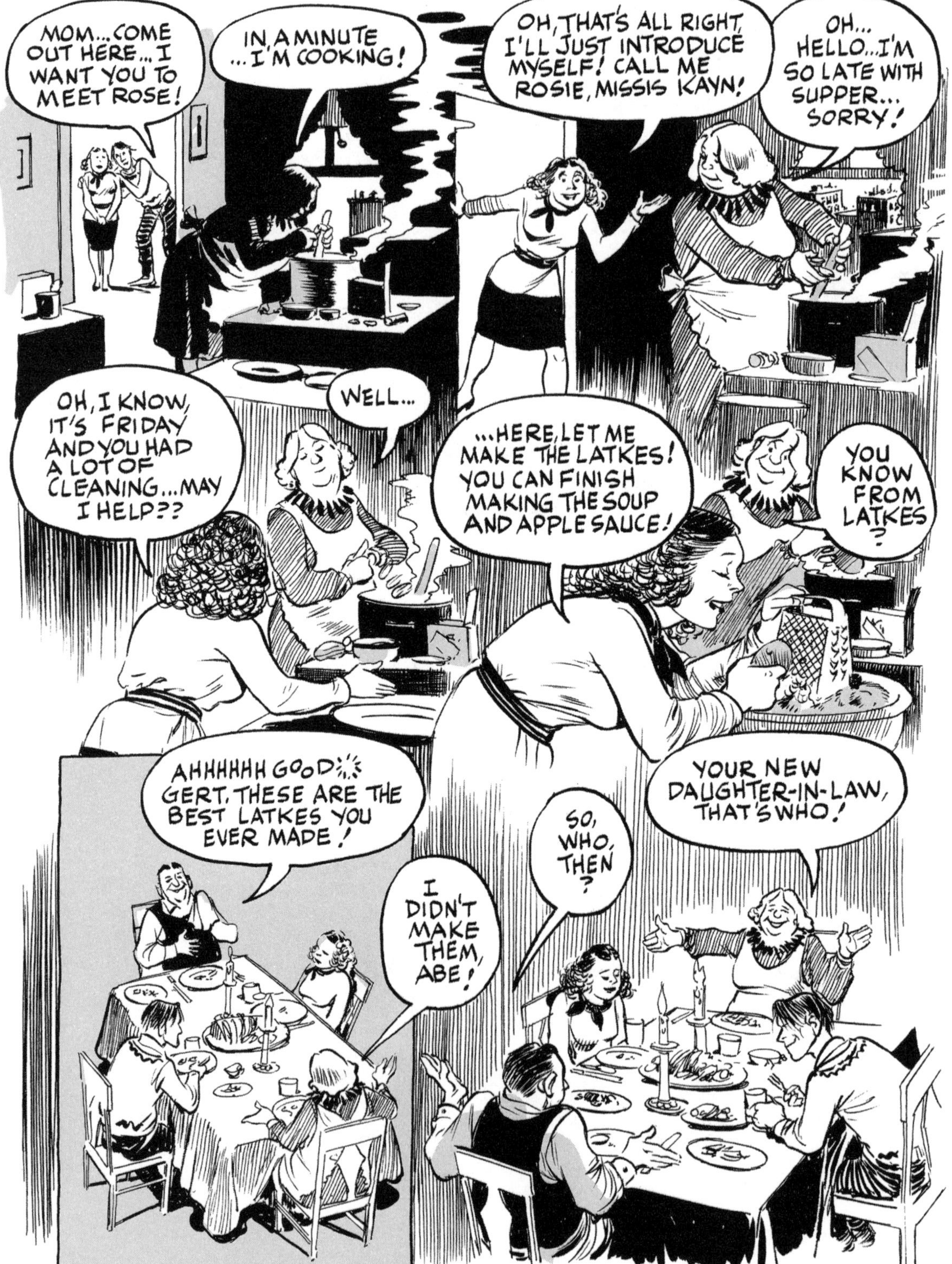
MOM...COME OUT HERE...I WANT YOU TO MEET ROSE!
IN A MINUTE ...I'M COOKING!
OH, THAT'S ALL RIGHT, I'LL JUST INTRODUCE MYSELF! CALL ME ROSIE, MISSIS KAYN!
OH... HELLO...I'M SO LATE WITH SUPPER... SORRY!
OH, I KNOW, IT'S FRIDAY AND YOU HAD A LOT OF CLEANING...MAY I HELP??
WELL...
...HERE, LET ME MAKE THE LATKES! YOU CAN FINISH MAKING THE SOUP AND APPLE SAUCE!
YOU KNOW FROM LATKES?
AHHHHHH GOOD! GERT, THESE ARE THE BEST LATKES YOU EVER MADE!
I DIDN'T MAKE THEM, ABE!
SO, WHO, THEN?
YOUR NEW DAUGHTER-IN-LAW, THAT'S WHO!

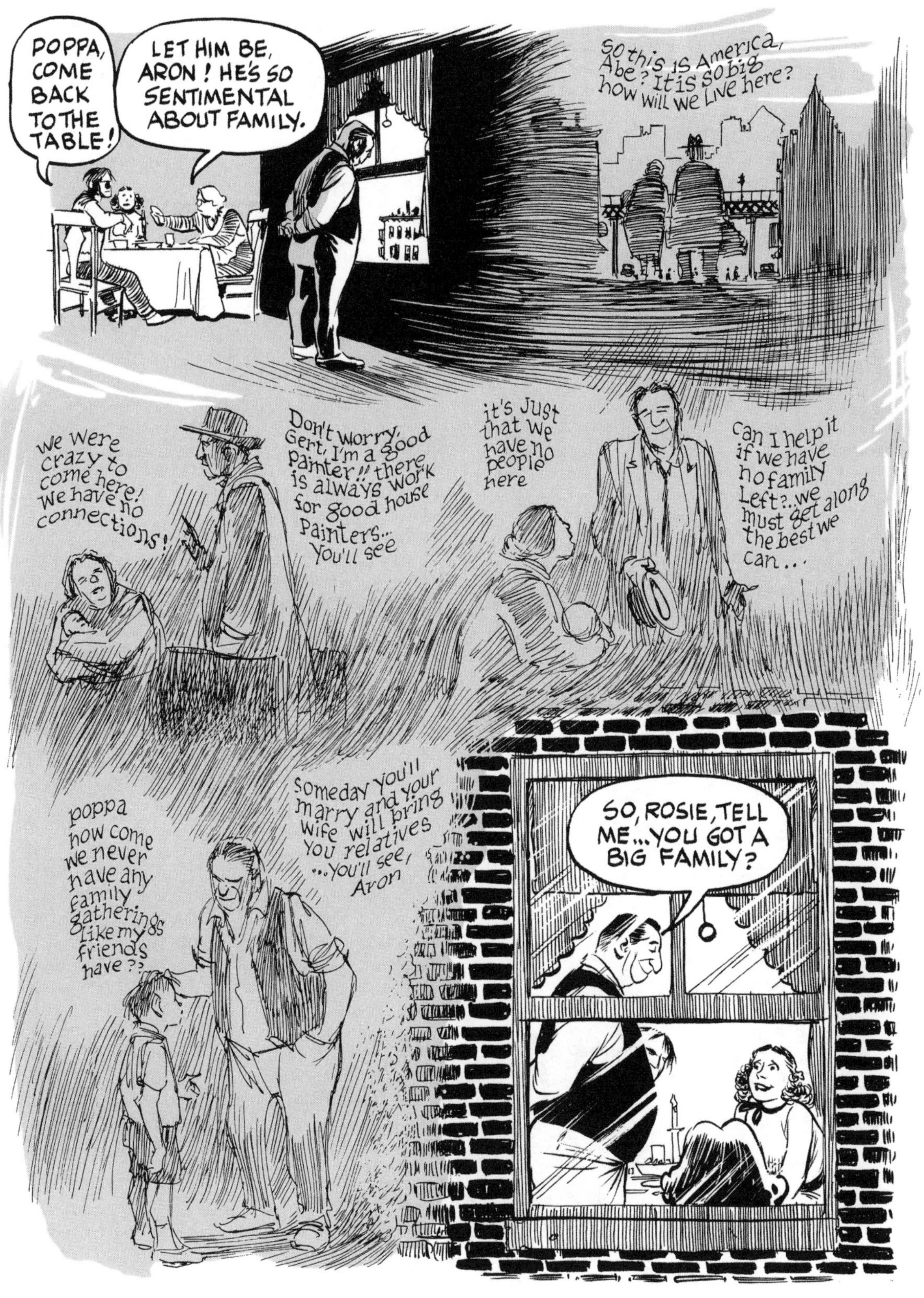
POPPA, COME BACK TO THE TABLE!
LET HIM BE, ARON! HE'S SO SENTIMENTAL ABOUT FAMILY.
So this is America, Abe? It is so big how will we live here?
We were crazy to come here! We have no connections!
Don't worry, Gert, I'm a good painter!! there is always work for good house painters... You'll see
it's Just that we have no people here
Can I help it if we have no family Left?.. we must get along the best we can...
poppa how come we never have any family gatherings like my friends have??
Someday you'll marry and your wife will bring you relatives ...you'll see, Aron
SO, ROSIE, TELL ME... YOU GOT A BIG FAMILY?

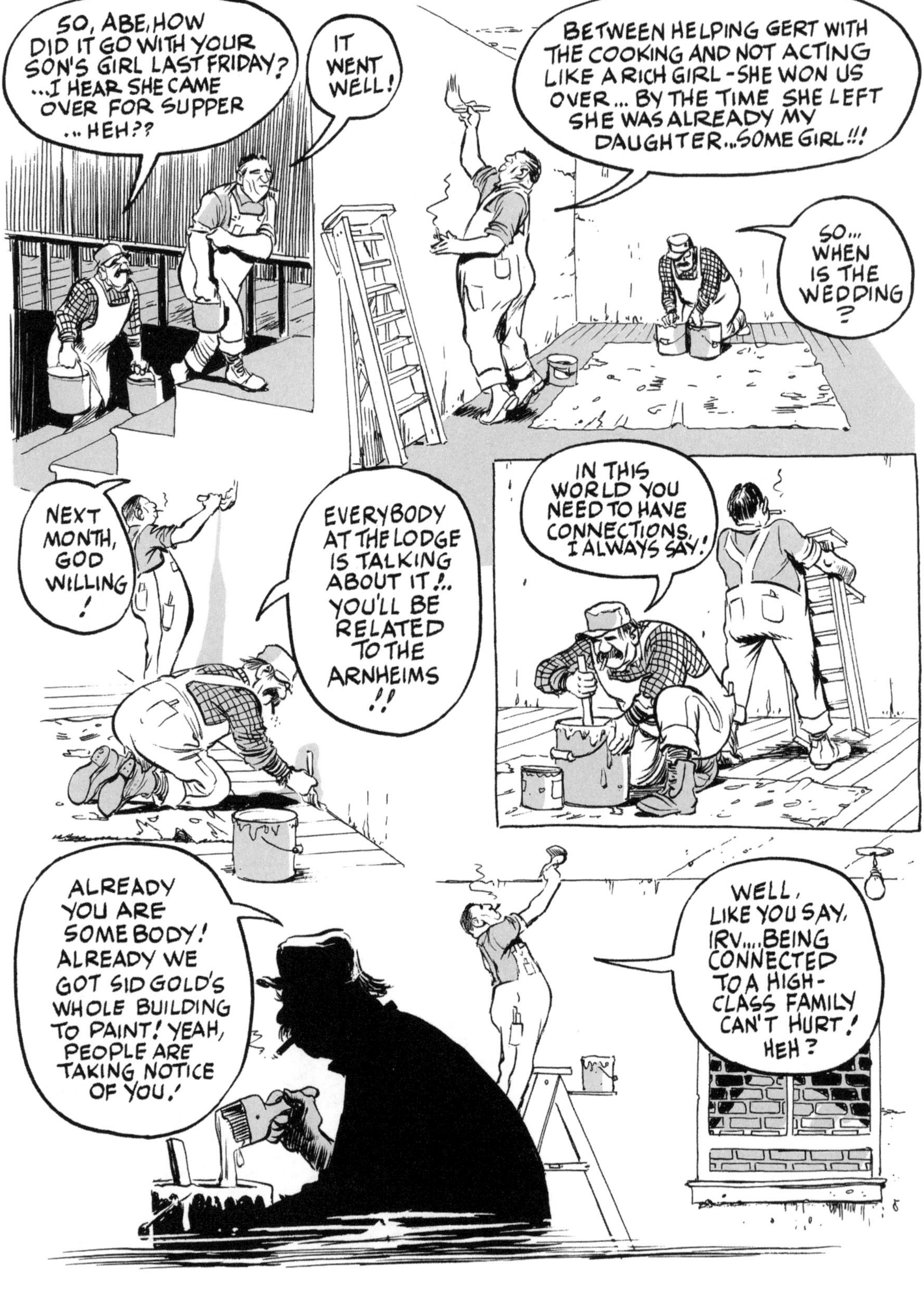
SO, ABE, HOW DID IT GO WITH YOUR SON'S GIRL LAST FRIDAY? ...I HEAR SHE CAME OVER FOR SUPPER ...HEH??
IT WENT WELL!
BETWEEN HELPING GERT WITH THE COOKING AND NOT ACTING LIKE A RICH GIRL - SHE WON US OVER... BY THE TIME SHE LEFT SHE WAS ALREADY MY DAUGHTER...SOME GIRL!!!
SO... WHEN IS THE WEDDING?
NEXT MONTH, GOD WILLING!
EVERYBODY AT THE LODGE IS TALKING ABOUT IT!.. YOU'LL BE RELATED TO THE ARNHEIMS!!
IN THIS WORLD YOU NEED TO HAVE CONNECTIONS, I ALWAYS SAY!
ALREADY YOU ARE SOMEBODY! ALREADY WE GOT SID GOLD'S WHOLE BUILDING TO PAINT! YEAH, PEOPLE ARE TAKING NOTICE OF YOU!
WELL, LIKE YOU SAY, IRV.... BEING CONNECTED TO A HIGH-CLASS FAMILY CAN'T HURT! HEH?

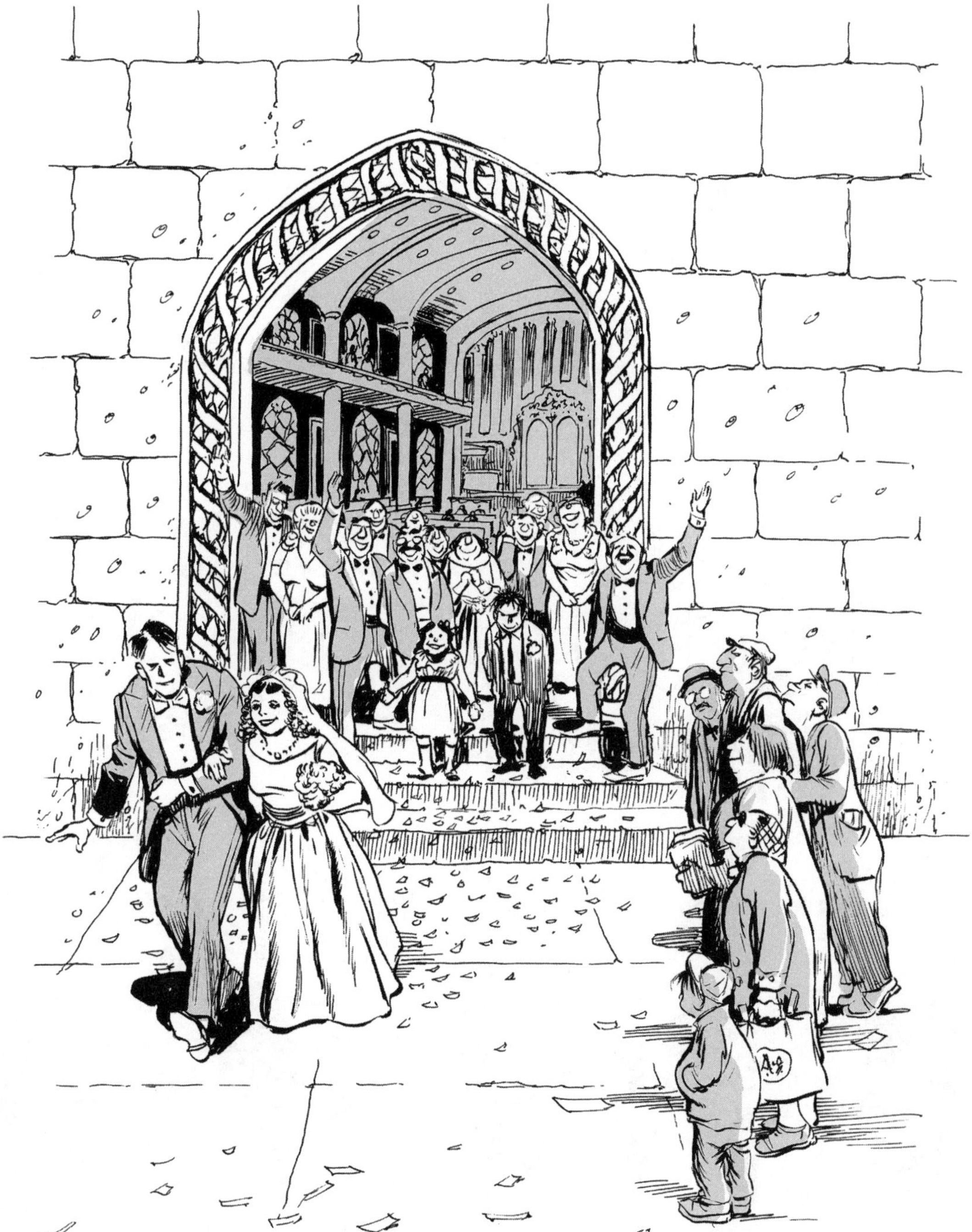

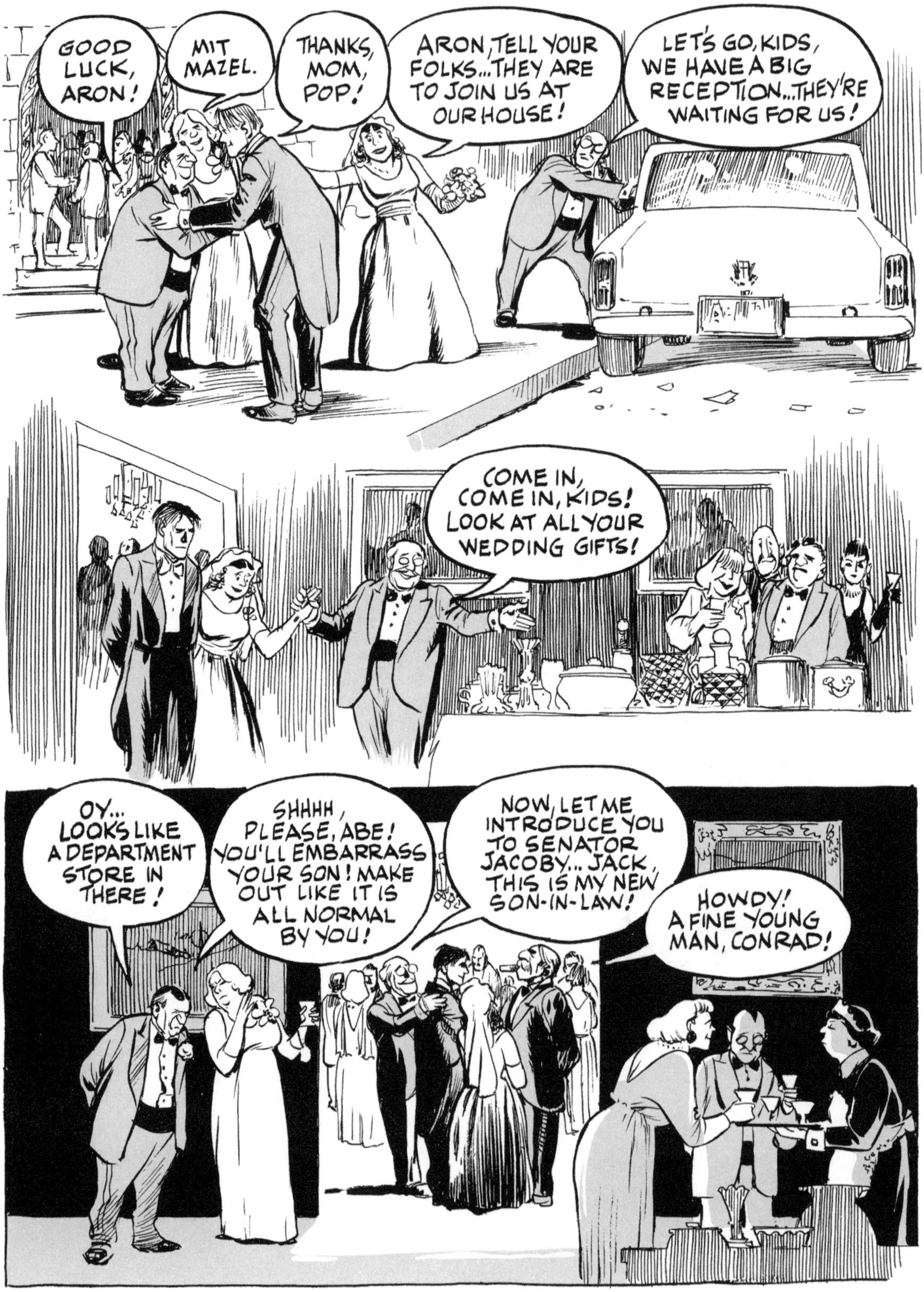
GOOD LUCK, ARON!
MIT MAZEL.
THANKS, MOM, POP!
ARON, TELL YOUR FOLKS... THEY ARE TO JOIN US AT OUR HOUSE!
LET'S GO, KIDS, WE HAVE A BIG RECEPTION... THEY'RE WAITING FOR US!
COME IN, COME IN, KIDS! LOOK AT ALL YOUR WEDDING GIFTS!
OY... LOOKS LIKE A DEPARTMENT STORE IN THERE!
SHHHH, PLEASE, ABE! YOU'LL EMBARRASS YOUR SON! MAKE OUT LIKE IT IS ALL NORMAL BY YOU!
NOW, LET ME INTRODUCE YOU TO SENATOR JACOBY... JACK, THIS IS MY NEW SON-IN-LAW!
HOWDY! A FINE YOUNG MAN, CONRAD!

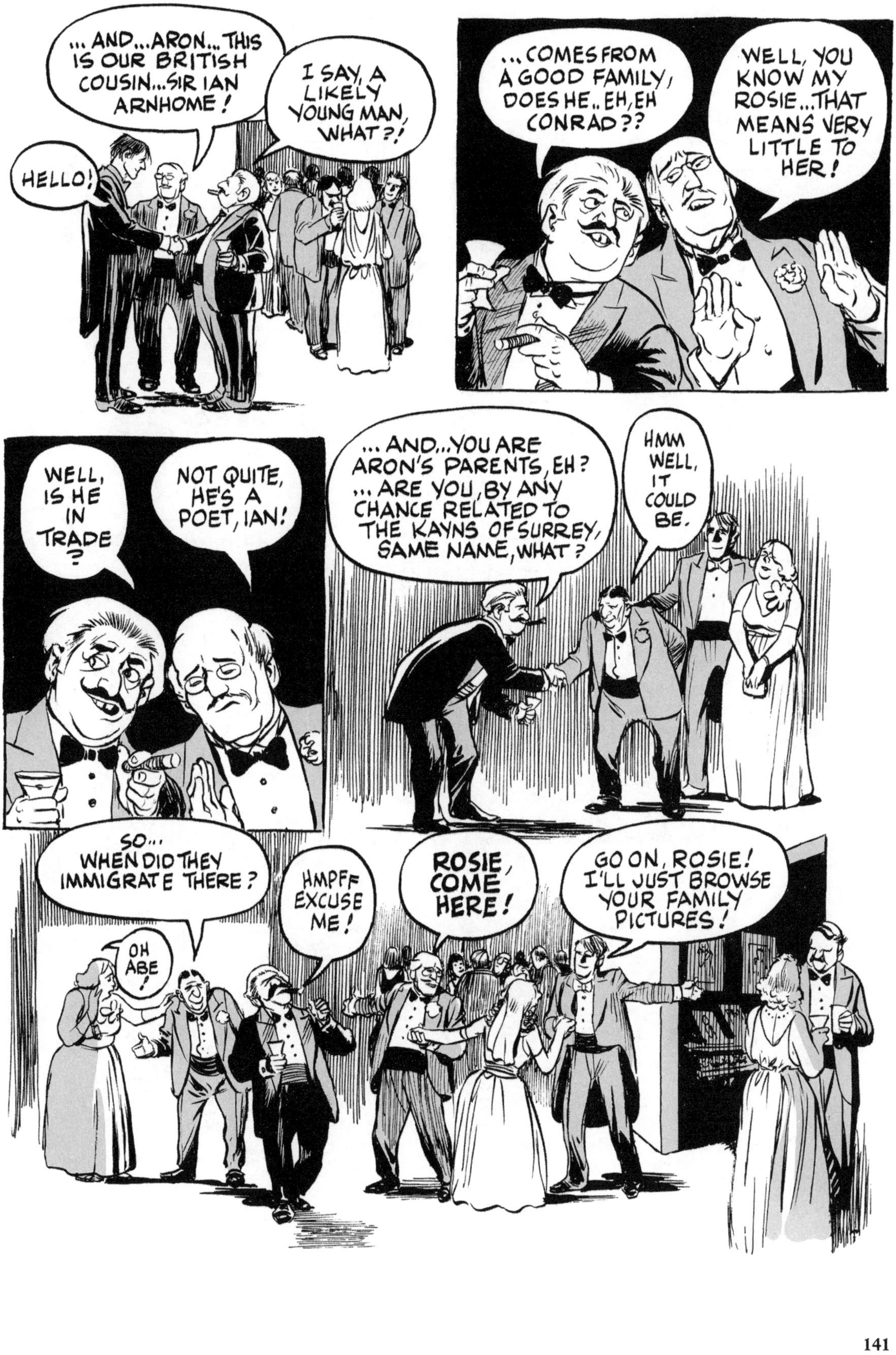
... AND... ARON... THIS IS OUR BRITISH COUSIN... SIR IAN ARNHOME!
HELLO!
I SAY, A LIKELY YOUNG MAN, WHAT?!
... COMES FROM A GOOD FAMILY, DOES HE.. EH, EH CONRAD??
WELL, YOU KNOW MY ROSIE... THAT MEANS VERY LITTLE TO HER!
WELL, IS HE IN TRADE?
NOT QUITE, HE'S A POET, IAN!
... AND.. YOU ARE ARON'S PARENTS, EH? ... ARE YOU, BY ANY CHANCE RELATED TO THE KAYNS OF SURREY, SAME NAME, WHAT?
HMM WELL, IT COULD BE.
SO... WHEN DID THEY IMMIGRATE THERE?
OH ABE!
HMPFF EXCUSE ME!
ROSIE, COME HERE!
GO ON, ROSIE! I'LL JUST BROWSE YOUR FAMILY PICTURES!

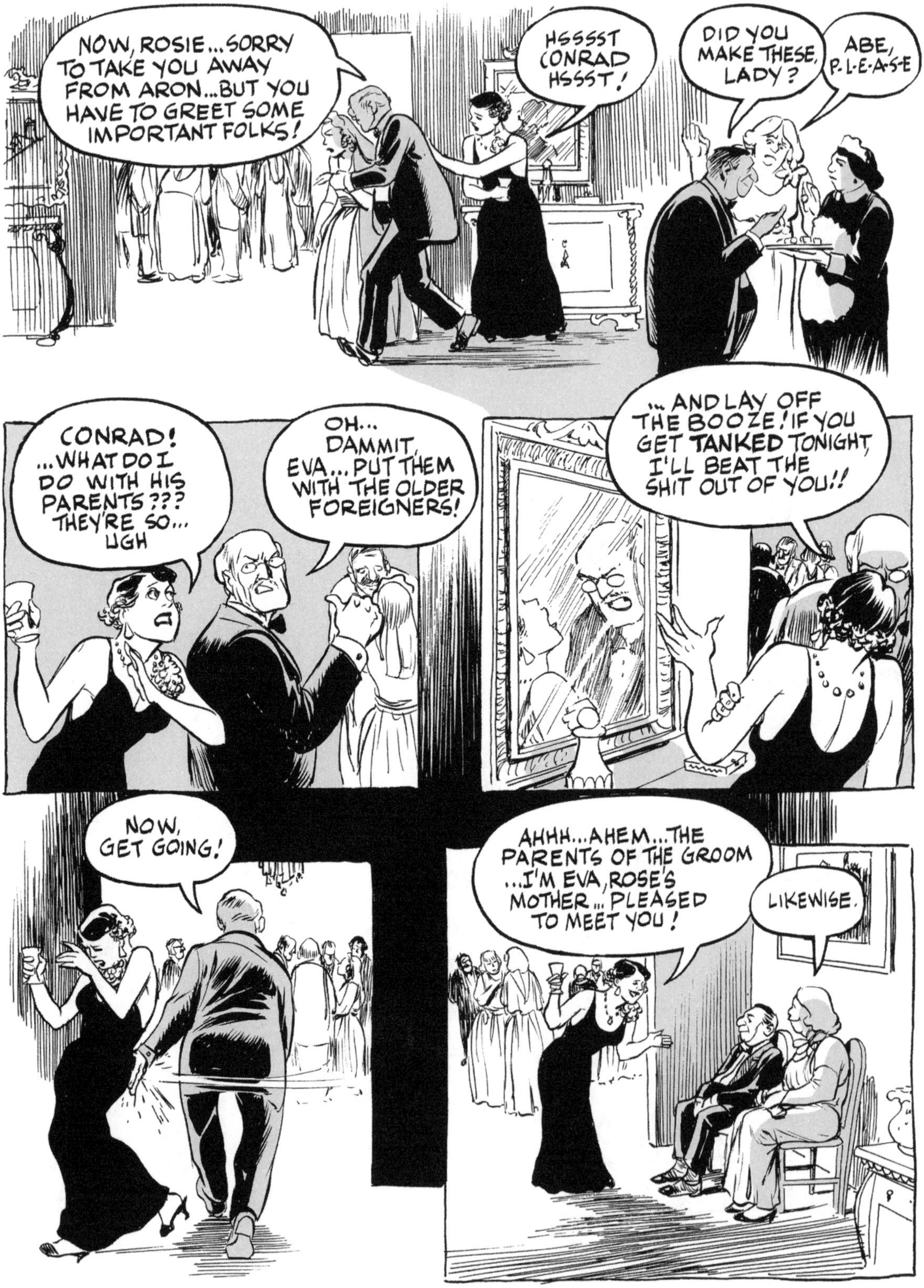
NOW, ROSIE...SORRY TO TAKE YOU AWAY FROM ARON...BUT YOU HAVE TO GREET SOME IMPORTANT FOLKS!
HSSSST CONRAD HSSST!
DID YOU MAKE THESE, LADY?
ABE, P-L-E-A-S-E
CONRAD! ...WHAT DO I DO WITH HIS PARENTS??? THEY'RE SO... UGH
OH... DAMMIT, EVA... PUT THEM WITH THE OLDER FOREIGNERS!
... AND LAY OFF THE BOOZE! IF YOU GET **TANKED** TONIGHT, I'LL BEAT THE SHIT OUT OF YOU!!
NOW, GET GOING!
AHHH...AHEM...THE PARENTS OF THE GROOM ...I'M EVA, ROSE'S MOTHER... PLEASED TO MEET YOU!
LIKEWISE.

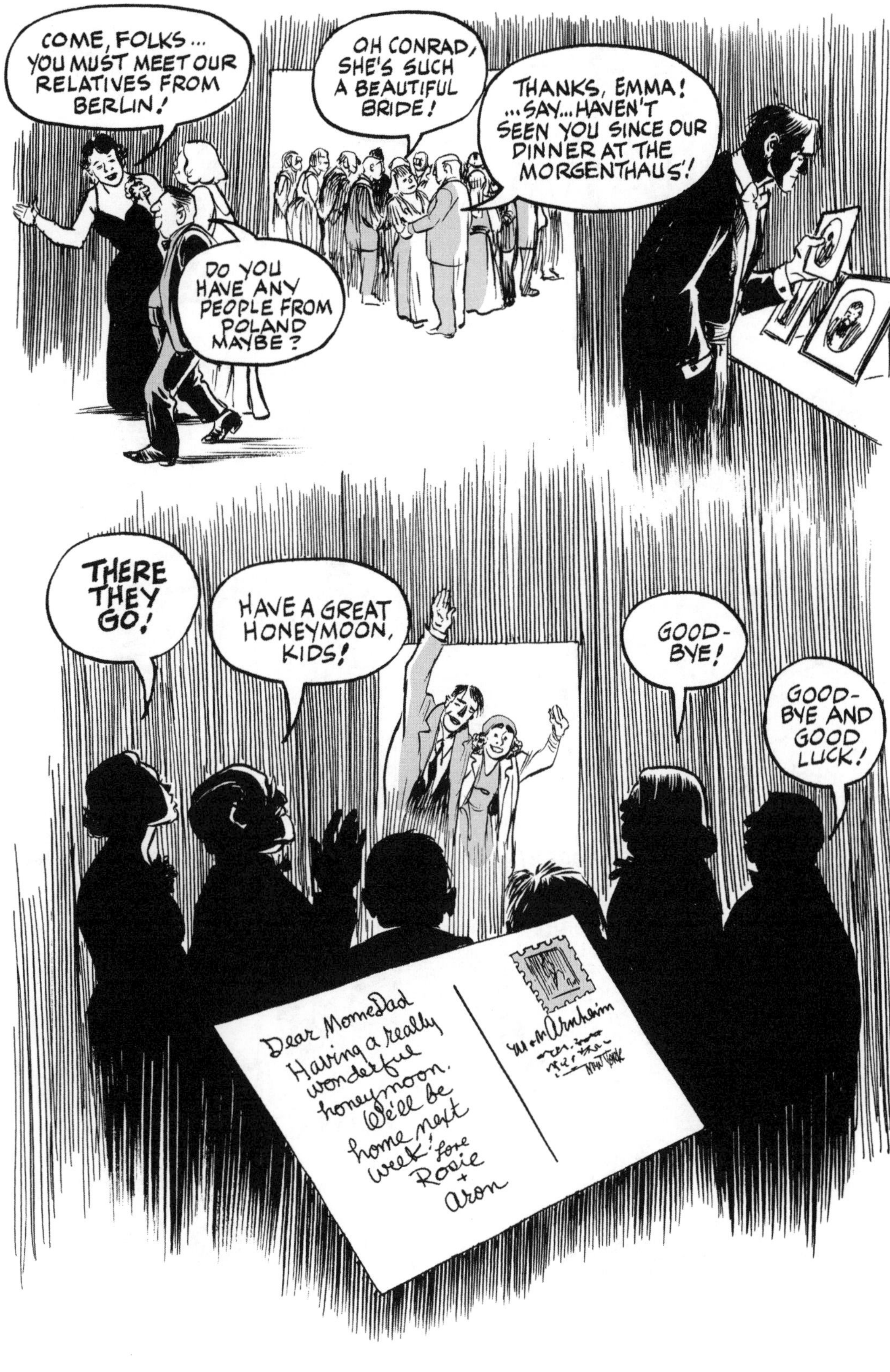
COME, FOLKS... YOU MUST MEET OUR RELATIVES FROM BERLIN!
OH CONRAD, SHE'S SUCH A BEAUTIFUL BRIDE!
THANKS, EMMA! ...SAY... HAVEN'T SEEN YOU SINCE OUR DINNER AT THE MORGENTHAUS'!
DO YOU HAVE ANY PEOPLE FROM POLAND MAYBE?
THERE THEY GO!
HAVE A GREAT HONEYMOON, KIDS!
GOOD-BYE!
GOOD-BYE AND GOOD LUCK!
Dear Mom & Dad
Having a really wonderful honeymoon. We'll be home next week! Love Rosie + Aron

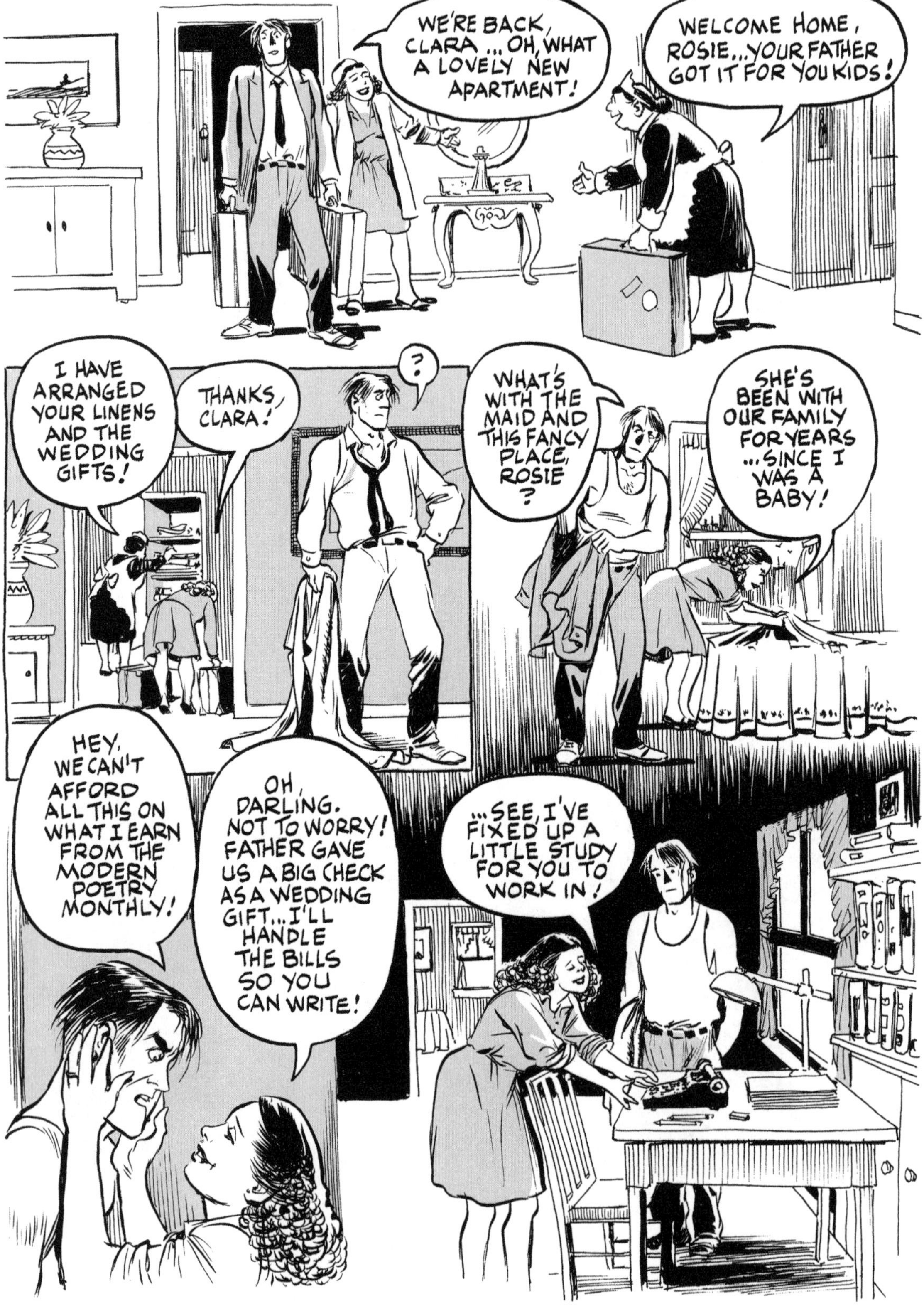
WE'RE BACK, CLARA ... OH, WHAT A LOVELY NEW APARTMENT!
WELCOME HOME, ROSIE... YOUR FATHER GOT IT FOR YOU KIDS!
I HAVE ARRANGED YOUR LINENS AND THE WEDDING GIFTS!
THANKS, CLARA!
?
WHAT'S WITH THE MAID AND THIS FANCY PLACE, ROSIE?
SHE'S BEEN WITH OUR FAMILY FOR YEARS ... SINCE I WAS A BABY!
HEY, WE CAN'T AFFORD ALL THIS ON WHAT I EARN FROM THE MODERN POETRY MONTHLY!
OH, DARLING. NOT TO WORRY! FATHER GAVE US A BIG CHECK AS A WEDDING GIFT... I'LL HANDLE THE BILLS SO YOU CAN WRITE!
...SEE, I'VE FIXED UP A LITTLE STUDY FOR YOU TO WORK IN!

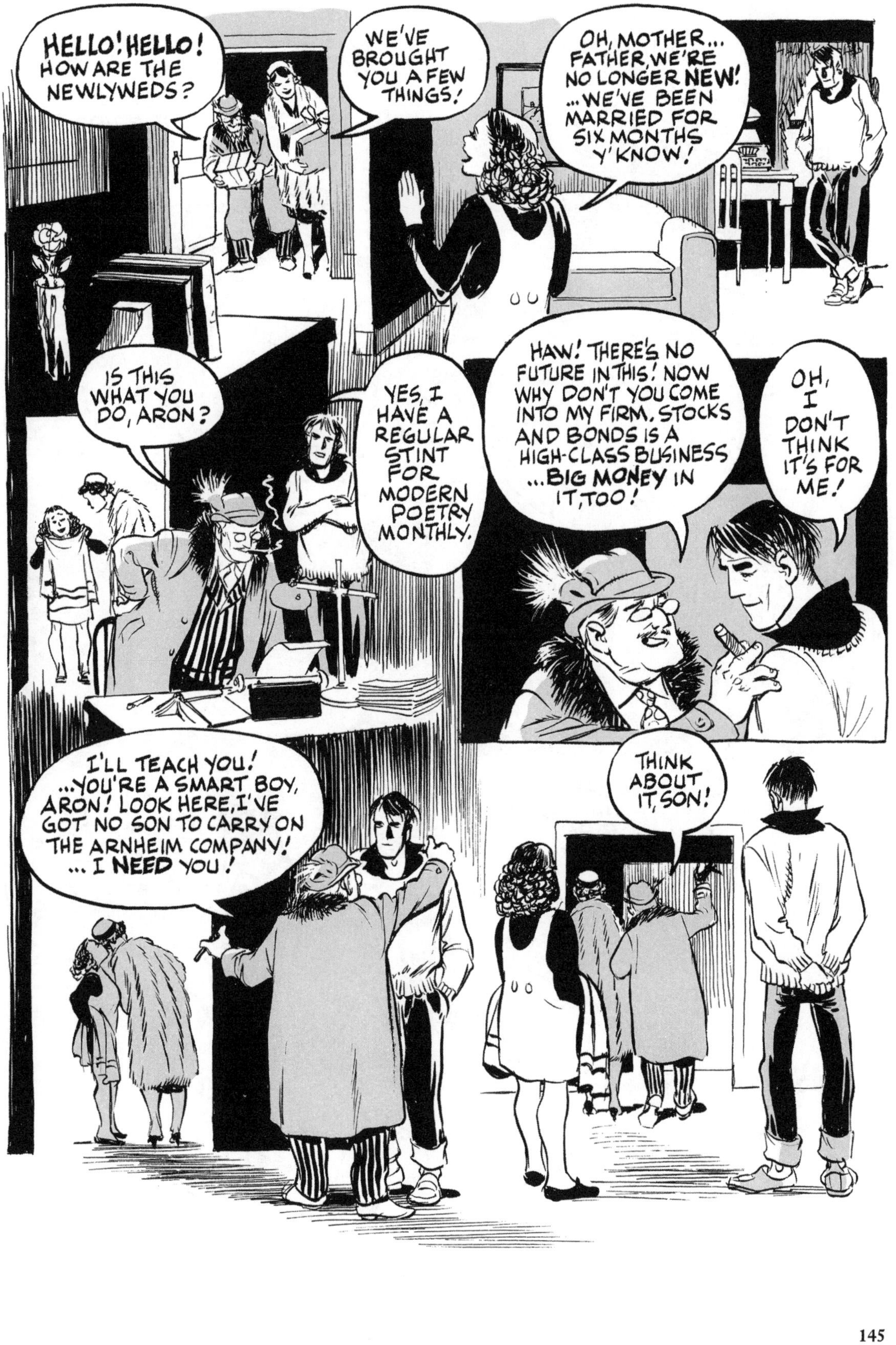
HELLO! HELLO! HOW ARE THE NEWLYWEDS?
WE'VE BROUGHT YOU A FEW THINGS!
OH, MOTHER... FATHER, WE'RE NO LONGER NEW! ...WE'VE BEEN MARRIED FOR SIX MONTHS Y'KNOW!
IS THIS WHAT YOU DO, ARON?
YES, I HAVE A REGULAR STINT FOR MODERN POETRY MONTHLY.
HAW! THERE'S NO FUTURE IN THIS! NOW WHY DON'T YOU COME INTO MY FIRM. STOCKS AND BONDS IS A HIGH-CLASS BUSINESS ...BIG MONEY IN IT, TOO!
OH, I DON'T THINK IT'S FOR ME!
I'LL TEACH YOU! ...YOU'RE A SMART BOY, ARON! LOOK HERE, I'VE GOT NO SON TO CARRY ON THE ARNHEIM COMPANY! ... I NEED YOU!
THINK ABOUT IT, SON!

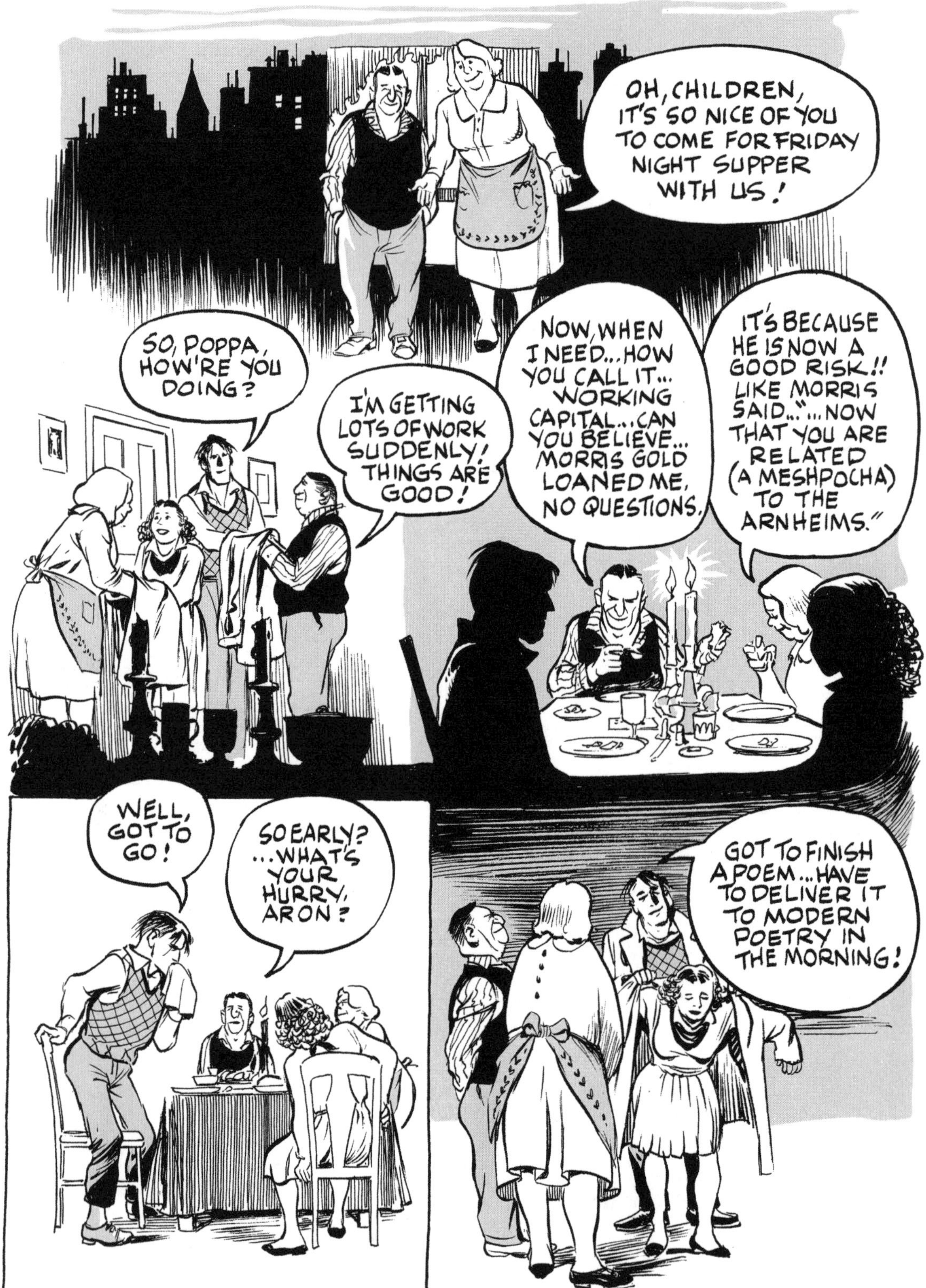
OH, CHILDREN, IT'S SO NICE OF YOU TO COME FOR FRIDAY NIGHT SUPPER WITH US!
SO, POPPA, HOW'RE YOU DOING?
I'M GETTING LOTS OF WORK SUDDENLY! THINGS ARE GOOD!
NOW, WHEN I NEED... HOW YOU CALL IT... WORKING CAPITAL... CAN YOU BELIEVE... MORRIS GOLD LOANED ME, NO QUESTIONS.
IT'S BECAUSE HE IS NOW A GOOD RISK!! LIKE MORRIS SAID..."...NOW THAT YOU ARE RELATED (A MESHPOCHA) TO THE ARNHEIMS."
WELL, GOT TO GO!
SO EARLY? ...WHAT'S YOUR HURRY, ARON?
GOT TO FINISH A POEM... HAVE TO DELIVER IT TO MODERN POETRY IN THE MORNING!

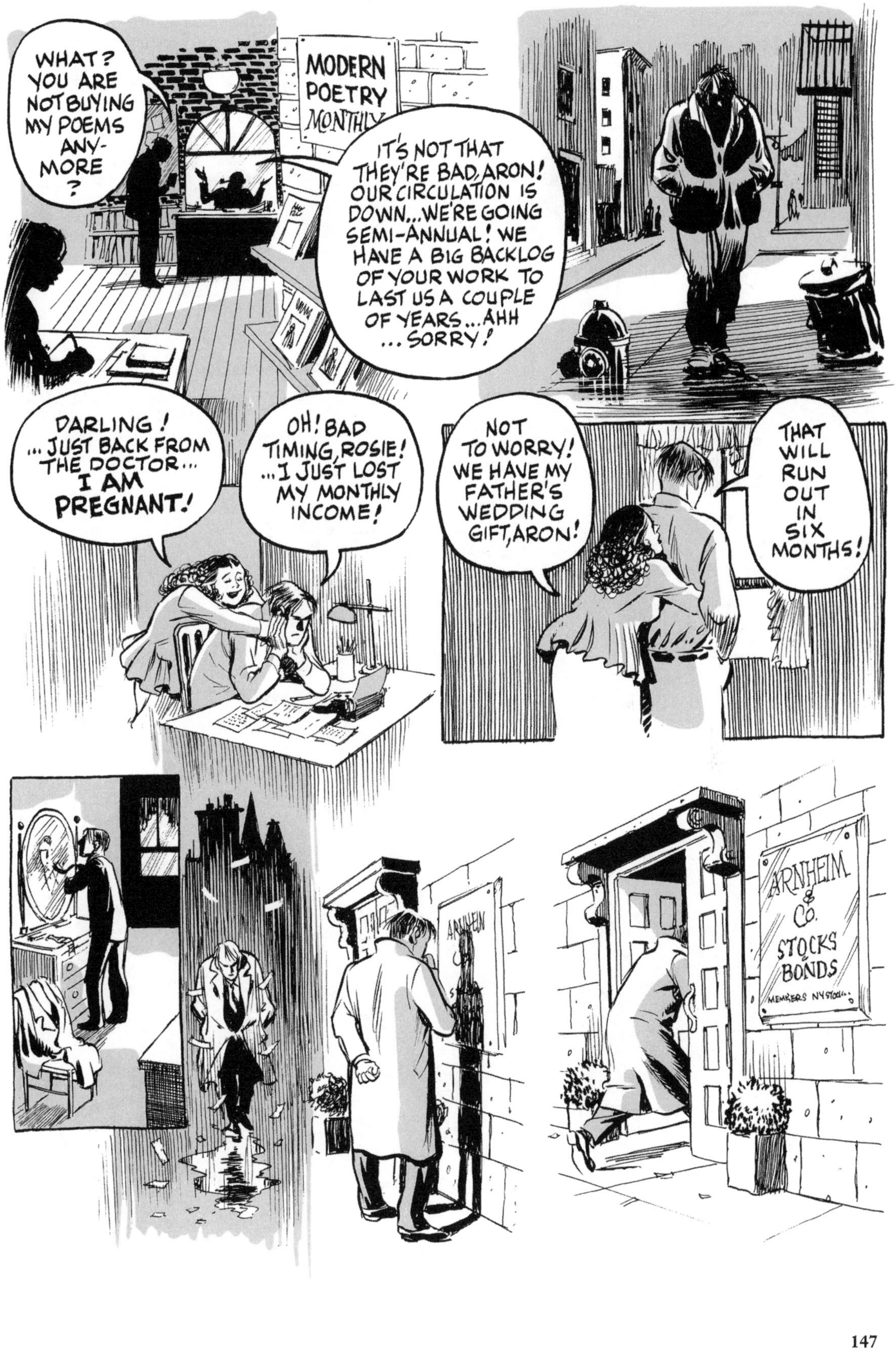
WHAT? YOU ARE NOT BUYING MY POEMS ANY-MORE ?
MODERN POETRY MONTHLY
IT'S NOT THAT THEY'RE BAD, ARON! OUR CIRCULATION IS DOWN... WE'RE GOING SEMI-ANNUAL! WE HAVE A BIG BACKLOG OF YOUR WORK TO LAST US A COUPLE OF YEARS... AHH ... SORRY!
DARLING! ... JUST BACK FROM THE DOCTOR... I AM PREGNANT!
OH! BAD TIMING, ROSIE! ...I JUST LOST MY MONTHLY INCOME!
NOT TO WORRY! WE HAVE MY FATHER'S WEDDING GIFT, ARON!
THAT WILL RUN OUT IN SIX MONTHS!
ARNHEIM & Co. STOCKS & BONDS
MEMBERS NY STOCK...

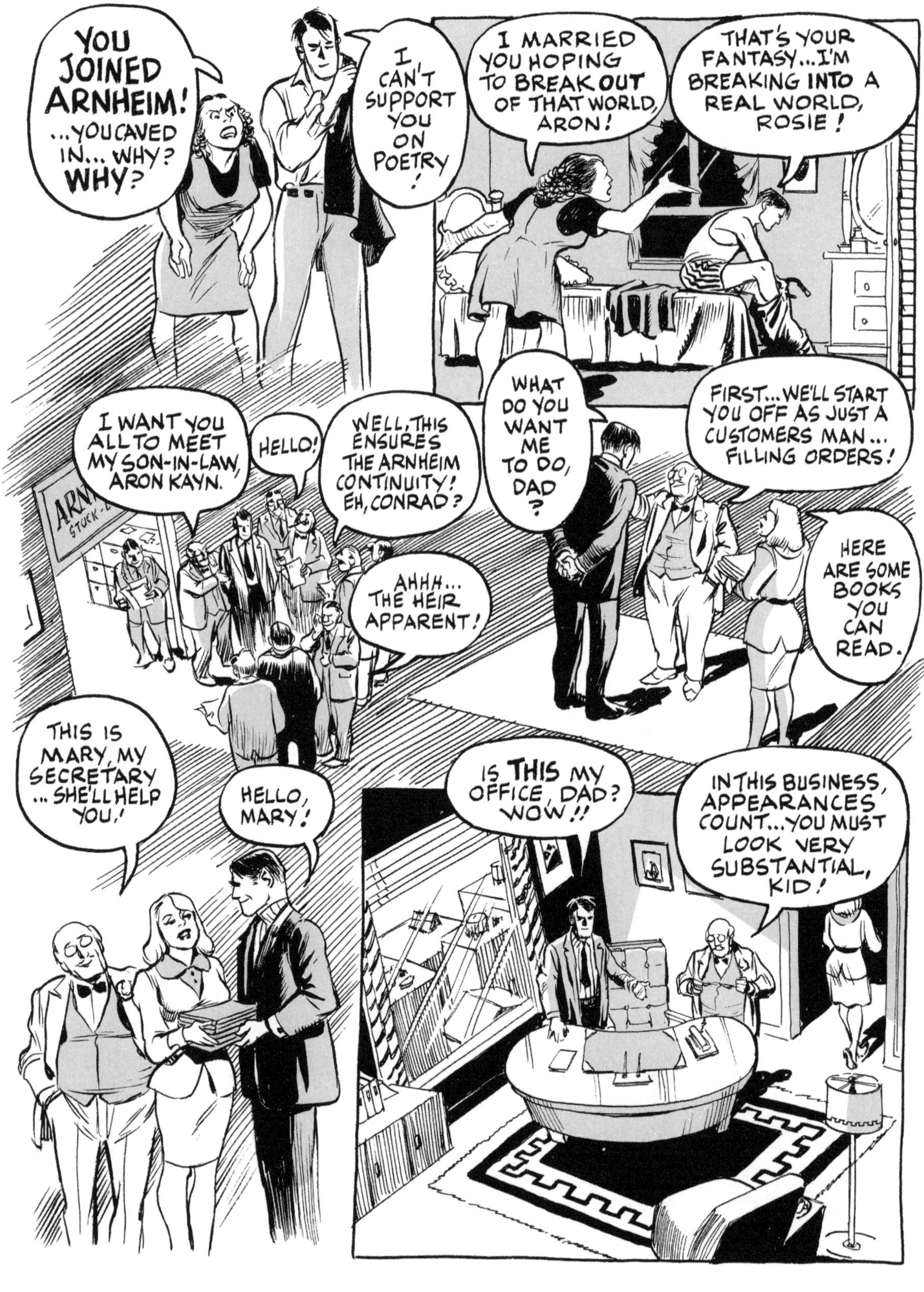
YOU JOINED ARNHEIM! ...YOU CAVED IN... WHY? WHY?
I CAN'T SUPPORT YOU ON POETRY!
I MARRIED YOU HOPING TO BREAK OUT OF THAT WORLD, ARON!
THAT'S YOUR FANTASY... I'M BREAKING INTO A REAL WORLD, ROSIE!
I WANT YOU ALL TO MEET MY SON-IN-LAW, ARON KAYN.
HELLO!
WELL, THIS ENSURES THE ARNHEIM CONTINUITY! EH, CONRAD?
AHHH... THE HEIR APPARENT!
WHAT DO YOU WANT ME TO DO, DAD?
FIRST... WE'LL START YOU OFF AS JUST A CUSTOMERS MAN... FILLING ORDERS!
HERE ARE SOME BOOKS YOU CAN READ.
THIS IS MARY, MY SECRETARY ... SHE'LL HELP YOU!
HELLO, MARY!
IS THIS MY OFFICE, DAD? WOW!!
IN THIS BUSINESS, APPEARANCES COUNT... YOU MUST LOOK VERY SUBSTANTIAL, KID!

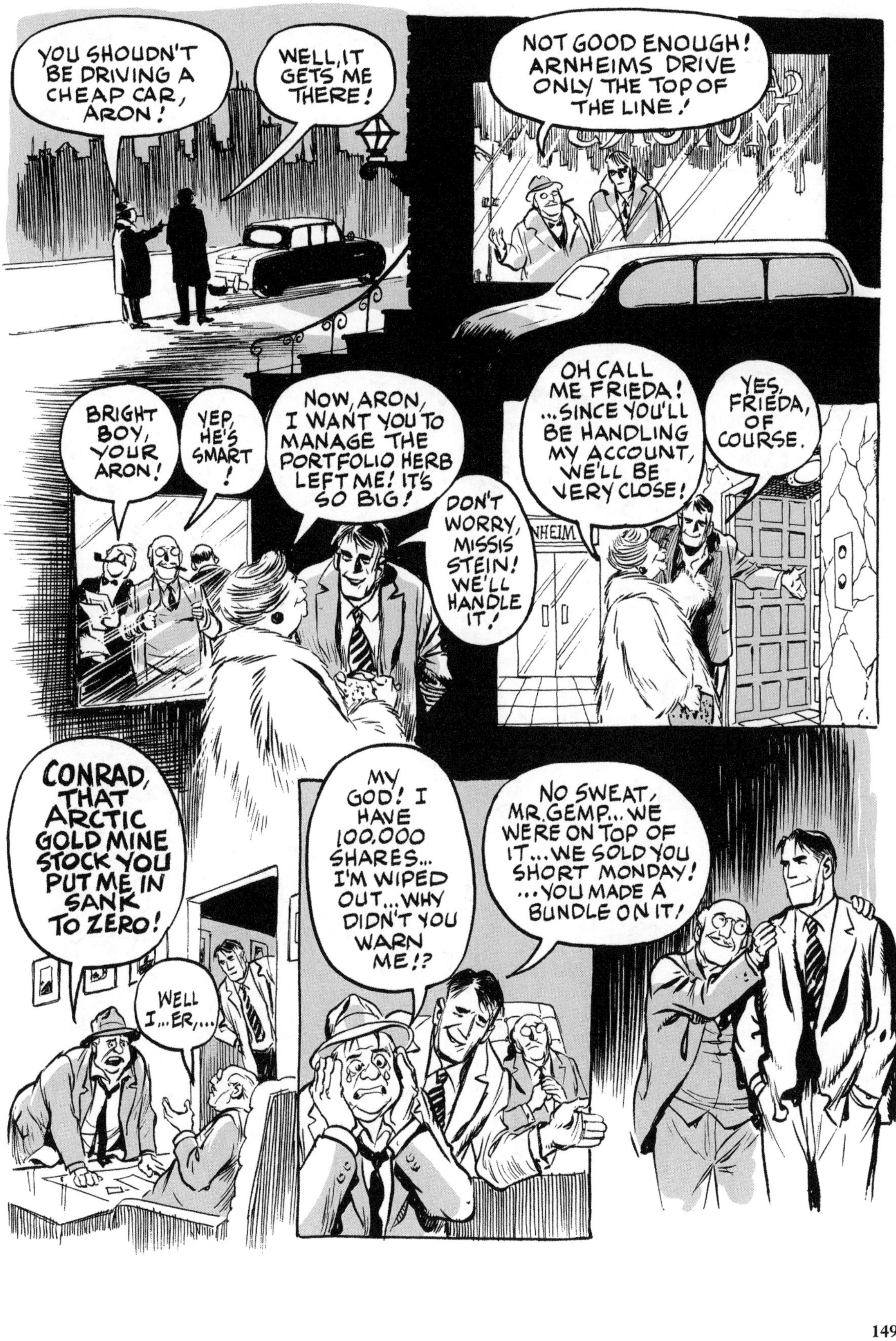
YOU SHOUDN'T BE DRIVING A CHEAP CAR, ARON!
WELL, IT GETS ME THERE!
NOT GOOD ENOUGH! ARNHEIMS DRIVE ONLY THE TOP OF THE LINE!
BRIGHT BOY, YOUR ARON!
YEP, HE'S SMART!
NOW, ARON, I WANT YOU TO MANAGE THE PORTFOLIO HERB LEFT ME! IT'S SO BIG!
DON'T WORRY, MISSIS STEIN! WE'LL HANDLE IT!
OH CALL ME FRIEDA! ...SINCE YOU'LL BE HANDLING MY ACCOUNT, WE'LL BE VERY CLOSE!
YES, FRIEDA, OF COURSE.
CONRAD, THAT ARCTIC GOLDMINE STOCK YOU PUT ME IN SANK TO ZERO!
WELL I...ER,...
MY GOD! I HAVE 100,000 SHARES... I'M WIPED OUT...WHY DIDN'T YOU WARN ME!?
NO SWEAT, MR. GEMP... WE WERE ON TOP OF IT...WE SOLD YOU SHORT MONDAY! ...YOU MADE A BUNDLE ON IT!

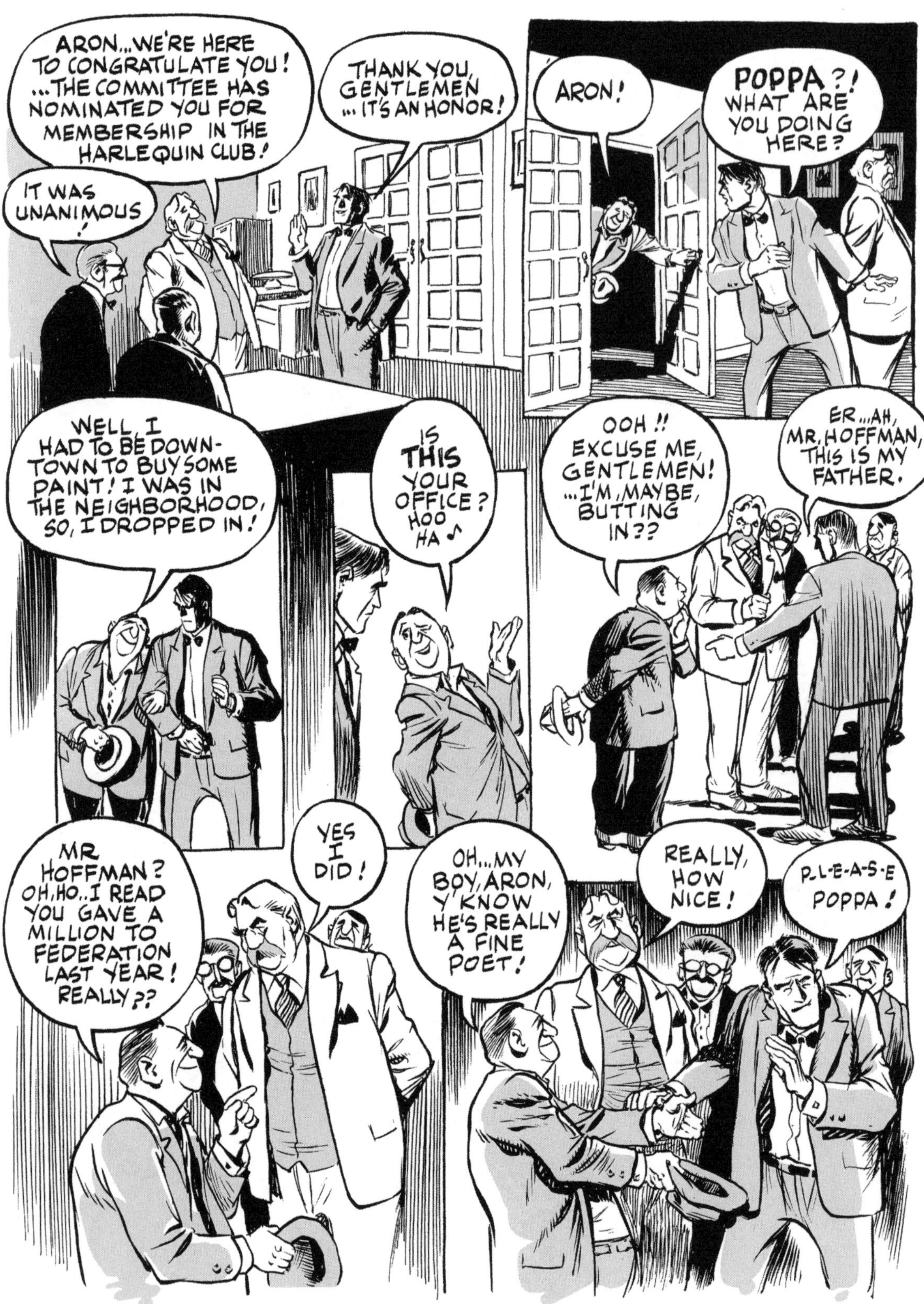
ARON... WE'RE HERE TO CONGRATULATE YOU! ...THE COMMITTEE HAS NOMINATED YOU FOR MEMBERSHIP IN THE HARLEQUIN CLUB!
IT WAS UNANIMOUS!
THANK YOU, GENTLEMEN ...IT'S AN HONOR!
ARON!
POPPA?! WHAT ARE YOU DOING HERE?
WELL, I HAD TO BE DOWN-TOWN TO BUY SOME PAINT! I WAS IN THE NEIGHBORHOOD, SO, I DROPPED IN!
IS THIS YOUR OFFICE? HOO HA ♪
OOH!! EXCUSE ME, GENTLEMEN! ...I'M, MAYBE, BUTTING IN??
ER...AH, MR. HOFFMAN, THIS IS MY FATHER.
MR HOFFMAN? OH, HO.. I READ YOU GAVE A MILLION TO FEDERATION LAST YEAR! REALLY??
YES I DID!
OH...MY BOY, ARON, Y'KNOW HE'S REALLY A FINE POET!
REALLY, HOW NICE!
P-L-E-A-S-E POPPA!

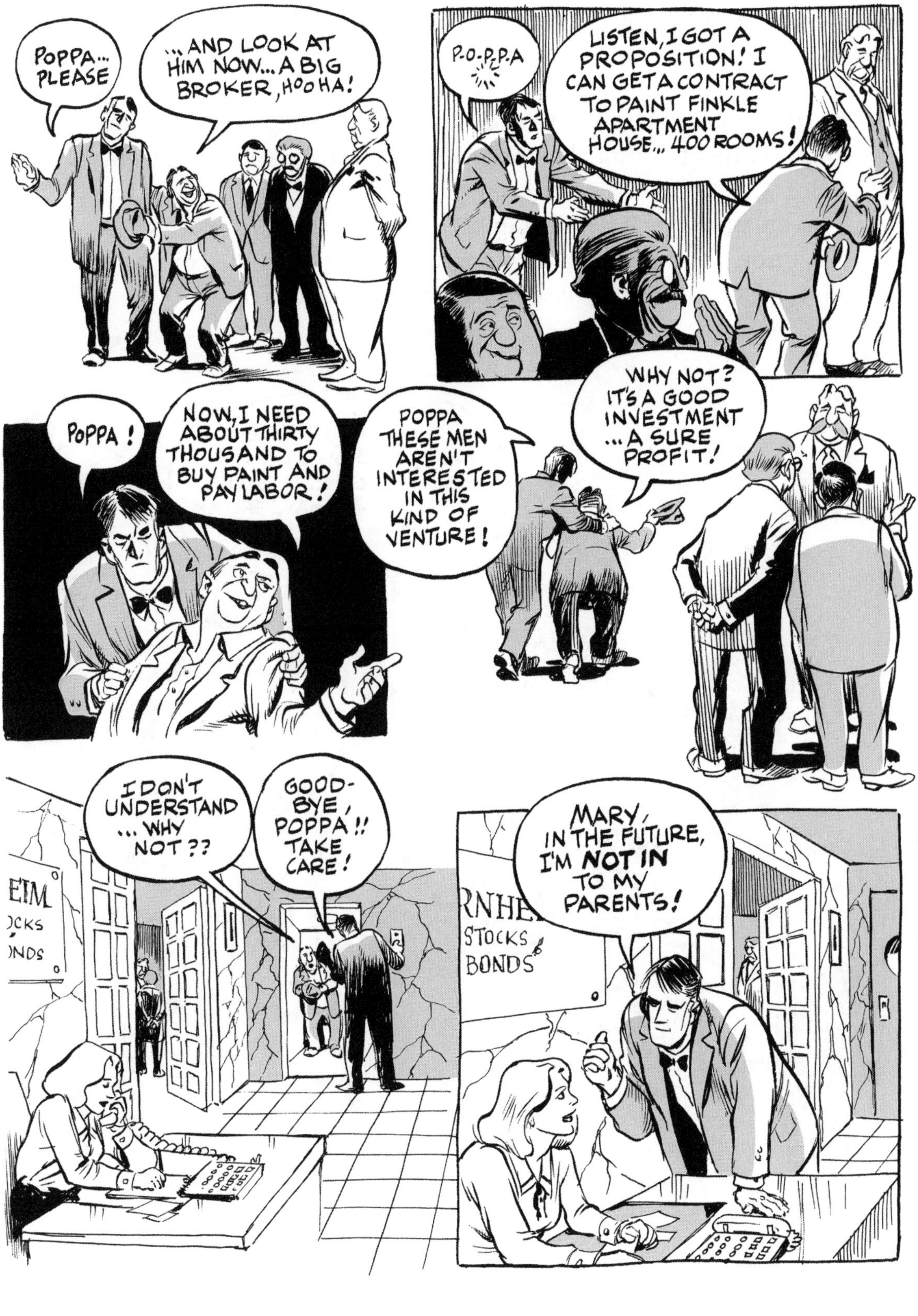
POPPA... PLEASE
...AND LOOK AT HIM NOW... A BIG BROKER, HOO HA!
P-O-P-P-A
LISTEN, I GOT A PROPOSITION! I CAN GET A CONTRACT TO PAINT FINKLE APARTMENT HOUSE... 400 ROOMS!
POPPA!
NOW, I NEED ABOUT THIRTY THOUSAND TO BUY PAINT AND PAY LABOR!
POPPA THESE MEN AREN'T INTERESTED IN THIS KIND OF VENTURE!
WHY NOT? IT'S A GOOD INVESTMENT ...A SURE PROFIT!
I DON'T UNDERSTAND ...WHY NOT??
GOOD-BYE, POPPA!! TAKE CARE!
ETM
OCKS
ONDS
MARY, IN THE FUTURE, I'M **NOT IN** TO MY PARENTS!
RNHE
STOCKS
BONDS

Aron's control of the Arnheim Company increased each year. He had mastered the skills necessary to lead the small-investor and widow-dependent firm to a more lucrative estate business. And he was clever enough to keep the company's following alive with the social set that traditionally provided its "bread and butter" income.

This enhanced the relationship between Aron and Conrad. Aron also made a point of keeping Conrad's identity with the company alive, which, of course, pleased Conrad and kept clients.

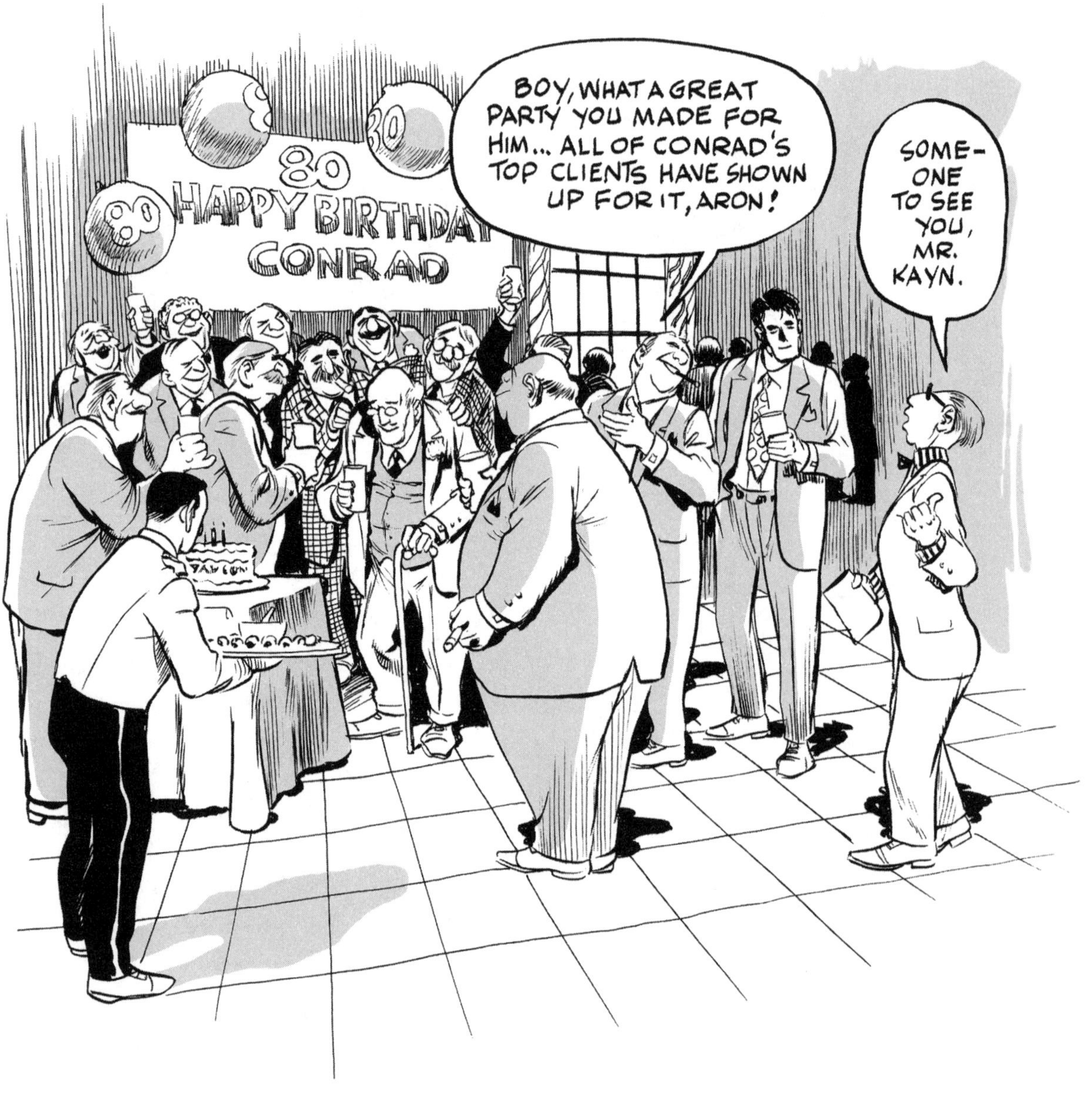
80
HAPPY BIRTHDAY
CONRAD
BOY, WHAT A GREAT PARTY YOU MADE FOR HIM... ALL OF CONRAD'S TOP CLIENTS HAVE SHOWN UP FOR IT, ARON!
SOME-ONE TO SEE YOU, MR. KAYN.

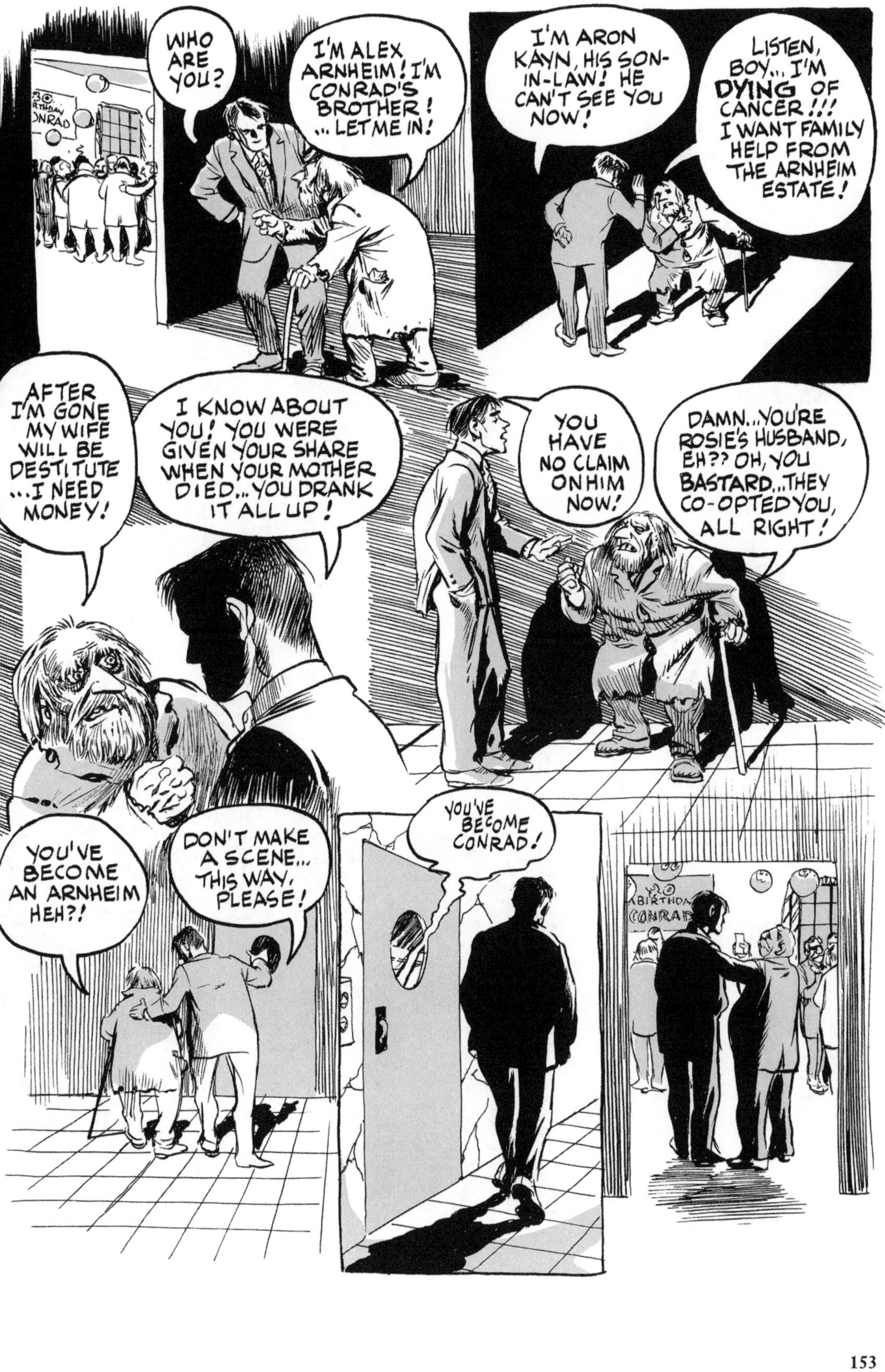
WHO ARE YOU?
I'M ALEX ARNHEIM! I'M CONRAD'S BROTHER! ... LET ME IN!
I'M ARON KAYN, HIS SON-IN-LAW! HE CAN'T SEE YOU NOW!
LISTEN, BOY... I'M DYING OF CANCER!!! I WANT FAMILY HELP FROM THE ARNHEIM ESTATE!
AFTER I'M GONE MY WIFE WILL BE DESTITUTE ...I NEED MONEY!
I KNOW ABOUT YOU! YOU WERE GIVEN YOUR SHARE WHEN YOUR MOTHER DIED... YOU DRANK IT ALL UP!
YOU HAVE NO CLAIM ON HIM NOW!
DAMN... YOU'RE ROSIE'S HUSBAND, EH?? OH, YOU BASTARD... THEY CO-OPTED YOU, ALL RIGHT!
YOU'VE BECOME AN ARNHEIM HEH?!
DON'T MAKE A SCENE... THIS WAY, PLEASE!
YOU'VE BECOME CONRAD!

Aron and Rosie's marriage began to reflect the life style Aron thought the business demanded. In an almost magical way, Aron gradually assumed Conrad's style and manner. The Kayns were succumbing to a transformation. More and more, their behavior conformed to the attitudes and mores of their enviroment.

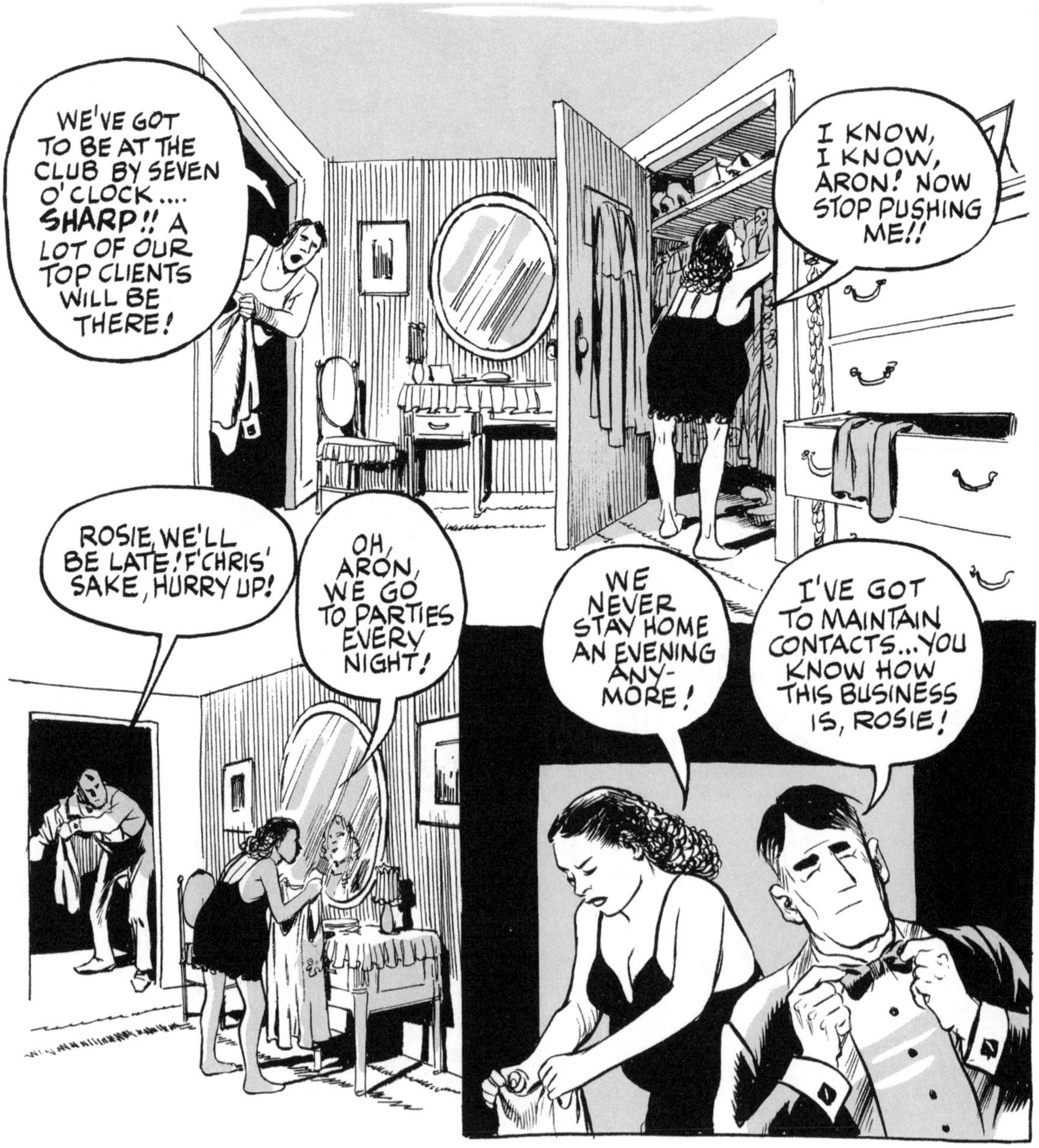
WE'VE GOT TO BE AT THE CLUB BY SEVEN O'CLOCK.... SHARP!! A LOT OF OUR TOP CLIENTS WILL BE THERE!
I KNOW, I KNOW, ARON! NOW STOP PUSHING ME!!
ROSIE, WE'LL BE LATE! F'CHRIS' SAKE, HURRY UP!
OH, ARON, WE GO TO PARTIES EVERY NIGHT!
WE NEVER STAY HOME AN EVENING ANY-MORE!
I'VE GOT TO MAINTAIN CONTACTS...YOU KNOW HOW THIS BUSINESS IS, ROSIE!

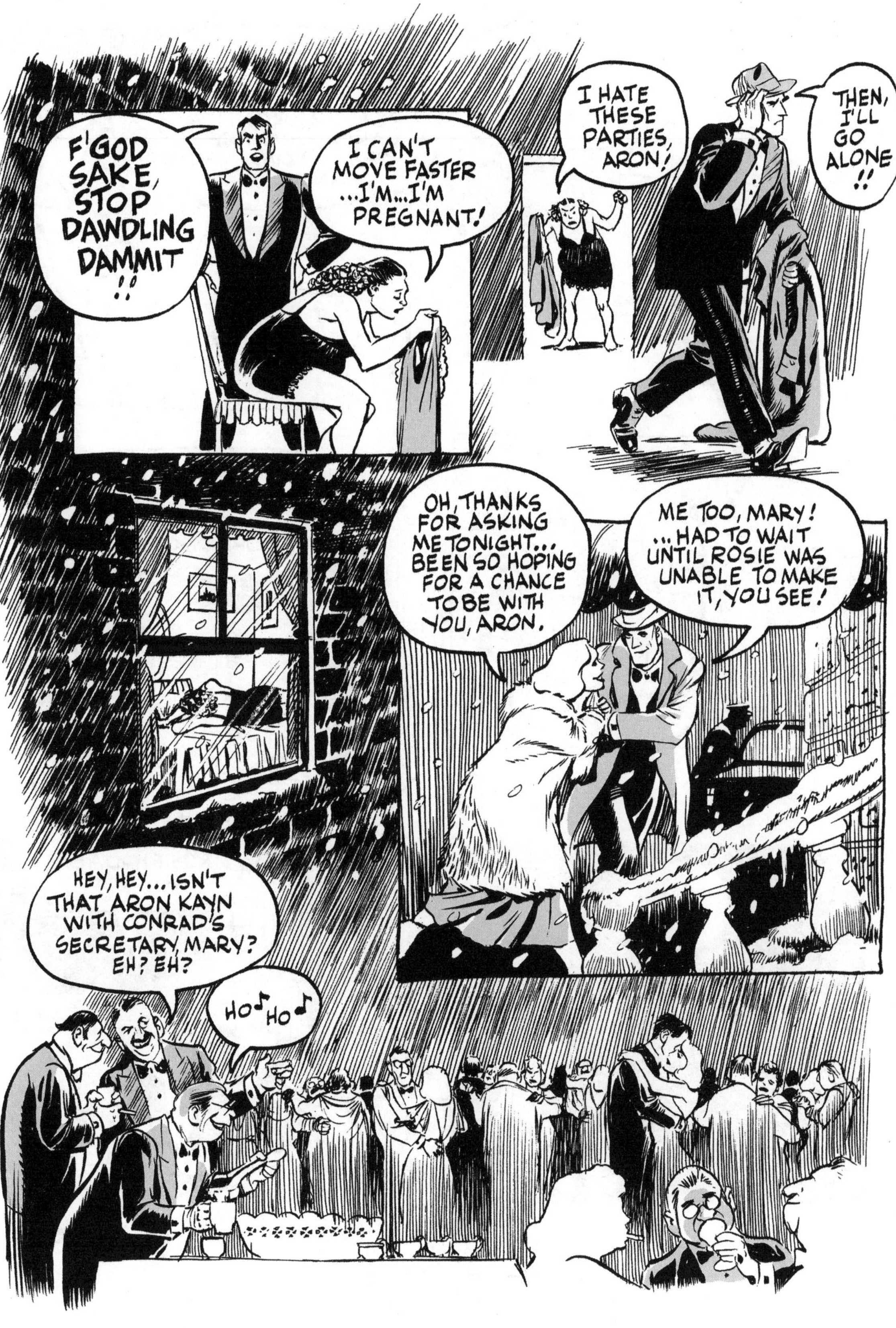
F'GOD SAKE, STOP DAWDLING DAMMIT !!
I CAN'T MOVE FASTER ...I'M...I'M PREGNANT!
I HATE THESE PARTIES, ARON!
THEN, I'LL GO ALONE !!
OH, THANKS FOR ASKING ME TONIGHT... BEEN SO HOPING FOR A CHANCE TO BE WITH YOU, ARON.
ME TOO, MARY! ...HAD TO WAIT UNTIL ROSIE WAS UNABLE TO MAKE IT, YOU SEE!
HEY, HEY...ISN'T THAT ARON KAYN WITH CONRAD'S SECRETARY, MARY? EH? EH?
HO♪ HO♪

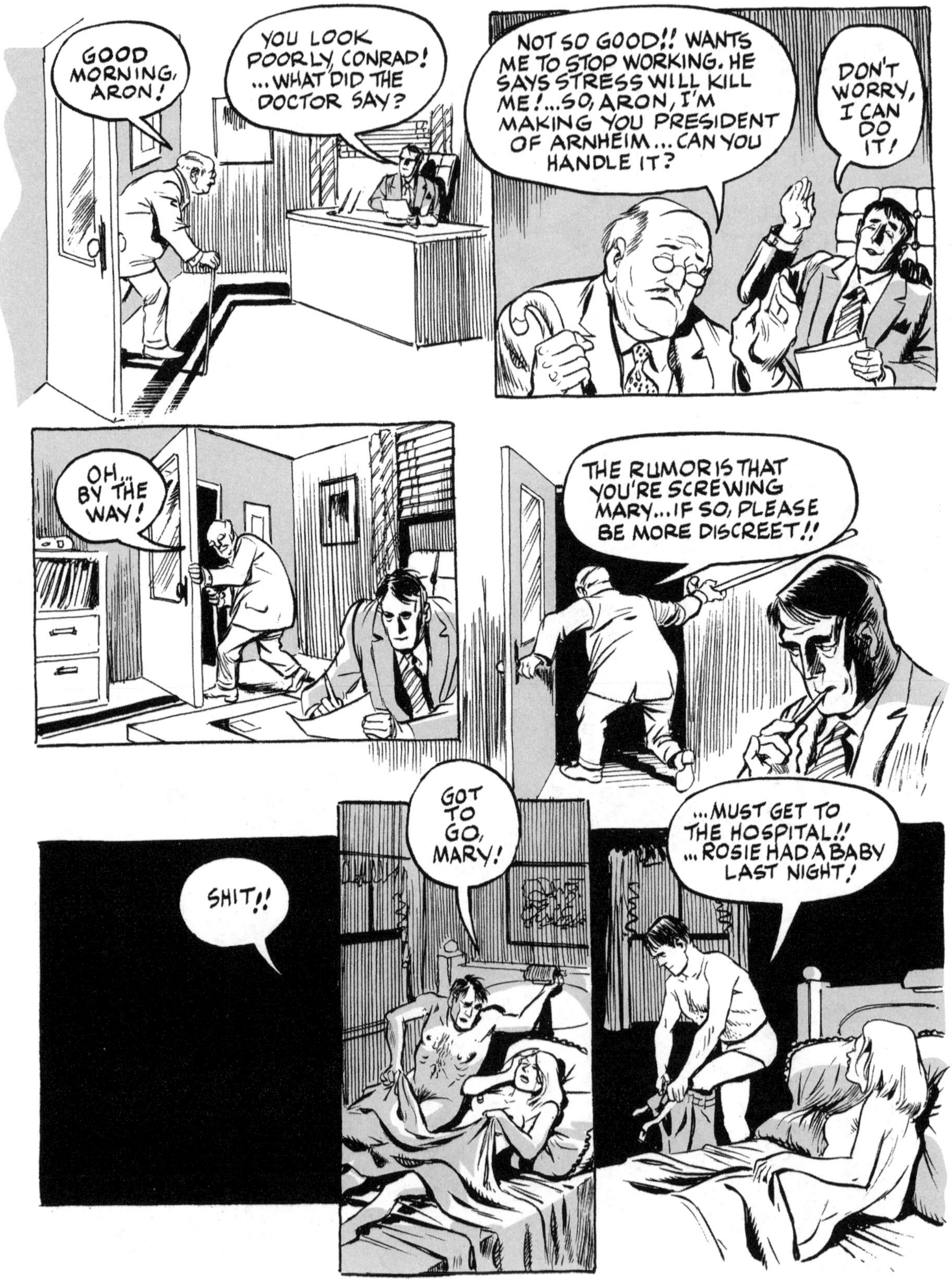
GOOD MORNING, ARON!
YOU LOOK POORLY, CONRAD! ...WHAT DID THE DOCTOR SAY?
NOT SO GOOD!! WANTS ME TO STOP WORKING. HE SAYS STRESS WILL KILL ME!...SO, ARON, I'M MAKING YOU PRESIDENT OF ARNHEIM... CAN YOU HANDLE IT?
DON'T WORRY, I CAN DO IT!
OH... BY THE WAY!
THE RUMOR IS THAT YOU'RE SCREWING MARY...IF SO, PLEASE BE MORE DISCREET!!
SHIT!!
GOT TO GO, MARY!
...MUST GET TO THE HOSPITAL!! ...ROSIE HAD A BABY LAST NIGHT!

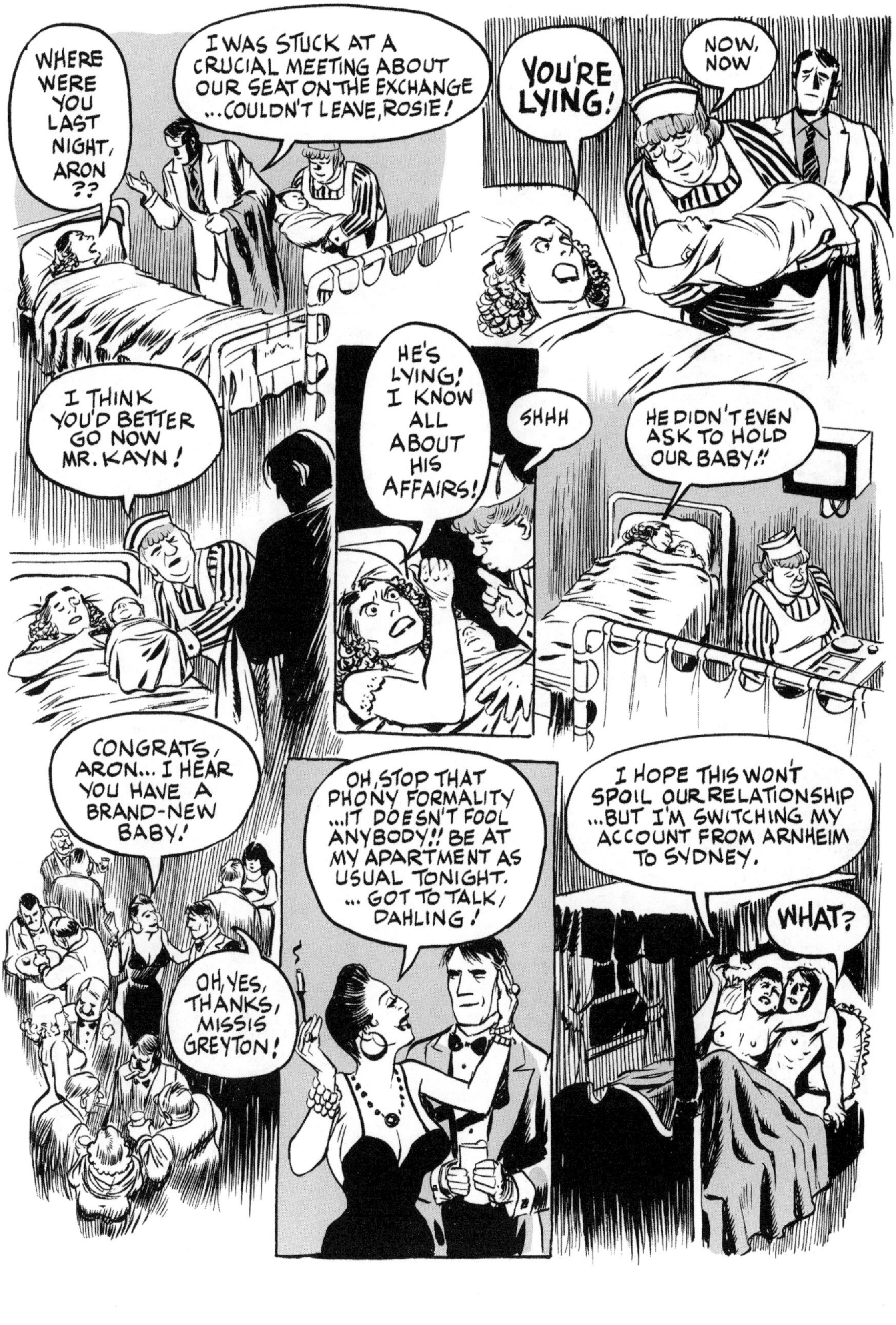

WHERE WERE YOU LAST NIGHT, ARON ??
I WAS STUCK AT A CRUCIAL MEETING ABOUT OUR SEAT ON THE EXCHANGE ...COULDN'T LEAVE, ROSIE!
YOU'RE LYING!
NOW, NOW
I THINK YOU'D BETTER GO NOW MR. KAYN!
HE'S LYING! I KNOW ALL ABOUT HIS AFFAIRS!
SHHH
HE DIDN'T EVEN ASK TO HOLD OUR BABY!!
CONGRATS, ARON... I HEAR YOU HAVE A BRAND-NEW BABY!
OH, YES, THANKS, MISSIS GREYTON!
OH, STOP THAT PHONY FORMALITY ...IT DOESN'T FOOL ANYBODY!! BE AT MY APARTMENT AS USUAL TONIGHT. ... GOT TO TALK, DAHLING!
I HOPE THIS WON'T SPOIL OUR RELATIONSHIP ...BUT I'M SWITCHING MY ACCOUNT FROM ARNHEIM TO SYDNEY.
WHAT?

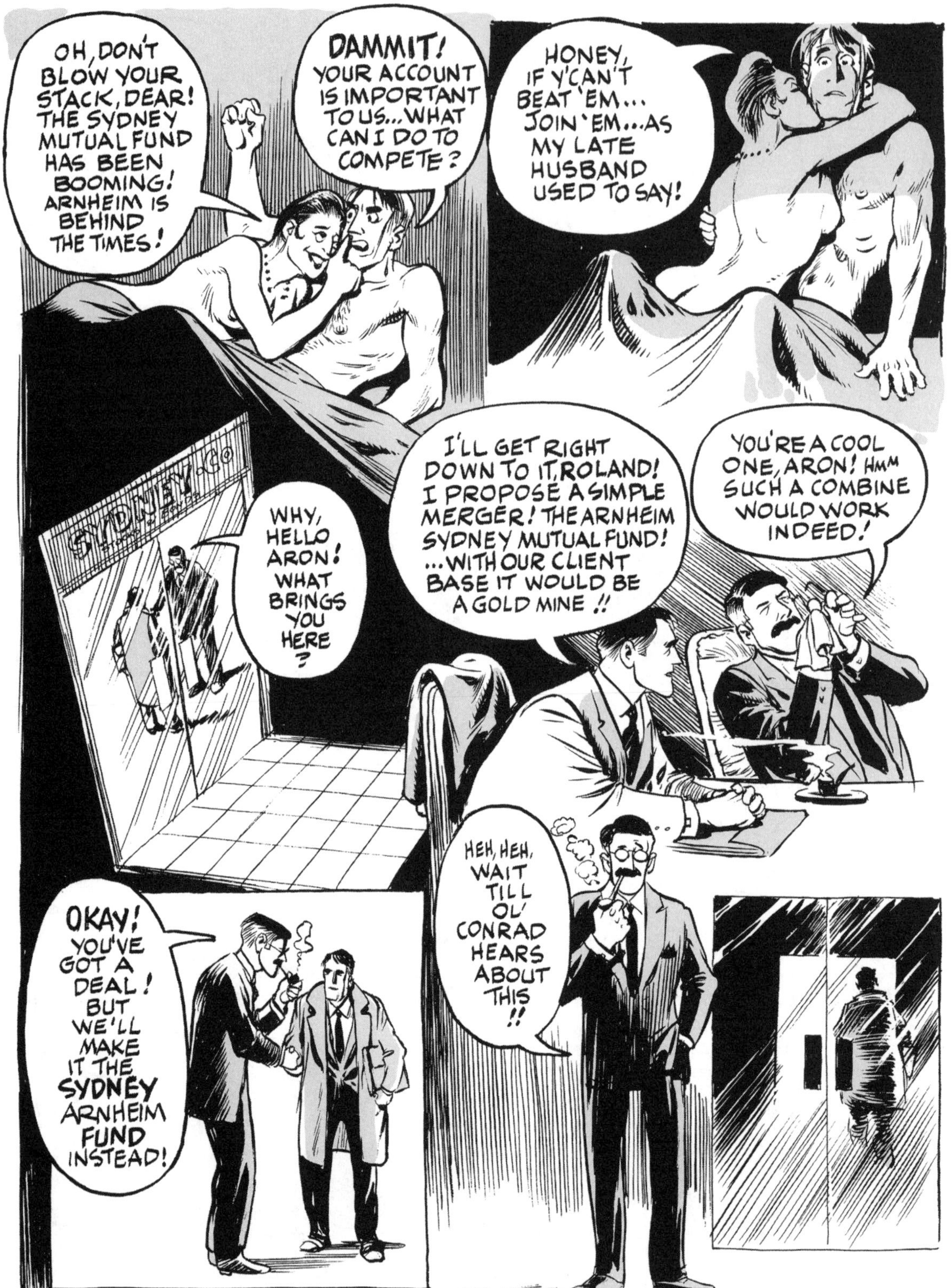
OH, DON'T BLOW YOUR STACK, DEAR! THE SYDNEY MUTUAL FUND HAS BEEN BOOMING! ARNHEIM IS BEHIND THE TIMES!
DAMMIT! YOUR ACCOUNT IS IMPORTANT TO US... WHAT CAN I DO TO COMPETE?
HONEY, IF Y'CAN'T BEAT 'EM... JOIN 'EM... AS MY LATE HUSBAND USED TO SAY!
SYDNEY CO
WHY, HELLO ARON! WHAT BRINGS YOU HERE?
I'LL GET RIGHT DOWN TO IT, ROLAND! I PROPOSE A SIMPLE MERGER! THE ARNHEIM SYDNEY MUTUAL FUND! ...WITH OUR CLIENT BASE IT WOULD BE A GOLD MINE!!
YOU'RE A COOL ONE, ARON! HMM SUCH A COMBINE WOULD WORK INDEED!
OKAY! YOU'VE GOT A DEAL! BUT WE'LL MAKE IT THE SYDNEY ARNHEIM FUND INSTEAD!
HEH, HEH, WAIT TILL OL' CONRAD HEARS ABOUT THIS!!

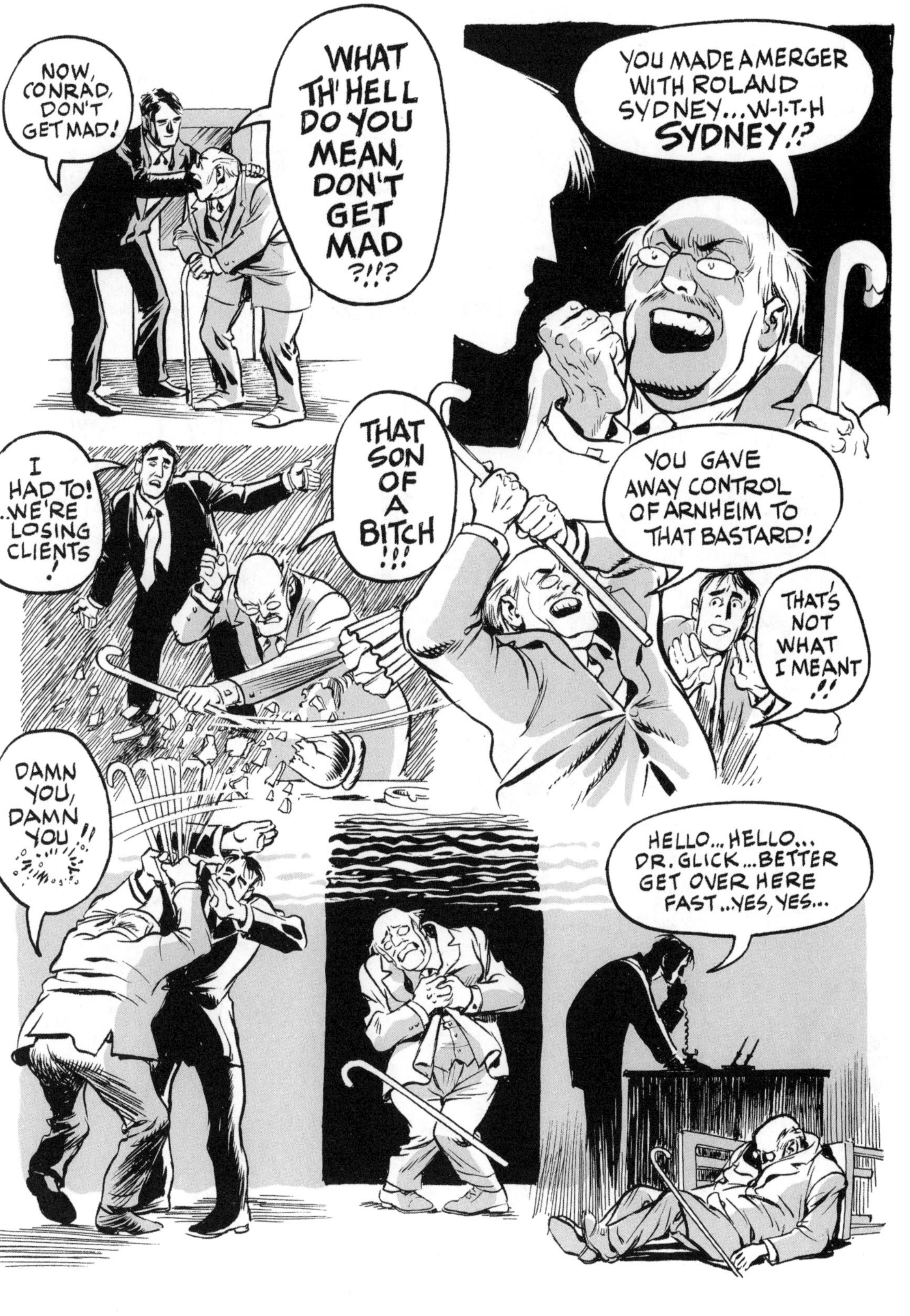
NOW, CONRAD, DON'T GET MAD!
WHAT TH' HELL DO YOU MEAN, DON'T GET MAD ?!!?
YOU MADE A MERGER WITH ROLAND SYDNEY... W-I-T-H SYDNEY!?
I HAD TO! ...WE'RE LOSING CLIENTS!
THAT SON OF A BITCH!!!
YOU GAVE AWAY CONTROL OF ARNHEIM TO THAT BASTARD!
THAT'S NOT WHAT I MEANT!!
DAMN YOU, DAMN YOU!!
HELLO... HELLO... DR. GLICK... BETTER GET OVER HERE FAST... YES, YES...

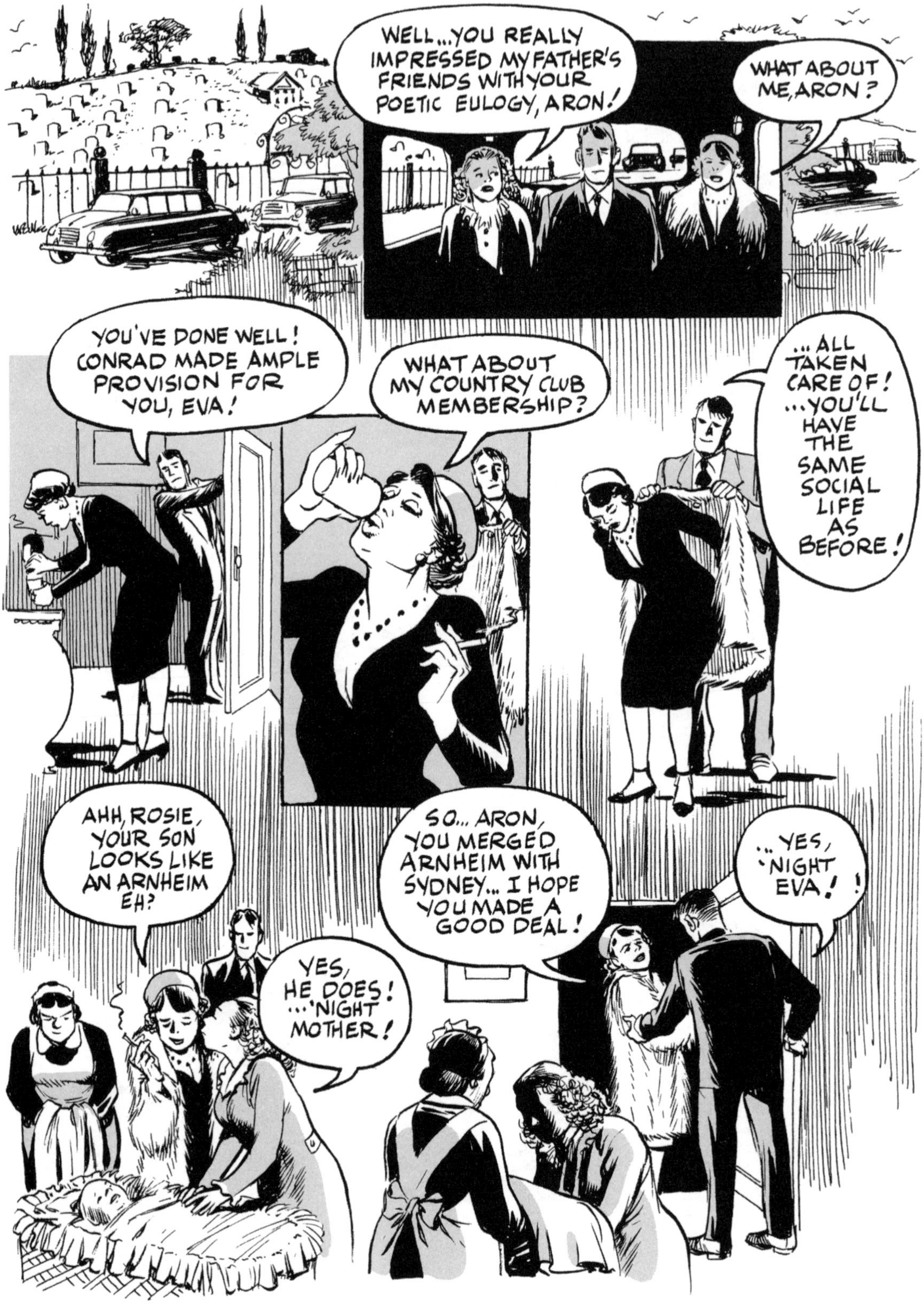
WELL...YOU REALLY IMPRESSED MY FATHER'S FRIENDS WITH YOUR POETIC EULOGY, ARON!
WHAT ABOUT ME, ARON?
YOU'VE DONE WELL! CONRAD MADE AMPLE PROVISION FOR YOU, EVA!
WHAT ABOUT MY COUNTRY CLUB MEMBERSHIP?
...ALL TAKEN CARE OF! ...YOU'LL HAVE THE SAME SOCIAL LIFE AS BEFORE!
AHH, ROSIE, YOUR SON LOOKS LIKE AN ARNHEIM EH?
YES, HE DOES! ...'NIGHT MOTHER!
SO... ARON, YOU MERGED ARNHEIM WITH SYDNEY... I HOPE YOU MADE A GOOD DEAL!
...YES, 'NIGHT EVA!

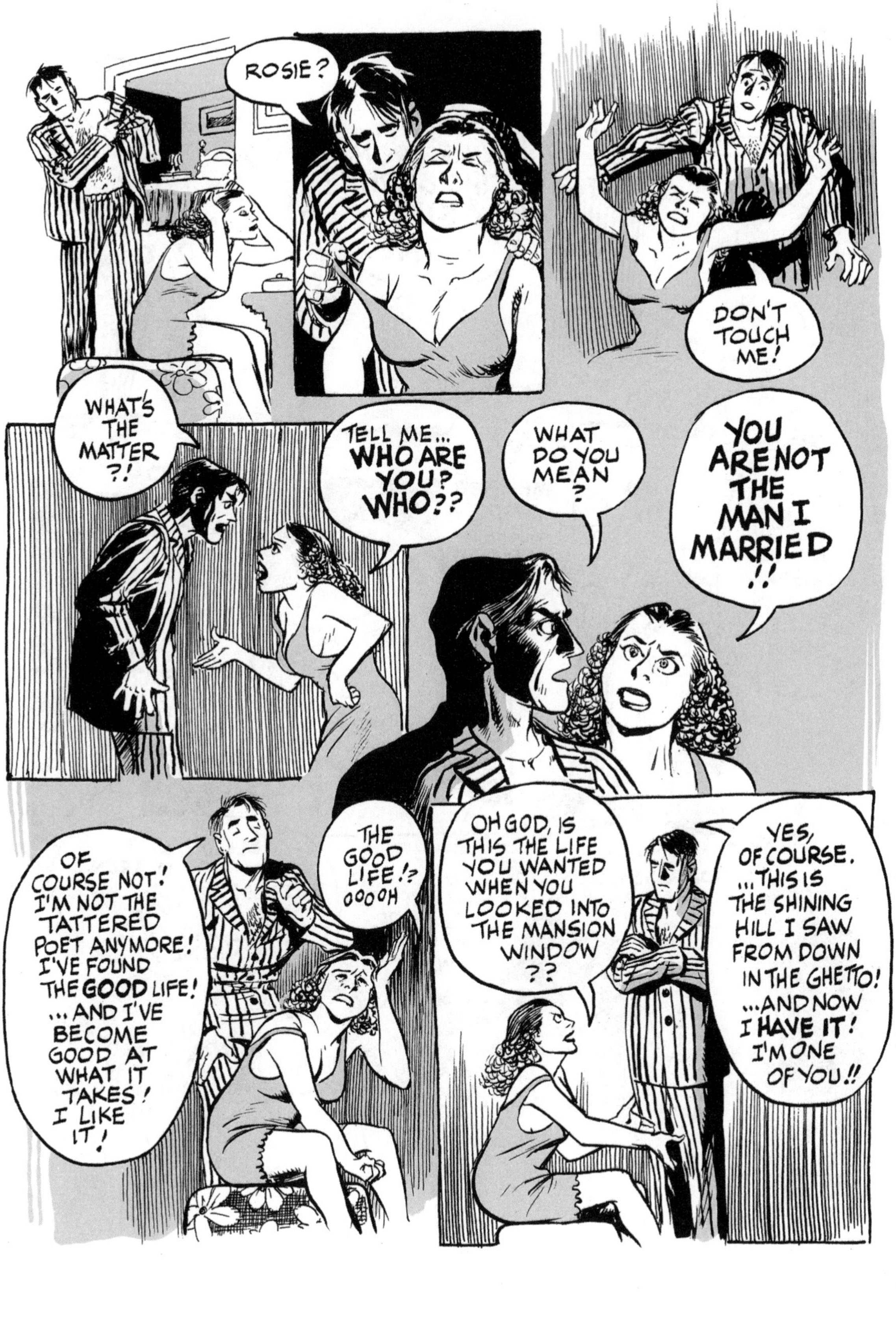
ROSIE?
DON'T TOUCH ME!
WHAT'S THE MATTER ?!
TELL ME... WHO ARE YOU? WHO??
WHAT DO YOU MEAN ?
YOU ARE NOT THE MAN I MARRIED !!
OF COURSE NOT! I'M NOT THE TATTERED POET ANYMORE! I'VE FOUND THE GOOD LIFE! ...AND I'VE BECOME GOOD AT WHAT IT TAKES! I LIKE IT!
THE GOOD LIFE!? OOOOH
OH GOD, IS THIS THE LIFE YOU WANTED WHEN YOU LOOKED INTO THE MANSION WINDOW ??
YES, OF COURSE. ...THIS IS THE SHINING HILL I SAW FROM DOWN IN THE GHETTO! ...AND NOW I HAVE IT! I'M ONE OF YOU!!

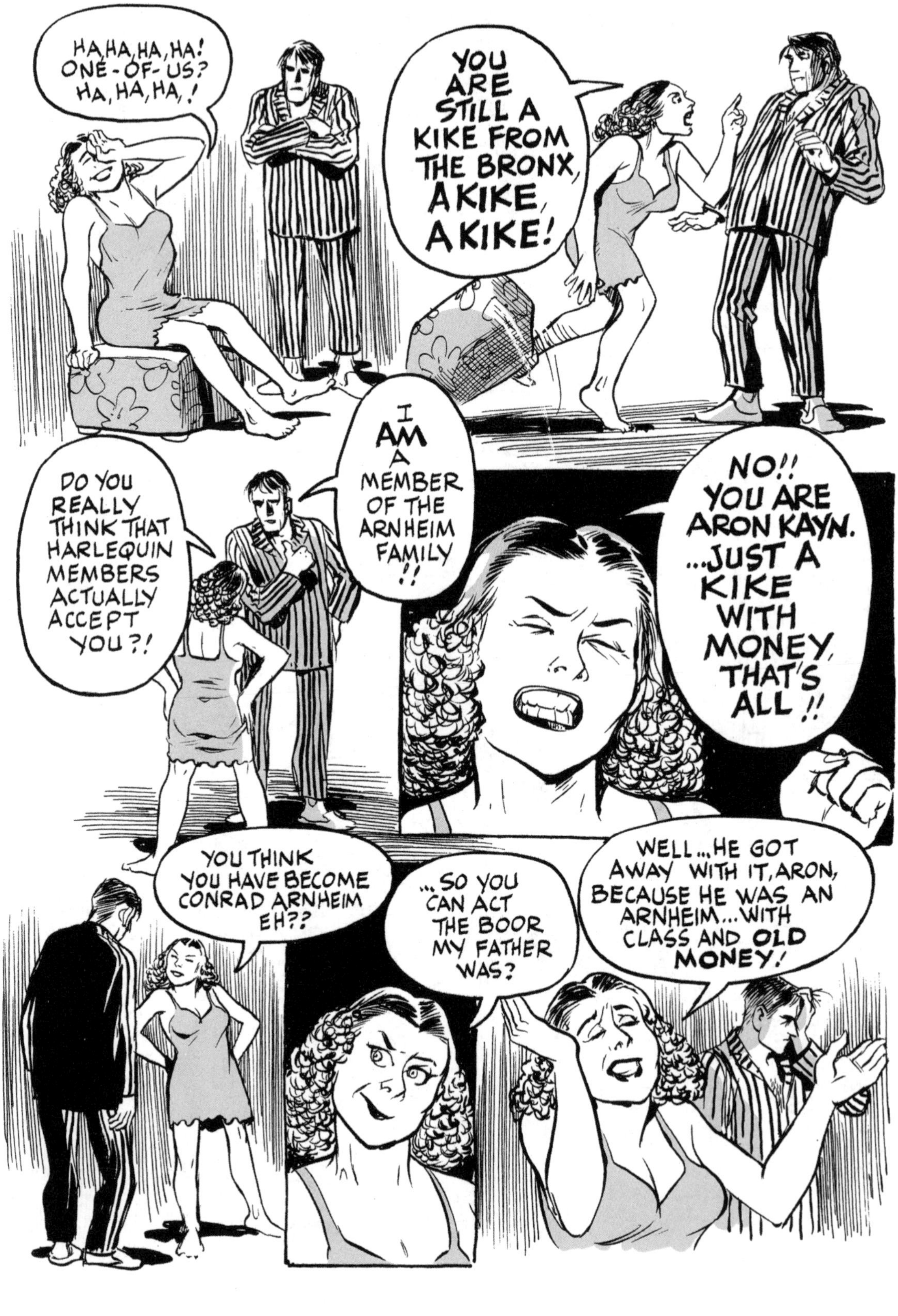
HA,HA,HA,HA! ONE-OF-US? HA,HA,HA,!
YOU ARE STILL A KIKE FROM THE BRONX, A KIKE, A KIKE!
DO YOU REALLY THINK THAT HARLEQUIN MEMBERS ACTUALLY ACCEPT YOU?!
I AM A MEMBER OF THE ARNHEIM FAMILY!!
NO!! YOU ARE ARON KAYN. ...JUST A KIKE WITH MONEY, THAT'S ALL!!
YOU THINK YOU HAVE BECOME CONRAD ARNHEIM EH??
...SO YOU CAN ACT THE BOOR MY FATHER WAS?
WELL...HE GOT AWAY WITH IT, ARON, BECAUSE HE WAS AN ARNHEIM...WITH CLASS AND OLD MONEY!

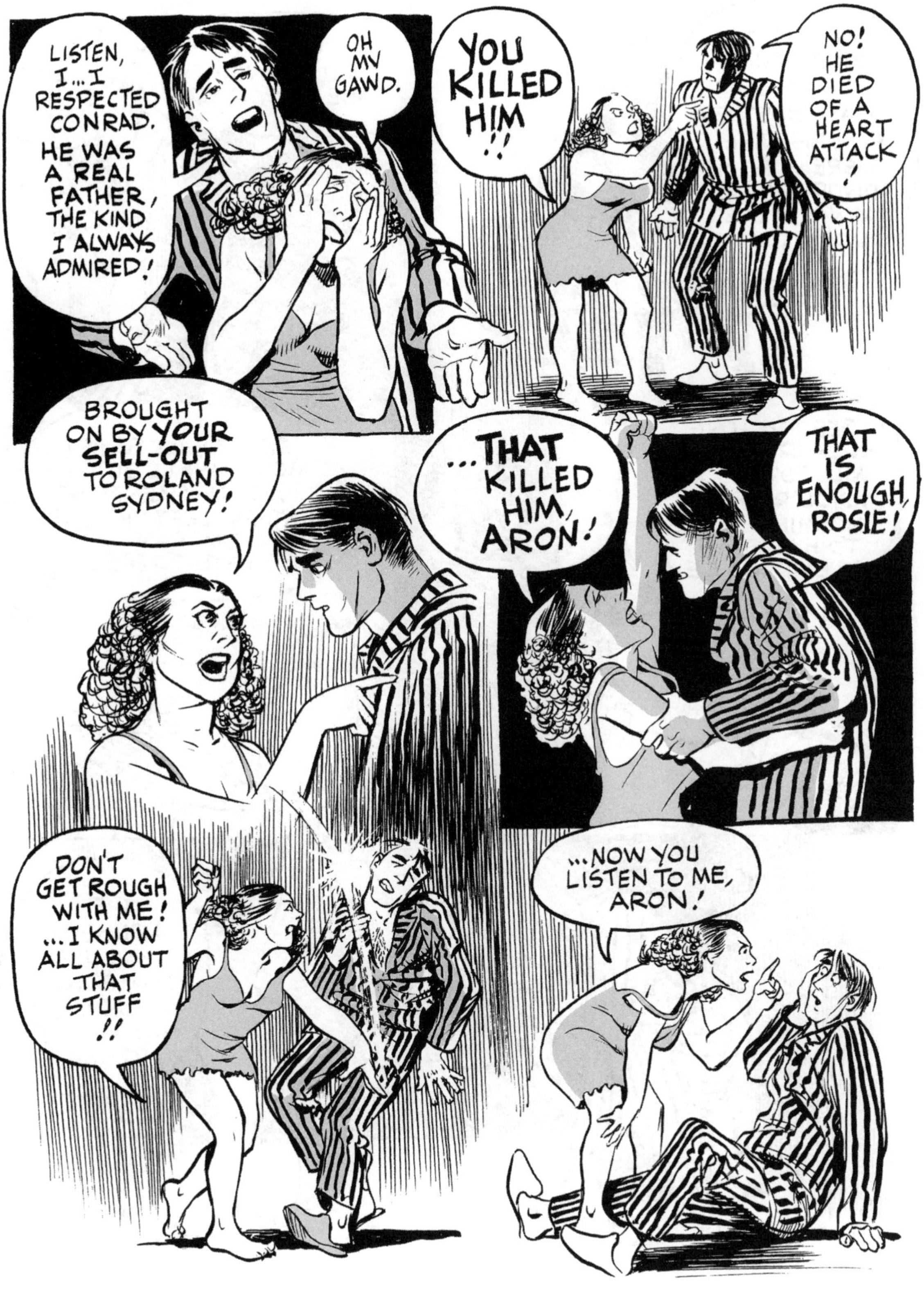
LISTEN, I...I RESPECTED CONRAD. HE WAS A REAL FATHER, THE KIND I ALWAYS ADMIRED!
OH MY GAWD.
YOU KILLED HIM!!
NO! HE DIED OF A HEART ATTACK!
BROUGHT ON BY YOUR SELL-OUT TO ROLAND SYDNEY!
...THAT KILLED HIM, ARON!
THAT IS ENOUGH, ROSIE!
DON'T GET ROUGH WITH ME! ...I KNOW ALL ABOUT THAT STUFF!!
...NOW YOU LISTEN TO ME, ARON!

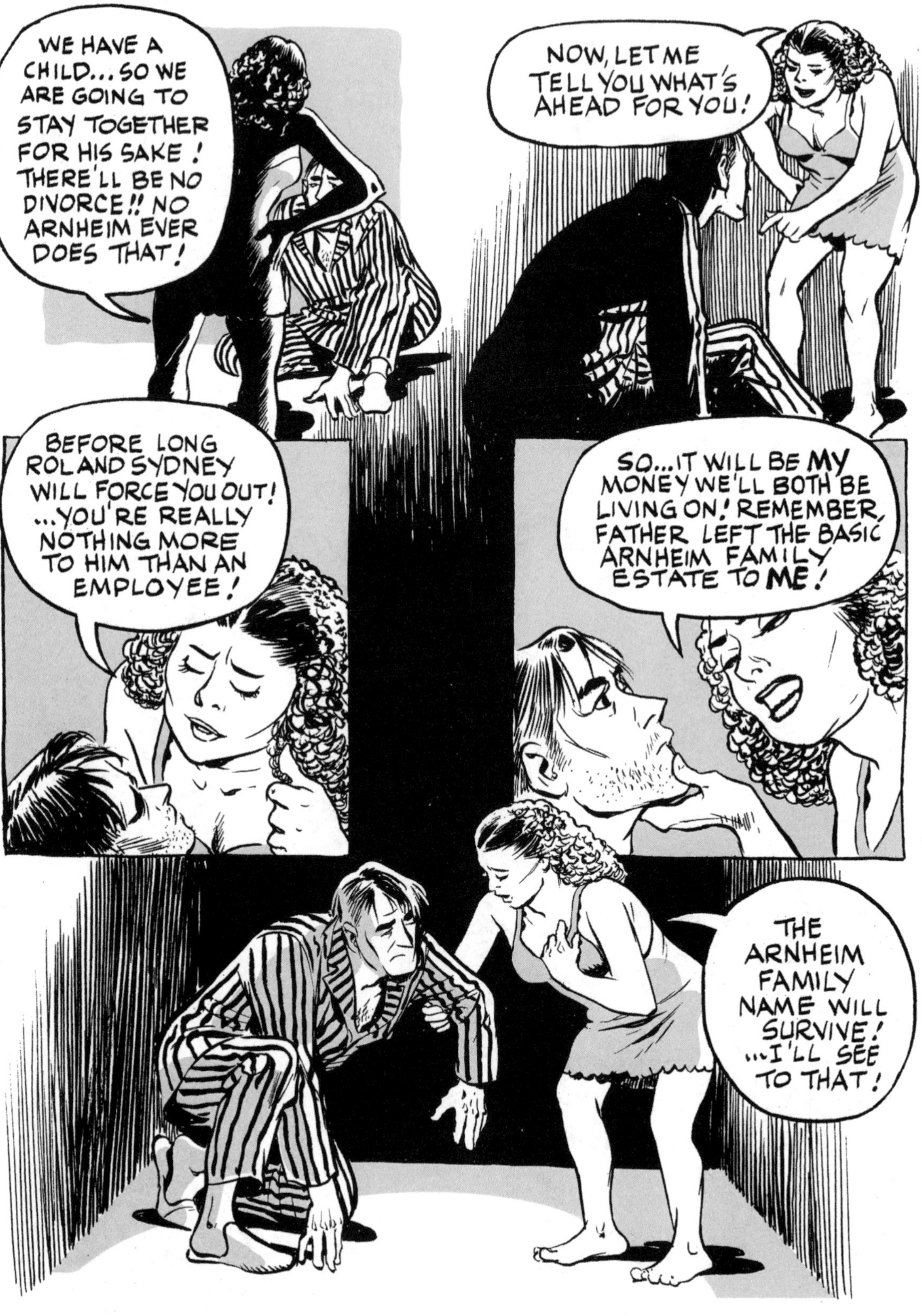
WE HAVE A CHILD... SO WE ARE GOING TO STAY TOGETHER FOR HIS SAKE! THERE'LL BE NO DIVORCE!! NO ARNHEIM EVER DOES THAT!
NOW, LET ME TELL YOU WHAT'S AHEAD FOR YOU!
BEFORE LONG ROLAND SYDNEY WILL FORCE YOU OUT! ...YOU'RE REALLY NOTHING MORE TO HIM THAN AN EMPLOYEE!
SO... IT WILL BE MY MONEY WE'LL BOTH BE LIVING ON! REMEMBER, FATHER LEFT THE BASIC ARNHEIM FAMILY ESTATE TO ME!
THE ARNHEIM FAMILY NAME WILL SURVIVE! ...I'LL SEE TO THAT!

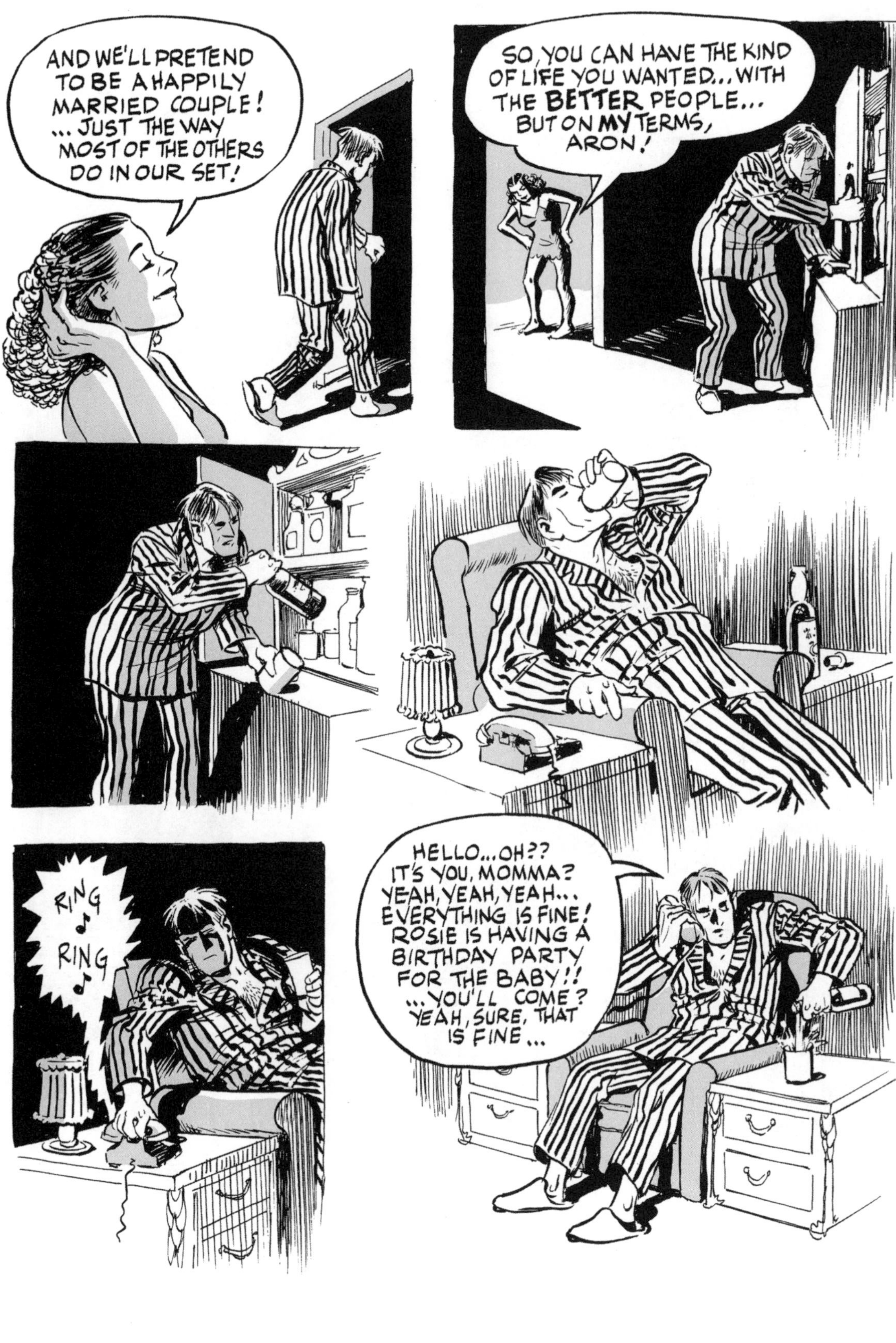
AND WE'LL PRETEND TO BE A HAPPILY MARRIED COUPLE! ... JUST THE WAY MOST OF THE OTHERS DO IN OUR SET!
SO, YOU CAN HAVE THE KIND OF LIFE YOU WANTED... WITH THE BETTER PEOPLE... BUT ON MY TERMS, ARON!
RING RING
HELLO... OH?? IT'S YOU, MOMMA? YEAH, YEAH, YEAH... EVERYTHING IS FINE! ROSIE IS HAVING A BIRTHDAY PARTY FOR THE BABY!! ...YOU'LL COME? YEAH, SURE, THAT IS FINE...

And that is how the Kayn family was elevated from its lowly station. True, they would always remain an appendage to the prominent Arnheims. But, in the scheme of things, they would enjoy the peripheral social benefits that came from such a connection.

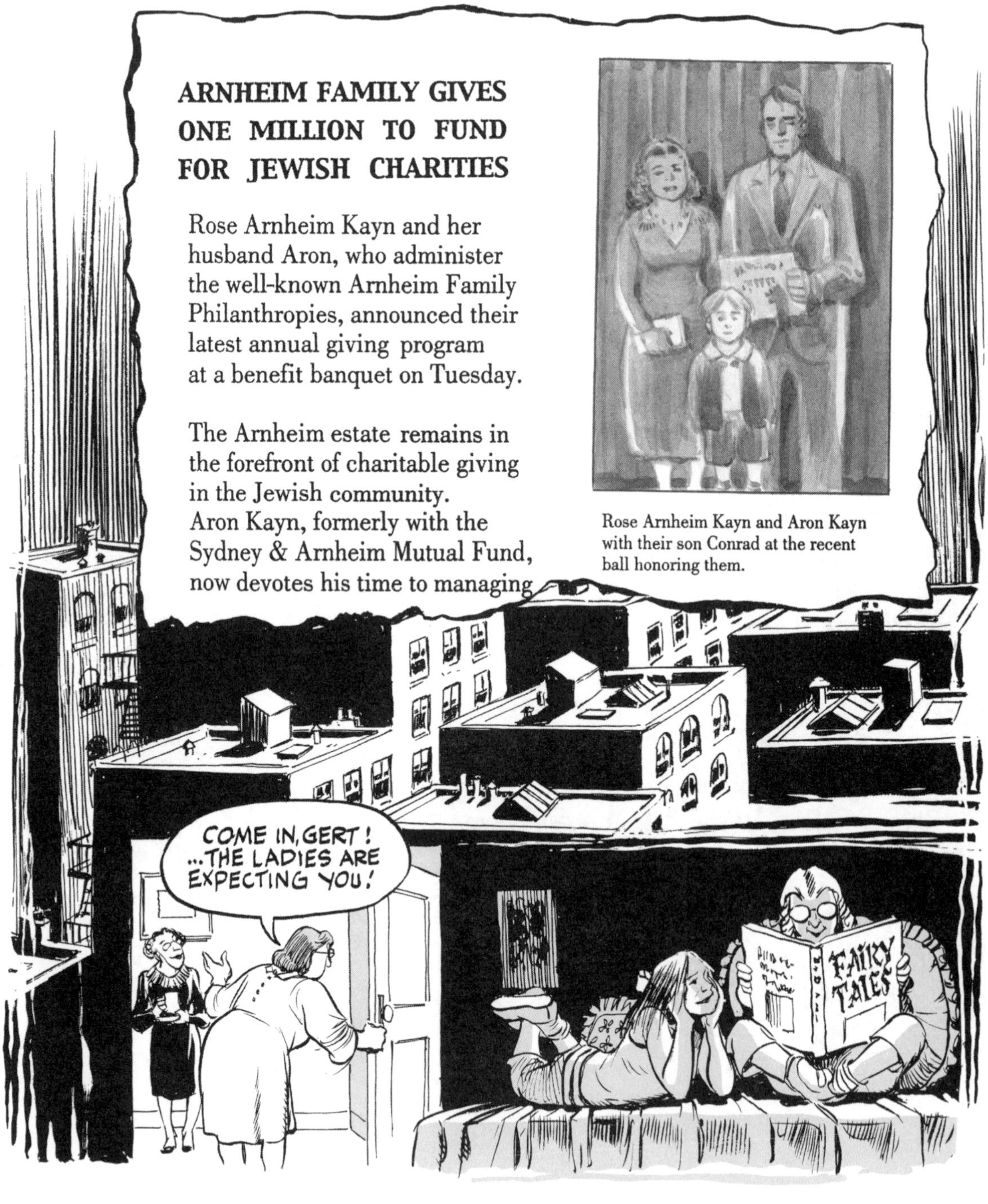
ARNHEIM FAMILY GIVES ONE MILLION TO FUND FOR JEWISH CHARITIES
Rose Arnheim Kayn and her husband Aron, who administer the well-known Arnheim Family Philanthropies, announced their latest annual giving program at a benefit banquet on Tuesday.
The Arnheim estate remains in the forefront of charitable giving in the Jewish community. Aron Kayn, formerly with the Sydney & Arnheim Mutual Fund, now devotes his time to managing
Rose Arnheim Kayn and Aron Kayn with their son Conrad at the recent ball honoring them.
COME IN, GERT! ...THE LADIES ARE EXPECTING YOU!
FAIRY TALES

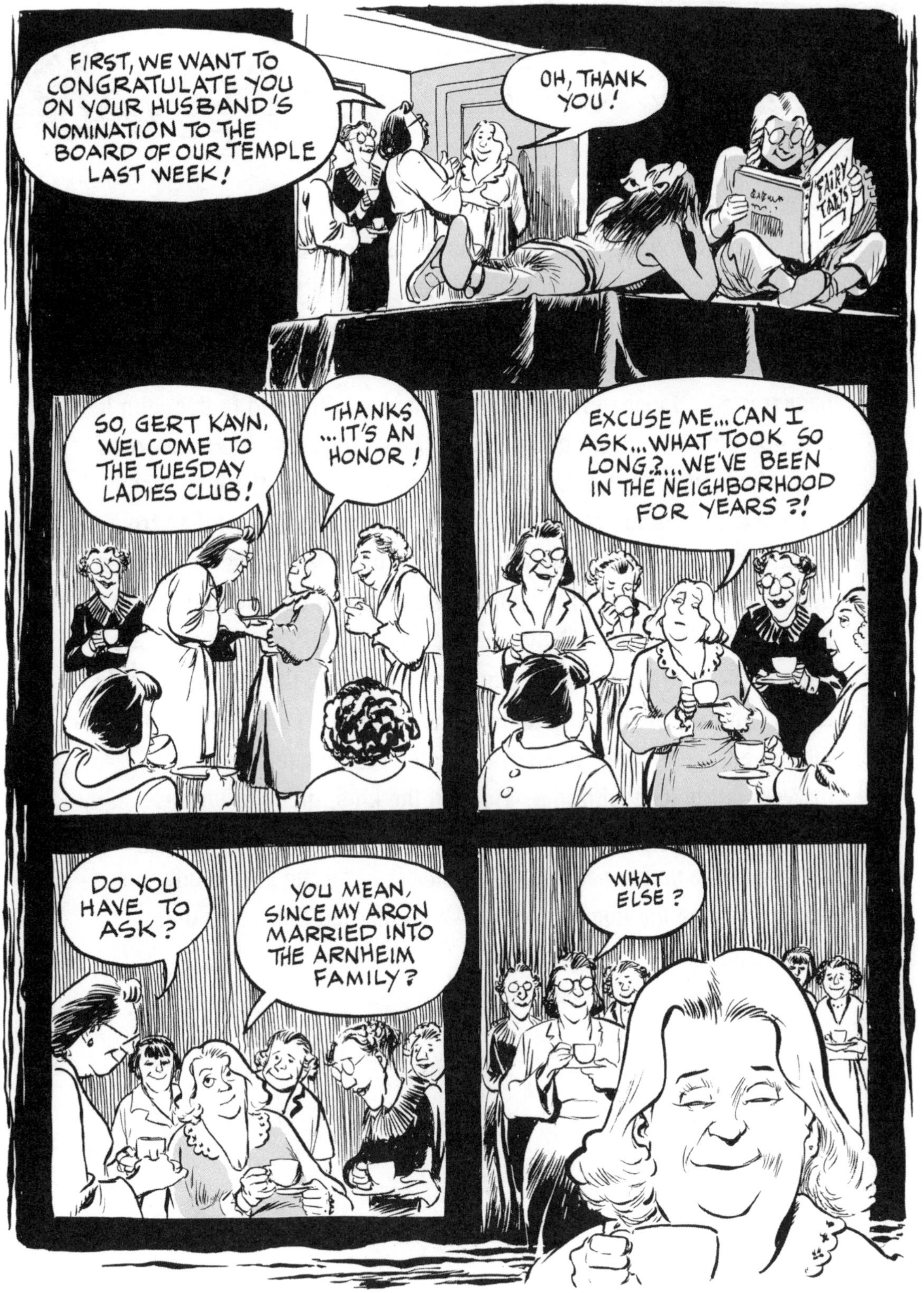
FIRST, WE WANT TO CONGRATULATE YOU ON YOUR HUSBAND'S NOMINATION TO THE BOARD OF OUR TEMPLE LAST WEEK!
OH, THANK YOU!
FAIRY TALES
SO, GERT KAYN, WELCOME TO THE TUESDAY LADIES CLUB!
THANKS ...IT'S AN HONOR!
EXCUSE ME...CAN I ASK...WHAT TOOK SO LONG?...WE'VE BEEN IN THE NEIGHBORHOOD FOR YEARS?!
DO YOU HAVE TO ASK?
YOU MEAN, SINCE MY ARON MARRIED INTO THE ARNHEIM FAMILY?
WHAT ELSE?

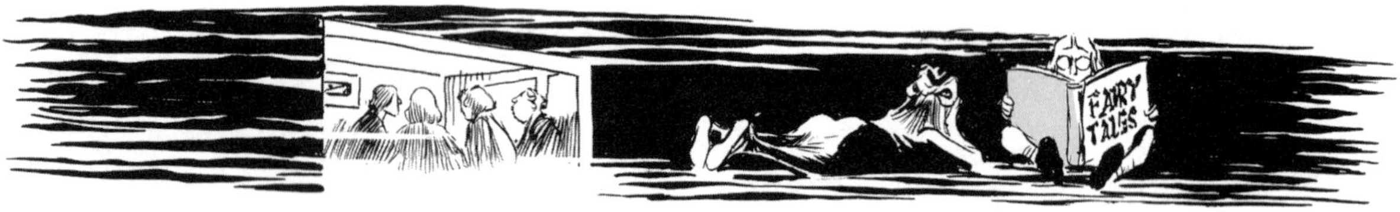
FAIRY TALES

There was once, in ancient times, a mighty king who ruled a great land which was handed down to him by his parents who so spoiled him that he expected everything to go his way. His first marriage was arranged with the princess of another royal family from a lower kingdom. In time, the couple had a daughter. But the king was uninterested. So when his queen died, he sent the child to live with her grandparents in their kingdom. A few years later, the king remarried a great beauty who did not want children at all. But the king wanted to have a child in his castle so the king had his daughter taken from her grandparents and brought to live with him. When she grew older, the girl found a suitor. She wanted to marry him but the king broke them up simply because the young man was not of royal blood. The daughter was so heartbroken that she died. Later, the king's new wife had a child -- a beautiful and outspoken princess. And it came to pass that a poor, handsome woodworker wandered by one day. The princess fell in love with him. By then the king, guilty about his treatment of his first child, offered his daughter's hand in marriage to the handsome young peasant. They married and the king made him a prince. In time the humble woodworker inherited the crown and became king.

And they lived happily ever after.

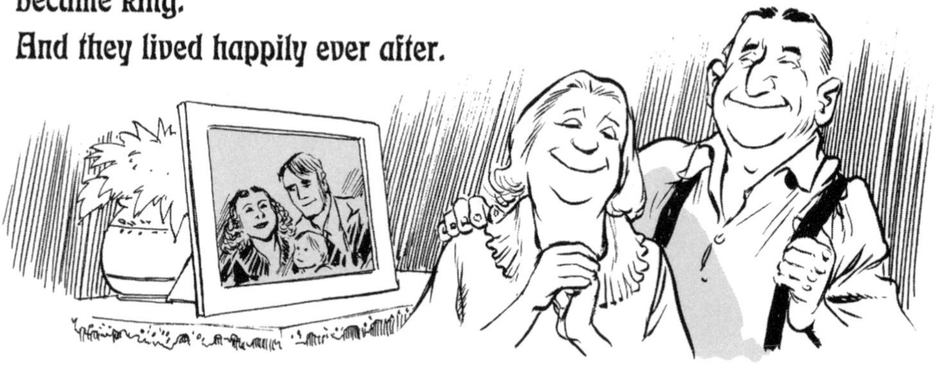

About the Author

Will Eisner (1917–2005) was the grand old man of comics. He was present at the birth of the comic book industry in the 1930s, creating such titles as *Blackhawk* and *Sheena, Queen of the Jungle*. He created *The Spirit* in 1940, syndicating it for twelve years as a unique and innovative sixteen-page Sunday newspaper insert, with a weekly circulation of 5 million copies. In the seven decades since, *The Spirit* has almost never been out of print. As a Pentagon-based warrant officer during World War Two, Eisner pioneered the instructional use of comics, continuing to produce them for the U.S. Army under civilian contract into the 1970s, along with educational comics for readers as diverse as General Motors employees and elementary school children.

In 1978 Eisner created the first successful "graphic novel," *A Contract With God*, launching a bold new literary genre. Nearly twenty celebrated graphic novels by him followed. Since 1988 the comic industry's top award for excellence has been "The Eisner." He has received numerous honors and awards worldwide, including, ironically, several Eisners and only the second Lifetime Achievement Award bestowed by the National Foundation for Jewish Culture (2002).